Individual choice and the structures of history

Alexis de Tocqueville is recognized as one of the most important nineteenth-century historians. In this study, Harvey Mitchell examines afresh Tocqueville's works, in particular the *Souvenirs* of 1848 and his voluminous correspondence, to shed new light on Tocqueville's philosophy of history. Professor Mitchell exposes the tensions which Tocqueville perceived between determined actions and choice, continuity and change, asking what happens to individual liberty if it is impossible to make a clean break with the past, and if past developments continue to influence the future. Professor Mitchell argues that it was Tocqueville's related concern with liberty in a modern democratic age which led him to write his *L'Ancien Régime et la Révolution*.

Drawing on the full range of Tocqueville's writings, *Individual choice and the structures of history* reveals in them a unity of thought and a deep involvement with the philosophical questions raised by historical continuity and change.

Individual choice and the structures of history

Alexis de Tocqueville as historian reappraised

Harvey Mitchell

Emeritus Professor of History
The University of British Columbia

CAMBRIDGE
UNIVERSITY PRESS

Published by the Press Syndicate of the University of Cambridge
The Pitt Building, Trumpington Street, Cambridge CB2 1RP
40 West 20th Street, New York, NY 10011-4211, USA
10 Stamford Road, Oakleigh, Melbourne 3166, Australia

First published 1996

Printed in Great Britain at the University Press, Cambridge

A catalogue record for this book is available from the British Library

Library of Congress cataloguing in publication data

Mitchell, Harvey.
    Individual choice and the structures of history : Alexis de
Tocqueville as historian reappraised / Harvey Mitchell.
        p.   cm.
    Includes bibliographical references and index.
    ISBN 0 521 56091 8
    1. Tocqueville, Alexis de, 1805–1859 – Philosophy.   2. Tocqueville,
Alexis de, 1805–1859 – Political and social views.   3. Historians –
France – Biography.   4. Revolutions – Philosophy.
5. Decentralization in government – France. I. Title.
DC36.98.T63M57   1996
944′.007202–dc20   95-33642   CIP

ISBN 0 521 56091 8 hardback

For Sheryl, Naomi, Steve, Norman, Reuben, Hannah, Rebecca, Molefe

Contents

Acknowledgments

My interest in Alexis de Tocqueville dates back several years to when I first thought about the nature of the French Revolution, the problems of understanding the political thought of the past and the philosophy of history. My views on these questions have been transformed over the years. The result is a study of a thinker whose demands on me were such that I often felt I could not meet them. Even now I feel that Tocqueville will continue to elude final judgment, all the more so as his linkage between contingency and necessity, choice and determinateness, painfully yet fruitfully exposes the ways in which historical study leaves many questions in a state of uncertainty.

Without the extraordinary support of the Social Sciences and Humanities Research Council of Canada from which I benefited over the years, this book would have surely had a more traumatic birth. In Paris, I had generous and gracious help from, as well as fruitful discussions with, François Furet and Françoise Mélonio who gave me permission to study copies of Tocqueville's manuscript notes for the two volumes of *L'Ancien Régime et la Révolution*. A visit to the Beinecke Rare Book and Manuscript Library at Yale University, where I consulted the Tocqueville repository, was eased by Vincent Giroud, curator of the Library's Modern Books and Manuscripts. I wish to acknowledge, as well, the impressive historical collections of the University of British Columbia Library, and the assistance I was given by its friendly librarians on this project as well as on others over the years.

Expressions of gratitude are also owing to John Bowditch and Alfred Cobban who originally stimulated my interest in French history. When I began my studies with Alfred Cobban, I suggested that I might begin a study of Tocqueville. Though I was politely overruled, I did not lose sight of the possibility, and returned to the idea with a greater appreciation of the difficulties posed by bringing it to fruition at a time when the definitive edition of his works was still on the drawing board.

I have been particularly lucky in being able to exchange ideas with individuals whom I count as my friends, colleagues and students, many of whom are all three. I am thankful to Kim Adam, Keith Baker, Marco Diani, Michèle Fogel, Marc Glouberman, Chava Glouberman, Iain Hampsher-Monk, Lynn Hunt, Douglas Johnson, Jean Laponce, Paul Nelles, Edouardo Nolla, Dorinda Outram, Ben Redekop, Roger Seamon, Martin Staum, Kay Stockholder, Steve Straker, Charles Tilly and Geoffrey Winthrop-Young. Ed Hundert submitted the manuscript to an incisive critique from which I gained much. I owe him a great debt. David Bates's reading of it opened up aspects of Tocqueville's thought that I might have overlooked. For his graceful and unstinting help, I am thankful. Thanks are also due to Richard Fisher of Cambridge University Press for his unfailing courtesy, and to Karen Anderson Howes, who, as copy-editor, paid remarkable attention to the manuscript's intricacies. Above all, I wish to express my appreciation to Ruth Mitchell for her encouragement and sympathetic understanding.

Portions of this book first appeared as articles: "Tocqueville's Mirage or Reality? Political Freedom from Old Régime to Revolution," *Journal of Modern History*, 60 (1988), pp. 28–54; "The Changing Conditions of Freedom: Tocqueville in the Light of Rousseau," *History of Political Thought*, 9 (1988), pp. 31–53; "Alexis de Tocqueville and the Legacy of the French Revolution," *Social Research*, 56 (1989), pp. 127–59 [also in *The French Revolution and the Birth of Modernity*, ed. Ferenc Féher (Berkeley, Los Angeles and Oxford, 1990), pp. 240–63]. The arguments I advance in them appear in various chapters of the book, often in their original form, but just as often in different, expanded and revised versions. Permission to use these materials was granted respectively by the University of Chicago Press, all rights reserved; *History of Political Thought*; *Social Research*; and the University of California Press.

Abbreviations

AT	The collection of manuscript notes for *L'Ancien Régime et la Révolution* conserved in the private Tocqueville archives. The third volume of the Pléiade edition (see below) will include all or the bulk of them.
BYT	The Yale Tocqueville Collection in the Beinecke Rare Book and Manuscript Library, Yale University.
Beaumont edn.	The first edition of Tocqueville's *Oeuvres complètes*, ed. Gustave de Beaumont, 9 vols. (Paris, 1864–78).
Nolla edn.	I and II, *De la Démocratie en Amérique*, critical edn., ed. Edouardo Nolla, 2 vols. (Paris, 1990).
OC	This definitive edition of the *Oeuvres complètes*, prepared under the supervision of the Commission nationale pour la publication des Oeuvres d'Alexis de Tocqueville, is nearing completion (Paris, 1950–). Only the volumes from which I cite are listed below.

I, pts. 1–2, *De la Démocratie en Amérique*. Introduced by Harold J. Laski. Preliminary note by J.-P. Mayer (1951).

II, pt. 1, *L'Ancien Régime et la Révolution*. Introduced by Georges Lefebvre. Preliminary note by J.-P. Mayer (1952).

II, pt. 2, *L'Ancien Régime et la Révolution. Fragments et notes inédites sur la Révolution*. Edited and annotated by André Jardin (1953).

III, pt. 2, *Ecrits et discours politiques*. Edited, annotated and introduced by André Jardin (1985).

III, pt. 3, *Ecrits et discours politiques*. Edited, annotated and introduced by André Jardin (1990).

V, pt. 1, *Voyages en Sicilie et aux Etats-Unis*. Edited and prefaced by J.-P. Mayer (1957).

VI, pt. 1, *Correspondance anglaise. Correspondance d'Alexis de Tocqueville avec Henry Reeve et John Stuart*

Mill. Edited and annotated by J.-P. Mayer and Gustave Rudler. Introduced by J.-P. Mayer (1954).

VI, pt. 2, *Correspondance anglaise. Correspondance et conversations d'Alexis de Tocqueville et Nassau William Senior.* Edited and annotated by H. Brogan and A. P. Kerr. Introduced by H. Brogan. Notes by J.-P. Mayer. Preface by Lord Roll (1991).

VII, *Correspondance étrangère d'Alexis de Tocqueville.* Edited by Françoise Mélonio, Lise Queffélec and Anthony Pleasance (1986).

VIII, pts. 1–3, *Correspondance d'Alexis de Tocqueville et de Gustave de Beaumont.* Edited, annotated and introduced by André Jardin (1967).

IX, *Correspondance d'Alexis de Tocqueville et d'Arthur de Gobineau.* Edited and annotated by M. Degros. Introduced by J.-J. Chevalier (1959).

XI, *Correspondance d'Alexis de Tocqueville et de Pierre-Paul Royer-Collard. Correspondance d'Alexis de Tocqueville et de Jean-Jacques Ampère.* Edited, annotated and introduced by André Jardin (1970).

XII, *Souvenirs.* Edited, annotated and introduced by Luc Monnier (1964).

XIII, pts. 1–2, *Correspondance d'Alexis de Tocqueville et de Louis de Kergorlay.* Edited by André Jardin. Introduction and notes by Jean-Alain Lesourd (1977).

XV, pts. 1–2, *Correspondance d'Alexis de Tocqueville et de Francisque de Corcelle. Correspondance d'Alexis de Tocqueville et de Madame Swetchine.* Edited by Pierre Gibert (1983).

XVI, *Mélanges.* Edited by Françoise Mélonio (1989).

XVIII, *Correspondance d'Alexis de Tocqueville avec Adolphe de Circourt et Madame de Circourt.* Edited by A. P. Kerr. Revised by Louis Girard and Douglas Johnson (1984).

OCR *Oeuvres complètes de Jean-Jacques Rousseau,* ed. Bernard Gagnebin and Marcel Raymond (Paris, 1959–).

Pléiade edn. pt. 1, Alexis de Tocqueville. *Oeuvres.* I. Edited under the direction of André Jardin with the collaboration of Françoise Mélonio and Lise Queffélec (Paris, 1991).

Pléiade edn. pt. 2, Alexis de Tocqueville. *Oeuvres.* II. Edited under the direction of André Jardin with the collaboration of Jean-Claude Lamberti and James T. Schleifer (Paris, 1992).

The following English editions of Tocqueville's works were used for the English translations in my study, but I replaced them with my own when I believed they were more faithful to the original:

Democracy in America. The Henry Reeve text, revised by Francis Bowen, now further corrected and ed., with introduction, edited notes, and bibliographies by Phillips Bradley, 2 vols. (New York, 1945).

Democracy in America. Ed. J. P. Mayer, trans. George Lawrence (New York, 1969).

The Old Régime and the French Revolution. Trans. Stuart Gilbert (New York, 1955).

The European Revolution and Correspondence with Gobineau. Ed. and trans. John Lukacs (New York, 1959).

The Recollections of Alexis de Tocqueville. Trans. A. T. de Mattos (New York, 1959).

I

Introduction

1 Frameworks

A Klee painting named "Angelus Novus" shows an angel looking as though he is about to move away from something he is fixedly contemplating. His eyes are staring, his mouth is open, his wings are spread. This is how one pictures the angel of history. His face is turned toward the past. Where we perceive a chain of events, he sees one single catastrophe which keeps piling wreckage upon wreckage and hurls it in front of his feet. The angel would like to stay, awaken the dead, and make whole what has been smashed. But a storm is brewing from Paradise; it has got caught in his wings with such violence that the angel can no longer close them. This storm irresistibly propels him into the future to which his back is turned, while the pile of debris before him grows skyward. This storm is what we call progress.[1]

For I am convinced that though they (the French) had no inkling of this, they took over from the *ancien régime* not only most of its customs, conventions, and mode of thought, but even those very ideas which prompted our revolutionaries to destroy it; that, in fact, though nothing was further from their intentions, they used the debris of the old order for building up the new. Thus if we wish to get a true understanding of the Revolution and its achievement, it is well to disregard for the moment the France of today, and to look back to the France that is no more.[2]

Alexis de Tocqueville has achieved a certain kind of iconic power. He can bear the burden. The real ordeal rests on those who appeal to or reject him. If they do either, they must reckon with his instinct and genius for locating the links between the past and future of his own time. We are left to debate whether he was right to say that, in the modern world of democratic equality, people would either face or turn away from the paradoxes of private and public liberty, and that they might prove either able or unable to meet the challenge of crafting the political weapons to make the decisions affecting them all as a community. The engagement with such a sweeping responsibility could, he was convinced, be found only in a

---

[1] Walter Benjamin, "Theses on the Philosophy of History," Thesis IX, in *Illuminations*, ed. Hannah Arendt, trans. Harry Zohn (New York, 1969), pp. 257–58.

[2] *OC*, II, pt. 1, p. 69.

culture that stressed the importance of origins, laws and transcendent goals. But none of the latter could be known without the historical imagination that would open modern self-consciousness to their importance and that needed the help of clear-sighted guides. Tocqueville counted himself among these select few.

Tocqueville was not one of those thinkers who prepare and identify their life's work along a single axis. Most who have written about him have adopted a specific aspect of his thought, whether it be political philosophy, sociology, morals and religion, the history of early American democratic institutions or the coming of the French Revolution. His major works are largely treated as separate units in his life, with the result that they stand like solitary and isolated figures in our mental landscape. Tocqueville's own compass was always much wider. No matter what inquiry he undertook, it was invested with a taste for its distant horizons where he could let his mind wander freely over problems that nest within rich layers of meaning. Any analysis oriented toward one of those isolated points of light is thus certain to be limited, especially if, in tracing the sources of his complexity as a thinker, it succeeds merely in reaffirming that he is an important thinker – a fact we all know but don't know as fully as we might.

This book is an attempt to consider and to support Tocqueville's claim in the last decade of his life that it was principally as a historian that he wanted to be remembered. Only the study of history, he came to believe, promised the route to an unraveling of the meaning of the democratic age, whose most urgent need was to set in place a foundation for avoiding its tendency to put on trial and exhaust the capacities of modern men to preserve and enhance the conditions of their liberty. Present historical consciousness could not live without this foundation, and the study of the past would show how liberty and history needed each other.

The extraordinary power of Tocqueville's thought may be illumined by looking at his view that the wholeness of his ideas, transcending its discrete and constituent parts, contained certain important truths of the world, and that these truths rested on understanding them historically. Studies of his ideas about the past have been restricted for the most part to *L'Ancien Régime*. A few modern assessments stand out from the rest. Alfred Cobban leaves us in no doubt that for him Tocqueville's work owes its enduring quality to the fact that he was a "man who had thought long and deeply on the problems of government, and that it was also the first history to be based upon a study of some of the administrative records in which the *ancien régime* was so rich."[3] As for Tocqueville's philosophy of

---

[3] Alfred Cobban, *Aspects of the French Revolution* (London, 1968), p. 42.

history, Cobban does not refer to *L'Ancien Régime*, but to the *Souvenirs*, lending weight to my view that it is not only in his last work that one may find answers to his thoughts on history. Cobban further anticipates my own arguments for a synthesized view of an individual's ideas, whether they are to be found in one work or scattered throughout several. He uses Tocqueville's musings on the weaknesses of his fellow-historians' and fellow-politicians' failure to give more than token importance to causation, reducing it either to the activities and intentions of individuals, or to more enigmatic, hence irrecoverable, first causes.[4]

François Furet underlines why Tocqueville might command renewed interest on a new plane altogether.[5] Beyond Tocqueville's literary skills, and the Tocquevillian thesis that the Revolution carried the centralizing tendencies of the French monarchy to new heights, and therefore was not revolutionary enough – both of which ideas figure prominently in Cobban – Furet sees in Tocqueville a thinker who gave extended importance, not only to the social and administrative, but to the primacy of the political and the ideological, sources of the old society in crisis. Tocqueville initiated the idea that one had to look at the evolution of the specific dialectic between the state and civil society in order to grasp why France uniquely succumbed to revolution. Cobban takes the line that social and political factors were more significant than ideas in launching the Revolution on its course.[6] Furet does not disagree with the first part of Cobban's position, and he gives the political even more weight. But he disagrees that ideas had only a secondary role. He is also far more probing in his analysis of Tocqueville's knowledge and understanding of the *ancien régime*'s administrative structure, and critical of his idealized version of the aristocracy's self-image. In Furet's overall evaluation, Tocqueville powerfully intuited how the "veil of ideology hides most completely the real meaning of the events from the protagonists" and that this insight was the "fundamental contribution of *L'Ancien Régime* to a theory of revolution."[7] Tocqueville's failure to enunciate a fuller theory of the Revolution lay, according to Furet, in his inability to tie events in themselves to the ideologies that rationalized and justified them. He did not succeed, in short, in grasping the operations of the cultural dynamic that transformed minds and values, because he had become too wedded to the idea that administrative structures are in the end more determining.

Like Furet, Lynn Hunt stresses the political dimensions of the crisis facing a besieged monarchy anxious to retain its authority. She implies, in

---

[4] Ibid., p. 94.
[5] François Furet, *Interpreting the French Revolution*, trans. Elborg Forster (Cambridge and Paris, 1981).   [6] Cobban, *Aspects of the French Revolution*, p. 20.
[7] Furet, *Interpreting the French Revolution*, p. 159.

addition, that Tocqueville's main point was that, after emasculating the aristocracy, the crown had little room to maneuver, thereby opening up space for revolutionaries of all types to continue the process of consolidating state power. Almost as an afterthought, she challenges Furet's failure to appreciate Tocqueville's narrative intentions and force, but she adds little to Furet's critique of Tocqueville's failed attempt to bring events, actors and structures into a coherent whole. For Hunt, by implication more open to breaking the law-like chain, Tocqueville was a prisoner of "the necessary course from origins to outcomes,"[8] so that he consequently stood on, but could not cross, the threshold of a political interpretation of the Revolution itself. George Armstrong Kelly resolutely says that Tocqueville turned his back forever on the perspectives of historical actors, because it was subversive of modern history writing to which he was committed in his conscious repudiation of aristocratic modes of historical reconstruction. There is for him, in short, no problem for Tocqueville after this putative decision.[9]

Both in an older work, but more emphatically in a more recent collaborative essay, Theda Skocpol appears to be the most faithful follower of the Tocquevillian idea that the Revolution transformed France into a more highly centralized and bureaucratic state.[10] Revolutionary France moved in that direction as much from the impact of international as from internal conflict – perhaps, even, more from the former. Tocqueville is praised for identifying the bureaucratic state and the movement toward modernity as the most enduring legacy of the Revolution, while Lynn Hunt is criticized for not perceiving the links between that achievement and French revolutionary politics. Skocpol and Kestenbaum argue for a closer fit between Jacobin political mobilization and the mobilization for international war. Tocqueville may have erred in drawing a direct line from the proclivities of old régime state power to revolutionary bureaucratization, but that does not affect his major achievement as a theorist of modern state formation. Tocqueville emerges from the Skocpol–Kestenbaum analysis primarily and most importantly as a sociologist of revolution, rather than as a historian concerned with such questions as intentionality and their intersection with long-term historical forces.

[8] Lynn Hunt, *Politics, Culture and Class in the French Revolution* (Berkeley, Los Angeles and London, 1984), p. 10.

[9] George Armstrong Kelly, *The Humane Comedy: Constant, Tocqueville and French Liberalism* (Cambridge, 1992), pp. 232–35.

[10] Theda Skocpol, *States and Social Revolutions: A Comparative Analysis of France, Russia and China* (Cambridge and New York, 1979), and Skocpol and Meyer Kestenbaum, "Mars Unshackled: The French Revolution in World-Historical Perspective," in *The French Revolution and the Birth of Modernity*, ed. Ferenc Fehér (Berkeley, Los Angeles and Oxford, 1990), pp. 13–29.

One may see that a crucial anxiety is at work in Hunt's account as in Cobban's and Furet's, but far less so in Skocpol – namely, the problem of how Tocqueville's sense of history was clearly marked by the problem of how to deal with individual choice and larger structures. Françoise Mélonio, who traces Tocqueville's overall reception down to the present time, also remarks on, but takes for granted, Tocqueville's supposed lack of interest in political actors in *L'Ancien Régime*.[11] What is, however, just as significant, from my point of view, is that these historians did not take this question further, because they confined themselves to interpretations of Tocqueville as historian of the Revolution's origins.

One of the obstacles to the assessment of an individual's thought that may in some way do justice to its totality (which is my task in this book) lies in the danger into which an inquirer might be lured by the hope of valorizing the subject's critical self-consciousness to the point of imagining that it exists independently of what he experiences; or in the acts in which the subject, inquiring about his own past, himself engages. While people try to bring sense to their thoughts and actions over time, their efforts combine the haphazardness of memory, the temptations of rationalization and, no matter how much care is taken to avoid it, some form of tunnel vision – all of them risks shared by subject and investigator alike. But, for subject and critic both, these risks, embedded in the nature of the enterprise, need not, Tocqueville rightly believed – and I concur – induce paralysis or an extreme skepticism. His way of thinking will only be intelligible when as many of its facets as can be dealt with under a broader canopy are brought together. I do so on the supposition that there was an intellectual structure to start with.[12]

Tocqueville plunged into the problems raised by the mounting attacks throughout the eighteenth century on the seemingly imperishable, integrative power of custom, which ended in revolution, with its after-shocks of unpredictable severity. This study explores how and why Tocqueville thought the problems of post-*ancien régime* society undergoing change were formed both by particular and concrete events and by law-like structures and processes. Historians often, if indeed invariably, plot their inquiries along one, not both, of these trajectories. Tocqueville tried to

---

[11] Françoise Mélonio, *Tocqueville et les français* (Paris, 1993), pp. 146–56. See also Mélonio, "Tocqueville: aux origines de la démocratie française," which is not confined to *L'Ancien Régime*, in *The Transformation of Political Culture*, Vol. III, *The French Revolution and the Creation of Modern Political Culture*, ed. François Furet and Mona Ozouf (Paris, 1989), pp. 595–611.

[12] As I worked on this study, I found much to agree with in Karl Jaspers's Introduction to his study of Nietzsche, *Nietzsche: An Introduction to the Understanding of His Philosophical Activity*, trans. Charles F. Wallraff and Frederick J. Schmitz (Tucson, 1965), especially pp. 4–5, 15 and 17.

travel along both. At both the particular and macrostructural levels, Tocqueville's idea of history is cradled, to a degree which has hitherto not been fully perceived, in an intellectual structure embracing purpose, choice, necessity and historical indeterminacy or contingency – questions that he tried to grapple with all his life. Focus on these elements exists in the foreground in my analysis of all of Tocqueville's works. His reflections on the sources of revolutionary change brought these metahistorical elements in his ideas to the surface and made them an integral part of his thought. For me, it is clear that his ideas will remain accessible only at a superficial level if we ignore the fact that these elements had a real place in his imagination, the positions he took on continuity and change and in his speculations on the future course of democracy.

To see Tocqueville as a thinker intellectually engaged in this way might be viewed as granting greater importance to him as a theoretical thinker than is warranted by his professed disdain for philosophy and, as one might argue, his limitations as a full-fledged philosopher of history, or finally by the contention that his ideas are more interesting in their details than in their conclusions.[13] It is impossible to ignore, but it is also possible to exaggerate, his own earliest declarations of alienation from philosophy. He wrote in this vein to a few of his friends from America where he was trying to confront the juxtaposed realities of the old and new worlds. Philosophy, he told Le Peletier d'Aunay, was the "essence of all gibberish,"[14] and to Charles Stoffels he characterized it as "an agony that man chooses and agrees to . . . inflict on himself."[15] The fact is that he inflicted it on himself. Even as he made these confessions, he told Ernest de Chabrol how frightened he was by the fact that human beings are capable of acquiring only infinitesimal fragments of certainty:

There is no subject that is not enlarged in proportion to the [energy] with which one penetrates it, neither fact nor observation at the bottom of which one cannot discover some doubt. All the objects in this life appear to us, like certain decorations in the opera, only through a veil, preventing us from apprehending their contours with precision. There are people who enjoy living in this perpetual twilight; as for me, it tires and depresses me; I would like to hold the political and moral truths the way I hold the pen . . . I place human misery in the same order of chronic illness, death and doubt.[16]

Encapsulated in this passage is a reluctant but resigned submission to doubt in human affairs, but also some resistance to the depression that concern with ultimate questions induced in him. Just as unmistakably,

---

[13] For the last view, see Jon Elster, *Political Psychology* (Cambridge, 1993).
[14] Draft of a letter from Tocqueville to Le Peletier d'Aunay, November 8, 1831, *BYT*, B.I.a. (1–2).   [15] Tocqueville to C. Stoffels, October 22, 1831, *Beaumont edn.*, VI, p. 370.
[16] Tocqueville to Chabrol, November 19, 1831, *BYT*, B.I.a. (1–2).

the letter to Chabrol offers more than a hint that the veil needed to be pierced, not by accepting the clichés and pieties that obscured life's meanings, but by questioning them. And the immediate and long-term lessons that the journey to America gave Tocqueville, lessons to which he returned for the remainder of his life, will be missed unless his need to get as close to the bottom of the doubt as possible is recognized. Much of this book is devoted to Tocqueville's struggle with this and related questions.

II

In assembling the pieces of an argument signifying the many themes in Tocqueville's approach to history, the question of how each of them might be unpacked, enlarged and glossed had to be faced. I had no problem in deciding to place the conceptual issues to the fore and deliberately to avoid the more traditional chronological conventions. Following the latter approach in fact tends to obscure the quality of Tocqueville's interpretive powers. Furthermore, in deciding that the *Souvenirs* are absolutely central to Tocqueville's handling of the tensions between individual choice and historical structures, I am taking the next step and wagering that there is some considerable advantage in treating them not in the chronological order in which Tocqueville's works appeared. The *Souvenirs* captured a personal record of a major political crisis. They brought together many formerly tentative ideas with which Tocqueville felt he had to come to terms. While the proximate and long-term meaning of the Revolution of 1789 was never far from his thoughts, the *Souvenirs* proved to be a decisive turning point in that they led directly to his study of the breakdown of the *ancien régime*. They acted as a kind of prism through which he could see into the past and into the future, sometimes with a clarity that startled him. The second reason for avoiding a straight chronology is that it runs the risk of distorting how many people actually order their ideas and conduct their inquiries. Tocqueville felt no commitment to obeying the dictates of a traditional chronology that would nurture the belief that events follow a system and an order. His very deep need to reach out for psychological verisimilitude and to assert his intellectual integrity fought against such an approach.

There is, in other words, a better way to achieve a reenactment of Tocqueville's concerns. There are foundations to be unearthed, as he was fond of saying when he evoked Georges Cuvier's paleontological research,[17] but many of the disinterred pieces take on their sharp edges only after several revisits, not only to their original sites, but to the new

---

[17] Tocqueville to Beaumont, November 22, 1836, *OC*, VIII, pt. 1, p. 175.

sites where Tocqueville fitted the pieces into his continuing imaginative rediscoveries of the themes that filled his life. The ten years ending in 1850 gave him newer ways of seeing the past than at the time he was writing the *Democracy*, especially in his belief that he had something even more meaningful to say about how human beings act in the mass.[18] It was not that he had any sense, as he grew older, of repudiating any of the fundamental principles that he had laid down in the 1830s. There were "irrevocable propositions and maxims" which formed the gritty ingredients common to all serious ideas. What eluded him, and remained a mystery, he remarked wryly, was how his own mental transformations over a lifetime had occurred.[19] He came somewhat closer to solving this enigma by speaking about how work and continuing relationships and interest in the world insulated the soul against the cold hand of death and presumably made him more patient. To succeed demanded, as he said repeatedly, constant scrutiny of the ideas that guided life in the past in light of the ideas that were changing society and thoughts about it.[20]

To convey some notion of what this meant for Tocqueville, it is therefore best to make the journey from the narrative of the *Souvenirs* to *L'Ancien Régime* by means of apparent detours to lines of inquiry he had started when he was younger. If necessary, the same terrain will be crossed more than once to ensure that the insights he collected and stored to bring them out at the right moment are not lost. As he candidly admitted, he had no expectation that his view of recapturing the past was either fully consistent or coherent. If striving for either consistency or coherency satisfied an aesthetic longing, the result should not, he felt, be confused with a notion that a final historical reality followed historical inquiry.

Lynn Hunt rightly intimates that Tocqueville does not entirely eschew the narrative form in *L'Ancien Régime*. His use of it in the *Souvenirs* presents a version of events and individuals interacting during periods of short duration, but he also shows that he knows they are being touched by underlying structural contexts, as in his constant appeals not only to the immediate past and future of what he narrates, but also to the more distant events of 1789 and 1830. His story should not therefore be seen exclusively as a narrative of short duration wherein quotidian choices are considered. The methodological boundaries supposedly separating that kind of narrative from the narrative of long duration are important but

---

[18] Tocqueville to Kergorlay, December 15, 1850, *OC*, XIII, pt. 2, p. 229.
[19] Tocqueville in a conversation of February 16, 1854, recorded by Mrs. Grote, *OC*, VI, pt. 2, p. 415.   [20] Tocqueville to Kergorlay, February 3, 1857, *OC*, XIII, pt. 2, p. 325.

not impermeable. If this view is plausible, his description of the durable and slowly changing structures of the *ancien régime* should itself therefore be seen in no small part as a narration of events that brings those structures to historical consciousness and cognition. Together these two aspects – though they are not totally distinct – of narrative enable one to grasp important features of Tocqueville's conception of history. He did not, it seems to me, wish to free himself entirely from what Furet calls the "tyranny of the historical actors'" own conception of their experience; and the difficulty of the "mingling of genres" – the mixing of narrative and analysis – troubled him a good deal.[21]

My use of "narrative" also denotes not only what Hayden White conveniently sums up as "the way in which a historical interpretation is achieved and the mode of discourse in which a successful understanding of matters historical is represented."[22] White finds support from Louis Mink's description of it as "a primary cognitive instrument . . . rivaled, in fact, only by theory and by metaphor as irreducible ways of making the flux of experience comprehensible."[23] I believe it is also particularly useful to conceive of narrative in a wider sense as carrying with it an ideological load, especially, as we shall see, the high degree to which Tocqueville's tastes and political preferences provide the energy of his *Souvenirs*. In arguing for the presence of the argumentative idiom in historical narrative, Alasdair MacIntyre casts additional light on what I believe were Tocqueville's intentions. "A tradition not only embodies the narrative of an argument, but it is only to be recovered by the argumentative retelling of the narrative."[24] Once Tocqueville chose narrative as his methodology for the *Souvenirs*, he came face to face with the structure of a preexisting narrative. He worked within it but not without making it work for him, shaping it by selecting and omitting incidents, events, char-

[21] I am questioning the first of Furet's views, and greatly qualifying the second. See *Interpreting the French Revolution*, pp. 15, 18. Reinhart Koselleck reminds us that no privileged status should be ascribed to historical narrative. He isolates the theoretical differences between narrative and description, coupling the first with "events," and the second with structures. At the same time, he points out that in practice the boundary between the two methods is not sealed tight. See his essay, "Representation, Event and Structure," in Koselleck, *Futures Past: On the Semantics of Historical Time*, trans. Keith Tribe (Cambridge, Mass., and London, 1985), pp. 105–15.

[22] See Hayden White, "The Politics of Historical Interpretation: Discipline and Desublimation," in *The Politics of Interpretation*, ed. W. J. T. Mitchell (Chicago and London, 1983), p. 122. Tocqueville was understandably not concerned with, nor could he have been cognizant of, "the conceptually underdetermined sort [of historical knowledge] that appears in the form of a conventional narrative."

[23] Louis Mink, "Narrative Form as a Cognitive Instrument," in *Historical Understanding*, ed. Brian Fay, Eugene O. Golob and Richard T. Vann (New York, 1987), p. 185.

[24] Alasdair MacIntyre, "Epistemological Crises, Dramatic Narrative and the Philosophy of Science," *Monist*, 60 (1977), p. 461.

acters and actions, claiming, as any author would, some special knowledge that carried with it the gravity of authoritativeness.[25]

The personal narrative of his *Souvenirs* thus provides a bridge from his
earliest ideas and works to what I shall call a narrative of structures in
L'Ancien Régime et la Révolution. What I found an obstacle at first, but in
time saw as an opportunity for unlocking this historical problem, was to
understand the relationship between, on the one hand, how the individual, through thoughts, affects and actions, and existing institutional and
psychological structures, participates in and in part creates knowingly, so
to speak, a "narrative" universe; and, on the other hand, how structures
appear to engulf the individual. Tocqueville revealed both processes
amply and often poignantly in the unfolding of the events of 1848. It was
in *L'Ancien Régime* that he chose to move deliberately from the particular
actions of historical actors to the general and subterranean forces shaping
historical change.

By this move, he brought narrative to another level. The shift need not
be thought of either as a betrayal or as a logical contradiction of the narrative form. Narratives need not be confined to the stories of individuals.
Societies, large and small, have their life histories. Tocqueville, exploiting
the narrative form, brought to critical consciousness the history of his
own society and that of its neighbors. Knowing imperfectly, to be sure,
that his own emotional and intellectual development was linked with the
challenges, strains and crises of his own society, he sought to perceive,
define and reflect upon those linkages. By extension backwards in time,
he also connected them with what was for him a seminal point in the
history of a society from which he had sprung. As a particular individual –
though an individual with a powerful urge to understand the past – he
attempted to lay bare the values and practices of that culture, the eventual
sources of its breakdown and its final death throes, though not without
leaving strong traces of itself in his present. He gave a highly precise voice
to what everyone in a community, small or large, tried to come to terms
with in their own lives. In doing so, they perceived that communities, like
the individuals which form them, are fragile, live and die; and hence have
narratives as well.

I make the *Souvenirs* bear as much of the burden as *L'Ancien Régime* –
sometimes a larger part – in recreating Tocqueville's self-understanding
as a thinker who worked out a mode of historical inquiry whose contours
took on greater sharpness as he defined its capacities to deal with these
aspects of a restoration of the past. My book may be read as a study of
how Tocqueville found, through his personal experience of 1848, that

---

[25] Cf. David Carr, *Time, Narrative and History* (Bloomington, 1986).

these two senses of narrative could not be kept apart. Each implied the other, but the personal one made manifest the close but never closed links between active choice, which operates within narrow limits that heighten the sense of possibilities, and deeper structures. The impersonal one kept choice and possibilities in the background but never out of sight. It was as if Tocqueville stretched himself out along the string of these two narrative poles which loosened and tightened their grip on his historical mind. This tension is plain to observe in his great longing to reveal the meaning of the events, rather than to remain content with a mere display of the events that themselves made up the 1789 Revolution and its reverberations.

His major historical work has claimed most attention in this regard. The reasons are themselves unexceptionable. He invested *L'Ancien Régime* with a high regard for the intellectual act of discerning general historical laws. He executed his intentions with a strong element of self-conscious cunning, exploiting his foresight, experience, courage and, occasionally, resorting to concealment of his reliance on others who had been over the terrain before him. His approach to history at times shows some of the epic qualities that are usually associated with remembrance of the feats of the ancients. His rhetoric sometimes fits that outlook. It also fits other sides of his temperament, the ones that sought out and found the ironies and tragedies and, sometimes, the comic in history. This side of his historical understanding constitutes the second way he identified structures and processes, and is to be found preeminently in the personal narrative of his *Souvenirs,* where he majestically discerned the relationship between human frailty and "error." He saw the last in three principal ways: sometimes as a deviation, as in his depiction of revolution as *un mal*; second, he related it to the deceptions and self-deceptions of historical actors; finally, he sometimes put it within the problematic of what we today tend to call "necessitarianism" and "voluntarism."

Tocqueville linked these meanings of "error" to the problems of conceptualizing a historical *telos*. He embedded it in his notion of "points of departure" – his metaphor for his search for the common foundations of Western societies – the rise of the modern state and its points of intersection with the rise of personal consciousness and modern political culture in the contrasting histories of France, America, England and Germany. He discussed these questions under such rubrics as "ends" and "beginnings." He was also much taken by a sense of incompleteness, as he considered how best to speak about each of these moments of time. He was satisfied neither with a seamless temporality, nor with a concept of time positing sharply defined boundaries between one historical period and another. Neither offered promising explanations for the origins and decline of aristocratic cultures and the sources and uncertain futures of democratic ones. He would not finally commit himself to a precise temporal framework to ease the process of extricating the presence of traces and continuities and the existence of apparent repetitions and ruptures.

This skeptical stance stimulated reflections on what he referred to as historical "reenactments," not only in the sense of theater or as replay, but also as momentary and flawed instances of the metahistorical. "Reenactments" conjure up the idea of acts embedded in a past from which people might try to struggle to free themselves with varying degrees of success. Or they might succumb to the burden of the past in resignation. Possibly, even more usually, they might believe they are doing the first while actually doing the second. Tocqueville saw the problems of choice and determinateness as entangled with repetition and reenactment in history, and wondered if the historical actors could see the truly transformative events that broadened liberty and opened up the possibility of enhancing the human condition, instead of subjecting themselves to the futile agony of endless repetitions that led nowhere. This semi-agnostic epistemology did not deter him from trying to keep the image of liberty alive through his own *imaginaire*, unlike the false *imaginaire* that he believed had led the generation of French revolutionaries astray, and confused their heirs. The prophetic and the predictive are recurrent themes, because he saw them as integral to his vision of historical time, his search for coherence and his struggles with randomness and order.

There was an unmistakable sense of unease in Tocqueville's search for an adequate historical treatment of the clash between the premodern and modern worlds that would do justice to their dialectical relationship and to a probable future issuing from it. In fact, he has not left a misleading analysis of the French Revolution as a simple battle between two opposing cultures with opposite political visions. Rather, as he saw it, remnants of the past clung to the specifically French and European democratic outcomes of the struggle. There was no absolute triumph of one set of imaginary or mythical abstractions over another. Democracy, as it appeared in America, on the other hand, marked for him a new chapter in the development of society, but even so it was in part the offspring of an older English religious and political culture. The kind of historical inquiry he made his own had as its source of energy the belief that, however elusive the meaning of the human condition in cultural and transcendental terms was, it could be glimpsed bit by bit – though never, of course, with any certainty that the whole of its meaning would yield itself to the scrutiny of the human beings who were haphazardly shaping it. To some of his contemporaries, who embraced an unreflective determinism, and who therefore saw historical change in non-dialectical terms,[26] he opposed a highly nuanced sense of the restraints imposed on choice, based on a particular view of how reality might be perceived and bound. No sense of resigned fatalism nor of cynical nihilism invaded his sense of historical change. Even if, at the same time, he was never far from feelings of inadequacy, he was always intrigued by the problems of fathoming the ways in which the past could be discerned, and in light of them, of plotting solutions to the present.

The oft-quoted passages from *Democracy in America*, where he aligned himself with the forces of the new against the old, show him reflecting on the paradox that the liberating forces leading to the modern age might be posing new threats to liberty in an untried political and economic context. The remarkable developments in commerce and technological expansion, long in the making, impressed him as an unstoppable force. Were the new forces controllable? He was inclined to doubt whether the class that had raised itself to wealth and power had all the qualities needed to exercise its prudence and restraint.[27] He asked the question in the spirit of a man who was convinced that material well-being was a byproduct of liberty, and not the reverse. The middle class alone – for there was no other, he argued, with the minimal qualifications to apprehend this truth – would have to draw resolutely on its pool of enlightened views to take up the challenge of putting liberty first. The question, as he put it later in *L'Ancien Régime*, was whether it would:

> Nor do I think that a genuine love of liberty is ever quickened by the prospect of material rewards; indeed, that prospect is often dubious, anyhow as regards the immediate future. True, in the long run liberty always brings to those who know how to retain it comfort and well-being, and often great prosperity. Nevertheless, for the moment it sometimes tells against amenities of this nature, and there are times, indeed, when despotism can best assure a brief enjoyment of them. Those who value liberty only for the material benefits it offers have never kept it for long.[28]

What could not be discounted completely, he said once *L'Ancien Régime* was published, was the fact that all mass movements, even the crudest, are initiated by metaphysical ideas, even quite abstract ones, a fact that history, he said, bears out. For that reason, there was still reason to believe that ideas should be circulated, "in the hope that, if they are correct, they will, little by little, end in transforming themselves into passions and into facts. I ask God to let me live to see that transformation,

---

[26] Cf. R. G. Collingwood's discussion in *The New Leviathan*, rev. edn., ed. David Boucher (Oxford, 1992), pp. 206–08. Collingwood incorrectly made no exception in his general critique of nineteenth-century historians whom he challenged for their failure to think dialectically.   [27] *Nolla edn.*, p. 205.   [28] *OC*, II, pt. 1, p. 217.

though to tell the truth, I hardly hope to."[29] In the *Democracy*, he was readier – although he did not suppress his uncertainty about such a transformation – to think that, however much the consequences of an unlimited equality troubled him, it was hard to deny that "the greater well-being of all" was more important than the "particular prosperity of the few . . . Equality may be less elevated, but it is more just, and in its justice lies its greatness and beauty."[30] The coupling of justice and equality was rarely stated with such assurance by Tocqueville. The association he made at this time may be related to his later musings on the power that liberty and equality might have in their ideal forms: each would not encroach upon, but would instead energize, the other. Though not fully conceptualized, his idea of justice as a transforming power is what he believed was at stake.[31]

In taking this stance, the aristocrat paradoxically became the analyst of the mixed sources of modernity and its discontents. He was not an intellectual in the critical *fin de siècle* spirit of a Nietzsche, pointing to modernity's dangerous, as well as its liberating, points, daring all for an indefinable future; instead, he was more of a protomodern kind of critic, aware of swiftly changing prospects for Western and, in the long run, for some sections of non-Western humanity. He was, as it were, permanently caught between finding a way of preserving or duplicating the best of the old – above all the spirit of excellence in human striving that was inseparable from liberty – and giving due recognition to democratic equality, which he thought inevitable. He could only speculate on the full consequences of the trade-off between the probable stability of life in democratic society, engendered by its cultivation of retreat into passivity, and the grandeur of the human spirit, expressive of the best in aristocratic cultures.

He confessed, in one of his moments of depression, that the alternations between trust and mistrust in his own powers came from the same source – an extreme desire to be noticed. Being a whole person meant recognition of this weakness.[32] There is a strong implication in this self-revelation that Tocqueville meant it to signal an act of freedom. To be free meant forcing oneself to recognize the power of contingency – not to celebrate it but soberly to make it part of the consciousness of one's own

---

[29] Tocqueville to Odilon Barrot, July 18, 1856, *Beaumont edn.*, VII, p. 395.
[30] *Nolla edn.*, II, p. 280.
[31] There are of course many extended passages in Tocqueville's work on the less metaphysical aspects of justice, the law and the courts. In the *Democracy, Nolla edn.*, I, p. 109, for example, he writes that, "The great purpose of justice is to substitute the rule of law for the idea of violence, to place intermediaries between the government and the use of physical force."   [32] Tocqueville to Mme. Swetchine, October 6, 1855, *OC*, XV, pt. 2, p. 264.

history and the history of the species. His allusions in his *Souvenirs* to sea change, driftlessness and lack of direction give full scope to his deepest beliefs in the uncertainty of the human condition, including, of course, the uncertainties of historical explanation. That sense of disorientation came from his immersion in the practical and theoretical problems released by the Great Revolution:

Shall we ever – as we are assured by other prophets, perhaps as delusive as their predecessors – shall we ever attain a more complete and more far-reaching social transformation than our fathers foresaw and desired, and that we ourselves are able to foresee; or are we not destined simply to end in a condition of intermittent anarchy, the well-known chronic and incurable complaint of old peoples? As for me, I am unable to say: I do not know when this long voyage will be ended; I am weary of seeing the shore in each successive mirage, and I often ask myself whether the *terra firma* we are seeking does really exist, and whether we are not doomed to rove upon the seas forever![33]

There is more than a feeling of aimlessness in the image. Tocqueville condemned the politicians of 1848 who thought they were rowing their boat along a river, when in fact they were adrift in mid-ocean, confused and even more uncertain over their destination than the passengers.[34] The Platonic metaphor of the ship of state, floundering in a confusion of misplaced authority, is an obvious point of comparison. The greater point that Tocqueville made relates to the question of the end of history, or the near end of history, when the struggles associated with successive historical epochs not only change over time, but will cease altogether, or at least take on a shape not perceivable to contemporaries. As he told Gobineau, just as it is impossible in the absence of written records to trace the various paths from the earliest periods of primitive human existence to the present, so too was it a purely hypothetical exercise to speak with certainty about the evolution of the various races of humankind, to ascribe to the white race an inherent superiority and, not least, to speak as if the study of the human sciences had achieved perfection.[35]

So he had already said unequivocally a decade earlier. "Man, with his vices, weaknesses, that muddled mixture of good and bad, low and high, honesty and depravity, is still on the whole the worthiest object of examination, interest, compassion, affection and admiration to be found on earth, and since angels are missing [from the world we inhabit], we can attach ourselves to nothing that is greater and worthier of our attention than our fellow beings."[36] There was more precision in some of his other

---

[33] *OC*, XII, p. 87.   [34] Ibid., p. 100.
[35] Tocqueville to Gobineau, November 17, 1853, *OC*, IX, p. 202.
[36] Tocqueville to E. Stoffels, January 3, 1843, *Beaumont edn.*, V, pp. 447–48.

reflections. Human beings are drawn to the particular. By limiting their affective selves to those they can know intimately, they satisfy a felt need for human solidarity. Only then can they grasp humanity in the abstract and take steps to secure their own well-being. There are not, however, any necessary direct links between particular and general affects. Individual passions are the key to how much human beings will reach inside themselves to display enthusiasm, energy and durability in achieving social cohesion. And people will only respond generously if a useful cause common to the human species is involved. They act in accordance "with their passions and their interests," and in the long run are good only insofar as doing good serves their needs.[37] The history of the French Revolution, seen in these terms, is a history of narrow views and personal egoism – its violent and dark side – as well as a history of its generosity and disinterestedness – its powerful, grand and irresistible side.[38] The questions of human nature and the uses of reason, for Tocqueville, did not lie wholly in the realm of metaphysics, but neither was history an unambiguously anti-metaphysical branch of inquiry. So he did not feel compelled to take up an intransigent position on the need to "drain" history of metaphysical concerns – a wholly false position as far as he could see.

On a matter closer to the issue, he took some considerable pain to give what he thought was Christianity's due in an effort to extract permanent values from it, and to relate them to his belief that modern human beings ignored their spirituality at great risk to their higher selves. Christianity's earliest institutionalized forms and political practices were almost all reprehensible, but had nevertheless assumed less vicious forms as time progressed. Nearly everything that was valuable in the human struggle to extend spiritual vitality and enlightened modern morality came from Christianity, despite a plethora of brutal episodes in its movement toward dominance. The oldest and purest Christian principles chose, developed, identified and united fragmentary Greek and Oriental ideas and made them part of a unique moral doctrine. Clearly the movement toward modern liberty was part of Christianity's humanizing message.[39] The future of liberty was not assured, but Tocqueville was not ready to say that it was lost, so long as human beings could exercise choice and see that it was bound up with their selves as spiritual beings. If anything, this belief

---

[37] Tocqueville used this phrase in June 1853. See *AT*, 43B, Dossier K, "Idées divers."

[38] *OC*, II, pt. 2, pp. 346–50. From these beliefs Tocqueville never departed. He repeated them, for example, in October 1856. See *AT*, 45B, "Première chemise. Marche de travail."

[39] Tocqueville to Gobineau, October 2, 1843, and October 22, 1843, *OC*, IX, pp. 57–62, 67–68.

became more intense as he grew older, when he said that "God has permitted us to distinguish [good and evil] and given us the liberty of choosing; but beyond these clear notions, everything that moves beyond the boundaries of this world seems to me to be shrouded in overpowering darkness."[40]

The primary legacy of Christian belief in individual conscience and self-realization, though now largely but not totally secularized in form, remained, however, as he said in the *Democracy*,[41] the best assurance for the survival of human morality and spirituality. For the latter depended on faith in a transcendent power – a basic human need. There was the possibility that this feature of humanity might be obfuscated and eventually buried by a tendency in modern life to identify material satisfactions with liberty. It was also possible that the elective process, especially under new, more intrusive forms of authority – the modern despotism that he feared – would actually be manipulated to make them appear deceptively as an expansion of the realm of liberty. To modify or avoid this tendency in modern life, Tocqueville urged that commitment to the idea that people should deploy liberty as an anchor against such intrusions needed to be joined to a concept of the exercise of liberty. In practice this meant that liberty would gain energy when individuals turned to the problem of how self-interest could actually deepen their consciousness of their ties to each other, extending their respect for the various paths to self-expression of their fellow beings. Tocqueville's ideal liberty could indeed not subsist without that fundamental respect for one's fellow beings. Liberty withered and despotism flourished when opinion of them descended into contempt.[42]

Tocqueville did not shrink from using redemptive images to identify the powerful feelings of regeneration expressed by the early authors of the Revolution. He may have been trying to have it both ways: he may have used such metaphors to avoid the problem of an unambiguous assertion of the place of providence in history. But it must also be said that he did not always cloak providence in Christian garb. He was content to leave this question in an indeterminate state. In his musings about the future, he had thoughts about posthistorical time, when, with the final achievement of a perfected liberty, due to the work of human agency, liberty itself might cease to be a matter of practical or moral urgency. The perfect form of liberty was the work of the spirit and the imagination; but its inescapable rootedness in history mattered as well. His view of the probable outcome of the symbiosis between science,

---

[40] Tocqueville to Mme. Swetchine, February 26, 1857, *OC*, XV, pt. 2, p. 315.
[41] *Nolla edn.*, I, pt. 2, esp. pp. 226–29.   [42] *OC*, II, pt. 1, p. 76.

technology and materialism in democracies affords a glimpse of how he looked at this question.

He must have been aware of the fragility of his earlier proposition that the goal of science in aristocracies is "to give pleasure to the mind, but in democratic ages to the body,"[43] for he modified his negativity. It was too early to conclude that democracies could not cultivate, through "enlightenment and liberty,"[44] a taste for pure science and produce the truly questing mind. Democracies might, he added, succumb to the momentary demands of utility and fail to keep the need for theory at the center of human thought and action. Were that to happen, the barbarians, ending one phase of civilized existence, would not come from outside democratic society, but from within. As if he knew that the questions he raised were difficult, he ended his speculations with the admonition that, so long as the proper balance between theory and practice in science were preserved, the danger to the life of the mind, and hence, to the preservation of liberty, would be diminished.

Tocqueville imagined, albeit imprecisely, a time when technical-industrial civilization would reproduce itself unthinkingly and mechanically, but the idea that humanity was caught in a Faustian pact was far from his mind. So he kept open the possibility that democratic societies, in which merit and excellence would find their true reward, and hence preserve themselves from falling prey to mindless anti-elitism, need not lose themselves in the exclusive pursuit of the sensual. By exerting all their powers to keep the temptations of immediate satisfaction in check, democracies could find other means to show their creativity. For Tocqueville poetry was one representation of the ideal.[45] Could poetic sensibility make itself felt in a democracy? Seeing themselves as being much alike, democratic peoples tend to see all their fellow human beings, *en masse*, as it were, and therefore see themselves as part of a greater whole. They dream about a future embracing all of humanity. This was a positive good. He let his aristocratic imagination run as freely as he dared.[46] He put cautious store in a future time when the individual, "not tied to time or place, but face to face with nature and with God, with his passions, his doubts, his unexpected good fortune and his incomprehensible miseries," turned his mind to human destiny, the "chief and almost

---

[43] *Nolla edn.*, II, pp. 50–51.   [44] Ibid., p. 52.   [45] Ibid., pp. 72–78.

[46] He had been even more cautious as he neared the completion of his first volume, when he was quite prepared to trade a love of poetry and a sense of greatness for order and morality, so long as a democratic future could preserve itself against disorder, depravity and violence, or find itself "bent under a yoke heavier than all those that have weighed on men since the fall of the Roman Empire": Tocqueville to E. Stoffels, February 21, 1835, *Beaumont edn.*, V, pp. 425–27.

the sole subject of poetry."[47] Moderns could not be expected to take seriously the idea of divine intervention; it was a metaphor and poetry was its instrument.

In language that was not always clear, he ascribed to poetry the power to "change, enlarge and embellish what exists. It does not create what does not exist; and if it seeks to do so, it will only amuse or surprise, but it will no longer have the power to move and will become the puerile plaything of an indolent imagination."[48] In its modern setting, poetry gave humanity the capacity to recognize "in the action of each individual a trace of the universal and consistent plan by which God guides mankind."[49] In democratic societies, the impulse toward transcendence could also come from the action of humanity upon the modern self prone to the crudest manifestations of individualism. By such a route Tocqueville thought some of the sense of emptiness, isolation and fragmentation in modern society might be reduced. All sense of human grandeur, he wrote in a review of the life of Poussin, is given to human beings by God, and armed with that gift they can cultivate it through a sense of duty and virtue.[50]

Tocqueville seemed to be close to speaking about a time when, if history was not approaching its end, a heightened human consciousness might leave historians little to do. In a democratic age, poetry might expand the languages of human knowledge and have a transforming effect upon all of humanity, and not only for privileged sections of it. If democratic equality were the inevitable future of the human condition, Tocqueville was still far from saying that people would have to face a stark and irrepressible choice, that of either willingly falling prey to a kind of hyperindividualism or, by disciplining themselves to prize liberty, miraculously perceiving its necessary links with a responsible sense of the social. Nurtured by the ideals of poetry and pure scientific inquiry, such a society might be inspired by an acute sense of the common human predicament and value liberty all the more.

Tocqueville tried to avoid the trap of carrying out his ideas to their "utmost theoretical conclusions, and often to the limits of the false and impracticable,"[51] by affirming that the theoretical constructs of historical inquiry are inherently unstable. As one for whom history was largely, but not exclusively, the generation and reception of political ideas, Tocqueville often agonizingly understood that a theoretical framework purporting to give a consistent account of each could be a transparent artifice. There is good reason to believe that he assumed that writers work within

[47] *Nolla edn.*, II, p. 77.   [48] *Nolla edn.*, II, p. 73.   [49] Ibid., p. 76.
[50] *OC*, XVI, pp. 310–11.   [51] *OC*, I, pt. 1, pp. 13–14.

the parameters of language, construct theories of human action in accordance with them, invest their theories with the appearance of unassailability, but also run the risk of becoming prisoners of their own constructs.

In many respects, Tocqueville believed that *L'Ancien Régime et la Révolution* was freer from the "privileged" understandings that other historians, such as Mignet, Thiers and Lamartine, claimed lay within their grasp. He took much pride in the magisterial and economical perspective of *L'Ancien Régime*. He came to believe that individuals had little choice but to come to terms provisionally with the mysteries of probability and contingency, just as he accepted the sense of incompleteness in his unrequited yearning for certainty.[52] This was matched by his resignation, almost amounting to stoicism, that the mysteries of the unknown could be borne by a faith in human power to sense the good.[53] Taste for this kind of speculation may be seen as a pervasive theme in his emotional being; and it found intellectual expression in his project to interpret the Great Revolution as the starting point of a struggle between impersonal forces and liberty. Tocqueville was unwilling, as he wrote to Royer-Collard, to believe in human decline in the face of the counterevidence of human progress in so many areas of life.[54] He consequently rejected the very idea of settling for a seemingly coherent account of the revolutions of the past that would distort the nature of the struggle for liberty in an uncertain universe. In daring to reach a less false account of it, he exposed himself to enormous anxieties. To this will to absorb into himself and to understand the sources and outcomes of the Revolution must be added his doubts in finding an understanding audience.[55] The responses to his work never quite lived up to his search for the multivalent meanings of the Revolution. Hence the disappointment that he had not been understood never left him. To this day, *L'Ancien Régime* remains a major challenge, but my purpose in this book is most emphatically not intended as a project to locate it in the historiography of the coming and the course of the French Revolution.

III

The major elements of Tocqueville's understanding of history, which are to be found in his major works, but in his preparatory notes and

---

[52] One of the earliest indications of Tocqueville's concerns with these questions may be inferred from a letter to Tocqueville from Kergorlay, January 6, 1838, in *OC*, XIII, pt. 1, pp. 119–24.   [53] Tocqueville to Corcelle, August 1, 1850, *OC*, XV, pt. 2, pp. 227–30.

[54] Tocqueville to Royer-Collard, September 15, 1843, *OC*, XI, pp. 114–16.

[55] Tocqueville to Henry Reeve, February 6, 1856, *OC*, VI, pt. 1, pp. 160–61.

correspondence as well, are introduced in part II of the book. There I look at how he approached the tensions between law/determinateness, and contingency/choice. These perplexing questions were embedded in, rather than located on the surface of, his detailed narrative of event and individual action, and his analysis of structures in which he shifted the focus from the individual and placed it on external forces.

In the third part of the book, I explore the ways in which Tocqueville struggled with the play of the major elements in his analysis of crisis and change in the *Souvenirs* and the *Democracy*. The first chapter in this section explores in some detail the contingency of the actions of the key historical actors in 1848. Even if Tocqueville were simply the narrator of the *Souvenirs*, and not, in addition, the observer of and participant in the historical events, his vision was inevitably restricted by being inside them, despite his efforts to take an objective stand outside them. I find it imperative to see in what state of mind Tocqueville found himself in 1848–49, before proceeding to the next stage of how he conceptualized the great rupture in the ancient history of France. In skeletal and incomplete form, the *Essai* of 1836 contains the clues to his later, mature analysis. That is why I consider it directly after the *Souvenirs*, even though he wrote it some dozen years earlier. The *Essai* turns on the more general structural forces that were at work in France, and moves, as it were, from individual choice within historical frameworks to an analysis of the frameworks themselves. The *Essai* canvasses the decline of a once powerful aristocratic ethos whose vital force was derived from conceptions of honor and shame that could not survive an internal and external *crise de conscience*. Tocqueville's early analysis of the breakdown of the Old Régime is linked with the future of Revolutionary France after the Terror for two reasons. First, because that question is what he turned to before he decided to shift his attention to the society of the *ancien régime*. Secondly, because it was yet another instance of crisis, another example of self-deception and rejection of the past by early liberals, like Cabanis and others who, in Tocqueville's mind, may have suffered psychological traumas similar to those experienced by the actors in 1848.

Tocqueville's purpose in telling the story of the breakdown of the structures of the old society was constantly in my mind as I worked on how he dealt with its disintegration. I take the risk of making a detour to test my conception of his major ideas in *Democracy in America*. The roles of providence, determinism, fatalism and choice in understanding historical change stamp its every page. The metaphysical and the existential, I conclude, were never far from the sociological, political and historical Tocqueville. This chapter restores these features as part of the *Democracy*'s essential foundations and weaves them into the fabric of

Tocqueville's eloquent invocations of liberty and his acute, even if occasionally overdeductive, analysis of equality.

These questions were in the background and often in the foreground of Tocqueville's synthesis of the American democratic experience. With Louis de Kergorlay he debated the issues of certitude and probability; and he conducted what may be called an internal conversation with Pascal over the Augustinian's rejection of skepticism and his surrender to faith. Both comprised an unmistakable part of, but assumed a transformed form in, Tocqueville's thoughts about the nature of change. Resistance to it by reviving and recasting earlier moral struggles was, however, not a solution he could embrace: an Enlightenment and post-revolutionary world drove him away from any kind of nostalgia for a lost past. In this chapter, I also introduce Rousseau, whose neo-Pascalianism brings into relief the affinities between the two major prerevolutionary thinkers who were important to Tocqueville's intellectual formation in ways that Montesquieu, however important he was to Tocqueville, failed to be.

Rousseau's ideas were important in another respect. His detestation of modern commercial society aroused similar feelings in Tocqueville who, however, accepted the inevitable reversal of older traditions and values. He argued only that the new culture might yet find ways to minimize its worst effects, and perhaps even prevent the fragmentation of community and personality. The concluding section of this chapter treats Tocqueville's comparison between the manifestations of caste, honor and shame in aristocratic, and their ultimate transformation in democratic, cultures. Not only were these problems first adumbrated in the *Essai*. They are basic to his thought, but were not fully exposed until Tocqueville embarked on his last explanation of the fissures that ended in revolution.

The fourth part of the book concentrates on Tocqueville's theory of revolution. It is further evidence of his earlier efforts to erect firm laws of historical change, which he could accommodate only in a theoretical framework that had the effect of diminishing the importance of individual action. Thus in his last work, history as event and process gave way to history as social structure and social expression. Tocqueville developed his theory of modern state centralization within the framework of structural mechanisms. I examine them in the light of his analysis of Western and Central European aristocratic societies. Important is how Tocqueville wavered in determining the relative decisiveness of an impersonal state power moving "naturally" to fulfill itself, and the fault lines of the aristocratic ethos built on ideas of honor. The last chapter on ideas and public opinion centers on the argument that the force of ideas was ultimately decisive for Tocqueville, both in his idea of history and his care for liberty of thought. His dissection of a series of concrete instances in the dissemination of opinion was his solution to the problem of giving a greater sense of immediate personal involvement by a number of public figures hoping to shape the flow of history.

II

Paradoxes in Tocqueville's idea of history

Toward a theory of history

Time is in flight; those who are clever have known this for a long time. Monstrous things have happened: the world has suffered great trans-formations silently and noisily, in the quiet pace of the day and in the storms and eruptions of revolution; monstrosities will occur, greater things will be transformed.[1]

What would be most original . . . would be . . . a freely ranging judgment on our modern societies and forecast of their probable future . . . I must find somewhere a solid and continuous basis for my ideas, which I can only find in writing history . . . But the difficulties are immense. The one which troubles my mind the most arises from [the problem] of blending history properly so called with the philosophy of history [la philosophie historique].[2]

Recurrent themes in Tocqueville's major works

The traditions of philosophy of history – for it is clear that Tocqueville's inversion of the words ("la philosophie historique") was not intended to challenge their proper ordering – or the equally familiar legitimate sub-jects of inquiry for a *histoire raisonnée* or speculative history, had taken root in the eighteenth century, which had borrowed much from the

---

[1] E. M. Arndt, *Geist der Zeit* (Altona, 1877), p. 55; cited in Reinhart Koselleck, " 'Neuzeit': Remarks on the Semantics of the Modern Concepts of Movement," in Koselleck, *Futures Past*, p. 252.
[2] Tocqueville to Kergorlay, December 15, 1850, *OC*, XIII, pt. 2, pp. 230–32. In his notes for his speech on April 3, 1852, to the Académie des Sciences Morales et Politiques, Tocqueville used the term "histoire philosophique," *OC*, XVI, p. 234. In *Alexis de Tocqueville: Selected Letters on Politics and Society*, ed. and trans. Roger Boesche (with James Taupin) (Berkeley, Los Angeles and London, 1985), p. 256, the term is translated as "historical philosophy." This rendering does not do justice to Tocqueville's meaning nor to his intentions. See also Jean-Claude Lamberti, *Tocqueville and the Two Democracies*, trans. Arthur Goldhammer (Cambridge, Mass., and London, 1989), p. 38, who con-tends that Tocqueville was interested in constructing "a new political science," not a phi-losophy of history. By confining Tocqueville's assessment of his purposes to the period of the *Democracy*'s composition, Lamberti may not only be taking too narrow a position about Tocqueville's goals as a historian, but also neglecting how much of Tocqueville's first great work was suffused by an acute concern for the movement of history.

seventeenth century's incipient interest in the travel literature and ethno-
graphic studies of non-European cultures. But until the eighteenth
century, history remained a series of stories, not related to other kinds of
stories (of nature, the earth, space), or with humanist philology and the
study, mainly by magistrates and lawyers, of laws and institutions.[3]
Philosophic history's purpose became in large part teleological, concerning itself with bringing together a number of discrete subjects, all deemed
to be related to the expansion of human knowledge, with the promise of
enlightening humankind and ensuring its happiness: in short, to extract
some meaning or significance from historical events and actions. The
study of "philosophical history," though not yet fully legitimized, was a
vast attempt to embrace explanations of humanity's stadial ascent from
its primitive and putatively natural origins to its adoption of more sophis-
ticated practices of social exchanges, the laying down of the structures of
a civil society and the expansion of the state, and, in addition, for some
writers, prescriptive accounts of the distribution of political power. But it
also took into its compass – and this surely counts for a good deal for its
"philosophical" content – the vast process of time in which man was only
a small speck.[4] *History* had displaced histories. Writers as diverse as
Voltaire, Montesquieu, d'Alembert, Turgot, Rousseau, Condorcet and
Gibbon influenced historians of the next century after more than a
generation of revolution and war. The study of the immediate turbulent
past and its distant origins was given an unprecedented urgency. It did
not owe its origins to the Ecole des Chartes, founded in 1822, but to the
availability of archival documentation, which conferred a kind of scientific legitimacy upon the study of history. And it was during the
Restoration that historians, among them Augustin Thierry and Jules
Michelet, and translations of Herder and Vico,[5] gained an audience concerned both with the distant past – a concern only for a few, like Vico, in

[3] For the last, see Donald Kelley, *Foundations of Modern Historical Scholarship: Language,
Law and History in the French Renaissance* (New York, 1970).
[4] See, *inter alia*, studies by Ronald Meek, *Social Science and the Ignoble Savage* (Cambridge,
1976); Michèle Duchet, *Anthropologie et histoire au siècle des Lumières* (Paris, 1977);
François Furet, "The Birth of History in France," in *The Workshop of History*, trans.
Jonathan Mandelbaum (Chicago and London, 1984), pp. 77–98; Stanley Mellon, *The
Political Uses of History: A Study of French Historians in the French Restoration* (Stanford,
1958); Hayden White, *Metahistory: The Historical Imagination in Nineteenth-Century
Europe* (Baltimore, 1973); and see the articles by Koselleck, "Historia Magistra Vitae:
The Dissolution of the Topos into the Perspective of a Modernized Historical Process,"
and "Historical Criteria of the Modern Concept of Revolution," in Koselleck, *Futures
Past*, pp. 21–54.
[5] See, for example, Jouffroy's essay, "Bossuet, Vico, Herder," *Mélanges philosophiques*, 3rd
edn. (Paris, 1860), pp. 59–63. Michelet brought out an abridged version of the *Scienza
nuova* in 1827, and in 1835 published selected works from Vico's writings. See also
Tocqueville to Princess Belgiojoso, [1844], thanking her for sending him a copy of her

the previous century – and with speculations about the contours of a dis-turbing present.

Kant, Fichte and Hegel were indeed some of the earliest intellectuals upon whose thinking the multiple and conflicting ideas and strains of Enlightenment ideas and the surprise of the Revolution itself made an extraordinary impact; and it is around their philosophies of historical meaning that much critical writing has rightly centered.[6] Tocqueville knew about their work, at best, only in small fragments, first in the 1840s through Arthur de Gobineau, later during the summer of 1854 in conversations with Christian-August Brandis and Charles Monnard, German university professors, but only after he had achieved his own intellectual bearings.[7]

More immediately, Théodore Jouffroy, the eclectic philosopher and liberal, suggested in the last years of the Restoration that modern histori-ans were rightfully revolutionizing history by studying customs and polit-ical and religious institutions, the arts, industry and private life, instead of

---

translation of the *Science nouvelle*. He added that Vico was "the genius with the most mas-culine turn of mind there ever was" [le génie le plus viril qui fût jamais], *OC*, VII, pp. 300–01, and note 14.

[6] For a useful analysis of the status of philosophy of history as a subject of inquiry, includ-ing the crucial importance of the Revolution to the development of Fichte's, Kant's and Hegel's philosophies of history, see Luc Ferry, *The System of Philosophies of History*, Vol. II, *Political Philosophy*, trans. Franklin Philip (Chicago, 1992).

[7] See Gobineau's "Coup d'oeil générale sur l'histoire de la morale," *OC*, IX, pp. 309–28. The "essay" was written in 1843 in response to Tocqueville's request for a summary of German contributions to philosophy of history: Tocqueville to Gobineau, August 8, 1843, and September 5, 1843, *OC*, IX, pp. 43–48. In Tocqueville's record of his discus-sions in Germany, Brandis told him that academic interest in philosophy had declined, and that the study of the natural sciences was now occupying intellectual life. He added that Hegelianism had had no influence on German politics, and that, if the Hegelian school had spawned revolutionaries, they were not revolutionaries in the true sense, because their main interest was philosophy rather than revolution. Monnard spoke about, as he termed it, a violent reaction against all materialist, atheistic and demagogic doctrines in Hegel's philosophy. Tocqueville's notes also refer to Lessing and Herder in the context of the spread of new ideas in the eighteenth century, akin to those in circula-tion in France, but the appearance of the former was especially startling, Tocqueville added, because of the rejection of the pietism of the past, which had been so strong in Germany. Tocqueville was impressed by the efflorescence of German philosophy, repre-sented magisterially by Kant, Fichte, Schelling and Hegel, and showed some familiarity with the "Left" Hegelians. He gained much of this information from Saint-René Taillandier's *Etudes sur la Révolution en Allemagne* (Paris, 1853). For these details, see *AT*, 43 B, Dossier Q, "Allemagne. Travaux sur l'Allemagne faits en Allemagne en juin, juillet, août et septembre 1854 . . . Idées et aperçus qui, bien que suggérés par l'Allemagne ne se rapportent que peu ou point à elle, mais à mon ouvrage en général." Tocqueville's further references to the ferment of German philosophy and German interest in the Revolution may be found in *OC*, II, pt. 2, pp. 243–46, 252–65. It does not seem that Tocqueville read anything that Victor Cousin, who took credit for introducing Hegel to French philosophers, had to say about Hegel. See *Specimens of Foreign Standard Literature*, ed. George Ripley, 2 vols. (Boston, 1838), I, p. 86, for Cousin's claim.

the chronicles of kings – all the questions that, as we shall see, Tocqueville, and before him, Guizot, were to say constituted history's true subject matter.[8] Montesquieu was, Jouffroy said, the exemplar of the first kind of history; Titus Livy was the legitimate historian of ancient times.[9] Tocqueville would have concurred in Jouffroy's admiration for Montesquieu. In addition, Jouffroy, like Tocqueville, was as much interested in the claim of modern historians to be "philosophic historians" in the fullest sense, that is, when they turned, as Jouffroy believed they should, toward the penetration of the "laws" underlying the movement of ideas.[10] There was no certainty that "human intelligence, which is the law of human power, has [the characteristics of] regular development . . . Changes that are the work of human beings . . . resist the scrutiny of science and will remain, if not forever, at least for a long time, in a floating and fragmentary condition [confined] in the reservoir of history." Presumably history was an inquiry resisting the promise of full clarity. If, however, regular laws governing human actions could be ascertained and established, "history will perish totally; it will no longer possess an object [of study]; science will have taken its place in the area dealing with the changes in humanity, as it already has in the domain of changes in nature."[11] Jouffroy entertained the thought that history might disappear once human beings had reached the perfection implied in possessing a scientific knowledge of the regularities of human actions that should logically eliminate struggle as a feature of human existence. True to his affinities with the Idéologues, it was to a future small, but prescient, band of thinkers that Jouffroy turned in his imagination to reveal the destinies and tendencies of humanity. They would enable people to see, had they but the capacity to see beyond the transitory truths of their own epochs, how "the truth, beauty and morality freed from all [historical] forms pass[ed] from one form to another without changing."[12] Poetry could reveal the truths of sublime mysticism and even Christianity, and perhaps also reveal them to the true initiate, but pure truth was beyond poetry's powers.

But how were historians, with the rare qualities Jouffroy said they

---

[8] For these aspects of Jouffroy's ideas, see his "Réflexions sur la philosophie de l'histoire," in *Mélanges philosophiques*, pp. 36–58. In 1838, Jouffroy supported Tocqueville's election to the Académie des Sciences Morales et Politiques, citing his admiration for the *Democracy*. See his letter to Damiron, April 23, 1836, in *Correspondance de Théodore Jouffroy, publiée avec une Etude sur Jouffroy par Adolphe Lair* (Paris, 1901), p. 396. I have been unable to trace any references to Jouffroy by Tocqueville, but both were members of the Académie.   [9] Jouffroy, "Réflexions," p. 52.

[10] Ibid., p. 40. In general, by "philosophy of history," Jouffroy meant the forces that were thought to be moving civilization from one stage to another.   [11] Ibid., pp. 40–41.

[12] Ibid., pp. 56–57.

needed, to regard the errors or dogmas that were piled up in vast mounds of historical debris, a locution he was fond of using? The answer is to be found in an essay discussing the morphology of dogmatism,[13] written at about the same time as the "Réflexions." Jouffroy took his cue from the Revolution, and before that, the Enlightenment. He reviewed both as a set of challenges to ancient dogmas, and he analyzed the Restoration as a rearguard action to salvage as much of the *ancien régime* as possible. Transferring the metaphor to a broader canvas, Jouffroy saw each pile of debris being buried under successive faiths. The movement of history proceeds through such successive stages. New spokesmen, determined to keep old dogmas alive, arrive on the historical stage. The people become embroiled in the ensuing conflicts, but are powerless to determine their outcome. They soon learn how to survive the onslaughts of the warring factions, but they can no longer tell if the advocates of the new faith are the authentic guardians of truth. Hence they adopt a stance of pure skepticism and disbelief that injures the spirit of human dignity. The work of providential forces, the ensuing corruption serves as a prelude to new life. Human beings can thus look forward to life's transformation from which truth will emerge. The secret power of providence takes care to ensure that small groups of individuals escape from the general malaise. In their self-imposed isolation, they develop the germs of noble sentiments, virtues, moral, political and religious truths – all destined to govern the world. The spark of new life, of truth, follows no humanly prescribed path. Its exact timing is not predictable, but it is inevitable. It will illuminate society once it catches fire.

Jouffroy was moved by the theory that ideas are the moving force of history. It was clear for him that, however long dogmatism would take to die out, there was movement toward intellectual perfection. In the shorter run, a theoretical framework that supposed the fatalism of historical events, including the very distinctive fatalism of human passions and ideas, must be the working ground for historians. In a near-Manichean metaphor, Jouffroy deployed the fatalism of ideas as civilization's claim to progress by means of the light that ideas bring to the human condition. Humanity would surely bring darkness upon itself if it gave up the search for seminal ideas and gave way to the uncontrolled exercise of the passions. The bare bones of Enlightenment thought were resurrected, but they came to life in the company of Bossuet, who was right after all, Jouffroy stated. What Bossuet called providence, and others called destiny, while still others the force of things, did not compromise individual liberty, but rather assumed its existence, and was expressed only

---

[13] Jouffroy, "Comment les dogmes finissent," in *Mélanges philosophiques*, pp. 3–19.

through action in the world. Acknowledging fate was a step toward freedom. When reasonable and free, human beings can deliberate, reflect, choose and conceive ideas that rise above passions. In the absence of the conscious exercise of liberty, or if liberty were to suffer conscious suppression, "the fatalism of sensory intuitions"[14] would supersede the fatalism of ideas; and sensual man would triumph over reflective man.

As we shall see, Tocqueville would soon turn to these questions, indeed, as early as his composition of the *Democracy*. In his earliest maturity, Tocqueville, however, was drawn to Guizot, who said that in his studies he looked only for general results, for the chain of causes and effects hidden under external manifestations. Guizot sought his analogies not in anatomy but in physiology, which allowed him to think of the interconnectedness of events as comparable to the body's interrelated structure – a favorite device that Tocqueville would employ in his discussions of the breakdown of monarchies and aristocracies.[15] Guizot was not, however, totally absorbed in these questions. He turned toward the past for other reasons as well, especially to the feudal past of Europe, with some of the same sweeping gaze that inspired the work of the writers of the previous century, but with a greater sense of certainty of what lay at the end of history and historical speculation. In the most immediate sense, Guizot looked at the breakdown of English feudalism as an object lesson for France. He had a political agenda as well. For Guizot and like-minded liberals of the Restoration, 1688 was vaunted as the symbol of what France could become. A starting point for modern English liberties, it could also serve as one for French constitutional practices. Tocqueville's comparisons of the rise of an aristocratic feudalism with Guizot's owed something to him, but Tocqueville did not fully accept Guizot's politics.[16] And his exposure to American democracy widened his perspective too much not to make him feel uncomfortable with the more limited conception of the future that Guizot envisioned.

[14] Jouffroy, "Réflexions," p. 53.

[15] François Guizot, *Cours d'histoire moderne: Histoire de la civilisation en France depuis la chute de l'empire romain jusqu'en 1789*, 5 vols. (Paris, 1829–32), II, pp. 267–68. See Douglas Johnson, *Guizot: Aspects of French History 1787–1874* (London and Toronto, 1963), chap. 7, esp. pp. 374–76, for the view that Guizot avoided the "abstractions" that permeated the philosophy of history in French historical writing in the nineteenth century. See also Shirley M. Gruner, "Political Historiography in Restoration France," *History and Theory*, 7 (1969), pp. 346–65.

[16] On this and the further point of the greater freedom Tocqueville had in developing his own agenda – he was born after the Revolution and had familial attachments to pre-revolutionary France, and therefore could look more dispassionately at the meaning of 1688 – see François Furet, "Naissance d'un paradigme: Tocqueville et le voyage en Amérique (1825–1831)," *Annales, E.S.C.*, 39 (March–April 1984), pp. 225–39.

Tocqueville also made some observations of his own about some of the earliest manifestations of feudalism, which, it seemed to him during this early phase of his intellectual development, could not have come into being except as an emanation of a preexisting principle: feudalism emerged from the midst of the northern peoples of Europe fully armed, "as Minerva from the head of Jupiter." If this judgment elevated ideas as a central source of historical movement, he saw them less as the work of individual decisions than as the consequence of the power of the condition of things, a kind of natural development of entities in the world. The study of history demanded a knowledge of these inexplicable forces, but by themselves they were incapable of accounting for the universalization of a common feudal law for all of Europe. In his mind, that law came into being as a result of human decision.[17] These two ideas existed side by side. The twenty-three-year-old Tocqueville told Beaumont that for them the history worth studying was the history of men, especially the history of men who were their immediate predecessors.

The first kind of history was worthwhile insofar as it disclosed "some general notions about the whole of humanity" and how man could be enlightened for a life in politics. As if in anticipation of the idea of the *longue durée*, with its emphasis on demographic and geographic determinants, Tocqueville wrote about the mysteriousness of the sheer physicality of events. Their resistance to immediate comprehension could perhaps be dispelled, he reflected, by a study of human geography. Such an inquiry could doubtless also say much about the distribution of physical resources and their uses by peoples, to the point perhaps of revealing how their choices were located in a more, rather than less, specific determinateness. Nonetheless, what human beings did with their choices could be visualized only by looking for and reflecting upon evidence on how they used the resources they possessed. In turn, this demanded a knowledge of the conditions in which the revolutions over the previous 200 years shaped their preferences, instincts and *moeurs*.[18] The first, most protean and most durable restraint within which human beings acted was custom itself, an omnibus term Tocqueville adapted from Montesquieu's *moeurs* and *manières*, which he would later say in the *Democracy* had more meaning for him if it were expanded to mean, not only "the habits of the heart," but "the various notions and opinions current among men and to the mass of those ideas which constitute their character of mind." Under

---

[17] Tocqueville was commenting on Guizot's University of Paris lectures in his "Rédaction d'une grande partie des leçons de M. Guizot, auxquelles j'ai assisté depuis le 11 avril 1829 jusqu'au 29 mai 1830," *OC*, XVI, pp. 441–534. See also Tocqueville to Beaumont, October 5, 1828, *OC*, VIII, pt. 1, pp. 51–57.

[18] Tocqueville to Beaumont, October 25, 1829, *OC*, VIII, pt. 1, pp. 92–94.

this term, he comprised "the whole moral and intellectual condition of a people."[19]

In so expanding the reach of *moeurs*, indeed, by endowing them with so much power to determine human agency, Tocqueville may have created some difficulty for himself when he insisted that *moeurs* need not be imprisoning; as he did, when, in his readings of the Frankish period, he thought that Guizot did not give enough amplitude to the decisive, even if accidental, interventions of important leaders in revolutionary times, and, indeed, in earlier periods.[20] These were the early ideas of the young Tocqueville, during the dying days of the Restoration, before he embarked on his journey to America. His mind was already fixed on comparative history when he returned from his first voyage outside France to Sicily in 1826–27, where the relics of feudal latifundia impressed themselves on his mind, not as objects of a tourist's nostalgia, but as an instructive example of how certain landholding patterns may stunt initiative and freeze social relations in so permanent a way as to foreclose any ideas of improvement.[21] He was turning to some of the key ideas that would inform his mature view of history.

By the time he turned to the study of history as a way to integrate his work, what Tocqueville found more impressive than Guizot's books and lectures was the monumental work of Montesquieu. He looked to him not only for concepts of liberty, but for Montesquieu's delineation of the makeup of civil society, as Tocqueville observed when he commented on the shape it assumed in the American republic, whose origins ironically were partially to be found in the aristocratic institutions and practices of England. Just as significantly, the model for the genre in which he thought he would choose to write his history of *L'Ancien Régime et la Révolution* was Montesquieu's history of the Romans.[22] But he knew that, because the time span he was going to traverse was smaller than Montesquieu's, he would have to find other concepts and forms. So he told Louis de Kergorlay, perhaps the person who came closest to sharing his interest in such questions.[23] A little more than a week later, on December 26, 1850, Tocqueville speculated further on his historical project. This time, confiding in Gustave de Beaumont, he did not use the term "la philosophie historique." The man who often said of himself that he had very little in his temperament that took easily to philosophy[24] found that the term "la

---

[19] *Nolla edn.*, I, p. 223. Tocqueville distinguished, as did Montesquieu, *moeurs* and *lois*.

[20] "Rédaction d'une grande partie," *OC*, XVI, p. 444.

[21] *Pléiade edn.*, I, pp. 5–26, esp. pp. 11–12 and 20–25.

[22] *Considérations sur les causes de la grandeur des Romains et de leur décadence*, first published in 1734.   [23] Tocqueville to Kergorlay, December 15, 1850, *OC*, XIII, pt. 2, p. 233.

[24] Tocqueville to Edouard de Tocqueville, August 24, 1842, in *Beaumont edn.*, VII, p. 197.

philosophie de l'histoire" served his purposes better than "la philosophie historique." There was a venerable precedent for the term. Voltaire had used it in his *Essai sur les moeurs* of 1756 – and many others were to use it – but Tocqueville gave it his own, more specific, meaning by speaking about finding the way "to blend facts and ideas, the philosophy of history with history itself."[25]

A narrow construction of his intention might construe this as a search for the way to understand how the Revolution was affected by the inter-action of ideas and facts – to see, in other words, how those who were concerned with rationalizing or questioning political theories and prac-tices before the Revolution threw everything open to discussion, with the result that politics entered a new phase after 1789. A wider construction is hardly out of the question, however, for such a project need not exclude the view that Tocqueville not only sought to reimagine this linkage of ideas and facts, but to comprehend how the Revolution was a unique moment in history, an authentic point of departure. It was not only his argument that ideas motivate human beings and give shape to history. Recall, he said in a speech to the Constituent Assembly in September 1848, "the terrible and glorious origins" of the Revolution, "the very beginnings of our modern history." Was it in answer to "material needs" that the Revolution achieved "the great things that have left their mark on the world?" No, it was by speaking "of virtue, generos-ity, disinterestedness, glory, that it accomplished these great things . . . There is only one secret to make men do great things, and that is to appeal to great sentiments."[26] Tocqueville saw history moving mysteri-ously through the act of the Revolution toward the expansion of liberty in the modern age, though its movement was not without obstacles and a fair share of errors, and perhaps, even, permanent detours, unknown to and often against the intentions of, human beings, whether as agents or subjects.

The unraveling of that past, Tocqueville came to believe, would give some unity to his life's work. The compulsion to dip deeply into it became all the more insistent as he pursued his journey to self-knowl-edge and knowledge by asking questions meant to enlighten both the self and the larger community. His way of making that experience part

[25] Tocqueville to Beaumont, December 26, 1850, *OC*, VIII, pt. 2, p. 343. Cf. Tocqueville to Freslon, July 30, 1854, *BYT*, D.III.a. To Freslon he wrote about how his detailed examination of the facts of the origins of absolutism in the German states "led me pre-cisely to the same conclusions as those that I was made to draw from the philosophy of history."

[26] "Discours prononcé à l'Assemblée constituante dans la discussion du projet de Constitution sur la question du droit au travail. Séance du 12 septembre 1848," *OC*, III, pt. 3, pp. 171–72.

of the reality of the human condition that the historian must rediscover meant building on his existing broad expanse of common conversation with chosen others, not only his lifelong friends, Beaumont and Kergorlay, but with individuals whose perspectives he did not always share. He sought from and with them the means to test his own views through a process of comparative judgment. Tocqueville hardly welcomed the opinions of all those with whom he was intimate, even less so the figures for whom he had a marked distaste, either on grounds of personality or beliefs, whether they were politicians and historians like Thiers, or socialists of virtually every conviction. His rejection of their contributions to an incipient comparative analysis need not be seen as an imperious craving to make his own ideas prevail, only his expectation that there was some prospect of reaching historical objectivity, beginning in individual histories, and then moving outward to acknowledge other individual histories, and then to the histories of larger collectivities. A study of these held out the possibility of establishing what he believed were the rational grounds for an objective understanding of the past.

Springing from the same impulse to compare his judgment with that of his peers was a lifelong conviction that societies could not be studied in isolation. The point of the exercise was to turn his gaze from the national features, social dynamics and patterns of state power in the distinctive cultures of England, America and the German states back toward his own. The expansion of his transcultural perspectives gave him a vantage point from which to think about the dangers of national complacency. The benefit that Tocqueville derived was some capacity for self-criticism, the ability to see how a formulation of the ways of life of different societies might illuminate "alternative possibilities in relation to some human constants" at work in all societies "through the language of perspicuous contrast." This is an idea I borrow from Charles Taylor, who thinks it to be a fair method for overcoming problems of incommensurability.[27] Taylor's perception usefully illuminates Tocqueville's like-minded preference for seeking comparisons. Tocqueville was engaged in such a dialogue, especially with his English friends, on the need for, but the difficulty of, grasping differences in national concepts of justice and the national styles that expressed them. Not the least of the problems was the presumption that Englishmen and Frenchmen were best able to judge the foundations of their own political

---

[27] See Charles Taylor, "Understanding and Ethnocentricity," in *Philosophy and the Human Sciences: Philosophical Papers*, 2 vols. (Cambridge, 1985), II, pp. 118–33. The citation is from p. 125.

cultures. Could the mind rise above such a myopic, short-lived self-infatuation? He wondered whether the citizens of one society could break through their unconscious and unquestioned assumptions to rise above forests of detail and see things whole, or to make room in the whole for the details that modify it.[28]

Tocqueville's memories of himself in a finite sense of place – his family, his class and the larger settings of French and Western society – were, as we may gather from his youthful correspondence, his journeys and the retrospective moments of his later correspondence, constantly shaping his feelings, his thoughts and his acts. It is not only his inheritance that is important. That is only one side of the equation. In a sense, it is possible to say that a moral, intellectual and social position – *moeurs* – inhabited him, just as they inhabited societies. In all of his endeavors, he had already taken a number of turnings that led him to the precincts of, and finally his immersion in, the problems of historical explanation. Yet it was only as he approached the problem of finding the links between his individual experience within the larger settings of the "community" that he turned toward what might be called a formal, but, in his hands, a highly unique, study of the French Revolution. It was the opening, and therefore most crucial, event of three generations of political and social disruptions in which he had a personal stake. He did not doubt that the Revolution was, in itself and in representations of it in its immediate temporal space and in succeeding generations, an event of universal historical significance, one which he never tired of saying would shape life far into the future. As he moved more and more into the interior of this, his last great work, seeking the solitude for his intense periods of reading and reflection on its antecedents, he felt the release of an explosive mixture of apprehension and exhilaration. But he repressed it in favor of a more measured style, which distinguishes *L'Ancien Régime et la Révolution*, the notes for additions to it and the notes for the unfinished volume on the Revolution itself.

The sober and dry, often Olympian style of *L'Ancien Régime* stands in sharp contrast to the heart-pounding textures of feeling in his *Souvenirs*. That the first was intended to bare its face in public, while the second was meant to be a private recollection, safely hidden from the gaze of friends and enemies alike, tells us a bit about Tocqueville's need for privacy. Yet his personal revelations to selected friends about some of the events he described in the *Souvenirs* slightly blur the boundaries between the

---

[28] Tocqueville to Mrs. Grote, January 31, 1857; Tocqueville to Greg, October 1, 1858, *Beaumont edn.*, VI, pp. 365–69, 454–58.

private and the public.[29] It may also be that Tocqueville thought of leaving
them to future generations of audiences to be his ultimate and fairest
judges;[30] and he did agree to permit them to be published after his
death.[31] He gave every appearance of yielding to an irrepressible need to
overcome the distance between these two realms of life, and unhesitat-
ingly to acknowledge that his own experiences were part of a larger
canvas. Still, the most distinctive features of the two works, in particular,
the conventional – but, as I pointed out in chapter 1, the problematic –
narrative elements which give the first its richness and fascination, and
their apparent absence in the second, is an excellent way of focusing the
question of the place that Tocqueville accorded to narrative in evoking the
past. The personal narrative form of the *Souvenirs* fairly breathes the
exaltation of being newly alive after the torpor of his activities as a legislator, though he did not wholly regret the practical experience he had
gained, nor the contributions he made in debates on domestic and foreign
affairs. But this does not answer the question of his allowing a subordinate part to narrative in *L'Ancien Régime*, in which he tried to adopt a
stance of cool detachment, bearing down against much of the play of personality and place – those constituent parts of events as these may be
reconstructed through the shifting prisms of one mind.

The stories or recollections that persons used to recreate their own
lives, Tocqueville believed, gave them a sense of what it was to be a
person, and connected them with humanity. The *Souvenirs* show
Tocqueville making this connection through a process of argumentation,
both with himself and with his peers, friendly and hostile. It is otherwise

---

[29] There is ample evidence that the words Tocqueville used in letters and in conversations
with friends are very like, indeed, if not identical with, those in the *Souvenirs*. See
Tocqueville to Senior, December 1849, *OC*, VI, pt. 2, pp. 112–14; Tocqueville's
conversations with Senior, May 26, 1848, ibid., pp. 242–45; the notes kept by H. Grote,
April 1849, May 19, 1849, and February 11, 1851, ibid., pp. 248–51, 271, 347. See
Tocqueville to Kergorlay, December 15, 1850, *OC*, XIII, pt. 2, pp. 229–30: "I have no
need to tell you that the recollections of 1848 cannot appear before the public. The unfet-
tered judgments that I am bringing . . . on my contemporaries and on myself render
[their] publication impracticable, even if I were inclined to expose myself in any [piece] of
literary theater, which it [the *Souvenirs*] are assuredly not." Beaumont was the recipient
of a similar confidence, Tocqueville to Beaumont, January 5, 1851, *OC*, VIII, pt. 2, p.
352: "I am trying, as I told you, to make use of my mind, but without tiring it, and I am
succeeding. If I achieve something that pleases me, I will read it to you on my return. It is
delightful to work when you can do so at your ease, and when your wish is to please only
yourself, and not to write with the public in mind. The prospect of being judged by the
public spoils all the pleasure that works of the mind can give, at least as far as I am concerned."

[30] On the notion of a *superaddressee*, with absolute and just understanding, see M. M.
Bakhtin, *Speech Genres and Other Late Essays*, ed. Caryl Emerson and Michael Holquist,
trans. Vern W. McGee (Austin, 1986), p. 126.

[31] See Luc Monnier's Introduction to the *Souvenirs*, *OC*, XII, pp. 23–24.

when the inquiry begins with a reconstruction of human societies whose structures and dynamics do not operate at so primordial a level as subjective experience. What is it, however, that warrants the claim of distinguishing the dynamics of the "I" and the "We," especially when it is plain that persons seek to make the links between themselves and the societies in which they live? Why should such a shift occur, and why and to what degree does it occur in Tocqueville? The question is important. Tocqueville did not doubt the existence of the links. We find, at the very conclusion of *Democracy in America*, that he puts individuals and communities on an equal epistemological and moral footing. "It is true," he said, "that around every man a fatal circle is traced beyond which he cannot pass; but within the wide verge of that circle he is powerful and free; *as it is with man, so with communities.*"[32]

Why are those links wholly or partly concealed in what seems to be a process that intellectually absorbs the elements of events but refrains from putting them before the reader in their raw form – as if they exist at a lower level of cognition? Was it more fitting to filter them through the mind of the historian who is transformed, as it were, in the process into another kind of person with a qualitatively different project – evincing the contours of larger patterns of collective endeavor? Of course, the rawness cannot help from peeping through; it cannot be totally hidden even within the thick folds of high generality. And it is not entirely absent, as I argue, in *L'Ancien Régime*. In the latter, Tocqueville withdrew from narrative in the fullest sense that he deployed it in the *Souvenirs* in order to gain the detachment to discern the general laws and to place theory above practice. But he was unable to escape completely from the power of narrative in which the concrete particularities of personal exchanges are of central importance. Why he deliberately moved from one form of historical understanding and explanation to the other demands an examination of how he makes narrative work in the *Souvenirs*, where he presents some of the most exciting and self-revelatory moments of his life during the breakdown of the July Monarchy and during the events that followed. But the recollections do much more. They are revealing in a totally unexpected way. Without perhaps intending to do so, Tocqueville here introduced all the ingredients for a discourse on the nature of historical explanation.

Tocqueville saw the links of his own life and the links of the past, written large, as part of a larger unity. He thought the key to the impasses

---

[32] *Nolla edn.*, II, pp. 281–82. The emphasis is mine. On the transitions from the "I" to the "We," from the narrative of the subjective self to the narrative constituting communal experience, see the helpful discussion in David Carr, *Time, Narrative and History*, esp. sections 5 and 6.

into which modern historians had led their readers was concealed from them by their failure to see how the approaches to history by thinkers living in aristocratic times were to be distinguished from those writing in democratic ones. In general, historians in predemocratic times could not escape from the notion that great individuals were the makers of historical change, while historians living in democratic societies tended to see time as a compact and indissoluble reality, with generations bound to one another, in "an enormous chain, which girds and binds the human race." Such a way of understanding the past, Tocqueville argued, severely limits both how persons might conceive it on other grounds, and how a commitment to the doctrine of necessity consequently shapes their actions in the present:

To their [historians in democratic times] minds it is not enough to show that events have occurred; *they wish to show that events could not have occurred otherwise.* They take a nation arrived at a certain stage of its history and affirm that it could not but follow the track that brought it thither. *It is easier to make such an assertion than to show how the nation might have adopted a better course.*[33]

Setting aside how historians in democratic societies viewed the past, Tocqueville turned to the thoughts ordinary Americans had about its importance for them. A curious thing, he noted with a kind of wonder, happens in America: the ethos of individualism makes harsh demands, changes people and their relations with each other. It is an ethos that leaves human beings standing alone, solitary and bereft. The chains linking them both with their ancestors and their descendants are as quickly lost as they are formed. But, as if in compensation, they protect themselves by inventing and acting on the belief that they owe their fates to no one but themselves.[34] Thus, in their own lives, democratic men say they owe everything to their own efforts, but in understanding themselves as a nation, they say that what has brought them to their present condition is the result of forces beyond any person's control. This means a strange disregard for the past, and a higher regard for present-mindedness; it is as if history, in the sense of an acute historical consciousness, mattered less and less. America was producing a unique society and unique human beings willing, or being coerced by force of numbers, to identify themselves with the future, and seeing the future as the work of necessity.

For Tocqueville, as he closed his second volume of the *Democracy*, the meaning of the past could only be obscured if such an outlook were to triumph. He did not say if he thought French historians, such as Thiers

---

[33] *Nolla edn.*, II, p. 85 (my emphasis).   [34] Ibid., II, pp. 86–87.

and Mignet, whose histories of the Revolution were winning a large reading public in France, belonged to the school of "democratic historians." Thiers's history, portions of which he read toward the end of the Restoration, at about the same time as he was attending Guizot's lectures at the Sorbonne, reduced his doubts about taking very seriously the respective roles of determinateness, ideas and persons in history. Thiers's history repelled him because of its facile and shopworn allusions to persistent causes and accidents, and because of its overwhelming surrender to naive and undeveloped ideas about fatalism, necessity and inevitability in human events.[35] He also adamantly rejected Mignet's "idea of necessity, of fatality," and vowed "to explain how my system is perfectly compatible with human liberty."[36]

Tocqueville found an ally in John Stuart Mill. He admired Mill's work and his prolific output. Mill returned the admiration, devoting two

---

[35] See Adolphe Thiers, *Histoire de la Révolution française*, 4 vols., 8th edn. (Paris, 1839). Tocqueville consulted the second edition which appeared in 1828 for his "Notes sur la Révolution française de Thiers," *OC*, XVI, pp. 537–40. Tocqueville's low opinion of Thiers's history dates from at least 1831. An unidentified friend mentions the fact, and proceeds to call it "mediocre and monstrous," especially for its justification of "all the crimes of the Revolution because of an alleged necessity to save the Revolution and liberty": [?] to Tocqueville, February 22, 1831, *BYT*, B.I.C. Tocqueville was incensed no doubt for other reasons as well. The totality of Thiers's dismissal of the *noblesse* as an undifferentiated, monolithic class incapable of responding to change was an analysis he found too determining. "I was bursting," he later wrote to Royer-Collard, "with upright feelings natural to youth, and, moreover, the original intensity of family traditions had been preserved in my imagination": Tocqueville to Royer-Collard, December 6, 1836, *OC*, XI, p. 29. The specific inheritance in which he found himself comprised a family with deep roots in the ancient *noblesse*. His brothers and father took an intimate interest in Tocqueville's work. They gave him their opinions, usually stressing how he could make his arguments stronger. His father, comte Hervé de Tocqueville, wrote a distinguished history of the breakdown of the old society. See Robert R. Palmer, *The Two Tocquevilles, Father and Son: Hervé and Alexis de Tocqueville on the Coming of the French Revolution* (Princeton, 1987). Neither father nor son, however, consulted one another on their respective works on the Revolution.

[36] *Nolla edn.*, II, p. 281, note k. See François A. Mignet, *Histoire de la Révolution française, de 1789 jusqu'en 1814*, 2 vols. (Paris, 1824). On the deep hold of the doctrine of necessity among early nineteenth-century French historians, see Louis Halphen's view that pre-1830 liberals envisaged history fatalistically, and displayed a tendency to philosophical generalizations, *L'Histoire en France depuis cent ans* (Paris, 1914), pp. 34–35, 38–39; Yvonne Knibiehler, *Naissance des sciences humaines: Mignet et l'histoire philosophique au XIXe siècle* (Paris, 1973). Johnson, *Guizot*, p. 85, claims that Tocqueville was "a fatalist" and that he was "bored by the realities of government." Tocqueville was impatient with and often filled with disgust for his fellow deputies in the Chamber, but he consciously chose to be actively engaged in politics, because of his conviction that a man of letters needed that experience to speak with authority about the aims of politics. He can be called a fatalist only by ignoring his belief in choice as the only way to interrupt and shape fate and, not least, by overlooking his keen eye for the contingent. Cobban, *Aspects of the French Revolution*, p. 42, maintains that Tocqueville moved away from a belief in the "overriding forces of destiny."

lengthy reviews to the two parts of the *Democracy*.[37] He told Tocqueville that he had "changed the face of political philosophy,"[38] and, in an essay on Alfred de Vigny, he said that, like the poet, Tocqueville "learnt to take formulas for what they were worth, and to look into the world itself for the philosophy of it . . . That . . . the spirit of the modern world, triumphant in July 1830 must have gone for something in giving to the speculations of a philosopher like M. de Tocqueville the catholic spirit and comprehensive range which distinguish them, most people will readily admit."[39] He was more critical on another occasion, telling Tocqueville that "the thoughts" expressed in the second part of the *Democracy* "are much more recondite" than the first, but "whether one assents to them or not, [they] are brought from a greater depth in human nature itself, than those in your first publication. It constitutes still more than the other did, an era in science."[40] Mill was the leading interpreter to a British audience of French literary, philosophical and, not least, historical works. In his reviews of major French historians – Mignet, Armand Carrel, Michelet and Guizot – Mill spoke approvingly, but perhaps with some exaggeration, of the latter's capacity as "a theorizer."[41] Earlier in the same essay, wishing to focus on the French historians "who have written history, as well as written *about* history,"[42] Mill used a formulation very like the one Tocqueville was to use in 1850, when he spoke of combining history properly speaking with philosophical history. Mill adverted to historians who had "a more comprehensive and far-reaching character," doubtless thinking of Mignet, who, he wrote some years earlier, made "history subservient to philosophy, in which the narrative itself is but a secondary subject, the illustration of the laws of human nature and human history being the first." While Mill proposed that this approach was instructive, there was "an intermediate style, which endeavours to unite the gratification of both the others."[43] Mill hoped, as he told Tocqueville nearly two decades later, that French thinkers would, without sacrificing their "telescopic view to our microscopic one," "combine the two and make them reconcilable."[44]

---

[37] John Stuart Mill, "De Tocqueville on Democracy in America," *London and Westminster Review*, 30 (1835), pp. 85–129, and "De la Démocratie en Amérique," *Edinburgh Review*, 72 (1840), pp. 1–25.   [38] Mill to Tocqueville, May 11, 1840, *OC*, VI, pt. 1, p. 328.

[39] John Stuart Mill, "Writings of Alfred de Vigny (1838)," in *Autobiography and Literary Essays*, ed. John M. Robson and Jack Stillinger (Toronto and Buffalo, 1981), p. 466. This volume, henceforth cited as *CW*, is the first of the *Collected Works of John Stuart Mill*, ed. John M. Robson (Toronto and Buffalo, 1963–).

[40] Mill to Tocqueville, December 30, 1840, *OC*, VI, pt. 1, pp. 331–32.

[41] John Stuart Mill, "Michelet's History of France," *CW*, Vol. XX, *Essays on French History and Historians*, ed. John Robson (Toronto, 1985), p. 229. This volume has a perspicuous introduction by John C. Cairns.   [42] Ibid., p. 221.

[43] "Mignet's French Revolution," ibid., pp. 3–4.

[44] Mill to Tocqueville, December 30, 1840, *OC*, VI, pt. 1, p. 332.

Uppermost in Tocqueville's mind was the problem of fatalism, so when Mill's ambitious book on logic appeared in 1843, Tocqueville must have turned eagerly to its last chapter on the moral sciences, where Mill discussed liberty and necessity. He could not have missed Mill's treatment of chance and probability either, though his major concern at that moment, as he expressed it to Mill, was how logic could be applied to the study of human behavior. He apparently agreed with Mill that a simple theory of necessity was indeed incompatible with free actions, but that if the common misconceptions about the linkages between them were removed, there need not be any logical or experiential conflict between the causes of volition and the act of choosing. Mill challenged metaphysicians who rested much of their case on feelings of human pride: people are repelled by the idea that human choices cannot exist outside the chain of cause and effect. Tocqueville found supportive of his own position Mill's statement that the error on the vexing question arose from what he called "wholly an effect of the associations with a word . . . [as] inappropriate a term as Necessity. That word, in its other acceptations, involves much more than mere uniformity of sequence; it implies irresistibleness . . . When we say that all human actions take place of necessity, we only mean that they will certainly happen if nothing prevents."[45] Tocqueville understood Mill to be saying that he was distinguishing irresistibleness and necessity, and Tocqueville went on to equate "irresistibleness" with fatalism, and congratulated Mill for providing a basis for arguments against the notion of simple fatalism,[46] a position from which he recoiled all his life. He also hoped that the metaphysical and nonmetaphysical treatments of the question of human liberty and necessity would be advanced on the neutral ground which Mill had laid down for further discussion.[47]

Tocqueville's commitment to a concept of linkage between human choice and an underlying, if hidden, structure in human events, was matched by his refusal to yield to any divorce between his notions of

[45] John Stuart Mill, *A System of Logic, Ratiocinative and Inductive. Being a Connected View of the Principles of Evidence and the Method of Scientific Investigation*, 8th edn. (New York, 1881), p. 583.

[46] Cf. Hannah Arendt, *On Revolution* (New York, 1963), p. 259. It seems to me that she is almost but not quite right in her judgment that Tocqueville was persuaded "that revolution had been the result of an irresistible force rather than the outcome of specific deeds and events." He did not neglect nor minimize, and, in fact, treated with the utmost subtlety, the points of fusion between the concrete and the general.

[47] Tocqueville to Mill, October 25, 1843, *OC*, VI, pt. 1, p. 344. The italics are in the original. (Tocqueville did not say whether he agreed with Mill's antitheological position.) Mill replied that the chapter was the most important in his book, and that he was seeking a solid intellectual basis for discussing the sense of human responsibility: Mill to Tocqueville, November 3, 1843, ibid., pp. 346–47.

personal liberty and the liberty of societies. We shall see how he does not give this problem a simple reading in the *Souvenirs*. Tocqueville may be said to have shown the gifts of an artist, but he did this without sub-terfuge: he was not being artful. He was consciously involved in an act of writing that was at the intersection of a personal testament and a treat-ment of a larger historical event. This exercise was, moreover, not carried out at the price of reducing the complexities of civic reality to the very different complexities of personal experience. It was also not the same as saying that the Revolution was in some sense "invented" as it developed.[48] Tocqueville worked out his own narrative, his own account, his own reconstruction, exploiting rhetorical devices as a conscious stylist would. His "strenuous and conscientious" struggle to achieve this goal might best be seen in the larger context of a multitude of events in which other persons were making similar efforts. Hence his double involvement in the events of 1848 was, as he believed, to be seen as an illustration, both of the limits of the human mind to grasp the universe, and of the mind's continuing efforts to expand the limits of human understanding. The best proof of the boundaries of human action was to be found by compar-ing human intentions with their consequences. One could take a more expansive view of the notion of a master narrative transcending individual narratives, that is, by seeing that nebulous notion itself as a metaphor. If one were to argue in this way, Tocqueville could be said to have been pre-pared to concede that what he was doing in his act of rediscovery might in some way be congruent with a master narrative – with the workings of providence. But beyond believing that degrees of determinateness in history existed as subsets or were subsumed by providential signs, the master narrative itself, if one existed, could not but be concealed from human beings. Although Tocqueville could not avoid being on the side of epistemological modesty, he believed that truth was discovered, not invented.

Tocqueville's claim to be working on an acceptable fusion of history properly speaking and the philosophy of history would not be particularly illuminating if a simple tension is posited between the end of history and a restless search for its purpose. Tocqueville refused to believe that there is a state toward which humanity was moving, as if in fulfillment of a hidden design. If democracy as a social condition was indeed inscribed as the fate for most aristocratic societies, Tocqueville did not go so far as to affirm that the liberty which he valued more – and which he indeed thought would constitute a privileged state for humankind – was assured by

---

[48] See, in contrast, Keith M. Baker, *Inventing the French Revolution: Essays on French Political Culture in the Eighteenth Century* (Cambridge, 1990).

providence. If anything, the passage from the abstract conception to the concrete instantiations of modern liberty was much more problematic than the particular expressions of democracy, with which liberty had a troubled relationship and to whose totalizing power it might very well succumb. This was especially so in the light of competing opinions and debates over what elements in liberty might be considered provisional and dispensable. If proof were needed of the absence of certainty, Tocqueville sought it in his belief that liberty, however circumscribed, is available to human agents. Such an argument reinforces his anti-necessitarianism. In fact, Tocqueville's praise of an ideal liberty appears to place it outside all historical referents. Liberty existed of course within specific cultural contexts, but within them it could not but suffer degradation from which it needed to be reclaimed from those who invoked liberty without appreciating its fragility, above all its vulnerability to contamination, once it was identified permanently with any of its concrete representations. See how he lyricized liberty and endowed it with a timeless quality when he was thirty, traveling in England and Ireland:

In truth liberty is a *holy* thing. Only one other thing merits this appellation more, and that is *virtue*. Still what is virtue if not the *free* choice of what is good? Liberty seems to me to occupy in the political world the same place as the atmosphere occupies in the physical world. The world is peopled with a multitude of beings diversely organized, all howsoever living and prospering. Alter the conditions of the atmosphere and they [will] suffer. Set them down in another and they will die.[49]

More than twenty years later in *L'Ancien Régime*, he continued to think of liberty in these ideal terms. It had the power of "real instinct," "intrinsic glamour"; it had a "fascination . . . in itself, apart from all 'practical' considerations"; it was nothing "other than itself." It was something that "defies analysis," it was "something that one must feel," it was something in which "logic has no part," and it was incomprehensible to "meaner souls, untouched by the sacred flame."[50] Tocqueville conceived of liberty as an abstraction, auto-referential to be sure,[51] which must necessarily fall short of perfection in any historical manifestation; but at the same time it could only reveal itself in history. This was his only certain conviction.

In every other respect, the principle of certainty had no problematic significance, unless it was grounded in an overwhelming affirmation of religious doctrine. But, as in the earlier periods of his life, as in his last years, when he reflected on the end of the *ancien régime*, Tocqueville found

---

[49] *Pléiade edn.*, I, p. 514. The emphasis is Tocqueville's.   [50] *OC*, II, pt. 1, p. 217.
[51] Linda Orr, "Tocqueville et l'histoire incompréhensible: L'Ancien Régime et la Révolution française," *Poétique*, 49 (February 1982), p. 69.

certainty nowhere. Just as he was beginning to write the first part of his *Souvenirs*, he expressed a need for certain signs. Much as he desired a "recipe for belief," much as he wanted to end his doubt by simply surrendering his will, as others did, he could not, for, in all his "passionate" searches for certainty, all he encountered was "a large, black, depthless hole in which human opinions exist in a state of tumultuous agitation . . . If God has not given everyone the gift to judge the truth, he has at least accorded to all of us the power of being conscious of what is good and decent, and that ought to be enough to serve as our thread through the shadows."[52] The recurrent theme in all his speculations on the meaning of existence – speculations that demonstrated respect, laced with some resignation, for theology, metaphysics and science – was the thought that, "what we call man . . . has been given just enough light to show him the miseries of his condition," enough to endure them in spite of his inability to apprehend why the world existed in the first place; what rationale there was for its creation, "about which he knows nothing, not even [do we know anything] about our bodies, still less our minds . . ."[53] Knowing the miseries of the human condition was, if we recall Pascal's judgment, one of man's distinctive faculties; the other was the grandeur of the human spirit:

But even if the universe were to crush him, man would still be nobler than his slayer, because he knows that he is dying and the advantage the universe has over him. Thus all our dignity consists in thought. It is on thought that we must depend for our recovery, not on space and time, which we could never fill. Let us then strive to think well; that is the basic principle of morality.[54]

So demanding, but for Tocqueville inspiring, a message was at the center of his belief that there was a human essence capable of self-actualization. But it was not in any "monastic life" that human beings should seek it; the claustral life was in fact "supremely immoral," for human beings fulfill themselves and derive satisfaction through their public and private actions, which by definition must involve others.[55] Human identity lies in the freedom to make choices; the faculty of choice is God's gift to human beings; and we can know this without being drawn into the mysteries of existence. In this world, "life [is] inexplicable and in the next frightening." The terrors of doubt, present in acute or repressed form, need not have the power to immobilize.[56]

---

[52] Tocqueville to Corcelle, August 1, 1850, *OC*, XV, pt. 2, p. 29.
[53] Tocqueville to Bouchitté, January 8, 1858, *Beaumont edn.*, VII, pp. 175–77.
[54] Blaise Pascal, *Pensées*, ed. A. J. Krailsheimer (Harmondsworth, 1965), p. 95. Cf. André Jardin, *Alexis de Tocqueville, 1805–1859* (Paris, 1984), p. 63.
[55] Tocqueville to Kergorlay, August 4, 1857, *OC*, XIII, pt. 2, p. 328.
[56] Tocqueville to Swetchine, February 26, 1857, *OC*, XV, pt. 2, p. 314.

Philosophy of history, seen as a search for a transcendent unity, would certainly not exclude Tocqueville's kind of questing and, if we grant that there is an attempt to define human beings through their self-actualization in different historical epochs, then there is no reason to think that the questions associated with the philosophy of history failed to engage him. He would not let go of these questions.[57] The reaching for sincerity, the most striking of the opening words in the *Souvenirs*, is bound up with his notions of choice and identity. Tocqueville, though never a marginal figure in the world of academies which were hardly slow in granting him recognition, felt himself to be an outsider in another, more disturbing way. His conviction that the thoughts of the greatest number of his contemporaries ran along conventional lines, or along lines which, even if novel, he found were evading the great issues of the day, impelled him to find a clear and independent ground for his ideas which he never stopped believing were unpalatable to many of his political and intellectual peers. The position of an autonomous and original thinker which he sedulously cultivated contributed, however, to feelings of self-doubt. His patrician stance was also an isolating and lonely one. He dealt with it by thinking of himself, not only as an outsider, but as superior to most of his friends and colleagues. This point becomes the more forceful when we perceive links between his self-doubt and his need for fixity and certainty at the cosmic level. Ultimately he thought of the narrative he was writing in the *Souvenirs*, in both its autobiographical and general historical aspects, as a search for coherence, even if much of the human action he observed and criticized seemed to fall within the realm of the incoherent. He was aware that his story was only one among many and that his way of configuring fate, necessity and chance could be challenged, but he was not ready to admit that his narrative was not in its essentials true. In his narrative, he was led intuitively to what he unquestioningly assumed the stories of everyday, particular and concrete experiences would reveal about historical actors and history itself.

The idea that the only authentic history is that which is written from a solid basis in practical experience, from participation in the events themselves, instead of from the shelter of a study, and that the first, not the

---

[57] Cf. Albert Salomon, *In Praise of Enlightenment* (Cleveland and New York, 1962), pp. 282–309, 324–27, who argues that Tocqueville's ideas must be seen in a Christian frame, and that he did not elevate the philosophy of history above the philosophy of man, or philosophical anthropology. The latter may be briefly understood as an approach that moves beyond idealism and positivism in an effort to combine phenomenological and existential subjective perspectives with the objective viewpoint of the human sciences. Insofar as Tocqueville placed great stress on metaphysical questions, yet was respectful of the empirical grounds of inquiry, he could be called an early exponent of philosophical anthropology.

second, vantage point alone entitles the historian to instruct the reader, is almost Polybian in tone.[58] But Tocqueville's aims were less utilitarian and his intent far more speculative. It was not enough to register success or failure, and to believe that all human beings had to do was to apply lessons from the past to the present. Insofar as Tocqueville's major concern in the *Souvenirs* is to tell us how he lived through the events of 1848 and how he assessed the actions and psychology of his contemporaries, the issues to be raised in his narrative revolve around what they did, what they thought they were doing, and beyond both of these questions, why he gave importance to and understood the perception of choices, real and putative, and how they were perceived. To see the question from this angle permits a comparative examination of how other *possible* choices were in fact seen, and, of equal (and some would insist greater) importance, why the historical actors elected the decisions they did. This question was important for Tocqueville, who reflected on and judged human blind spots, wishful thinking and self-deception either as moral shortcomings, or as being enfolded in, but not invariably engulfed by, the broad and uncontrollable flow of history. By concentrating on relatively minute but dense fractions of time, he captured some of the textures of events and mentalities, and he forces the reader to ponder the double question of how the historical web is constructed and reconstructed.

Tocqueville inveighed against the biological determinism and materialism he found so repugnant in Arthur de Gobineau, whose espousal of such ideas seemed to Tocqueville an intolerable, as well as a crude, repudiation of the idea of persons choosing their liberty.[59] Liberty was endangered by political sterility and impotence, but could never be totally extinguished. It was by charting the patterns of possibility that he saw that the historian not only records events, but how they come into being through the cluster of choices and the emotions that, in some important but undetermined way, constitute them. Without explicitly considering

---

[58] Most of the following passage from Polybius would have appealed to Tocqueville: "The peculiar function of history is to discover in the first place, the words actually spoken whatever they were, and next to ascertain the reason why what was done or spoken led to failure or success . . . For it is the mental transference of similar circumstances to our times that gives us the means of forming presentiments of what is about to happen, and enables us at certain times to take precautions and at others by reproducing former conditions to face with more confidence the difficulties that menace us." For the citation, see Kenneth Sacks, *Polybius on the Writing of History* (Berkeley, Los Angeles and London, 1981), p. 94. Cf. Friedrich Nietzsche, *The Use and Abuse of History*, rev. edn., trans. Julius Kraft (Indianapolis and New York, 1957), p. 12: "Polybius is thinking of the active man when he calls political history the true preparation for governing a state; it is the great teacher that shows us how to bear steadfastly the reverses of fortune by reminding us what others have suffered."

[59] Tocqueville to Gobineau, January 24, 1857, *OC*, IX, pp. 277–81.

the role of possibility in history, Michael Oakeshott characterizes Tocqueville's intention in his account of the Revolution as a refusal to avow a simple demonstration of necessity or the "inevitable result of preceding events, but as an intelligible convergence of human choices and actions."[60] Oakeshott seems to grant primacy to events as mediating one circumstance to another, and not, as Tocqueville does, to the choices that make them up. Those choices and emotions needed, as far as I can see in Tocqueville's approach to the past, to be displayed, and narrative was his method of showing what they were.[61]

The *Souvenirs* embody, with a fair degree of consistency, this respect for, and awe before, the unknown which is uncovered in the telling of what happened and could still happen through the efforts of human actions. Tocqueville's narrative captures some of the ironic and tragic interaction between the expected and the unexpected, the possible and the impossible, contingency and necessity. Narrative as a way of recollecting the past can achieve some of the complexity of the struggle experienced by human beings when they are players in their own histories and the histories of others. Narrative has another great advantage. It is particularly good in paradoxically revealing the limits of the narrator. It is a method that lights up certain aspects of human conduct, including its moral dimensions in heightened political situations, but at the same time its historical perspectives are foreshortened. As we shall also see, the political and moral quandaries Tocqueville encountered severely tested his own calculation of what was at stake for him personally. All these perplexing questions are also present in Tocqueville's apostrophes to the "miracle" of 1789 – "that historic date of glorious memory" – which was the perspective he wanted to keep in mind at all times, and which for a moment broke loose from its moorings, as they did in the less inspired, but still not wholly ignoble, mood of the early moments of 1848. As it did so, the desired historical perspective Tocqueville sought was put to a great strain.

As Tocqueville closed the last pages of *L'Ancien Régime*,[62] he linked memories of the lyrical mood inspired by the hopes of the early days of the

---

[60] Michael J. Oakeshott, "The Activity of Being an Historian," in *Rationalism in Politics and Other Essays*, new and expanded edn. (Indianapolis, 1991), p. 172.

[61] Cf. Martha C. Nussbaum, *Love's Knowledge: Essays on Philosophy and Literature* (New York and London, 1990), pp. 5–7, 171. Nussbaum believes that fiction is a valuable source for examining moral choices in real life. I see no major critical difference in the approaches of novelists and historians when they confront the reader with the emotions and decisions – the realm of possibilities – of their protagonists. It is easier of course for novelists, presumably acting in their roles as master narrators, to imagine how their characters might envision choices, but novelists, too, are constrained by the limitations of their personalities and the societies in which they live.

[62] See the references to surprise, the unexpected, the startling and to the fall of the régime in *OC*, II, pt. 1, pp. 247–50.

Revolution with a sober reflection, not only of how the actors were puzzled by "surprising" and "startling" events, but what their successors found themselves doing when they dealt with the unanticipated. Even when they took the greatest pains to restore a sense of order, they were never quite able to shake off the feelings of marvel. Tocqueville's urge was to disenchant the past by speaking of "foregone conclusions," once the historian delved deeply enough. But when he gave reasons for the transformation of civilized and good intentions into savage violence – one of the many critical ways in which Tocqueville characterized the road the Revolution took – he was not entirely certain that he could do so. When he introduced, as if in an afterthought, "the peculiarities of the French temperament," he presents us with a uniquely French socio-psychological cast of mind, which proves to be only a summation of how French people surprise both themselves and non-French people alike. Thus revolutions are happenings in which the unpredictable reigns unchecked. The "fall" of the Old Régime opened up a period of possibilities, one of which might have led to a new order, embodied, for Tocqueville, in democracy's appropriation and proper uses of liberty. At the same time, much as the new carried with it the features of the old, the processes of how the old were incorporated in the new remained to challenge the historian's imagination, as he pushed away the "shadows" to see the "grandeurs and miseries" of the old society (one is reminded of Montesquieu's title for his study of the grandeur and decadence of the Romans).

Tocqueville also implied more – a commonplace for present-day readers, but not yet so for most of the contemporaries he addressed, who he believed had yet to place their own delicate political situation within the wider perspective of a revolutionary past. Not only were the Revolution's achievements traceable to antecedents in the Old Régime, but, by building on the modern institutional features that were introduced through state consolidation, France entered the path of revolution because of the unexpectedness and stubbornness of human actions which were themselves supervening. Human actions, in short, could work both ways – to prevent disaster as well as to cause it. The force of ideas he saw in the same way. In 1842, in his inaugural address to the Académie française, he noted the blindness of political leaders to the power of ideas. They are always surprised to find that "the general law" binding great intellectual ideas to great political movements – revolutions, in short – stares them in the face too late. Leaders are always surprised; they are never prepared for the new.[63]

---

[63] "Discours de M. de Tocqueville prononcé dans la séance publique du 21 avril 1842, en venant prendre séance à la place de M. le Comte de Cessac," *OC*, XVI, p. 255.

This returns us to the question of possibilities, to the "counterfactual" problem, but this time to what possible outcomes existed for people facing and in a position to deal with the dilemmas of prerevolutionary France. For, once the question of possibility is raised, so too is that of intentionality. How deeply Tocqueville considered why intentionality involves the "simultaneous consideration of several possible states of affairs or courses of events,"[64] will be seen in his narrative of the 1848–49 crisis, and again in his work on the *ancien régime*. For the moment, it is enough to note that he linked the problem of intentionality and possibility with the element of surprise. He struggled with the perception – hard to grasp in all its complexity – that, once we accept that "surprise" is never missing from human events, we may find that there are no surprises at all in a retrospective sense. No surprises, once the Revolution's "suddenness," its "frantic and thoroughgoing" nature, its "changes of direction, its anomalies and inconsistencies," which are deeply embedded in the French past, are disinterred, recollected and reconstructed. Still, while Tocqueville, working with the past, saw it as holding the key to the surprises, he was frustrated by the bluntness and imperfection of his instruments. Feelings of bafflement were never erased. Better cognitive tools and greater mounds of evidence, offering more adequate explanations, always beckoned to him. Would they reveal why certain choices made in the past appear to be deeply unsettling, while others seemed straightforwardly conventional?

---

[64] See Jaako Hintikka, *The Intentions of Intentionality and Other New Models of Modalities* (Dordrecht, 1975), p. 195.

3   Tocqueville's conceptualization of moral choice and the particular

---

There is often no more logic in the course of events than there is in the plans of men, and this is why we usually blame our luck when things happen in ways that we did not expect.[1]

Order and disorder: a matrix for historical inquiry

It was not until Tocqueville experienced the 1848 revolutionary crisis and transmuted it in his recollections that he was able to reflect on how human beings weighed their intentions within frameworks of possible action. Tocqueville wrote the first part of his *Souvenirs* in the family chateau in Normandy in July 1850, following his departure from a brief and unhappy tenure as ministre des affaires étrangères. The second part was written in Sorrento at the end of that year and completed in March of 1851. He began the last section in September in Versailles after the prorogation of the National Assembly. He composed the first part quickly, without the mental anguish that would precede his search for, and the doubts he expressed about, the most rewarding methods for confronting the immensity of the history of the 1789 Revolution. Not absent from the *Souvenirs*, however, are breaks in the narrative, which he used for reflective comments on the nature of the conflict. It was not, however, until he got to the calm of Italy that he felt easy enough, after periods of apprehension, to look at the causes leading to February 24. But, on that day itself, he wrote that he was "thinking of the events themselves, and sought less for what had produced them than for what was to follow."[2] And, when he resumed the narration in the second part, he mixed narrative and explanation, as in the first. The third part follows the same structure, but with a greater emphasis, already discernible at the end of the second part, as we shall see, on Tocqueville as a person in a position of power.

---

[1] From Pericles's Funeral Oration, in Thucydides, *History of the Peloponnesian War*, trans. Rex Warner (Harmondsworth, 1986), p. 119.   [2] *OC*, XII, p. 86.

While he tried to isolate the hidden sources of the explosive political maneuvering in 1848, what stirred Tocqueville so deeply and with such immediacy, and what he wanted to record with emotional fidelity, was the fractured spectacle in which events and human beings appeared at times to move together, as if seamlessly. At other times, events appeared to overwhelm individuals, brutally undermining their actions, including his own. Yet, in other instances, persons seemed to move against the current, conferring on themselves the power of free action. The most striking feature of this most private work, including his disclosures to his closest friends, is to be found in its sketches of and comments on the characters of the actors. He did not do so as a fabricator of fictional drama who knows the outcome of his characters' actions beforehand, yet who must, to be convincing, keep the spectators guessing. Rather, in Tocqueville's use of the narrative form, he cautioned himself to be sensitive to the historical veracity of the actors, showing them in encounters with one another and conspiring in ways, known only dimly to themselves, to respond to and to help shape events. At the same time, by deploying the narrator's art, he knew that he must present his history as a process, which might or might not be related to a specific outcome. Process and outcome would thus exist in mutual and tentative tension. He wrote almost languidly about the composition of his recollections. Already, as he reflected with resignation, the five months of his ministry at the Quai d'Orsay had vanished into a kind of nothingness. What stirred his memories more was the thought that only by being so close to the things he witnessed could he have grasped their singularity. Just as stimulating for him was the promise of understanding the "physiognomy" of the persons he had observed: "There are enough sordid models [for me] to be able to produce a sufficient number of mediocre portraits, but a gallery of contemporaries often gives more pleasure than the most beautiful portraits of the most illustrious dead."[3] From viewing their conduct and inferring their motives, his putative readers would gain some edification from the historian's skill in introducing the contingent and the unexpected as reflections of historical reality.

The first pages invoke his intentions, which are couched in late eighteenth-century conventions of realistic portrayal, using images with the power to capture the past as he lived it – the spectacle of history in action. Promised are a "tableau," a "painting," a "mirror" and the "authenticity" through which to regain some of the realities of a "labyrinth" of emotions and judgments, and, above all, to confront the blurred "physiognomy" of

[3] Tocqueville to Beaumont, December 26, 1850, *OC*, VIII, pt. 2, p. 343.

his time,[4] blurred because of the ultimate impossibility of knowing the larger frameworks of human actions and possibilities. "Remembering," for Tocqueville, was a fleeting condition. Indeed, Tocqueville chose not to call his work *mémoires* but rather *souvenirs*, which denotes more broadly the sense of recollection.[5] Recollection is not a mere act of remembering, for memory is a minimal kind of faculty. Nor can it be an act of reproduction, producing a clairvoyant and unproblematic rendering of the past.[6] It does not have the comprehensiveness of memory that is said to be found in the epic, which can "absorb the course of events." It is more like reminiscence, and, for that reason, deserves the term "art."[7] Recollection may thus be seen as a highly conscious and imaginative act of reconstruction. Tocqueville's disclaimer that his recollections would "be a form of mental relaxation and not at all a work of literature"[8] is somewhat disingenuous if taken literally. He enjoyed crafting his style, but above all he wanted to find the authentic mode for his own biography.

The more closely we look at the *Souvenirs*, the more it seems certain that recollection for Tocqueville was an act of creative reconstruction of the self's thoughts, wishes, intentions, actions and their criss-crossings with those of other selves. He looked for an unwavering and relatively stable reference point in himself, to be attained by finding an exit from his personal "labyrinth." If he could be true to himself – true to his most secret thoughts, emotions and feelings – he could begin to be true to his subject. In choosing an "unmoved" point in himself, he did not claim that other points external to himself were subordinate to his will, but only that the world of self and others outside it were in a constant state of flux, and that individuals must have a starting point, for they have no choice but to adopt a metaphysical fixity to make possible an interpretation of the empirical world. The maneuver was a heuristic device to confirm the

[4] Ibid., p. 29.
[5] Cf. Søren A. Kierkegaard, *Stages on Life's Way*, ed. and trans. H. V. Hong and E. H. Hong (Princeton, 1988), pp. 9–12, who makes the point that recollection is stronger than unstructured remembering.
[6] A similar argument is advanced by Hayden White, *Tropics of Discourse: Essays in Cultural Criticism* (Baltimore and London, 1978), pp. 90–91. For the many questions raised by the claim that Tocqueville's image of the secret mirror would reflect his inner thoughts, and where such a cognitive and psychological device led him, see Larry E. Shiner, *The Secret Mirror: Literary Form and History in Tocqueville's "Recollections"* (Ithaca and London, 1988). Shiner also believes (p. 7) that Tocqueville preferred the rhetorical to the narrative form. He contends that Tocqueville could not end the narrative in the *Souvenirs*, because of "certain discursive combinations" that lent themselves more easily to his moral sense (pp. 200–01). Tocqueville's strong moral consciousness is undeniable, and I will be arguing that the reason for the narrative's incompleteness is traceable to his brooding over questions of choice and necessity.
[7] For this distinction between comprehensiveness of memory, memory and reminiscence, see Walter Benjamin, "The Storyteller," in *Illuminations*, pp. 97–98.   [8] *OC*, XII, p. 29.

intersubjectivity of such entities as the public and private, the social and the personal. The image of the labyrinth carried for him an even greater source of emotional and epistemological energy. It is impossible to see the image fully outside his need to put it in universalistic terms, to attach the thread of the recollections of his personal existence to "the chain of history."[9]

Tocqueville declares his intention to depict the élites among his contemporaries, as he would paint himself, "without flattery," or as he also described his purpose, *sincerely*. Almost immediately, he interrupts the narrative with another, more grandiose, declaration of purpose. He is determined to locate his narration of the petty incidents, ideas, passions and personal views in the imbricated contexts of France's revolutionary past and its latest manifestations in the political life of the post-1830 era in which politicians listened only to their own needs. Their egoism had become a natural instinct shaped by a virtually unimpeded and absolute control over all the manifestations of the country's culture, which appeared to run as effortlessly as a machine.[10] But that symptom of the régime's undoing Tocqueville did not perceive fully until a few weeks before 1848.

In 1842, six years earlier, when he was very far from believing that the Revolution of 1830 was failing to establish a stable order, Tocqueville compared the 1688 English Revolution and settlement with the events leading to and including 1830. Twelve years after the final extinction of the Bourbons, he gave some small inkling of how the political malaise he detected in his own country offended him, taking as his example for the comparison he thought worth making Tobias Smollett's "pedantic" history of England from 1688 to the accession of George II. His main lesson, from his survey of England's experience, was that, "The role played by egotistical passions, the absence of principles, the inconstancy of opinions, the demoralization and almost constant corruption of politicians in this constitutional history of England is immense. The power of individual intrigues, the pettiness and particular ugliness of passions, during periods of calm when events failed to produce great efforts and to bring great personalities to light, are infinite." Extraordinarily, in spite of these vices, the English nation proved itself capable of great achievements

---

[9] Ibid., p. 47. Cf. Italo Calvino, "Riccordo di un battaglia," *La strade di San Giovanni* (Milan, 1990), pp. 81–82. Calvino was fearful "that as soon as some remembrance forms, it will immediately appear in a faulty light, contrived, war and youth as sentimental as always, and become a segment in the story with the style of that time, which cannot tell us how things really were but only how we thought we saw them and said them" (cited by Carlo Ginsburg, "Microhistory: Two or Three Things That I Know about It," *Critical Inquiry*, 20 [1993], p. 30).   [10] *OC*, XII, pp. 29–30, 36.

because of its respect for political liberty. In the absence of such a political tradition in France, the futility of political wrangling was simply more glaring. Politicians tormented themselves looking for subjects upon which to disagree – an allusion to the poverty of political discourse in post-1830 France, but also proof of the significance Tocqueville gave to the emotional climate of individual decisions and the role of the unexpected.[11]

Tocqueville brought this attitude to the Chamber to which he was elected in March 1839, locating himself between Thiers's center-left and Odilon Barrot's dynastic left.[12] The charms of writing, and the firm reputation he had established as a modern-day prophet, were, he felt, not the only way to experience life. In political action, much could be done to restore or to initiate the kind of debates capable of bringing ordinary citizens into public life. In 1836, when he had already begun the second part of the *Democracy*, Tocqueville told Eugène Stoffels that, more than any man, he feared the recrudescence of the revolutionary spirit. What he believed could be achieved was the expansion of liberal ideas, "with as much freedom as possible left to individual action, to personal initiative," and he also thought a hereditary monarchy, rather than a republic, could promote "both direct and indirect exercise of very extensive political rights . . . I want citizens to be involved in public life to the extent that they are deemed capable of making a useful contribution, rather than kept out at all costs."[13] But some three years later, the parliamentary life for which he had longed infuriated him, pushing him to an uncharacteristic outburst. He wanted more passion in his life:

A state of revolution is a thousand times more preferable than the misery in which we find ourselves, and from which I cannot see any exit . . . Will we ever again see the wind of truly passionate politics . . . those violent, hard, often cruel, but great, disinterested, promising passions; passions which are the soul of the only parties I understand and to which I will gladly give my time, my fortune and my life? I cannot accustom myself in any way to what we are now witnessing. I will never accustom myself to it.[14]

A slightly more sober persona resurfaced a little later, as he settled down to contemplate the chances for non-revolutionary change. So long as circumstances remained unchanged, unless some accident occurred to

[11] Tocqueville to Kergorlay, October 25, 1842, *OC*, XIII, pt. 2, pp. 108–09.
[12] Odilon Barrot, one of the leaders of the 1847–48 banquet campaign launched in criticism of the government, defended the régime in its last trials. Deputy to the Constituent and Legislative Assemblies in 1848 and 1849, he was to become minister of justice under Louis Bonaparte. He left politics after the latter's coup d'état.
[13] Tocqueville to E. Stoffels, October 6, 1836, in *Beaumont edn.*, V, pp. 436–38.
[14] Tocqueville to Corcelle, October 19, 1839, *OC*, XV, pt. 1, pp. 137–40.

change them, no useful nor decisive stances could be struck. He longed for the unexpected to happen to satisfy his desire to express great political passions.[15]

It was not revolutionary passion he longed for, however much he wished to experience some of the energy it released. When the second volume of the *Democracy* was published, readers could find his first thoughts on the probabilities of future revolutionary turmoil. In a note to himself, he defined the revolutionary spirit or mentality as comprising a taste for rapid change and the use of violence to effect it. To complete the picture, he added that such a mentality was not impervious to tyrannical aspirations. The revolutionary mind exhibited an indifference concerning the means to achieve ends and satisfied itself by surrendering to brutal appetite. From the psychological roots and manifestations of the revolutionary mentality, he posited a negative relationship between the revolutionary mind and liberty. He suggested that the revolutionary mentality, feeding on the natural shortcomings of democratic societies, not only finds them intolerable and holds them in detestation, but in the process puts liberty in terrible jeopardy.[16] In 1840, he remained confident that the revolutionary spirit had exhausted itself, and that revolutionaries would commit a great error in hoping for its revival, while the peaceful members of society would waste their energies in fearing it.[17]

His prose was deliberate, even a bit orotund, in his talk to the Académie française in the spring of 1842. He declared that revolutions always promised more than they delivered, and that it was rare, even when they were most necessary and most victorious, for those who led them to live with pleasant or unambiguous memories of them. The future needed only a few final touches to complete the achievements of 1789.[18] In six articles published in *Le Siècle* in January 1843, he expanded his ideas. With some tentativeness, he conceded that the only revolutions lurking on a distant horizon might arise from the frustrations of the growing industrial class of workers.[19] In his preparatory notes for the 1844 session of the Chamber, he wrote that "the ideas of disorder, violence and tyranny to which all revolutions give birth were weakening." Simultaneously, "devotion to the country, liberty, independence and

[15] Tocqueville to Corcelle, November 14, 1839, ibid., pp. 140–45.
[16] *Nolla edn.*, pt. II, p. 276, note u. On Tocqueville's views on the unlikelihood of revolution, see Seymour Drescher, "Why Great Revolutions Will Become Rare: Tocqueville's Most Neglected Prognosis," *Journal of Modern History*, 64 (1992), pp. 429–54. Drescher stresses the famous chapter 21 of the third book of the second volume of the *Democracy*. The note to which I refer appears toward the very end of the third book.
[17] Tocqueville to Corcelle, September 26, 1840, *OC*, XV, pt. 1, pp. 147–52.
[18] "Discours de M. de Tocqueville," in *OC*, XVI, p. 255.
[19] These articles are to be found in *OC*, III, pt. 2, pp. 95–121.

fraternity" was weakening and a cause for concern.[20] The nation's indifference to politics was a sign of deep malaise, of death itself. He resumed the theme the next year. His analysis of the isolating and parlous effects of American individualism on political life clearly informed his diagnosis of French political life. The modern passion for amassing wealth was the greatest single motive force of societies. It was so powerful that it bred indifference to any other concern. It separated persons from one another and enervated the foundations of political life. This profound somnolence was making the achievements of the 1789 Revolution "problematic" and dangerous, since it dramatically raised the question of whether its final outcome would strengthen liberty or "give despotism the most perfect and hypocritical of forms."[21]

Nothing, except universal wishful thinking, could conceal the evidence that the hermeticism of parliamentary life was directly linked to the massive and unchecked displays of economic greed. In the Chamber, politicians, totally oblivious to their responsibilities, had become undisguised actors, disingenuously intent only on perfecting their own performance, but stumbling in front of the footlights because of their glaring lack of conviction, or insincerity as Tocqueville preferred to call it.[22] The themes of theatricalism and sincerity, expressed in his letter to Beaumont at the end of 1846, were to be sounded frequently in the *Souvenirs*. By late 1847, the depths of political complacency forced Tocqueville to the conclusion that the country had been pierced to its very bones by contempt for a government that was selling itself to the highest bidders. "We are not close to revolution, but this is assuredly the way revolutions are prepared."[23] And a month later, he was filled with "terror." For the first time since the July Revolution, he expressed the "fear that we will have some revolutionary experiences to live through. I admit that I cannot see how the storm could take shape and sweep us away, but it will blow up sooner or later, if something does not put new life into minds and lift up . . . souls."[24]

By the time he gave his prophetic speech in the Chamber on January

---

[20] Ibid., p. 217.   [21] Ibid., pp. 213–14.

[22] Tocqueville to Beaumont, December 14, 1846, *OC*, VIII, pt. 1, pp. 600–06. The Romantic Tocqueville would have found it difficult to agree with Iuri M. Lotman, "The Decembrist in Daily Life (Everyday Behavior as a Historical-Psychological Category)," in *The Semiotics of Russian Cultural History: Essays by I. M. Lotman, L. Ia. Ginsburg and B. A. Uspenski*, ed. A. D. Nakhimovsky and A. S. Nakhimovsky (New York, 1985), pp. 95–149: "The contemporary observer would see the everyday behavior of the Decembrist as *theatrical*, that is to say, directed toward a spectator. But to say that behavior is *theatrical* does not imply that it is insincere or reprehensible in any way" (p. 105).

[23] Tocqueville to Corcelle, August 27, 1847, *OC*, XV, pt. 1, pp. 235–36.

[24] Tocqueville to Corcelle, September 29, 1847, ibid., pp. 236–41.

27, 1848, portions of which he reproduced in the first chapter of the *Souvenirs*, he was sure that the apparent calm in the country was deluding the deputies, and that they were blind to what they had failed to do, and deaf to the lost possibilities of forming the kinds of political coalitions that could do real political work. In the few months before the January speech, Tocqueville turned wearily to what he deemed the principal sources of the descent into revolution. The first was the total absence of any real debate between two opposing parties, which he believed was the necessary lubricant of liberal politics. Instead, the nation witnessed politicians speaking about its problems as if they were children of the same family busying themselves with petty domestic things. In the absence of political dialogue focused on real issues, the time would come when a new upheaval would create two parties, but this time they would be locked in a violent struggle over the rights of property.[25] The *Souvenirs*, as we shall see, would advance his argument to another level. Just as he inveighed against the old aristocracy for its exclusiveness, the porousness of the middle class, he thought, attracted support from the great majority of property owners, but excluded everyone else. This was why it was not invulnerable; this was why it was coming under attack.[26]

Choice, necessity, contingency and possibility

The general causes of the breakdown in 1848 were, at least from Tocqueville's vantage point and self-ascribed prophetic powers, more easily discernible than the accidents precipitating it. Accidents are never predictable. Looked at in this way,[27] historical accidents cannot be dismissed. If in fact they are unforeseen (because of their very nature), accidents might indeed be seen as the decisive rather than as the secondary sources of an historical event, for logic dictates that in their absence the historical event could not come to completion. Resting the matter there, however, Tocqueville said, would put a premature end to the debate on choice and decision. If it is important, as it seems to be in the *Souvenirs*, to attach significance to concrete human actions, either by individuals or groups, we may say that whenever Tocqueville was able to detect their conscious intentions, he saw them as working within a web of underlying historical causes. It was hence difficult to view their actions as wholly autonomous variables. Tocqueville took the view that, in a less developed

---

[25] These thoughts are scattered in a series of notes Tocqueville wrote in 1847 and prefigure the January speech. They may be consulted in *OC*, III, pt. 2, pp. 720–41.

[26] *OC*, XII, pp. 63, 94. Tocqueville, it should be noted, would have some problems in sustaining the argument that the *ancien régime* aristocracy was locked into an absolute exclusivity.   [27] Ibid., pp. 12, 41.

sense of its meaning, accident is what persons and groups do in an absence of a full knowledge of what is at stake. To illustrate his point, he recalled the monarchy's fall in 1789. He set aside "the particular mischance . . . of the act of some man . . . the deficit, the oath in the Tennis Court, Lafayette, Mirabeau" as the expressions and acts of men riding the surface of things. Human beings were wrong when they beckoned to a naive, instead of a more complex, concept of chance. If they considered the first notion with care, they would soon discover that it was a primitive code word for their ignorance.[28]

In this instance, he echoed the Laplacean view that chance was a crude invention, masking ignorance. Pure chance possessed no explanatory power. Its arbitrariness in making everything in the causal field hinge on itself destroyed the very notion of causality. Chance, he thought, should be seen as a kind of external power, and could not be logically allowed to roam freely, as a kind of *deus ex machina*. It needed to be integrated into an explanation that would assign a proper ranking to it. The fall in 1789, for example, was due to a "governing class [that] had become incapable . . . of governing the country."[29] So the collective actions of classes carried more weight than the chance actions of individuals. But, even as he thus concluded, he did so in the context of his famous speech predicting breakdown in 1848. He could not have risen in the Chamber of Deputies without giving importance to his own efforts to shape the processes of government in the months before February. Human actions and utterances could thus count for something, a fact that Tocqueville did not dismiss when remarking that human beings tend to make the error of believing that they possess the power of clairvoyance. He punctuated this point from the very start: first, in his commonplace observation that individuals may see clearly as far as the horizon, both literally and metaphorically, but are incapable, because of their single-mindedness, of seeing that the real horizon is constantly changing.[30] Secondly, in their interactions, individuals "mutually push each other away from their respective plans," as if in accidental interference with one another, so that "the destinies of the world proceed as the result, but often as the contrary result of the intentions that produce them . . ."[31] Then, to give the coda an even greater paradoxical quality, he added, with an exquisitely polite but firm critique of his contemporaries who saw events only in their fragmented parts, retreating from a more complex whole:

---

[28] Ibid., p. 84.   [29] Ibid., pp. 38–39.

[30] Ibid., pp. 44–45. What prompted his remark was his meeting with Duvergier de Hauranne, a prolific writer on politics.   [31] Ibid., p. 50.

I have lived with men of letters, who have written history without taking part in public affairs, and with politicians, who have only concerned themselves with actual events without thinking of describing them. I have observed that the first see general causes everywhere, while the others, living in the midst of disconnected daily facts, are prone to imagine that everything can be reduced to particular incidents, and that the petty strings they pull are the same that move the world. It is to be presumed that both are equally deceived. For my part I hate those absolute systems which derive all the events in history from great first causes, link one to another in a chain of destiny and, so to speak, eliminate men from history. I find them narrow in their pretended greatness, and false under their air of mathematical truth.[32]

The 1848 revolutionaries were in part stuck in a scenario from the past; in fluctuating degrees, and, in a chaos of fluttering poses, they were prisoners of its signs and behavioral practices. Tocqueville characterized the dilemma of the subject or the self in the familiar terms of self-interest and lack of distance preventing one from seeing oneself as one is; the "views, interests, ideas, tastes and instincts that have guided [the self's] actions" wove the intricate network of a veil or a screen.[33] He wanted to use the power of the past, rather than bury it in personal lives and social settings, in order to grasp something even more difficult. He has left us with an impression that if he could in some way emerge from the maze with a heightened understanding of where he had been, he could help rescue his countrymen from their labyrinth, tell them where they had been, where they were likely to be going and prepare them for the democratic future.

Tocqueville tried to assure himself that he was freer than his co-actors from the lures of self-deception. In the first place, he set aside the idea that any theory of general causes entails necessity. There is no absolute "chain of fatality." In criticizing those who made claims to understand the workings of "great first causes" with "mathematical exactness," he probably had Laplace in mind.[34] Thus, while refusing, as we saw earlier, to accept a crude version of chance, he was equally resistant to vulgar notions of necessity. To underscore his opposition to necessitarianism, he stated in the second place that:

many important historical facts can only be explained by accidental circumstances, and . . . many others remain totally inexplicable. Moreover, chance, or rather that tangle of secondary causes which we call chance, for want of the knowledge of how to unravel it, plays a great part in all that happens on the

---

[32] Ibid., pp. 83–84.   [33] OC, XII, pp. 101–02.

[34] Cf. the reference in chap. 2 to Tocqueville's familiarity with John Stuart Mill's *System of Logic*, in which Mill discusses Laplace. Laplace's ideal was an explanatory law connecting the state of the universe at any particular moment with its state at any other moment, past or future.

world's stage; although I firmly believe that chance does nothing that has not been prepared beforehand. Antecedent facts, the nature of institutions, the cast of minds and the state of morals are the materials from which are composed those impromptus which astonish and alarm us.[35]

The idea of randomness was something he found intolerable; the search for certainty, a lost cause. What was left were probabilities. When, as is their natural propensity, human beings search for determinate causes, they try to lessen the weight of probability. Tocqueville put his thoughts with biting irony to Gobineau, who claimed to have discovered an infallible science of humankind. As he made his major point, Tocqueville briefly adverted to his belief in the uncertain status of the physical sciences:

A hypothesis which permits the prediction of certain effects that always reoccur under the same condition does, in a way, amount to a demonstrable truth. Even the Newtonian system had no more than such a foundation. If you really have discovered such an important secret which has been vainly searched for during several centuries, and if this is admitted by the world of scholarship, this will certainly give you the highest reputation.[36]

Tocqueville's kind of seriousness did not take him to the edge of the absurd. He was more attuned to the tragic and ironic. His understanding of the long-term effects of revolutionary change also offers scant proof that he espoused a full-fledged futility thesis, namely, that the present simply rearranges the debris of the past, or that human history is a chronicle of catastrophes. One of his own aphorisms appealed to him, but he did not allow himself to be utterly captivated by it: "Societies and men walk around in rings and the image of human destiny is a circle."[37] He preferred another image of the circle, one which opens up, rather than closes off, the opportunity for making choices. In its ultimate sense, choice is not a necessary revelation of human weakness nor of strength, either in terms of dealing with a particular instant or in a retrospective analysis of it. For this reason, he was inclined never to pose the problem of choice starkly or conventionally. Viewing it in such a manner wrongly polarized choice and determinateness instead of seeing them more plausibly as the inner and outer, or internal and external, forms of an interlocked process. The room for choice was therefore circumscribed but not without effect.

Accident was not without effect either. It retained its force no matter how much historians, or anyone for that matter, imposed closure on the

---

[35] OC, XII, p. 84. See also p. 89.

[36] Tocqueville to Gobineau, August 5, 1858, OC, IX, p. 295.

[37] AT, 43A, Dossier J, "La France avant la Révolution. Miscellanés." In these notes Tocqueville wrote about how temporary laws imperceptibly become permanent.

search for the sources of human decisions by prematurely limiting their contexts of inquiry. Contexts could be widened, even if they could never be complete. The human mind cannot grasp the realities of all the particles of existence, but is nevertheless tempted to fill in the unknowns by attributing an element of decisiveness to the accidental. The accidental may thus be built into the act of rediscovering the dynamics of the past, but the exact contours of the accidental could still not be discerned. Tocqueville tried to work from this premise. He knew that, by trying to assemble all the elements that make up revolutionary situations, let alone their outcomes, some, in fact many, of the facts would inevitably fall through the cracks.

Chance, accident and general causes are thus conjoined in intricate, and mysterious, ways. Neither those who blithely subsume the first two under the third, or who are so naive as to think that their privileged selves are acting in concert with some ineluctable destiny, are conceiving of the relationships correctly. Related to this problem were the important truths, Tocqueville believed, that could be derived from studying the concrete and particular manifestations of human activity in the public, as in the private, realm. Narrative released some of these truths. Contingency, as experiential and existential and, as he also thought, as historical, was important for him only insofar as, in the dress of either chance or accident, it informs human beings that the choices they make are moral choices. The extent to which Tocqueville held that contingency in all these aspects had cognitive value cannot be settled: he argued sometimes, as we have just seen, that it does. And, in a few moments, we will find him saying the opposite.

The ethical content of contingency stimulated his imagination as a much more compelling question. The act of reconstructing the tragic, ironic and comic elements of 1848 amounted to a condemnation of "the degradation of public morality" that expressed the sickness of the régime, but beyond that, his act of recollection, because it was more personal, more bitingly indicted the deputies for their complacency, their indifference and calm, and not least, their complicity in creating and reaping the rewards from a vicious society. Such a scene could not be captured except by reviewing his own actions and those of his friends, colleagues and opponents, as individuals or in groups. This meant that he gave a good deal of thought to alternatives, to pondering over different courses of action; in short, to possibilities. His recollections of the events of 1848 were told from the inside, as it were. The breakdown of the *ancien régime* he examined from a greater distance. Still, because of Tocqueville's conviction that 1789 was continuing to have repercussive effects, the differences in his treatment of the "purity" and near-mythic quality of

1789 and the more prosaic elements of 1848 ought not to be exaggerated. The issues raised by considering the possibilities in relating the sources, processes and outcomes of historical events figure in both.

At this point we must ask how, in Tocqueville's view, the realm of possibilities and the contingent are related. Possibilities may be considered as existing in the minds of historical actors with some grasp – which can be accorded only a problematic rational or irrational status – of the choices before them. In turn, the flow of information or the facts available to them helps to govern their choices. These conditions apply equally to historians, but not quite in the same way. Contingency comes into play at all times, for actors and historians alike, because total information is never available, except perhaps in closed, very finite systems. In the case of historians, new facts may come to light or, what is more likely, old ones may be seen in a new light. Hence causal explanations must be considered provisional, and always incomplete. Such would be the worst scenario if one were to pin one's hopes on achieving an iron-clad causal explanation, that is, when there is a presumption that all aleatory elements are wiped out of existence. This not being the state of affairs, possibility and contingency may, if considered together, yield a more fruitful understanding of historical actors. The relationship between contingency and possibility is, however, an unstable one, since in seeking explanations that take both into account, the greater the attention given to the unstable cognitive and emotional situations of individual actors, the greater will be the incidence of alternative actions, not only in their minds, but in the mind of a later commentator who might also be a participant – the position in which Tocqueville found himself when examining the actions of his contemporaries.

Geoffrey Hawthorne argues that, as our depth of explanatory powers is improved by juggling an increasing number of possibilities, that is, by including some but not others from coherent accounts, their number paradoxically not only diminishes, but increases on the grounds that every explanation suggests alternatives. Whatever that might lead to in the long run, historical and social theory might, on this argument, be liberated from both necessitarian and holistic positions.[38] Tocqueville did not quite reach the same position, but he seemed to come close to it. How

---

[38] Cf. Geoffrey Hawthorne, *Plausible Worlds: Possibility and Understanding in History and the Social Sciences* (Cambridge, 1991); Roberto M. Unger, *Social Theory: Its Situation and Its Task* (Cambridge, 1987); George A. Reisch, "Chaos, History and Narrative," *History and Theory*, 30 (1991), pp. 1–20; and Reinhart Koselleck, "Chance as Motivational Trace in Historical Writing," in *Futures Past*. Koselleck cites, on p. 116, from Raymond Aron, *Introduction to the Philosophy of History*, trans. G. J. Irvin (London, 1961): "The historical fact is essentially irreducible to order: *chance is the foundation of history*." In another place, Aron states that it is a mistake "to push history in one direction and individual acts" in

did he see the links between possibility and contingency? He isolated, as we shall see, what the actors perceived as alternatives by considering their choices within their networks of understanding, emotional preferences and inclinations or, more intuitively still, in what lay below their manifest acts. For him these were constituted by their communities as well, with their intergenerational memories. Thus individuals are related to and linked with one another contingently. He was not certain, however, that he himself or that they actually see themselves behaving entirely as contingent beings. They might, of course, try valiantly to remove contingency from their lives (in the specific but unrealistic sense of being totally free to determine their lives), but their experience would tell them to accept its presence as an inescapable part of life.

This would be so for humanity taken in the abstract as well as in any particular context: "So true is it that, if humanity is always the same, the mental frameworks [les dispositions] of peoples as well as the incidents of history are always different. The past is not able to teach us much concerning the present, and nothing good is produced when those old pictures are forced into new frames." Indeed, their memories may well lead individuals and societies astray. They act on false reconstructions of the past, as for example when, by trying to avoid what they see as past errors, they take a course of action opposite to that of their ancestors, but produce the same result. "People were often ruined," is Tocqueville's ironic comment, "through having too good a memory."[39] The weight of the past, he said, may repress creative responses, but people can never help themselves from committing errors even as they try to avoid them. An alternative way of ordering one's sense of human behavior was to think – as Tocqueville was clearly unable to do completely – of it as "rational" through a variety of providential belief. Having understood the past with greater accuracy, people might then have "rational" grounds for accepting themselves as contingent beings, with a fuller knowledge of the risks they were taking, but, in this case, "rational" would have to mean their willingness to accept the idea that they were contingent in a cosmic as well as in a historical sense.

He did not give up on history "rightly understood," to borrow a favorite phrase he used when speaking about self-interest, and he affirmed, in the act of recollecting and reflecting on his own and his contemporaries' reconstructions of the past, his belief in the possibility of

---

another, adding that, "The fact that at a higher level one finds a chain of events following satisfactorily one after another does not prove that accidents cancel each other out and that the course of the enterprise, in its broad outlines, was what it had to be, given the profound forces of European society and politics." See his *History, Truth, Liberty*, ed. Franciszek Draus (Chicago and London, 1985), pp. 41–42.   [39] *OC*, XII, p. 59.

producing better and perhaps the best account of it. At the same time, he seemed to subordinate the actions of people to some higher cosmic and historical laws, explicitly declaring that these have operated more or less regularly in their lives. He implied, as we saw a moment ago, that, even given a different mix of characters and a different time scheme, such laws would continue to exhibit some degree of regularity. He wished, nevertheless, to accord moral importance to what people actually do, for the existence of such laws does not remove responsibility from whoever is involved in any specific historical situation, but he did not believe that their actions are by themselves historically decisive. He was impressed by their shortcomings, by what he believed were their moral failures, which he saw as an inseparable part of their roles as social actors. Their actions were, nevertheless, not to be seen as moral shortcomings *tout court*. In a strong sense, by conducting themselves in the contexts of their traditions, histories and psyches, they followed their external and internal fates, including the accidents of fate.

The "fatefully accidental," ("the accidental that could be different but . . . cannot be changed, or changed very little," because it is a stroke of fate, which resists negation) and the notion of "usual practices" (the existing mores, customs, traditions of human activity) – these two central ideas of Odo Marquard's[40] concerning the play of accident as the essence of the human condition provide a useful device for thinking about Tocqueville's understanding of the relationship between necessity and choice. Tocqueville saw choice as the process of reaching decisions within "the fatal circle" – the image with which Tocqueville closed *Democracy in America*. He also sometimes saw persons as contingent beings – in some but not in every way as the sums of their accidental properties. These two premises made it possible for him to postulate that free decisions, when they are achieved, take on a greater, not a lesser, dignity. Thus, to the extent that he was critical of friends and opponents alike, he said that they could have conducted themselves differently, that they were responsible for seeing how they might imagine another course of action, responsible at crucial times for finding it within themselves to break free from their accustomed usages. He did not posit absolutely free actions, nor did he posit a theory of absolute accident. He would not have accepted the idea that human beings are more the playthings of accidents than they are agents. He wanted individuals to think of how, within the circle, they might find the way to free themselves from violent change as well. A less

---

40 See Odo Marquard, *In Defence of the Accidental: Philosophical Studies*, trans. Robert M. Wallace (New York and Oxford, 1991), particularly chap. 7, pp. 109–29. The citations that follow are located on pp. 5–7, 87–88, and 96–97.

undistorted view of how accepted usages come to form the matrix of human life was within human grasp. Starting with an image of a fatal circle within which the self can act, Tocqueville moved on to the idea of a fatal chain only to reject it. He returned to the first, much less restrictive, circle image to record more faithfully his notion that the chain of history should not be misconstrued in fatalistic terms. Human beings are not, he stated, locked into a timeless and predetermined continuum, because particular human beings supervene. To see how they do is to follow their stories, to be sensitive to their finitude, fallibility and contingency, but also to hold them to account as moral agents. Tocqueville's narrative in the *Souvenirs,* as we shall see in the next chapter, is so structured as – to use Paul Ricoeur's remarks on the nature of narrative – to hold us, as their stories unfold, in "suspense by a thousand contingencies," which "imply . . . alternatives, bifurcations . . . creat[ing] the feeling of surprise."[41]

[41] Paul Ricoeur, *Hermeneutics and the Human Sciences*, ed. and trans. John B. Thompson (Cambridge, 1981), pp. 277, 285, and in his chapter on "The Narrative Function," pp. 274–96.

III

Plotting crisis and change

4 Tocqueville's uses of intentionality and necessity in the *Souvenirs*

> Let me for a moment resume the chain of history, so that I may the more easily attach it to the thread of my personal recollections.[1]

Chronology of 1848

1848	February 22	Defection of National Guard
	February 23	Revolution in Paris; Guizot resigns
	February 24	Abdication of Louis-Philippe; universal suffrage proclaimed
	March 14	Elite units of National Guard dissolved
	March 16	Elite units of National Guard demonstrate
	March 17	Republican groups counterdemonstrate
	April 23	Election of Constituent Assembly
	May 15	Political clubs demonstrate; invasion of Assembly
	May 21	Festival of Concord
	June 22–26	June Days; government of Cavaignac
	July 28	Decrees restricting political clubs
	August 9–11	Decrees limiting freedom of the press
	November 21	Constitution of the Second Republic proclaimed
	December 10	Louis-Napoleon Bonaparte elected president; government of Odilon Barrot
1849	January 29	Dissolution of National Assembly
	May 14	Election of Legislative Assembly
	June 13	Attempted rising in Paris
	October 31	Resignation of Barrot cabinet
1850	May 31	Majority conservatives in Assembly disenfranchise about one-third of voters

Tocqueville saw 1848 and what followed in the first few months of the Revolution as a series of capitulations to chronic disorder. It was kept

---

[1] *OC*, XII, p. 47.

alive by forces at both extremes of the political spectrum. More threateningly, in the early stages of the turmoil, the instability was the work of radicals on the left, latter-day Jacobins, who were more numerous, and socialists of various stripes. More fervently, as events became more explosive, Tocqueville aligned himself with the moderates in the legislature to find the basis of a stable régime in a conservative republic capable of containing and, in time, eradicating revolutionary discontent. The challenge/capitulation scenario played itself out time and time again. First came the buckling of the July Monarchy's defenses that stood by powerless to halt the defection of the National Guard, the collapse of Guizot's ministry and the abdication of Louis-Philippe. These momentous events followed one another in three frenetic days between February 22 and 24. Then followed a jockeying for position among political groups to become the heirs of the defunct régime and bring an end to the power vacuum. A feeble attempt to save the Orléanist line, by setting up a regency under the duchesse d'Orléans, foundered on February 24, on the third day of the Revolution when the Chamber, under pressure from invading crowds, capitulated and proclaimed the establishment of the Second Republic. Among the first acts of the new provisional government was the announcement of the principle of universal suffrage, the "right to work" and freedom of the press and assembly. It also quickly called for elections for a Constituent Assembly for April 23 in the expectation that by then the political atmosphere would lead to the cessation of the crisis. Over the next few weeks, during March and early April, the government abolished slavery and opened up the National Guard to all adult males, a decision that provoked a short-lived protest from, and the dissolution of, the élite companies of the Guard. Turmoil increased, as during the same period peasants demonstrated in favor of forest rights, and workers attacked the railways and took part in tax revolts.

After the Assembly convened on May 4, the several challenges to the new régime were met with shows of force that put an end to the threats of radicalism in 1848. The Assembly's radical republican groups, challenging the conservative republican majority, found support from a coalition of working-class forces in the capital. A radically inspired invasion of the Assembly on May 15 was thwarted with the arrest of the radical leaders. As the Assembly's Constitutional Committee set to work in the last week or so of May and the first weeks of June, a new challenge from the radical elements gathered momentum, and led to the brief civil war of the June Days, precipitated by the government's closing of the National Workshops, which ended relief for thousands of unemployed workers. The government, unlike the hapless last ministry of the July Monarchy, decisively commandeered the support of the army and rural landowners who crowded into Paris to ward off radical threats to their property.

Before the debate on the Constitution began in September, decrees limiting the activities of political clubs, and others restricting press freedom, were passed at the end of July and the beginning of August. Thus some five months after the democratization and liberalization of political life had been proclaimed, restrictions limiting full political activity were restored. The new Republican Constitution, proclaimed on November 21, embodied resolutely conservative principles. Louis-Napoleon was elected president on December 10 under its terms. He used his powers to dissolve the National Assembly in January of the next year. To the surprise of all, elections the following May returned a large number of Montagnard deputies. To check the possibility of a fresh radicalization of politics, a moderate but internally divided coalition was formed to run the government. Yet it was sufficiently united to put down the short-lived insurrection of June 13, 1849. The cabinet then legislated even greater restrictions on the press and assembly. By the end of October, Barrot's moderate ministry resigned in protest against Louis-Napoleon's maneuverings to call into being a cabinet that would do his bidding. By mid-1850, with a conservative majority in the Assembly, a full third of the electorate was disenfranchised, and even more Draconian laws on the press and assembly were passed. By then Tocqueville was at work on the first part of the *Souvenirs*. For the most part, I confine myself to his participation in, and observation of, only those events and people he chose to include in the recollections.

Charting one's way through Tocqueville's byways and alleys is no easy task. Finding my way through his labyrinth to see how he emerged from it with the historical dimension of his thought enhanced is the guiding thread of this chapter. Larry Shiner, who is concerned with the "polarities between truth and literature,"[2] traces the voices of recollection and commentary by playing on the uses of voice in the *Souvenirs*, that is, the authorial "I," the confessional "I," the commenting "I" and the "I" that affirms universal moral truths. Within the context of my own inquiry, I incline to think of the last two – the commenting "I" and the "I" of wisdom – as the historian's "I"/eye. It is hard to disagree with some aspects of Shiner's theory of masks through which people speak through their several voices, but seldom in their "own" – but knowing what a person's "own" or authentic voice is, is even harder, if not impossible, to access. That the *Souvenirs* possess a presence is indisputable.[3] It is this presence, multifaceted and elusive, which must be grasped. I take its existence for granted and with little trepidation that I might miss the

---

[2] Shiner, *Secret Mirror*, p. 201.   [3] Ibid., pp. 136–38.

"essential" Tocqueville. For me it is important to see how his narrative of 1848 helped to release his historical sense and took him at least partway out of the labyrinth to transform him into the historian he was fully to become. In the process, he found he could say more about and tighten his grasp on the elements of choice and contingency in history.

The present tense, which I shall use in plotting these elements in his interpretation of the nature of history, is, I think, the most effective device to catch Tocqueville's different roles as actor/narrator/historian. I shall use the past tense when I interrupt my analysis to comment on how Tocqueville, as a historian/moralist, paused to tell us how he viewed matters. If I sometimes merge these tenses, it is because Tocqueville clearly does not distinguish the boundaries between his emotional responses from his stance as a historian who looks for the most effective way to distance himself from and objectify events and persons. In this respect, the *Souvenirs* are neither unambiguous nor consistent.[4]

The February Revolution as reenactment

Tocqueville's concern with particulars tumbles out in his description of the events. The tumult of February 24, which he recounts with a sense of danger, followed by despair, begins with his thoughts on the ingratitude of the middle class. He repeats his warnings from his January speech that the bourgeoisie had reaped enormous rewards from an indulgent government with which it had been associated from its inception, and had quite complacently, and in Tocqueville's estimate, corruptly, thrown in its lot with the anti-monarchical forces in an act of betrayal to save its skin. On the morning of February 24, as he makes his way to the Assembly, Tocqueville realizes at once from his exchanges with a battalion of the National Guard that their members had already calculated that the government had lost all claims on their loyalty and had no one to blame but itself. He feels that their decision to abandon it will lead to further chaos and disaster. Next, he describes his meeting with the military commander, General Alphonse Bedeau, whom he recalls he personally liked, but did not admire. As a man whose background should have given him the resources to deal with unanticipated events, Bedeau turns out instead, Tocqueville writes, to be a person without the powers of intellect and calculation to understand that what is needed in this desperate situation is a defiance of the orders he had been given to show no resistance to the violence in the capital. Tocqueville's reflection was harsh, but not unsympathetic, though his response was to soften at a later point in the

---

[4] Cf. ibid., pp. 120–24.

Souvenirs, when he comments on human fragility. Until then, he chooses to describe Bedeau as a man of undoubted merit, but without the "genius" to deal with revolutions.

In Tocqueville's words, the supreme qualification needed to understand and deal with revolutionary violence was to be able to "regulat[e] one's actions according to events." It was not from a stance of what may be called pure or absolute morality that, on reflection, he writes in condemnation of Bedeau's failure to act. The issue is given a more interesting twist if we take into account his earlier discussion of the unforeseen nature of 1848 – unforeseen by all, Tocqueville ruefully writes, but most of all by Louis-Philippe whose defect as a ruler for most of the eighteen years of his régime was to mistake "luck for genius."[5] Tocqueville, hostile to Machiavelli's principles of authority, uses them to explain Louis-Philippe's identification of luck or chance with sound policy, and, in addition, he condemns the king's unjustifiable equation of both with the quality of moral choice. Observing next that Louis-Philippe took the further step of believing that his "choice" was a mark of genius, Tocqueville devastatingly dismisses the aging king's wishful thinking: in fact the king's choice was, because it was non-intentional, simply chance acting itself out. It was not the sort of contingency that came from a weighing of what moral risks were involved in confronting the unexpected. To make his point even more starkly, Tocqueville reflected on the question of luck and morality. He tells us that Bedeau did not believe that luck was on his side, and saw no way to reverse the situation. Louis-Philippe was forced, like Bedeau, to the same conclusion. He also collapsed, but until that turning point, his error, Tocqueville stresses, lay in ascribing morality and genius to his own actions, from which he excluded the fact that sheer chance or luck had run out and left him totally unprepared for the reality he had now to face.[6]

After his conversation with Bedeau, Tocqueville resumes his journey to the Chamber of Deputies. Singling out individuals and politicians, the jostling crowds, the thunderous entrance of the National Guard, and his own reactions as he interacts with some of the key players in the Assembly, he presents his version of the confusion leading to the plight of the duchesse d'Orléans, who had come to seek support from the deputies for her son as heir to the throne; Lamartine's support for a provisional government, which ensured the establishment of a republic; and the events that were to follow later that day. Though the description is not without a

---

[5] *OC*, XII, p. 85.
[6] For a discussion of the elevation of absolute morality as a value in itself and the problems of seeing it in isolation from social and political aims, see Bernard Williams, *Ethics and the Limits of Philosophy* (Cambridge, Mass., 1985).

running assessment of the principal actors, his attempt to apply his judgment on the events is more arresting. It comes as somewhat of a surprise, however, that after telling us about his own part in the events, he portrays himself as an observer feeling little excitement. The form of the event obviously offended him, because it concealed "the terrible originality of the facts" under a veneer of theatricality, discernible to few but, as Tocqueville added, demonstrative of a national weakness. People everywhere looked, he writes, for models in literary and dramatic reminiscences of what they believed they should be doing in revolutionary situations.

Their tendency to confuse past and present was an important point for Tocqueville, but he made an even more acute one by saying that the distortions of the past, however they are produced and by whom, cast their shadow over the present. Reserving his sharpest criticism for Lamartine's history of the Girondins, he placed his own recollections of the first Revolution against the recollections of the 1848 participants, and found them quite destructive. Like provincial actors performing a bad tragedy, they were imitators, not creators. They were "acting the French Revolution, rather than continuing it."[7] "The terrifying originality of the facts remained concealed"[8] from them. They were still steeped, it seems clear from Tocqueville's judgment, in a version of *historia magistra vitae*, looking uncritically at the icons of the past to gain and justify their understanding of the present. The notion that history was instructive of life, and that its main use was to provide human beings with examples for conducting themselves, did not prepare them for the unexpected, but instead froze them in fantasies about the past.

More deeply reflective at this juncture in his narrative, Tocqueville said even more. The power of badly impressed models of 1789 on the minds of the participants threw them off track, deflecting them from what ought to have been their genuine goals. Continuing the Revolution would presumably have turned the next page – as Tocqueville wanted it turned – surrounding the liberal goals of ensuring liberty with proper constitutional safeguards. Instead the principal actors engaged in mimetic posturings. Their reenactment of 1789 in 1848 showed, he said, a profound misunderstanding of what the first revolutionaries had set out to achieve. The inferior tragedy that was stalking the historical stage sixty years later revealed a poverty of imagination and a desiccation of political morality. The year 1848, then, loses for Tocqueville its claims to be a genuine revolution, because those who are active in it had no clear vision of their purposes.

---

[7] For all of the above, see *OC*, XII, pp. 62–75. For Beaumont's view that Lamartine's book would be harmful to the interests of both moderate liberty and radical democracy, and instead serve despotism, see Beaumont to Tocqueville, August 30, 1847, *OC*, VIII, pt. 1, p. 612.   [8] *OC*, XII, p. 75.

We must, of course, admit the possibility that Tocqueville was not immune from self-deception of his own, but, since we have on record his speech analyzing the signs of a revolutionary situation and his hopes for the changes that would remove it, the safer conclusion is that he in fact possessed greater prescience and suffered from fewer degrees of self-deception when the explosion occurred. Tocqueville might have had, as Collingwood might have said in his discussion of the psychological structures of autobiography,[9] a better grasp of the past. Tocqueville's reenactment of his own part in the events of 1848, and of what brought on 1789, might have been more faithful to the realities of both, and superior to other historians – for instance, Lamartine, Thiers and Mignet, of whom he may have been thinking. In his opinion, their histories of 1789 fell short of feeling and knowing how past and present actors felt and thought. But this argument has its limits. Tocqueville's wishes and political program rested in significant part on a reconstruction of the past and should be subject to the same standards as those to which he submitted those of his opponents and his friends. His recollections blend, as we have already noted, the particulars of past events with reflections of how those events appeared to be working themselves out, and with a prognosis of their relationship to a future yet to be seen and further assessed. In the months following 1848, as he composed his recollections, Tocqueville judged what had happened, but he had only a limited kind of distance from the events. What he saw he plainly did not like. His political and historical selves blended. His correspondence acts as a check against his account of the significance of accident in the *Souvenirs*. It almost veered toward that fatal chain that he warned against as a historian – to see the events following February as the irreversible precondition for the development of a new political and social scene, furthering centralization and the economic and social entrenchment of the two aristocracies of wealth and of the ancient *noblesse*. Together they were bound, he predicted, to succeed in gaining the support of the newly enfranchised populace in the electoral process. Tocqueville almost slipped from a denial of the contingent into the hubris of omniscience.[10]

In defense of this interpretation, we have two sources. The first is to be

[9] Cf. R. G. Collingwood, *The Idea of History* (Oxford, 1946), esp. pp. 295–97. In addition, an interesting comparison might be made between Tocqueville and Bernard Groethuysen's imaginative use of the ideas of empathy (*Das Mitgefühl*), *Verstehen* and dialogue. They are not unlike Tocqueville's effort to kindle in his mind how other people, present and past, perceived the world. For an informative study of Groethuysen's importance, see Michael Ermarth, "Intellectual History as Philosophical Anthropology: Bernard Groethuysen's Transformation of Traditional *Geistesgeschichte*," *Journal of Modern History*, 65 (1993), pp. 673–705.

[10] Tocqueville to Senior, March 8, 1849, *OC*, VI, pt. 2, pp. 107–09.

found in a letter to Nassau Senior in December 1849 in which, more than a year after the fatal scene in the Chamber, Tocqueville wrote that, "Even on February 24, the monarchy could have been saved if it had been possible to delay the proclamation of the Provisional Government and the flight of the duchesse d'Orléans for one hour."[11] For the second, we may turn to that part of the *Souvenirs* in which he describes what he says were his only moments of real feeling. Those emotions, welling up in him unexpectedly, point up the importance of the unpredictable, this time as one person experiences it. His frank expression of his emotions at the time may be seen as complementing his assessment of what might have happened. His feelings are aroused when the duchesse retreats from the Chamber with the heir presumptive to the throne. Tocqueville reimagines her reactions as she watches the proceedings in the Assembly rush by her. It is a *pietà* scene that he paints, one in which a number of feelings, perhaps even an erotic element, is clearly present:

and when she had fled [with her child], the remembrance of the sweet, sad, firm glances which I had seen her cast upon the Assembly during that long agony came back so vividly to my memory, I felt so touched with pity when I thought of the perils attending her flight that, suddenly springing from my seat, I rushed in the direction which my knowledge of the building led me to believe that she and her son would have taken to seek a place of safety.[12]

Recalling his frustration at being unable to find her, he examines the reasons for his spontaneous actions. He confesses that he feels no shame for his response, only astonishment that he should have leapt in honorable defense of a member of a family that had no claims of loyalty from him or his family except, as he says, to serve the "public interest." He was overwhelmed, we might add, less by his avowed intentions than by the deeply ingrained memories of heroic and chivalric gestures making up the aristocratic code, which appeared to come to life for him as if from the deepest part of himself. He was powerfully moved by the sight of a great personage suffering misfortune.[13] Most revealingly, he admits that a deep current of feeling in him wants to bask in the light of the approval of princes, and he takes further pleasure in telling himself that neither they nor any one else will ever know what he had tried to do. It will be his secret. He tells himself that his act is a pure gift, and that such gratuitous

---

[11] Tocqueville to Senior, December 1849, ibid., p. 114.   [12] *OC*, XII, pp. 75–76.

[13] Tocqueville's act bears some comparison with Edmund Burke's famous description of Marie Antoinette. Burke tried to make the chivalric juices flow, but his effort was merely a rhetorical stratagem, recognized as such by most impartial contemporaries. See *Reflections on the Revolution in France*, ed. Conor Cruise O'Brien (Harmondsworth, 1968), pp. 164–71. Tocqueville's own responses to the duchesse put the lie to Burke's apothegm that the age of chivalry was dead. Tocqueville was familiar with Burke's great polemic, as well as some of his other anti-revolutionary tracts.

acts belong to a distant past, now unfortunately forgotten. On any view, it seems that Tocqueville responded to the events' semiotic structures, to the psychic hold they exerted on him. Exercising their power over him, as if from some unsummoned place in himself, they represent an almost perfect instance of the fusion of deep psychological structures and the contingent. Together they made up a kind of gratuitous act that had little possible future resonance, except that they gave him some knowledge of his deepest drives.

This time, needing it no longer, he dispensed with irony. He did not doubt that his act was genuine, a quality that he denied in the intentions of the others whose actions and speeches he described immediately after he returns from his fruitless search for the duchesse. His scorn was heavy. The confusion in the Chamber had not been dissipated. Indeed, though there appeared to be some movement toward a restoration of order, as Lamartine read out the names of the men who were to constitute the provisional government, Tocqueville again returned to the theme of play-acting. He invoked Shakespeare to prove that burlesque and tragedy intersect when "the people" rub shoulders with those occupying positions of authority. The situation was admittedly complex, since the authorities were not yet exerting power, and were themselves being ridiculed by the crowd, which Tocqueville may have seen as preparing the ground for a tragic outcome. His discerning eye catches Lamartine in a posture of embarrassment. The poet-politician finds himself the target of the crowd's newly found powers of articulation, shouting support or disapproval of his actions. From Tocqueville's vantage point at the time, and upon later reflection, the mutual exchanges between Lamartine's actions and the crowd's reactions revealed a man in perplexity about his next step. What is likely to happen next, he recalls asking himself. For a moment, Tocqueville fused reality and fiction, wearily acknowledging the futility of knowing the event in advance and perceiving how it might end and achieve completeness: "For in a rebellion, as in a novel, the most difficult part to invent is the end."[14]

Tocqueville did not hesitate to share out praise and blame. The specific end of that memorable day came, he concluded, with the exile of Louis-Philippe and Guizot, the hysterical and cowardly retreat of Thiers, and the heroic but futile attempts of Odilon Barrot to rally the barricades in defense of the monarchy. But whatever Barrot could have achieved with his eloquence and courage in favorable times, Tocqueville added, was swallowed up by events that outpaced the strength of personal intervention, as in the futile attempts of a pair of unlikely allies, General Victor

[14] *OC*, XII, pp. 76–77.

Oudinot and Alexandre-Philippe Andryane. Leading a column of National Guards to the Chamber, unaware that her fate had been sealed, these two came too late to help the duchesse.[15] For Tocqueville this was another ironic, but just as strongly comic, instance of how the "truth of events" cannot be known in periods of revolution or rapid change, and, moreover, how events change too quickly for any one to be able to keep up with them. "The incident is worthy of being told and noted among the incidents of fickle instability with which the history of revolutions abounds."[16] As Tocqueville ended the *Souvenirs'* first part, he took care to frame it within a conventional beginning, middle and end, as if in a piece of theater. But, as in life, he kept repeating, 1789 had its distant sources, and 1848 was hardly an end. He had in mind the larger issues he had been invoking, beyond the ends of individual events that he had been recollecting. He thought of 1848 as a phase of the great French Revolution: "Its end seems farther off and shrouded in greater darkness."[17]

There was much self-consciousness, and less irony, in his attempt to explain himself to himself. His encounters with friends and foes alike, as we have seen, came from a perturbed center in himself. His exchange with his friend Jean-Jacques Ampère after the day's events convinces him that he alone understands the dangers that lie ahead. Annoyed by what he thinks is Ampère's blind belief in the good will of the insurgents, Tocqueville reduced Ampère to the status of a mere and naive man of letters, who imported into politics a fatal preference for display and novelty, and who thought that they make up reality. Men of letters, Tocqueville more than implied, are by nature not only incapable of distinguishing the mask from the real: just as many in the French public like to live in a world of show, writers are in the habit of making themselves up.[18] Tocqueville believed that he was right in setting himself apart from these distorting tendencies: he was not the kind of person to don masks. The thread of his belief in his "sincere" reconstitution of his own person and in trying to gain the measure of his contemporaries begins in the very first words of the *Souvenirs* when, as if recalling Machiavelli's introductory remarks to *The Prince*, he announced that, following his removal from public life, he was "reduced in the midst of my solitude, to consider myself for a moment or rather to contemplate the contemporary events in which I was either an actor or a witness."[19] He was, however, not as reluctant an autobiographer as his qualified phrases suggest: "I am striving

---

[15] In 1849, Oudinot commanded the expeditionary force against the Roman Republic. Andryane had once been a member of the French revolutionary Carbonari.

[16] *OC*, XII, p. 78.   [17] Ibid., p. 87.   [18] Ibid., pp. 88–89.

[19] Ibid., p. 29. In his Dedicatory Letter to Lorenzo de'Medici, Machiavelli writes that he wishes to convince him of the need to understand that "I have not embellished this work

only to rediscover the traces of my actions, ideas and impressions during the course of this revolution."[20] He quite consciously laid down the groundwork for his recollection of his decisions, which he contrasted with those of men whose judgment he questioned: Thiers, Rémusat, Duvergier de Hauranne and Molé.[21]

Not surprisingly, his candor was hardly transparent, no more so than when in his promise to examine his motives, he anticipated that, if he spoke well of himself, he would be misunderstood. The phrase "mais qu'il est difficile de bien parler de soi" may also be construed as speaking candidly about oneself. In self-justification, Tocqueville did not think that his self-image – as a person driven by sincerity and authenticity – was incompatible with making a deliberate point that absolute sincerity demanded that he must leave nothing unsaid, and that speaking well of one's actions is an obligation, if in fact it mirrors the person's sense of his own reality. To support this version of the honest man, he called into question the memoirs of other men, most pointedly those of cardinal de Retz, whose motives, he says, were shaped by so overwhelming a need to be praised for his cleverness that he unintentionally revealed his hypocrisy. Weighed against the recollections of a person who had, Tocqueville concluded, no love of truth, only a "warped mind which involuntarily betrays the vices of the heart," he told himself that he was the more reliable, because he was the more authentic, person.

How would the public react to such a claim, he asked. They would, he responded, tend to recoil before such candor, because they would misunderstand its sources and hence would not be able to judge it. They would simply misconstrue it and feel that it must be a disguise for vanity. To elaborate this point in his own confessions, Tocqueville first talked

by filling it with rounded periods, with high-sounding words or fine phrases, or with any of the other beguiling artifices of apparent beauty . . . ; for my wish is that, if it is to be honoured at all, only its originality and the importance of the subject should make it acceptable" (cited in Niccolò Machiavelli, *The Prince*, ed. Quentin Skinner and Russell Price [Cambridge, 1988], p. 3).   [20]   *OC*, XII, p. 100.

[21] Charles de Rémusat, active in the politics of the July Monarchy, was deputy to the Constituent and Legislative Assemblies in 1848 and 1849. He retired to private life after the coup d'état of 1851. Historian and literary figure, his fourth volume of *Mémoires de ma vie*, ed. Charles H. Pouthas, 5 vols. (Paris, 1958–67), covers the period from 1841 to 1851. In vol. IV, pp. 44–45, Rémusat speaks admiringly about Tocqueville's independence of mind. He quite mistakenly says that Tocqueville read little and ignored the work of his contemporaries. He also believes that Tocqueville was passionately devoured by ambition. Prosper Duvergier de Hauranne took part in the banquet campaign and was deputy to the 1848 and 1849 assemblies, where he voted with the conservative right. He wrote voluminously on government and politics. The comte Louis-Mathieu Molé, who served Bonaparte and the Bourbons in turn, was for a brief period in 1839 Louis-Philippe's first minister, and for an even briefer time he served as Guizot's successor just before February 24.

about a pure heart and a clear mind. Then, casting his mind to more distant horizons, he alluded to the unavoidable boundaries surrounding every person's search for the motives of action. These were to be found in the hard and inescapable constraints of the "little foot-paths" that converged on the "main roads" that the will takes. No one is able to discern them. But it is, he convinced himself, by recognizing the inescapably hard fact that only by taking a journey to his inner being – through a process of self-examination as well as an examination of the other actors – that anything of lasting value can be created. Even if his account will be, as he says he hopes, freer from distortion, he wants to make it clear that he expects no rewards from submitting the threads of his life to laws of verification. Such presumption would be a clear misapplication of his purposes. In his conception of his recollections as a search for some authentic self, not only in telling his own story, but also in relating it to the historical events, he felt himself to be a semi-participant and a semi-observer, a player and a spectator. He knew that he was not unreservedly one nor the other. His self-scrutiny could not, he knew, take him totally outside the events he was describing. To his credit, however, he made the attempt, but not surprisingly he remained unsure of the difference between knowing the world as spectator – or how well he knew it – and how, as an actor, he actually inhabited a world.

In the *Souvenirs*, the one thing he sought above all was self-approval. He had a powerful hunger for it, and felt it to be health-giving in his struggle with his lack of self-confidence. As an afterthought, but a highly suggestive one, Tocqueville came to believe that his self-doubt was rooted in his pride, the pride of a man whose self-esteem could be wounded by the very individuals he so despised.[22] This self-protective pride, as Tocqueville revealed it in the *Souvenirs*, may have emanated from a self-defeating glorification of the self, and may also be viewed as a debased form of honor, the very passion which he understood so well in his psychological portrait of the Old Régime aristocracy.

Contingency and character: detachment and deceptions

When Tocqueville spoke of sincerity as the way to achieve unity in his public and private lives, he was not engaged, as was Rousseau, in composing a momentous act of revelation. Nor did he share Rousseau's suspicion of the stability of self-reflection, which deepened as he moved from one autobiographical mode to another. Tocqueville, moreover, had much less

---

[22] Ibid., pp. 101–05.

taste for paradox for its own sake.[23] Besides, Rousseau was not interested in historical particulars. Tocqueville was, no more so than in finding the grounds for a politics that could be situated in historical time. So much is evident in the *Souvenirs* where he reviewed his life in the decade or so before 1848. Politics had proven to be a bitter disappointment. It called on a temperament and a cast of mind which he had found he did not have. Indeed, 1848 proved for him an escape from the fatiguing demands made on him as a deputy. Regret, misunderstanding and increasing isolation dominated his memories of his life as a legislator. He could no longer bear its conventional civilities, the small talk, the artifices and the false cama-raderie of the Chamber – above all its staginess and its mediocrity. As he put it, in words that blur the boundaries between directness and oblique-ness and that show his deeply rooted *hauteur*, he congratulated himself that he did not have the necessary defects of politicians. In the distinction he drew, he tried to create and inhabit a special place for himself, free from the corruptions that the other deputies lived. He traced his defects as a politician to a sense of his own rectitude, his respect for the fragility of "truth," his aversion to placing it at risk in the obfuscating procedures and from the self-serving deputies in the Chamber.

Then, moving toward an even greater fusion of the personal and the political, he adverts to the chronic state of uncertainty in which politics, as it was conducted between 1830 and 1848, buried the "truth." The political process was to blame: it had increased his own uncertainty and doubt. It had been the product, he believes, of intellectual confusion – which he does not discuss further – not of a failure of courage. With the political slate now washed clean by the dangers of revolutionary disorder and the hope of bringing it to an end, doubt is no longer an option. It has become a luxury. If indulged, it will prolong the social disorder and confusion. The time for action has arrived, and he welcomes it. Thus, if his self-doubt finds its sources in his pride, the pressure of events brings out for him pride's positive aspects. While he still has doubts about the future politics of France, the two emotions represented in his self-analysis two opposing and colliding emotions and convictions. They had freed him from his self-doubt. Now, at last, feeling himself to be on firmer ground,[24] he stood successfully for election to the Constituent Assembly.

---

[23] These features of Rousseau's unquenchable taste for endlessly dissecting his own person-ality are best discussed in Jean Starobinski, *Jean-Jacques Rousseau: La Transparence et l'ob-stacle, suivi de sept essais sur Rousseau* (Paris, 1971). Tocqueville expressed his admiration for Rousseau's *Confessions*, "which would assure his glory," in February 1851 just as he was nearing the completion of the second part of his *Souvenirs*, *OC*, VI, pt. 2, p. 346. Also cf. Shiner, *Secret Mirror*, p. 135, who in his comparison between Rousseau and Tocqueville underestimates Tocqueville's belief that he was more interested than his con-temporary foes in knowing himself.   [24] *OC*, XII, pp. 103–05.

Noting how the hunger for power transformed the local conservative supporters of the July Monarchy into the eager servants of all those politicians who had longed for power for ten years and were on the point of reversing the balance in the Assembly, he now felt himself part of a common effort, reversing, as he welcomed the next stage in the political struggle, the sense of the loss of honor he had found painful.

Now more secure, Tocqueville tells us that he surveyed the scene at the opening on May 4 of the Constituent Assembly, "with only a very confused recollection of it . . . linger[ing] in my mind. It is a mistake," he conjectured, "to believe that events remain present in one's memory in proportion to their importance or their greatness alone; rather is it certain little particularities which occur, and cause them to penetrate deep into the mind, and fix them there in a lasting manner." These little particularities formed the rich texture of the events he describes, and there was nothing in his account to suggest that, whatever may have been the ways in which they were related to what he does not remember, he had any doubts that his was a true picture. He was fairly confident that the forces of order would prevail, and that he would be taking a key part in preserving democracy against demagoguery in an atmosphere in which the radical program, whether Montagnard or socialist, was striking terror into the hearts of all property owners. The symbols of the impending defeat of the radical egalitarians were their ludicrous imitations of the radical sects in the first Revolution. The prospect of a hundred thousand armed workers "dying of hunger" in Paris alarmed him, but he felt first that their spokesmen were inept, and second that the aroused bourgeoisie would not hesitate to use all their power to resist them. Tocqueville recalls without any difficulty the surge of strength he felt at the prospect of being on the winning side, and the notion that he will be saving the cause of "liberty and the dignity of mankind." Most of all he relishes the adventure of it all, the "spice of danger" that seems to him "the best seasoning that can be given to most of the actions of life."[25]

Tocqueville prefaced his recollection of the May Days with another of his illustrations of how character and chance produce surprising consequences. His portrait of Lamartine in the days preceding May 15 was not unlike the tenor of his earlier critique. This time he questioned whether Lamartine had pursued the most effective strategies to achieve his ostensible goal of emasculating the Montagnard–socialist alliance, adding strength to the moderates without giving any entrée to the conservatives of the old Chamber. At the time, he says that he had his own agenda for Lamartine: he wanted him to remove himself voluntarily from politics,

[25] Ibid., pp. 115–24.

leaving others to direct events. This would have constituted his greatest service to France. He remembers distrusting him as a person who was utterly without sincerity (the opposite of Tocqueville's self-image as "sincere"), consumed by ego, a desire to shine whatever the cost, dismissive of truth, indeed, incapable of telling, because not caring to know, the difference between truth and falsehood. But Lamartine remained very much *en scène*. Tocqueville described him maneuvering to gain friends, making promises, secretly conferring with all shades of politicians, and, as everyone else also seemed to be doing, creating and living off mirages.

What Tocqueville called "these unforeseen incidents in parliamentary life, [when] . . . parties [are] constantly deceived in the same way, because they always think only of the pleasure they themselves derive from their great orator's words, and never of the dangerous excitement they promote in their opponents"[26] did not come to him as a shattering revelation. Lamartine, provoked by Odilon Barrot's attempt to gain support from the moderates, intervenes for no other reason, in Tocqueville's mind, than to displace him. Carried away by his egoism, Tocqueville charged, Lamartine turns to Ledru-Rollin[27] as an ally and therefore runs the danger of weakening the moderate forces. This prompted Tocqueville to express his fury and fear. Lamartine's weakness of character, according to Tocqueville, clouded his judgment. Lamartine overestimated both the intensity of radical passions in Paris and rural indifference.

But, at this point in his recollections, Tocqueville admits some perplexity, perhaps another episode of self-doubt. "But I am not sure that I, on my side, did not overdo a point on the other side. The road we ought to follow seemed to me so clearly and visibly traced that I would not admit the possibility of deviating from it by error."[28] He seems to be conflating, as before, his emotional state, his political preferences and desired historical outcomes, though quickly adding in mitigation that his anger against Lamartine is lessened by recognizing that errors in judgment, not only intentions, can open up unforeseen consequences. He confesses that he had concluded, before Lamartine made what he called an error, that it was time for the moderate forces in the Assembly to take control of the government.[29] Ironically, Tocqueville remarks, Lamartine's error led to

---

[26] Ibid., p. 128.
[27] Alexandre-Auguste Ledru-Rollin, a republican leader during the July Monarchy, was minister of the interior in the provisional government set up after the February Revolution. He fell from power after the June Days. His candidacy for the presidency later that year won him fewer than half a million votes.   [28] Ibid., p. 129.
[29] Ibid. Tocqueville's language is very firm: "Il me paraissait évident qu'il fallait se hâter de profiter de la force morale que possédait l'Assemblée en sortant des mains du peuple pour se saisir hardiment du gouvernement, et, par un grand effort, de la raffermir; tout retard me paraissait de nature à diminuer nos forces et à accroître celles de nos adversaires."

his ruin and saved France, leaving his meaning and us in suspense until the next chapter. Tocqueville asks us to go along with a reconsideration and a reversal: Lamartine's error might not have been an error after all, for he was as much motivated by his fear of bringing on a civil war as he was by his ambition. Tocqueville ended this chapter on moral and political ambiguities by regretting that he had not deigned to listen to Lamartine's wife, whose opinions he ought to have respected, precisely because, as he laconically but arrogantly phrases it, her character repelled him.[30]

Lamartine had indeed effectively lost most of his power, but Tocqueville shifts his attention from him, withholding even the briefest, let alone an extended, treatment of the reasons for his eclipse. His few appearances in the narrative become incidental to Tocqueville's focus on the threats to the Assembly on May 15, followed by the events leading to the June Days, and the June Days themselves. But Tocqueville found the temptation to apply the harshest standards to Lamartine's impending disappearance from the political scene irresistible. He has left us an even more unsympathetic, if not utterly damning, picture of a man whom he observed in a small but telling personal gesture. Unable to assert his former power, Lamartine is reduced to a pathetic figure, worrying about his personal appearance. Tocqueville describes him in the process of rearranging his hair, disheveled by the intense heat of the Chamber. Then, Lamartine is further diminished by Tocqueville's acerbic remarks on the humiliation he suffers when the crowd rebuffs his harangues. He ought, according to Tocqueville, to have commandeered the support of the National Guard and rescued the Assembly from the insurgents. He didn't do so. But, amidst the cheers of the Chamber, Lamartine did announce his plan to march on the Hôtel de Ville and put down the insurrection. The day ended with the arrest of the chief leaders of the abortive insurrection, including Barbès.[31]

Tocqueville's last allusions to Lamartine are more unpleasant to read. Taking part in the Festival of Concord on May 21, which he ridicules as an empty and puerile spectacle, he conjures up Lamartine as an embarrassed recipient of an ode to glory recited by a woman, one of three hundred in virginal costume. In Tocqueville's acidulous prose, they are more like Amazons or washerwomen than adolescent girls. As the ceremonies drag on to their conclusion, Tocqueville watches Lamartine withdraw, accompanied by some shouts of approval – a testament, he observes

---

[30] Ibid., p. 130.
[31] Armand Barbès, a republican under the Orléanist régime, member of the Constituent Assembly, was arrested as one of the instigators of the May 15 uprising, and released from life imprisonment only in 1854.

contemptuously, not of loyalty to or affection for the erstwhile hero, but proof of how some people respond belatedly to yesterday's events. Lamartine leaves the scene, looking, in Tocqueville's unconvincing attempt to show compassion, "weary and care-worn." He makes one last appearance in the *Souvenirs*, trying to speak to the insurgents at a number of barricades set up in the street fighting in June, but being met with, and turned back, by shots.[32]

Tocqueville wrote as if he were not demanding, because he was not expecting, signs of sincerity or integrity from Lamartine, but he appeared to have momentarily believed that the political crisis that had brought the poet to the center of revolutionary action might have elicited some sign of political responsibility. In fact, as we saw, Tocqueville did not fail to acknowledge that Lamartine might have had, because he was at the center of power, information that made him decide in favor of fatal alliances. As events unfolded at the time, Tocqueville became certain that Lamartine's single-mindedness had nothing to do with integrity, sincerity or political practicalities, and that his hunger for adulation was his major fault. In judging his own weaknesses, Tocqueville did not hesitate to disclose that his own pride, which protects but alienates him from many members of the political and academic élites, often leaves him feeling hurt and defeated. Pride such as his, he told himself, is much less of a vice than Lamartine's unquenchable thirst for applause.

In Tocqueville's normative universe, these troubled times demanded the most scrupulous conduct consistent with one's beliefs. Thus when Tocqueville says that he was unable to find any evidence that Lamartine was coherent or consistent either as a thinker or a man of action,[33] he meant that the absence of moral content in Lamartine's behavior – about which Tocqueville showed no doubt – was in fact predictable, but even so regrettable. Unfortunately, Tocqueville wryly observed, there were no surprises. There is an air of self-congratulation in Tocqueville's superior stance, perhaps sparked by his experiencing surprise himself, when his loyalties were carried away by the plight of a doomed princess. Tocqueville's judgment may have been colored by contrasting his own behavior in 1848 and Lamartine's unsuccessful attempt in 1842 to have the duchesse d'Orléans appointed as regent. Tocqueville seems to write

---

[32] Cf. Senior's conversation with Tocqueville, May 26, 1848, *OC*, VI, pt. 2, p. 245. Just days after the Festival of Concord, Tocqueville revealed that he still was not sure that Lamartine had become a totally spent force. Tocqueville admitted he was still speculating about Lamartine's future actions, but clearly let Senior know that he found Lamartine unsuitable to deal with the crisis which he believed was about to break over Paris. His low esteem for Lamartine was almost universally shared by a number of politicians, among them leading liberals. For a sampling, see Kelly, *Humane Comedy*, pp. 190–96.   [33] *OC*, XII, p. 130.

his recollections in the single-minded (but unexamined) belief that his devotion to the truth is the necessary, even if futile, basis for eliciting it from others. He believed further that he had the moral resources to guard himself against any hidden subterfuges that would mar his self-image, as a man who thoroughly knew and could honestly admit his own blemishes and contradictions. In brooding over the form of his recollections, he gave enormous weight to this evocation of an apparently transparent sincerity, seeing in it proof of his commitment to give free expression to all his thoughts and actions, however painful. In this way, that is, by saying that he was confessing all, he told himself that he was saving himself from self-deception. This was his solution, he thought, to the problem of achieving a more secure knowledge of himself, as well as proving to himself that an individual like Lamartine, swept along by his vanity, was incapable of achieving the needed self-distance to admit elements of self-deception. And because Tocqueville felt his conscious desire and need to live in a moral universe which admits and understands frailties, but does not thereby excuse them, he had little difficulty in feeling he had a right and duty to put his contemporaries under a judgmental microscope.[34]

Tocqueville's judgments are consistently rendered in images of masquerade, in acts of self-concealment, in the reflexes of fear and faulty calculation that led politicians to retreat from the problems of returning politics to the realm of the practical. The theater cannot, he insisted, be a substitute for the realities of politics, yet it was theatricality that proved to be the moving force in the events of May 15, as of February 24. Indeed, in a phrase that was to resound more than once in his judgment on the dissolution of the Old Régime, the theatricality that he decried was an integral part of what Tocqueville liked to call a "semi-madness," a distinctive, perhaps decisive, feature of democratic revolution. This madness was something that was not to be minimized, he says, since it often led to success; but the revolution's next, more radical, phase was to be short-lived. The Assembly's invasion on May 15 by crowds of unemployed workers and radical agitators was ended by the intervention of the National Guard and the Gardes Mobiles, but not before the occurrence of one of those reenactments that Tocqueville argued clouds reality. The invading crowd's resolution to set up a provisional government, he condemned as "a parody of the 24th of February, just as the 24th of February

---

[34] For an all-too-brief discussion of sincerity and single-mindedness, see Jon Elster, *Ulysses and the Sirens: Studies in Rationality and Irrationality* (Cambridge, 1984), pp. 175–76. For an older, but still valuable study, see Henri Peyre, *Literature and Sincerity* (New Haven and London, 1963). Lionel Trilling, *Sincerity and Authenticity* (Cambridge, Mass., 1972), canvasses the question from Molière to Freud.

was a parody of other revolutionary scenes."[35] What the parodists did not see, but Tocqueville writes that he clearly perceived, is that their imitations were a foretaste of the impending civil war when the two sides in the democratic revolution, the confused and now leaderless moderate forces, and the radicals, taking up the desperate plight of the workers of Paris, would for the last time clash as classes on either side of a chasm in which differing conceptions of private property would become the single and commanding issue.

In Tocqueville's interpretation, the last days and weeks before the eruption of the class war were spent in a mood of caution to avoid any acts that would precipitate violence, and a sense of resignation that it could not be avoided. At this point in the *Souvenirs*, Tocqueville was almost as evasive as the deputies who failed, he believed, to confront the issue of the National Workshops. "This burning question . . . was treated daily, but superficially and timidly; it was constantly touched upon, but never firmly taken in hand."[36] We are left to wonder what he means when he uses the word "firmly." He had in fact been studying the various socialist sects for some time, and had expressed his disdain for, and extreme hostility to, them; but the *Souvenirs* show him equally incapable of suggesting solutions to end the misery of the urban workmen. He continued to regard their condition as due to causes inherent in the "laws" of political economy and beyond the control of positive state action. The Workshops represented for him an experiment guided by false principles and slogans proclaiming the right to work that ended by duping the workers and made them dangerous.[37] Yet he revealed an openness to the views of others on condition that they are informed. The greater the political uncertainty, the more important it was to acknowledge the dangers of one-sidedness. "Political parties never know each other; they approach, touch, seize, but never see one another." George Sand, a person he did not admire, brought this truth home to him, when she told him about "the condition of the Paris workmen, their organization, their numbers, their arms, their preparations, their thoughts, their passions, their terrible resolves."[38] Tocqueville first thought her picture exaggerated, but it proved to be accurate, as he admits in the *Souvenirs*.

Reclaiming order: banishing contingency

Tocqueville's fullest description of what the workers were up to is to be found, he argued, in their erroneous conflation of their wishes with the wishes of the "people" – the people, as he ideally saw them, constituted a

[35] *OC*, XII, p. 139.   [36] Ibid., p. 147.   [37] Ibid., pp. 151–52.   [38] Ibid., p. 150.

united body of responsible citizens, a description he was unwilling to extend to the workers. Tocqueville considered the claim that in their popular assemblies, the workers of Paris said that they had never completely alienated their political will to their representatives. In principle the claim was true, Tocqueville conceded, but they had drawn from it the false conclusion that *they were* the French people.[39] For him, the workers' minds, hearts and blood had in fact been captured by the socialist sects and were mouthing their slogans.[40] Tocqueville had no doubt that liberty would be the first casualty of socialism. Elucidation on these questions is not offered in the *Souvenirs*, but they may be found in his speech on September 12, 1848, to the Assembly and in his notes on socialism. What needs to be explained is why he considered democracy and socialism to be unalterably opposed political and social visions. Democracy extends, he said, the sphere of individual autonomy; socialism constricts it. Democracy invests each person with intrinsic value, while socialism transforms the individual into a cipher. The only thing binding the two is equality, but each conceives of it differently. Democracy seeks to found equality in liberty; socialism works to bind equality within a public sphere of constraint.[41] In a free democracy, everyone should assume responsibility for himself, and not look to the state to appropriate it on the premise that it would enlarge it. The state may nevertheless extend its assistance to those who have exhausted all their resources of self-help. Tocqueville did not doubt that such an attitude to policy is simply the application of Christian principles to politics, the opposite of a policy that would ask the state to intervene in peoples' lives to guarantee them work, impose new rules and also tyrannize them by these seemingly benevolent means, the better to govern them.[42]

Socialism was for Tocqueville a retrogressive social theory. Its various doctrines all advocated legislation to level the citizenry. It hearkened back to the infancy of the social art. Were there not analogies in the absolutist and Jesuit doctrines in Paraguay and in the histories of China and Morocco? He did not pursue this highly suspect comparative analysis, nor the comparisons he said existed between two kinds of socialism, but only went so far as to say that one kind was animated by the purest materialism and aversion for work. It was beneath his contempt. He did not get round to discussing the second kind which he didn't identify. He left the question in that state and suggested that the most important point requiring further thought was his hypothesis that socialism owed nothing to the spirit of the great Revolution, and indeed was alien to it. The Revolution

[39] Ibid., p. 131.   [40] Ibid., p. 157.
[41] "Séance du 12 septembre 1848," *OC*, III, pt. 3, p. 175.   [42] Ibid., p. 180.

had swept away everything the socialists wanted to restore, especially administrative centralization.[43] Socialism and centralized state institutions, for Tocqueville, grew from the same roots and had a similar objective in working toward the reduction of the free actions of citizens.

In their present defiance of the Constituent Assembly, the workers and their leaders were choosing to locate themselves outside the community. Holding this conviction, Tocqueville writes that he placed himself, along with partisans of the moderate republic, as its heroic defender. He tries to recapture the moods and sounds of the city in the fatal June Days, by blending his own memories of his actions with small but telling personal anecdotes. Here raw memories are more in evidence than the deliberate art of recollection. He tells of his impression, after the first day, of having survived as if in a dream – so quickly did events pass by – leaving him in a state of utter exhaustion as he walks through the empty and quiet streets toward his apartment at one in the morning.[44] Convinced that the insurrection's energy is being directed by an unnamable force, because it is so total, he speaks of it as a spirit which "circulated from one end to the other of this immense class, and in each of its parts, as the blood does in the body."[45] To personalize that spirit, and accepting the veracity of some rumors quite uncritically, he recounts stories of working-class people relishing the thought of enjoying the material gains of their victory. His encounter with an old woman whose face is contorted with furious anger symbolizes for him the frightening essence of revolutionary emotion; his critical sense returns in remembering his relief that Thiers's original plan to abandon the city to the insurgents and then retake it by force met opposition from the king; and he reveals his doubts about the declaration of the military dictatorship under Cavaignac, but he surrenders his hesitation once he realizes that his delicacy is unduly obscuring the need for appropriate military measures. But not wishing to relax his principles, he referred with undisguised bitterness to the fact that: "Never were people so delighted to be relieved of their liberty and their government;"[46] and, as if to comfort himself against this latest popular lapse into servitude, he called on his judgmental voice to condemn "what Lamartine's popularity had come to in less than two months."[47]

The chapter recounting the June Days is not without its dark humor, but it seems inappropriate for the first time. He falls back on it to describe the details of his forays to the insurgent parts of Paris, side by side with such unlikely defenders of the Assembly as Goudchaux, Cormenin and

[43] Ibid., pp. 189–95. These ideas are to be found in separate notes on "Socialisme," "Vielleries socialistes," "Esprit antisocialiste de la Révolution française" and "Socialisme et liberté."   [44] *OC*, XII, p. 156.   [45] Ibid., p. 157.   [46] Ibid., p. 165.   [47] Ibid.

Crémieux,[48] who were deputed along with other commissioners by the Assembly to deliver its decrees to the National Guard. From his tone, it seems plain that Tocqueville finds his association with them a bit hard to take, though he cannot help but reveal some sympathy for the first of – for him – his unusual companions. In their traversal through areas already in insurgent hands or about to be taken over by them, Tocqueville depicts Cormenin and Crémieux, in a mood of indecision, rationalizing a detour away from the most dangerous spots in the capital. Tocqueville remarks that he took great pleasure in observing that "others [who] are able to cover it [their cowardice] with a veil so delicate, so daintily woven with small, plausible lies" give proof of "this ingenious work of our intelligence."[49] Together with Goudchaux, Tocqueville keeps to his planned route.

His highly compressed account of the momentous nature of the revolutionary fighting denotes the selectivity of his narrative. He was plainly driven to the small detail in the hope that it could be revelatory. At the same time, one has the impression that he was aware of, but that he would not be deterred from deploying, the ambiguities inherent in narration, as he shifted to a more analytic and less personal mode, swinging his telescope in the direction of the army and the National Guard. He writes accurately about their suppression of the insurgents with the support of substantial and middling landowners, who came pouring into Paris from the countryside by rail. The mixture of black humor and historical analysis works well only as long as we are willing to remain impressed by Tocqueville's capacity to marvel at how the commonplace manages to survive in the midst of bloody events. The device begins to break down when he interrupts the narrative by an abrupt denunciation of the omnipresence of the forces whom he blames for nearly destroying the social order. Previously described with some sympathetic understanding, the threats to disorder now assume a sinister physiognomy. His demonization of the armed crowds waiting to take the defenders of the "city of antiquity" into slavery seems like a gross violation of his more balanced metaphorical style. By the end of the chapter, his account collapses into its own theatricality at the very moment that he ends his comments on the theatricality of a new scene in the Assembly, which keeps on meeting

---

[48] Michel Goudchaux, banker and deputy, voted with the republicans on the right in the Constituent Assembly. Minister of finances under the Cavaignac government, he failed to be reelected to the Legislative Assembly. Louis de Cormenin gained a reputation as an authority on administrative law. He survived several changes of régime, and served under the Second Empire. Adolphe Crémieux, a liberal under the July Monarchy, was a deputy in the Constituent and Legislative Assemblies, and briefly minister of finances in the provisional government.   [49] Ibid., p. 164.

irregularly during the insurrection. Sénard, a lawyer, presided, practicing what Tocqueville writes he knew best – the art of manufacturing emotion. Though this time, as the hapless man reads out the news of the crumbling strength of the insurgents and the heroic deeds of the army and its allies, Tocqueville grants that Sénard's feelings were probably genuine: "Never were the sublime and the ridiculous brought so close together: for the facts were sublime and the narrator ridiculous."[50] Tocqueville's own narrative, however, does not capture the terrible sublimity of what was taking place in the working-class districts of the city. His partisanship is too transparent. In resorting to the evocation of a one-sided emotion to justify his attribution of sublimity to the victorious side, while totally denying it the other, the account sinks into near melodrama.

Indeed, the final descriptions of the June Days mark a departure from the narrative's earlier, much greater, openness. From acquiring and presumably internalizing the insight that political parties grew incapable of speaking to and seeking some forms of an understanding with one another, as they retreat in panic from dialogue,[51] Tocqueville, in the flush of excitement he feels as the insurgents are defeated, falls a somewhat unwilling victim to the comforts of order restored by Cavaignac, about whose grant of dictatorial powers he had earlier expressed serious reservation. His adversaries were silenced; that is what mattered most for Tocqueville in his depiction of a civil war whose class nature reminded him of those in ancient times when the sacred and the profane met the same end. Such violence was the worst kind in Tocqueville's mind. It exercised and answered only to its own ferocious will. It needed, for that very reason, to be excised. So it was, but would it be the final confrontation, Tocqueville asks. We find in this chapter, possibly the most difficult he found to write, a conflation between the different voices of the narrator and the "We" of the victorious side. As Tocqueville recollects walking the streets, seeing for himself the destruction and the massacre, he alternatively felt alienated from, and the wish to participate in, the will to destroy the insurrection, yet exulting in the "sublime" act of General Lamorcière,[52] whose "magnificent rage" brought back his retreating troops to face the barricades.[53] "I shall say no more of the June combats," he wrote. "The recollections of the last two days merge into and are lost in those of the first." Tocqueville could not face the task of rendering them in their bloody details. Instead, his ancestral memories blotted them out. Waves of irrepressible sentiment wash over his encounters with the

---

[50] Ibid., pp. 167–68.   [51] See below, note 56.

[52] Léon Juchault de Lamorcière, famous for his subjection of Algeria, was named minister of war in the Cavaignac government, and in 1849, with Tocqueville in the foreign office, was sent on a mission to Russia.   [53] Ibid., p. 174.

provincial nobles who had come to the rescue, the men who "remembered that they had once formed part of a warlike and governing class." Then, as if to write finis to that distant epoch, he recalled the last hours of Chateaubriand, who "best preserved the spirit of the old races."

The June Days and Chateaubriand's death converge for Tocqueville as if plotted by history itself. A history without persons is now given privilege over a history of personal actions. The June Days are ambiguously designated as "necessary and disastrous." *They* deliver the nation. This metonymic device made it easier for Tocqueville to avoid further images of killings and death. From them, Tocqueville turned toward the problematic outcome of the June crisis. What changes are to come? Will liberty survive? The only hope for its restoration, Tocqueville declares emotively, and in a spirit contrary to his own respect for an historical accounting, rests in a removal and effacement of the "particular recollections of the Revolution of 1848."[54] Political amnesia is Tocqueville's solution, as if a shameful chapter in France's history cannot be looked at directly. So much of a departure from his promise to be frank is contrary to his promise of approaching all problems with sincerity, but Tocqueville seems to have some trouble seeing, or shows himself unwilling to consider, that sincerity and truth do not always coincide. This false conflation leads him astray. Sincerity now begins to look like a virtue with limitations. It turns its face away from what Tocqueville now calls "necessary." Does he now wish to assert the necessary as an expression of historical truth, or of the historian's wisdom in reaching a pact with the past? He was not so quick, up to this point, to see necessity and contingency as existing at polar ends of a dialectic, but rather as close relatives. Is contingency about to be swallowed up in a plethora of fatality? The coupling of the disastrous with the necessary suggests that a full surrender to the claims of necessity is not consistently in his mind. Disastrous the June crisis certainly was. But was it disastrous in the wider context of what led up to it, in the actualization of the June Days themselves or in the sequel that lay waiting in the wings?

As Tocqueville tackled the next parts of his *Souvenirs*, his narrative loses some of its earlier evenhandedness. He distributed blame as he saw it, and upon whomever, without partisan regard, he felt that it should fall. This is evident, not so much in his treatment of the actors, who remain mainly, as before, targets of his ironic wit, but in his almost imperceptible shift toward the status of full actor, moving from the periphery more closely to the center of power. Not surprisingly, he did not give up the stance of the more-or-less impartial observer who probes events and

---

[54] Ibid. All the materials and quotes come from chap. 10, esp. pp. 177–78.

actors with a relentless scalpel. But, as he moved more and more from observer to participant, the complex human motivations of those with whom he was in daily contact, working out positions and tactics, were seen more within fatally inscribed circles. Accordingly the narrative takes on a reduced sense of urgency and the actors slide into their predictable roles. The intertwining of intentions, chance, accident, contingency and fate, which had marked the *Souvenirs* up to this point, now loses its immediacy, and a more mechanical analysis surfaces. These points of the human compass appear to be a less pressing problem for Tocqueville, who comes to live in a political world solidly fixed on ensuring a society capable of resisting the futility of revolutionary violence. He does not lose his capacity to isolate the more extravagant errors of his colleagues and foes, as well as the atmosphere of reactive fear which he feels to be exaggerated; but his earlier passionate intensity is replaced by an icy, more calculating, tone. The diminution of narrative effect, which at its fullest depends on closely following the ties between actions and contingency, registers a visible increase of affect.

The change is noticeable even before Tocqueville sat down to write about his tenure as foreign minister. It may be seen in the last chapter of the second part of the *Souvenirs*, devoted to his participation in the Constituent Assembly's constitutional committee, which began its work after the May Days and before the June crisis. He penned the chapters on the June crisis first, explaining the interruption in chronology as a desire to focus his narrative on the events leading "so swiftly and directly to those days."[55] He clearly did not want to break the momentum of his narrative by introducing the more prosaic work of the committee. Nevertheless, Tocqueville tells us that it did most of its work before the eruption of the civil war, and was, as it turned out, to have a decisive effect on future political structures and practices. At the same time, as we are treated to his evaluation of the committee members, and his pessimism about their capacity to deal with the enormous problems of the project, any links between the committee's deliberations and the storm that was gaining force outside the committee rooms remain unexplored. Perhaps at the time the connections were not clear, and Tocqueville's omission, if it may be called that, is not really an oversight or obfuscation at all, but a faithful mirror of the fragmented nature of revolutionary confusion. Indeed, this may have been so much the case that one may say that contingency might have played an even greater role than before, but his customary fineness of touch abandoned him. The fatal circle seemed to have become much smaller,

---

[55] Ibid., p. 178.

and Tocqueville, working within it, saw the possibilities open to him reduced to the zero point.

It is difficult to imagine that, even as his energies were taken up by the committee's work, he so totally blocked out what was happening outside the Assembly. He confronted the juxtaposition of the two in a specific way: the turmoil in the streets became a justification for the committee's concentration on the restoration of order. The mental coupling – or perhaps it is more fitting to call it a mental disjuncture – becomes clearer still by contrasting the expository form that is used to deal with theories of political institutions and the narrative skills that are usually deployed to bring out the vitality of political events. However, the line between the expository and the narrative forms is fluid and should not have posed a barrier to an interweaving of the two. It is just as hard to say that Tocqueville's blindness was too profound to allow a more distanced perspective. This question is a variation on the voices available to Tocqueville himself. It brings to the surface in a fresh way the intersecting forces of intentionality and necessity as he conceived them in understanding his own actions. No quick answer is at hand.

In an opening footnote to the chapter on the debates of the Constitutional Committee, Tocqueville remarks that it did get down to "general principles,"[56] and did so with some wisdom and courage. But this concession to its work does not change the profound tone of misgiving and contempt that pervades his analysis: "I declare that I never witnessed a more wretched display in any committee on which I ever sat."[57] His governing concern continues to be the elaboration of a constitutional instrument with ample safeguards for political liberty. The specter of centralization, which he sees as the ruling principle of modern political life in France, is, for him, as omnipresent after February as before, and it is against government aggrandizement that he centers his opposition: even revolutions have no power over it, he writes. And "the pleasure it procures them [those who govern] of interfering with every one and holding everything in their hands atones to them for its dangers."[58] He confesses minimal confidence in his colleagues on the committee whom he compares unfavorably with the makers of the American Constitution.[59] The monarchists possess no real appreciation of republican theory, and the republicans wallow in popular, undigested notions. As for Lamennais, the great heretic who moved steadily leftward from the liberal Catholicism of L'Avenir, and Victor Considérant, a Fourierist socialist, who were the only Montagnards on the committee, the first resigns over a procedural matter (prompting Tocqueville to unburden himself with a

---

[56] Ibid., p. 179.   [57] Ibid., p. 184.   [58] Ibid., p. 182.   [59] Ibid., p. 180.

devastating critique of the clerical mind), while the second he dismisses as a blind, almost insane, visionary. His other colleagues fare no better. Armand Marrast, an old-time republican, now president of the Constituent Assembly, is described as a revolutionary to the extent that centralization promised the Revolution's consummation. He is a man who understands "the liberty of the people to mean despotism exercised in the name of the people."[60] But it is André Dupin, the prototypical politician of the July Monarchy and survivor of all change, for whom Tocqueville reserves his fullest satirical jabs. "I had seen him for ten years prowling round every party without joining any, and attacking all the vanquished: half ape and half jackal, constantly biting, grimacing, gamboling, and always ready to fall upon the wretch who slipped."[61]

The *Souvenirs* plot the committee's failures against a background of near futility, with the actors responding – more so than in the narrative to this point – with their well-worn reflexes. They seem to be behaving exactly in the way Tocqueville expects them to. This does not mark a fundamental departure from the earlier tone Tocqueville adopted, but in his previous portraits he conveys much more strongly both his tendency to confirm his anticipation of the actors' conduct, and the steps they take or the choices they make, usually in a state of confusion, to consummate them. There was one exception, he says. It arose in his discussion of the merits of a bicameral or a unicameral Assembly, and whether one or the other was the best barrier against the powers of the president who was to be elected directly by universal suffrage. The arguments on both sides were, in Tocqueville's assessment, hypothetical. There appeared to be no way of knowing which solution was the better. Tocqueville concluded that the advocates on either side had good arguments to make, but that the confusion which ensued might have been removed had popular opinion been ready to reduce presidential powers or grant the legislature the power to elect the executive.[62] But the public's near unanimity on the question of preserving the direct democratic will was, he declared, hard to resist.

After the June Days, he expressed his regret for actively supporting this clause in the Constitution, pleading that he had done so only because public opinion would not have tolerated any erosion of its supremacy. He recalled that, before the breakdown in June, he had tried, with some success, to mitigate the effects of such a clause by giving the legislature the power of choice in the absence of an absolute popular majority.[63] Along with Beaumont, he also argued and again with success, against a second term for the president on the grounds that it would lead to the

[60] Ibid., p. 182.   [61] Ibid., p. 186.   [62] Ibid., pp. 184–86.   [63] Ibid., pp. 188–90.

further consolidation of the enormous power, sanctioned by law and custom, in the hands of the executive branch of government. At this juncture in his account, Tocqueville regretted that he had failed to anticipate that, since the principle of direct election was already conceded, any attempt to question it in these secondary ways would most likely lead to a more passionate and thoughtless defense of the democratic will. In the circumstances, the transfer of the democratic will to the democratic despot in the person of the president was a foregone conclusion for Tocqueville. His irony seems more inferential than open. His self-critical gaze focused on his own misjudgment, tempered by a belief in a doomed scenario. The contingent was given a much slighter importance than earlier. He was, at the same time, harsher about his own failure to anticipate the future than he is with the failure of his peers from whom he expected less. It was, he says, "my most unpleasant memory of that period."[64] The atmosphere of futility of all the political maneuvering hangs heavily in these pages of the *Souvenirs*.

The closing pages of the chapter seem compressed, as if Tocqueville can barely wait to still his feelings of dismay and despair. The committee's belief that constitutional amendments should be difficult finds him taking the opposite position – that it is best to make them easy, just as it is "best to treat the French people like those madmen whom one should be careful not to bind lest they become infuriated by the restraint." In their wish to end its work, the committee decides, in Tocqueville's account, to treat its proposals as a sketch, with the intention of giving it definitive form at a later time. "But we did not retrace our steps, and the sketch," Tocqueville writes, "remained the picture."[65] With a few more closing remarks on Marrast's irresponsibility as secretary, and Cormenin's puerile belief in novelty for novelty's sake, Tocqueville gave voice to one of his most durable beliefs. As it did for the *littérateurs* of the eighteenth century, abstract symmetry appealed more to the literary mind than any concern to see politics as a series of challenges to find practical, not experimental, solutions.[66]

The third and final part of the *Souvenirs* introduces Tocqueville as a full-fledged cabinet minister, exercising power in the uncertainty of the aftermath of the 1849 elections which unexpectedly returned a sizable number, but still only a minority, of Montagnards, and a much larger heterogeneous group of conservatives, including Legitimists, Orléanists and more moderate deputies. Why had the election results confounded all the parties? Tocqueville's answer precludes any discussion of faulty predictions, missed possibilities and contingency in general – features

---

[64] Ibid., p. 190.   [65] Ibid., p. 192.   [66] Ibid., p. 193.

that had been so much a part of the earlier part of the narrative. The author of *Democracy in America* was at a loss to assess the motives of the democratic electorate. "It is difficult to say for certain, for great masses of men move by virtue of causes almost as unknown to humanity itself as those which rule the movements of the sea. In both cases the reasons for the phenomenon are concealed and, in a sense, lost in the midst of its immensity."[67] The French electoral ocean seemed for a moment more unfathomable than it was when Tocqueville had unraveled the expectations of the democratic American electorate.

That he feels himself so engulfed is surely due to similar feelings of incredulity in his description of what he calls the self-generating current of revolution in June that had, as we saw, astounded him at the time. The force of personalities and the discrete, or the series of linked, events seemingly therefore had nothing to do with their outcomes. Once he divests himself of these remarks, however, the allusions to how party decisions affect the results come cascading out, as if the grandeur of the metaphor, even if fittingly describing elections held in revolutionary times, is, even so, too rhetorical.[68] The rather prolonged remarks prefacing his decision to join the cabinet lead to passages giving importance to his own role, and that of his political friends, in weighing the chances of giving practical effect to their political agenda. Despite the difficulties, the prospect of becoming a minister, he says, is not an illusory act, because his reading of the past tells him what he can expect from the future.[69] This he tells himself should arm him against error, as will his resolution, he assures himself, to leave the government as soon as there are signs that by remaining in it, he will lose the power to be "true to myself."[70]

Tocqueville, it is clear, believed that by working toward an arrangement with like-minded moderates who, along with himself, were given three of the key portfolios in May 1849 in a politically heterogeneous cabinet, he was being true to his earlier passionate defenses of liberty. Indeed, he

---

[67] Ibid., p. 199.
[68] Cf. his remarks in *Nolla edn.*, I, pp. 151–52, where he laments the decline in the quality of statesmanship and the general talent of the citizens, ascribing the difficulties the lower classes face in making wise choices to lack of time and information, but mostly the necessities of work, resulting in the success of impostors. Some of the undesirable consequences could, however, be lessened in a system of indirect elections, and thereby ensure a minimal guarantee of quality in political life. See Tocqueville to Corcelle, sometime after October 15, 1835, *OC*, XV, pt. 1, pp. 56–57.   [69] *OC*, XII, p. 201.
[70] Ibid., pp. 202–03. The French reads that he wanted "pouvoir . . . rendre quelque service signalé à mon pays, et pour m'y grandir moi-même . . ."; and that he intended to do so "sans jamais subordonner au besoin de me maintenir celui de rester moi-même." Closer in time to the events he described in the *Souvenirs*, he expressed virtually the same sentiments to Corcelle, October 26, 1849, *OC*, XV, pt. 1, p. 473: "Jamais je n'ai été plus convaincu que je fais la seule chose utile à mon pays et honorable pour moi-même."

assumed something of the air of a power broker, intent on ensuring the survival of the Republic as the best defense against the possibilities of coups d'état from many sides. He isolated three obstacles to the foundation of a stable republican form of government. First, and above all, the threat came from Louis-Napoleon whose dictatorial ambitions were undisguised and who would, if given the right opportunities, assume full power, retaining the Republic in name only. The second threat to the Republic came from the Orléanists whose power could be held in check by supporting the Legitimists on certain issues, because the latter were ready to do almost anything to diminish the chances of an Orléanist revival. The final, but not the least, danger to the moderate Republic came from the Montagnards, some of whose socialist ideas Tocqueville was sure would introduce a new round of disasters, injurious to liberty and property alike. The idea of saving liberty by forbidding it to those who threatened his conception of it became Tocqueville's major concern. His preference for a constitutional monarchy was balanced by his aversion for an Orléanist coup that would amount to the triumph of the same venal middle classes, who had been in control since 1830, and lead them to replay the events leading to 1848.[71] But for him the danger was infinitely greater from a new round of revolutionary violence or a coup from the left than from the right. With the left, the chances of liberty "in a regular, conservative and absolutely constitutional way"[72] would, as he saw it, come to an end. In his words, there were no republicans in France; the Republic was thus difficult to maintain, "for those who favored it were, for the most part, incapable or unworthy of governing it. But it was also rather difficult to pull down."[73] The reasons lay, as Tocqueville saw them, in the three political groupings that detested one another more than the Republic, and therefore somehow kept it breathing. But this did not mean that it could simply survive on its own: the moderates alone were in a position to save the Republic against its supposed defenders and its real enemies. It was necessary to exploit their opportunities, lest, with its disappearance, liberty slipped into the abyss.

The Montagnards were put in their place, Tocqueville recalled with relief, in the second June insurrection of 1849, which was precipitated by their hope of gaining support in Paris against the cabinet's secret decision to attack Rome in violation of the Chamber's right to debate the question. (The French were intervening in Rome to restore the Pope, who had fled following the proclamation of a Roman Republic.) Tocqueville feels compelled to support the decision on the grounds that, even if it violates the Constitution, a contrary position will strengthen Ledru-Rollin, the

---

[71] *OC*, XII, pp. 209–10.   [72] Ibid., p. 202.   [73] Ibid., pp. 209–10.

Montagnards and the deputies further to the left. In defense of his assessment, Tocqueville adduced evidence of appeals to civil war that were being voiced in the Chamber. The anticipated renewal of civil war on June 13 was blocked by a well-timed declaration of a state of siege, but more important, Tocqueville claimed, by the failure of the Parisians to respond to appeals to defy the government. "In June 1848, the [revolutionary] army had no leaders; in June [1849], the leaders had no army."[74] Once the danger was disposed of, he had no problem in taking the next step supporting repressive measures to end political and social unrest in various parts of France, including Lyons and neighboring departments. The laws, if not as Draconian as during the June Days, found Tocqueville affirming, as he had once before but not with the same conviction, that "after so violent a revolution, [the only means] of saving liberty was to restrict it."[75] In the event, the press was muzzled (never before, as he noted, so severely) and the clubs suspended.

There is a curious slip in the narrative, when his voice is displaced by that of the veteran centrist, Dufaure, as if he cannot bring himself to utter the assertion that society has an inalienable right to protect itself by establishing a "parliamentary dictatorship."[76] He is ready to go further: to expel all the republicans "of indifferent capacity or bad character,"[77] but he fails to persuade Barrot. Tocqueville believes during the entire period of his tenure that the position he is advocating is both coherent and defensible. There are fewer, indeed, there are virtually no second thoughts about the course he is following. It is as if he is exaggerating the precarious position of the moderates to enhance his self-esteem as a prudent man of politics – a perch from which it proves harder to exercise his more characteristic self-vigilance. The uncertainty of the political scene in early 1848 had alerted his sense of the contingent and the risks of self-deception. A year later, while contingent factors had by no means been removed, he feels that the best way of reducing them is to take even more decisive action against the Montagnards. He is also ready to overlook the fact that this amounts to a surrender to the conservative demand for repressive action and, as a result, is undermining his own principles. When he writes of the need to save the Second Republic against its enemies at both ends of the spectrum, reserving his harshest criticism for the left, he may have had in mind the Republic of the Year II. In this difficult situation, the ministerial self replaces the detached observer, and the dangers of self-deception become a secondary concern. The dynamics of the narrative had changed.

Self-deception no longer worried him. In his résumé of his brief period

---

[74] Ibid., p. 219.   [75] Ibid., p. 225.   [76] Ibid.   [77] Ibid., p. 226.

of power as foreign minister, he presents us with a self-portrait of a man who successfully traversed the route from his earlier self-doubts as a deputy in opposition during the July Monarchy to a person whose self-confidence grows with the power he exerts, as if he has a privileged aristocratic right to it. This surprises him, but also increases his pleasure. He shows no hesitation in this new self-assessment: the greater the complications and the more serious the consequences, the fewer the periods of anguish. Imperatives of decision act on him, he writes, like a magnet, mobilizing personal capabilities he has always wanted to test, but till now could never exercise. He claims that he was – and this was not the least of the pleasures he gained from being a minister – in a position which brought out an unknown affability and cordiality in his exchanges with persons in the government and in the opposition. Formerly, he explains, he had only to do with the ideas of fools. Now the changed circumstances make him aware that their interests were not unimportant.[78] This was an echo of his conviction that men are best approached by appealing to their vanity and private interests,[79] though he wavered when he opined that men give in to what flatters their vanity more than they do to what serves their interests.[80]

It is hard to determine whether his newly found affability is, as he asserts, waiting to be released, or whether it is the mask he needs to achieve his goals. Tocqueville elides this question, but, on the other hand, he does not disguise what he thinks was at work in giving him the resources to carry out his responsibilities. Such an admission risks, he admits, an accusation of self-flattery, but it is as nothing compared with the self-flattery of his opponents.[81] Masks and theater are a natural part of political discourse, Tocqueville came near to saying, though he did not give any inkling that he saw any symmetry between his acute discernment of the strong elements of theatrical reenactments in February and June 1848, and his own contrived strategies. He did not, however, believe that he was falling prey to self-deception. There is an obvious pride he felt in picturing himself at the center of political decisions. Pride is his great weakness, he told us at the start of the *Souvenirs*. In the new circumstances, he is sure that he has expunged it. His belief that he is transforming it into an absolute source of strength is unmistakable, and must be compared with his earlier condemnation of his own pride as an unacceptable defect. He does not stop to consider how pride, which he regarded as a vice, really worked for him.

One of the unintended consequences of the Revolution, as it unwound itself, is to find Tocqueville caught up in the decisions that led to a curtail-

---

[78] Ibid., pp. 234–35.   [79] Ibid., p. 226.   [80] Ibid., p. 255.   [81] Ibid., pp. 236–37.

ment of liberty in France. Early on he feared that the chief leaders of the various factions and parties, through their misreadings of the past which shaped their misinterpretations of their present, would imperil liberty. He always brooded over the burdensome inescapability of the past, locking the present in a semi-vice, but not so fully as to preclude decisions other than those that are made. The contingent was never absent, except when the crudest forms of causal necessity permeated discourses and policies. The presence of the contingent could be overlooked, if it were seen simplistically, as being in primitive opposition to necessity. He hoped, as he had often said, for an expansion of the imaginative capabilities that would increase choice. His hope was an expression of guarded faith, but it was clouded over by his disappointments. In the *Souvenirs*, he clothes them in a language of ironic aphorisms about individual and group action, whether at the parliamentary level or in the streets. He issued his warnings against violence as expressive of collective psychopathology, of what he calls a revolutionary illness at times, and madness at others; and he justified the curtailment of liberty on the grounds that, in extraordinary circumstances, order had to come first. Strong feelings of futility touch his gloomy assessment of the survival of liberty in Europe. "On every side, the old powers were rising up again from amid the ruins which it [the Revolution] had made – not, it is true, the same as when they fell, but very similar."[82] What was to be done? In relations with the powers of central and eastern Europe, France must never "disown [her] principles of liberty and toleration . . . Thus France, while at war with the Revolution, did not lose her liberal attitude by which she was known among the peoples." By adding that, "It is true that this attitude was not of a kind to bring her immediate good fortune, for license had rather discredited the cause of liberty,"[83] Tocqueville unintentionally exposed some of the hypocrisy of France's claims to be speaking on behalf of liberty. He was uneasy in noting the massacre of revolutionaries taken prisoner in Germany, even as he pressed his familiar distinction between "anarchy and liberty." If he had any doubts about how the boundaries between them could be stated without contradiction, he did not express them.

The dynamics of the narrative had indeed changed. Though it fairly breathes a persona who rarely slipped from a position of knowing better than the characters who move through the pages of his recollections, he almost never deprived them of their qualities as "free" men, whatever errors they committed. As he ended the *Souvenirs*, Tocqueville continued to believe that he was able to see men as they "actually" are. Even if the "laws" of deception could not be breached, it is evident that he had fallen

---

[82] Ibid., p. 242.   [83] Ibid.

into a highly self-protective mode. In writing the *Souvenirs*, he followed a method which, until reaching the point where he justified his decisions as a minister, he would soon come to believe was not entirely appropriate to a study of the 1789 Revolution. The *Souvenirs* do not entirely betray his principle that the historical role of actors and their own conscious intentions must be dissonantly related to one another.[84] Because of his own role as an historical actor in the February Revolution, no matter how much the narrative falters in the last part of his recollections, that form is best suited to his purposes. He makes his point with some clarity, but in apparent forgetfulness of his sensitivity to the distortions wrought by self-deception. In this instance, his remarks carry unconscious irony. In search of the truth of 1789 and what followed, the recapturing of what the actors of the period actually said and felt – "the vibrations of which they can still sense in their minds and hearts" – were the raw materials, he notes to himself, for his reimagining and distancing himself from them. In fact, a double distancing is at work. The first is an inescapably constant feature of a relationship to the historical past, which is at once obscured by time but is still recoverable; the second demands not only detachment, but mental reenactment.

Five years after completing the *Souvenirs*, Tocqueville quite clearly had them in mind as a testament of how the "vibrations" of historical actors, including his own, exist on one plane, recollected or not, while those who come after them can only hear their echoes. Narrative was the best, if imperfect, way to record some of them, as originally uttered; others as they were recalled. As the promise of candor became tangled up with the demands of office and the critical scrutiny of the future, the tone in the narrative moves further and further away from the speculations prompted by looking at the particular, and more and more toward the defense of practical decisions, not in the name of a theoretical or ideal liberty, but in the name of France as the incarnation of Tocqueville's particular vision of it. Its universal quality would nevertheless come to the surface in *L'Ancien Régime*.

For Tocqueville, in an earlier period of his life, moral and political grandeur could be tested only by its adherence to a universal idea of liberty. He could not understand, he had said in 1836, why the love some people had for morality, religion and order, and that others had for liberty and equality before the law, had different and hostile partisans, whereas all of these goals were united indissolubly in the eyes of God.[85] Now, in an

---

[84] Cf. Furet, *Interpreting the French Revolution*, on his treatment of how Tocqueville saw the totality of the gap between human actions and the "real" meaning of the Revolution.

[85] Tocqueville to E. Stoffels, July 24, 1836, *Beaumont edn.*, V, pp. 429–30.

extreme moment of disappointment, he displaced a universalist ethos of liberty with decidedly religious overtones, with a nationalist one that ranked order more highly than both liberty and equality. The union of all three that he longed for in 1836, and that he had believed lay within the realm of the practical, appears to lose its sense of immediacy in an atmosphere that fed on fear of revolution. He seems to have lost his way, unable either to escape a sense of historical repetitiveness, or to see a clear exit from his sense that a rational politics was being washed over by events.

5 Toward the history of *L'Ancien Régime et la Révolution*

Newness is the realm of the historian who, unlike the natural scientist concerned with ever-recurring happenings, deals with events which always occur only once. This newness can be manipulated if the historian insists on causality and pretends to be able to explain events by a chain of causes which eventually led up to it. He then, indeed, poses as the "prophet turned backward" . . . Causality, however, is an altogether alien and falsifying category in the historical sciences. Not only does the actual meaning of every event always transcend any number of past "causes" which we may assign to it . . . ; this past itself comes into being only with the event itself.

What the illuminating event reveals is a beginning in the past which had hitherto been hidden; to the eye of the historian, the illuminating event cannot but appear as an end of this newly discovered beginning.[1]

The path from the *Souvenirs* to *L'Ancien Régime*

As Tocqueville composed his *Souvenirs*, he also thought of writing a new book. Musing in his solitude over the final shape of his recollections, he was led to renewed brooding over his own life's purposes. After ten years in the public arena, his regret, especially after the establishment of a presidential republic that claimed legitimacy in democratic forms, was tempered by some satisfaction of having gained an intimate knowledge of the actions of men in political life. The experience would prove valuable, he was sure, for the study of predemocratic politics, but he was still "dreaming" of a subject.[2] It was as though he were already plotting an alternative approach to the past from the one he had elaborated in the *Souvenirs*, a past so close in time to his present that the more distant past seemed to demand a frame quite different from the one enclosing the events of 1848–49. The way in which he might gratify his need for a more ambitious gaze into the misunderstood and mystified prerevolutionary era was

---

[1] Hannah Arendt, "Understanding and Politics," *Partisan Review*, 20 (1953), p. 388.
[2] Tocqueville to E. Stoffels, December 30, 1850, *Beaumont edn.*, V, pp. 462–64.

as yet barely conceived. Part of this new impulse was shaped by his changing conceptualization of the long-term significance of the 1789 Revolution. It had always loomed as a shattering event whose consequences would reverberate in time and continue to surprise. But how was it to be represented to explain both its singularity and its continuities?

Well into the 1840s, as we saw, Tocqueville was virtually certain that the 1830 Revolution was bringing an end to any future revolutionary challenges, though from time to time the political maneuvers of the ministerial party aroused his suspicions, while those of the opposition's anti-liberalism provoked his contempt. He went on more optimistically to hope that the "permanent instincts" of the country would suppress these aberrations.[3] With the 1848 outbreak and its aftermath, his confidence in the country's ability to achieve stability evaporated, and he came to see 1789 not only as a turning point, but as a kind of interminable point reaching into an indefinite future, a revolution without visible signs of exhausting itself, or one that would continue to take unexpected turns and twists. He now tended to see all the revolutionary expressions of violence from 1789 to his own day as one revolution. He was not about to accept the idea of a revolution in permanence,[4] but rather to ascertain why it was continuing to have such a long life. He could not reject the potential menace of renewed revolution, as he experienced his first period of fear that democratic despotism would take solid form under Louis-Napoleon. Though permanence as a word does not appear often in his correspondence after 1851–52, it is not hard to imagine that he was asking himself what alternatives, if any, there were, short of revolution, to the entrenchment of an anti-liberal government that could so successfully exploit a compliant population with promises of "democratic" consultation.

He groped for a solution. He gathered up, as it were – or, if he did not proceed with the task so deliberately – he prepared himself to make use of his earliest ideas on a number of pressing questions that he had stored up in his fertile mind, and which he was to retrieve from time to time to develop them more sharply. It is appropriate and illuminating to think of these moments in Tocqueville's life as constituting a period of transitions,

---

[3] Tocqueville to Mill, February 10, 1836, *OC*, VI, pp. 306–07.

[4] On the origins of the expression and progress of the idea of permanent revolution, see Koselleck, "Historical Criteria of the Modern Concept of Revolution," in Koselleck, *Futures Past*, pp. 39–54. It was first broached immediately after the 1830 Revolution by a German writer, K. H. L. Pölitz, and Proudhon was to give the idea his own reading. Tocqueville had already raised the question of the probabilities of permanent revolution in his famous chapter 21 of book 3 of the *Democracy, Nolla edn.*, II, p. 211. "Does the equality of social conditions habitually and *permanently* lead men to revolutions?" (my italics).

composed of several points of intellectual activity, which went back to those times when the questions that were to occupy him in the future first came to light. We must follow him back to that time when he first began circling the questions that were to figure in his history of the *ancien régime* to see how he came to write it in a form that claimed to give expression to underlying laws of historical development. As we make the reverse journey with him, we will find that, when he brought this baggage from the past into his preparations for the momentous task of piercing the enigmas of the old society, he had not thought of how the perceptions he had gained from imagining and observing the details of how human beings see themselves and engage in intersubjective communication could be integrated in such a study. While the insights he had gained in 1848 had become part of his mental makeup, he had thus far not resolved how he might and whether he should include in his account of France before the Revolution examples of the concrete and the particular, which mark the historical imagination of the *Souvenirs*. He thought it important for his purposes to move on to a historical form that removed people and their actions from the foreground, an approach that would bring into prominence the larger and more general, and, as he thought, more theoretically dignified, framework that envelops individuals in sweeps of a grandiose historical causality that he believed the Revolution, as a "prodigious enterprise," demanded. But it was not the kind of causality that the epigraph to this chapter dismisses as beyond the capabilities of the human mind.

The mysteries and symbolic forms of 1789 remained his major concern, as did the epoch from which it emerged and the period that followed it. Getting it right would perhaps go some way to answering the question of why it had fastened itself so firmly on the minds and determined the actions of successive generations. As he wondered how he might pursue his inquiry, he saw its real meaning buried under the "false colors" with which historians had chosen to paint over it. He continued to believe that he might be able to grasp the fullness of the Revolution by doing what he had always done – judging the facts, rather than confining himself to grasping their texture, though he did not understress the importance of the latter. This assessment of his powers would not have surprised anyone with a memory of his first extended analysis of the condition of France on the eve of the Revolution, an analysis which, by taking the long view, was executed in the same spirit that animated the first volume of the *Democracy*, indeed, so much so that he wondered if he could ever move beyond it. At that time he already feared that the analytic mode might bear too heavily on and smother the effects of narrative: the genre which he was even at that moment using in the *Souvenirs*. It is important to recognize that in 1836, as he told John Stuart Mill, he was already self-consciously asking how he might approach his subjects and the genres appropriate to each:

> I am afraid that my method is too French and little to the taste of your contemporaries, and that they are finding only that I have an overly pronounced penchant for general ideas. I had at first had the idea of struggling against this tendency, but the subject has, in spite of myself, driven me back to it. *Nothing forces you to ponder more about the general rules which are traceable in human societies. Besides, I believe that when I come [to deal] with the France of our own days I will find it easy to become more detailed and more practical.*[5]

The *Essai* of 1836: the formation and collapse of caste, honor and inequality

In fact, as we saw, Tocqueville came to adopt for the *Souvenirs* the mode that gave pride of place to the concrete to allow him some way of apprehending what he had experienced in 1848–49; and we also saw that he had quite an extraordinary gift for the texture of narrative to make a statement about what he thought was important – surprise, reversal and contingency, as well as the unexpected and the stubbornness of events that lay beyond human control. The 1836 essay, which was published in the *London and Westminster Review*,[6] came on the heels of his first volume on American democracy and provided Tocqueville with an interlude during which he could test his ideas on a subject as challenging as the new American experience. The essay lent itself to and seemed to demand the same kind of treatment that gave primacy of place to largely unwilled historical forces. Such was the focus of the first volume of the *Democracy*, and would remain the vision of the second. Tocqueville was intent on digging out hidden general laws, on seeing 1789 "as the culmination of everything that happened before, as 'fulfillment of the times.'"[7] The filiations between what we may call Tocqueville's 1836 prolegomenon to the *L'Ancien Régime* and the *Democracy* are unmistakable.

In another important respect, the filiations are less unproblematic. For

---

[5] Tocqueville to Mill, February 10, 1836, *OC*, VI, pt. 1, p. 307 (my italics). A few months later, when he thought about the next volume of the *Democracy*, Tocqueville told Mill how he worked. As a writer, he was not in the habit of committing himself to a single approach, and he proceeded somewhat "randomly toward [my] goal, allowing [myself] to be carried along genuinely from one inference to another. The result is that so long as the work is not completed, I don't know precisely where I am going and if I ever will get there": Tocqueville to Mill, September 19, 1836, ibid., p. 314.

[6] It may be read in its original French version in *OC*, II, pt. 1, pp. 33–66.

[7] Cf. Arendt, "Understanding and Politics," p. 388, who puts the problem of historical understanding this way.

if there is no doubt that Tocqueville's major purpose was a synthesis – conceived, as it were, from afar – of the "surprising" appearance of democracy as a state of society, he collected and retained a sharp memory of his meetings with the citizens of the countries he visited, and where he made lasting friendships. He was one of the earliest practitioners of oral history. He delighted in his interviews with Americans, and he traveled extensively to acquaint himself with the new country's diverse regions. These are wonderfully documented in the records he left.[8] Yet the personal conversations occupy little if any space in the completed work, as if Tocqueville feared that they would divert him from his purpose of presenting a "scientific" work: the style of a more abstract, more theoretical study demanded a rigorous exclusion of the personal he thought to be inappropriate for an adequate statement on what constituted the realities about societies undergoing change. But he did not see the two styles as mutually exclusive. The abstract mode is far from absent in the *Souvenirs*; and, as we shall see, the appeals to the concrete and particular are not wholly missing from *L'Ancien Régime*. If, however, the latter has few references to personal encounters, Tocqueville, we might say, used his recollection of them as a mental storehouse and distilled them through his own voice. He exploited to the full his "privileged" post as an impartial observer, one who had the added advantage of being able to bring to bear on his assessments of America insights rooted in a broader Western European context, of which the not least important feature was the convulsive force of the French Revolution, with its 1830 incarnation as a reminder of its continuing power.

The chance to repeat the magisterial mode that permeates the first volume of the *Democracy* came when Mill asked him to write on the French Revolution for an English audience. As in America, where he met and spoke with a great number of people, Tocqueville used his personal encounters in England, which he visited briefly in 1833, and again in 1835 for a longer period during which he traveled to Ireland as well, to expatiate publicly on the differences between the French and English aristocracies and the structure and workings of the institutional forms each had fashioned. He thought of both in conjunction with the absence of aristocratic forms and practices in America. It was their long presence in Europe that needed explanation. In England the aristocracy appeared

---

[8] For a sampling, see the *Pléiade edn.*, I. The Beinecke Collection of Tocqueville's papers and letters at Yale University contain many dossiers documenting his contacts. See *OC*, VII, for a selection of the American correspondence. For the best account of Tocqueville's American journey, see James T. Schleifer, *The Making of Tocqueville's "Democracy in America"* (Chapel Hill, 1980). George W. Pierson, *Tocqueville and Beaumont in America* (New York, 1938), remains indispensable.

to him distinctive because of its accessibility to men of wealth, no matter what its sources, permitting it to resist both royal and popular challenges to its social supremacy. It was, moreover, likely that its chances of survival were assured if it were to continue to exploit to its advantage infusions of wealth and the "instincts of the nation, and if it could give in the future, as in the past, material prosperity to the inferior classes." Since the "people" everywhere were incapable of making revolutions on the basis of their own strength, the English privileged classes realized the wisdom of remaining open to those who had acquired status, rather than relying on the presumed strengths of inherited status. Would this be the case as the expansion of wealth became such as to enlarge the mobile classes with the same wish to gratify their hunger for status? Could aristocracy in England remain adaptable, enabling it to absorb the democratic urge to equality, and to preserve and extend its own traditions of political liberty?[9]

Past English experiences of revolution were but one form of a wide-spread European revolution or, as he also put it, the "idea" of revolution assumes different forms – forms, in the English case, determined by the particular nature of their *moeurs*, customs and laws. The English borrowed French ideas at different times in the past, but cast them in their own mold; they "seek to assure their triumph and to apply them in their own way." Tocqueville made it clear that the nature of inequality had to be perceived before a full understanding of the irrepressible force of equality in France was possible. Once the differing paths followed by aristocratic societies became evident, it would be possible to posit general laws of social development and thus contribute to historical explanation. He stated these convictions in the original French opening of the *Essai*. They did not appear in the translation. The project Tocqueville had in mind was the discovery of the sources of, and the movements leading to, the extinction of inequality in 1789. The project was not focused on what was a very different phenomenon in America, where a sea change had occurred, making possible the *sui generis*-like appearance of equality: America did not need a revolution to find itself in a social condition of equality.

The uniquely American origins are not taken up in his 1836 essay; rather he deals with the impulse to end the conditions of inequality in aristocratic Europe. Secondly, by identifying the voluntary, revolutionary act in France ending inequality as "the new science," Tocqueville envisaged this new science not only as a willed act, but in and through that very act the living and purposeful expression of general laws. The revolutionaries insisted on the universal nature of truth, bounded neither by time

[9] *Pléiade edn.*, I, pp. 441–44.

nor space, and equated it with their understanding of science – as a stage in the continuing fulfillment of knowledge about the human condition. In his opinion, they were the first to exploit the philosophical method and they universalized it. In their hands that method became the science that universalized truth. They put themselves at the head of two great revolutions – political and philosophical. France incarnated both. It had not, however, sown the germs of revolution affecting all of Europe; it had set in motion those that were already there in embryo: "France has not been the God that creates, but the sun's ray that brings forth blossoms."[10] Tocqueville's teleology dictated the belief that liberty's only chance of survival rested on understanding the human urge to gain social equality, that is, when the ethos of inequality lost its support from aspiring classes which saw themselves prevented from escaping their fate in a general lottery of inequalities. The French then turned to give the impulse toward equality the dignity of a philosophy with universal claims, and, even more importantly, saw it as a scientific method. The significance of the Revolution was instinctively known by most observers, but Tocqueville wanted to provide it with a historical explanation. Using the image of a chain of time, binding one century to another, which was one of his favorite metaphors, Tocqueville wrote:

Invisible but almost all-powerful links connect the ideas of one century to those of the century preceding it, just as they connect the tastes of sons to the inclinations of fathers. One generation likes to declare war on the generations that came before it, [but] it is easier to make war against them than to [avoid] resembling them. It would therefore be hard to know how to speak of one nation at a given point in its history, without saying what it was a half-century earlier. This is especially necessary when it is a question of a people who, over the past fifty years, have been prey to almost continuous revolutions. Foreigners . . . are aware only of the great changes that took place in the bosom of this people, but they do not know what parts of their former condition have been abandoned, and what others have been preserved in the sphere of vicissitudes [experienced] over so long a time.[11]

From these remarks, Tocqueville moved rapidly to an examination of the origins and different shapes of European aristocracy, specifically its manifestations in France and England. His observations on the peculiarity of the notions and realities of the English nobility and gentry permitted him to assess and accentuate the differences between each and the French *noblesse*. As Tocqueville saw it, the term aristocracy in England, in its most common usage, was meant to include all of society's superior classes, and was not identical with the legal and societal complexity of the

---

[10] The suppressed passage appears in "Etat social et politique de la France," *OC*, II, pt. 1, pp. 33–34.   [11] Ibid., pp. 35–36.

French *noblesse*. The English aristocracy was a body with a sense of its superiority, but nonetheless did not shut itself off from the general population as did the French *noblesse*. Neither George Grote nor Mill felt as generously disposed toward their own aristocrats. The first told Beaumont that his book on Ireland greatly overestimated "the good workings of the aristocracy in England."[12] And Mill also told Beaumont that he had been "too favorable to the English aristocracy," but went on to say that his impression might have been due to the book's contrast with Ireland, "where all the natural evil tendencies of our institutions are so much aggravated."[13] Doubtless Tocqueville knew about his English friends' critique of their own superior classes. This did not deter him from pressing what for him was the key difference between the two aristocracies. The French *noblesse* was indeed an aristocratic body, but it did not constitute the aristocracy of the nation, since, broadly speaking, there were classes as enlightened, as rich and almost as influential as the *noblesse*, and who in very large measure were appropriating for themselves an aristocratic self-image. "The French *noblesse* was thus to the English aristocracy, such as it exists in our day, what the *species* is to the *genus;* it formed a *caste*, and not an aristocracy. In that respect, it resembled all the *noblesses* on the continent."[14]

The transformation of the French aristocracy into a caste, a term Tocqueville was to use frequently in the concluding volume of *Democracy*, and again in *L'Ancien Régime*, is a crucial leitmotif by means of which he elaborated his understanding of the long-term causes of the Revolution. It was the failure to make room for and to incorporate all classes claiming superiority in the aristocracy by various but controlled standards that led the French *noblesse* to take on some of the features of a caste. By its non-porous nature, a caste lives with its gaze turned inward; it appeals to its genetic particularity to justify its unique biological, and thus its mental and social, exclusivity. Blood-right was its shield. But unlike castes elsewhere, as in India, it was not possible in France to save the caste totally from "pollution." The most extraordinary mental feats were employed to accommodate a social hierarchy outside the proper limits of the *noblesse*, who devised a far from perfect set of mechanisms to strengthen boundaries within the *noblesse*. The various grades of nobility (those that had access, but no full claims, to becoming part of the original caste) found a temporary but unsatisfactory solution to the impasses facing them. Some of them found it advantageous to consolidate their own position, burying

[12] Grote to Beaumont, August 1, 1839, *BYT*, C.I.e.
[13] Mill to Beaumont, October 18, 1839, ibid.
[14] "Etat social et politique de la France," p. 37 (italics in the original).

their feelings of resentment by ignoring the caste's pretensions when they could, especially when they achieved high positions in the state or could impress by their vast landed fortunes. But these constituted a tiny group in the upper ranks. The greatest number lived at the lower margins of the *noblesse*. They retained only the simulacra of power – those of a ceremonial nature – for even their fiscal privileges were not safe from a state that was expanding its demands over the country's human and natural resources. Like their betters, they devised grounds for exclusivity, asserting their own superiority against those even further below them in the social scale. In the process, they tried to give the appearance of feeling closer to those above them.

The ethos of the *noblesse*, of the *gentilhomme*, was the old régime's social glue. It came unstuck, Tocqueville argued, as a result of three developments. The first was the mobility of wealth that actually penetrated the caste structure, helping to form, *in potentia*, as it were, "a democratic body sheathed in the rights of an aristocracy vis-à-vis the other classes."[15] The caste's aversion to commercial wealth was not unbreachable, as when it appropriated the new capital in one form or another from the Third Estate to make it part of an existing patrimony founded on the exploitation of the land. The second was the caste's resistance to any attacks on its exclusivity. It kept the powerful elements of the Third Estate at a distance and in fact alienated them. The caste saw intermarriage as a concession, never as a right. As the caste was losing its preeminence in real terms, the Third Estate was gaining more and more of the qualities that, in its view, should have entitled it to full membership among the families that for centuries had set the psychosocial tone of the nation and sanctioned its goals. The caste, finally, began to lose its raison d'être on other grounds as well. It could no longer claim realistically that it protected the servile and non-servile laboring classes on the land; the latter knew that it was the chief source of their impoverishment and oppression.

Tocqueville did not neglect the caste's inner social and economic divisions, as well as the shocks its collective psyche had to absorb from outside forces, leading it each time to rally its forces to defend itself. The passages in which he essays a mental portrait of the caste perhaps explain better than any strictly economic or social analysis the inner dynamic of its defenses and its self-doubt, which, he believed, led in time to suicide by default. Critical though he was of the *noblesse*'s inability to look outward, he wished to steer his course away from gratuitous judgment, moral or otherwise. A far more valuable form of judgment, he argued, was to imagine the viewpoint of one who acts in a particular way.

[15] Ibid., p. 44.

To exercise historical imagination with any success meant eschewing rigorously the idea of certainty in essaying the psychosocial substrata of order and change. "It is almost as dangerous for human morality to despise a prejudice because it is obstructive as to abandon a true idea because it is dangerous. The nobles at first were mistaken to believe that they were debasing themselves by marrying the daughters of commoners; and in the end, having this belief, perhaps their greater mistake was to marry them."[16] The strong implication was that an aristocracy can indeed feel secure under certain conditions. In Europe, or at least in France, a caste-like aristocracy did come into being; but being neither a true caste, nor an aristocracy with a more flexible ethos, as in England, it was doomed.

Tocqueville was ever a thinker with a consuming interest in the psychological and social dynamics of what, at any point in history, nourished the ethos of classes or more restricted social groups. From his early days when he was still thinking of the law as a career, the question of honor and shame arose in the explanation he gave for the persistence of dueling. He saw it as a socially barbarous, but an emotionally powerful, means of preserving the first and dealing with the second.[17] The elaborate ceremonies surrounding honor and its chronic vulnerabilities were emblematic of and reinforced the social conventions of the *noblesse*. Recourse to the courts to seek amends and retribution in the form of a cash settlement for a man whose honor had been damaged fell far short of justice. It was not enough, because it failed to respond to the stresses of heightened human instincts. Man enters society, Tocqueville argued, by concluding a contract with his fellow men, lending his individual power to, and expecting in return the protection of, society's considerable solidifying powers. But what should be said of a society that refuses to acknowledge the instincts of vengeance? Isn't the man whose honor has been impugned more unfortunate than guilty for choosing to restore it? Should such a person be punished for taking steps to repair his feelings of loss? Let divine justice determine the rights and wrongs of dueling.[18] Legislation to restrict it might unintentionally strengthen it. Why so? Because human beings are made of flesh and pride, and are therefore weak. Virtue and honor have, to be sure, presided over human societies of all kinds. Virtue, simple and natural like the truth, calm and tranquil like force, "existed in and for itself: its body is earth-bound, its head, sky-bound, it is the genius of small republics and moderate states.

---

[16] Ibid., p. 42.
[17] "Discours de rentrée des tribunaux sur le duel," [début novembre 1828?], *OC*, XVI, pp. 49–64.   [18] Ibid., pp. 57–58.

It is virtue that guided the chariot of Cincinnatus on the morrow of his triumph; in a word . . . it is genius."[19]

Tocqueville could not quite bring himself to look at virtue as coolly as some of the de-moralizing philosophers of the eighteenth century. It remained an ideal, and was not to be dismissed. In the absence of virtue, honor was heaven's greatest gift to men. Like virtue, it loved the good, but its dynamic was far different. For those who lived by the commands of honor, "Shame is feared more than evil. Public opinion is its life, and while simple virtue may be satisfied by a sense of inner approbation, peacefully awaiting the time when the future will recognize its power, honor is almost tempted to lose its self-confidence as soon as one gives up believing in it."[20] Moreover, just as the individual who lived by the aristocratic ethos might be psychically injured by his loss of honor, states might also perish if care were not taken to give honor its due in that part of the community from which the state drew much of its raison d'être. To be sure, the monarchy under Louis XIV took decisive steps to strengthen its monopoly of force and to reduce the privileges of the *noblesse*, including its use of the duel to maintain honor. The monarchy thus undermined one of the primary values of the aristocracy, yet not so thoroughly as to destroy it completely for it could neither dispense with it, nor was it averse to the preservation of honor both as a psychic and practical asset. Tocqueville recognized that such considerations lay behind the monarchy's decision to give the marshals of France, and not the ordinary courts, the duty to hear arguments from aggrieved persons. The question of honor and shame had not been put to one side by the Revolution; the *noblesse* lived by the dictates of both, but so did, in other ways, democratic societies, which Tocqueville was to specify in the second volume of the *Democracy*, and again, when he reached his most mature views on their power in the society of the *ancien régime*.[21]

Thus the emotional power of guarding honor and avoiding shame keep aristocratic societies intact, but by the same token the psychic demands may assume an exaggerated force and produce caste-like reflexes in the face of challenges that cannot be met pragmatically. Aristocracies become

---

[19] Ibid., p. 62. Tocqueville doubtless relied on Montesquieu's discussion of virtue and honor; see *De l'Esprit des lois*, in *Oeuvres complètes de Montesquieu*, ed. Roger Caillois, 2 vols. (Paris, 1949–51), I, book 3, chap. 6, and book 19, chap. 5. There is also a strong resemblance between Tocqueville's concept of honor and Adam Smith's ideas in *The Theory of Moral Sentiments* (Indianapolis, 1976). See chap. 6 below for a fuller discussion.

[20] *OC*, XVI, p. 63.

[21] For a refreshing study that questions the idea that shame and guilt cultures induced totally distinct notions of moral conduct, neither of which would be understood by people living in one or other of the cultures, see Bernard Williams, *Shame and Necessity* (Berkeley, Los Angeles and London, 1993).

castes to resist all change; and when they cannot maintain the resistance to change they fail to survive. To remain healthy, aristocracies may in fact not have to give up all inequalities. It is the nature of specific inequalities that human beings, who are its victims, find unendurable. If persons can continue to believe that they have a chance of becoming a part of the élite, they will tend not to question its rights, however much those rights are stretched. In fact the very vices of aristocracy (excluding its fall into caste-like postures) constitute its strength. It scarcely matters if the goal is the certainty of a small success rather than the possibility of making a great fortune. The more the difficulty of attaining the goal is increased, the less there is to fear from diminishing the chances of reaching it. However, the aristocracy's very divisions ensured that there could not be agreement on how best to ensure that inequality could be preserved. Tocqueville thought that the principle of equality would not have made progress but for these very specific weaknesses of the régime of privileges, and not only because the desire for equality was a deeply felt human need.

Tocqueville struggled to make a highly original point. The dysfunctional character of the French aristocracy unmasked its injustice, not the other way round. Equality came to be seen as a good not because of its innate moral superiority, but only when the good that inequality predicated failed to answer new needs. In short, Tocqueville did not see equality as an absolute good. "The Third Estate was one part of the aristocracy in revolt against the other, and it [was] constrained to profess the general idea of equality in order to combat the particular idea of inequality imposed upon it."[22] Egalitarian ideas thus found their home within and not outside the régime of privileges, and they gained force as they came to be viewed as an emanation of "the natural order of things."[23] In their propagation, individuals with literary talent took the lead, and they came from both aristocratic and plebeian ranks. They found in literature "a kind of imaginary democracy, where each individual relied only on his natural talents."[24] There they found a welcome relief from a losing struggle to participate in a political régime from which they had been effectively excluded by a professional bureaucracy.

The democratic tendencies born in the bosom of the old society, leading to the great political revolution, did not appear overnight. In addition to the struggles among the ranks of the aristocracy, changes in the way the sources of wealth were regarded were instrumental in altering the contours of French society. Tocqueville advanced the theory that the hunger for land, the ownership of which was seen as a value conferring honor and status, in small or large bits, and the need to satisfy degrees of

---

[22] "Etat social et politique de la France," p. 47.   [23] Ibid.   [24] Ibid., p. 49.

magnificence within the fragmented class of the privileged, created a fit that answered the needs of both. Land exchanged hands, but did not end inequalities. Tocqueville, on the lookout for general laws, theorized on the changing nature of wealth in the nation. The new wealth did not, however, shift the balance toward the commercial sector. Something more subtle, but no less dramatic, was happening. "The inequality [derived] from mobile wealth makes individuals wealthy, the inequality [derived] from land makes families opulent; it [inequality] links the rich from both groups, and between them the inequalities [of both forms of wealth] create a small group of people in the state, [living] apart [from the nation], but which always happens to obtain a certain power over it in the middle of which it is placed. It is precisely these things that harm a democratic government most."[25] The elliptical tone was Tocqueville's way of saying that democratic government and the particular nature of French inequality became incompatible.

Tocqueville gave a key role to the lawyers who were as important to the monarchy as they would become in creating a democratic administration in France. He used them – but this time more explicitly than in his analysis of changing patterns of wealth – to illustrate his belief that general laws govern all societies. Lawyers were to be found everywhere, ensuring that political bodies continued to function, no matter what their ideology. Borrowing from Cuvier the idea that all organized bodies exhibit the principle of a necessary relation among their parts, he concluded that, on the basis of such a principle, human beings are inclined to reconstruct the whole whenever any part is detached or is found to be missing. He told Beaumont that Cuvier's study on antediluvian animals had inspired his use of "philosophical deductions or analogies."[26] Cuvier's impression on Tocqueville remained with him throughout his life. In 1855 he was still using paleontology as an analogy for uncovering the buried sources of revolution.[27] Cuvier's law served as a successful example of the kind of inquiry capable of inspiring the search for general laws governing everything.[28] In all civilized societies from the time records were kept, kings and legists worked together, the first to command obedience, the second to gain the voluntary obedience of the ruled. Thus rulers without lawyers disrupt the organized body of the state.[29] With them, the state finds its completion.

[25] Ibid., p. 52.   [26] Tocqueville to Beaumont, November 22, 1836, OC, VIII, pt. 1, p. 175.
[27] Tocqueville to Mrs. Grote, November 22, 1855, Beaumont edn., VI, p. 243.
[28] In 1837, as he was working on chapter 14 of part 3 of the second volume of the Democracy, his notes reveal that Cuvier was on his mind when he proposed an analogy between the faculties making up moral man and the parts constituting his physiological being. See Nolla edn., II, p. 182, note c.   [29] "Etat social et politique de France," p. 58.

A third general law Tocqueville located in his perception of the long-term trends toward centralization. Democracy in France appropriated the centralizing tendencies of the monarchy and, with the propensities of a citizenry determined to defend equality, made centralization an even more imposing force. In the monarchy the lawyers acted as the crown's agents to keep the privileged orders in check. Once democracy was established they became in a sense its voice. By serving the royal power, they followed their own nature; they did the same when they consulted the interests of the class which they accidentally found themselves leading as France turned toward democracy.

Tocqueville's vision of the emergence of liberty from its origins in feudal society to its forms in democracies was not without its aura of historical generalization either. As the monarchy's institutions became more despotic, the practices of liberty were increasingly found in *moeurs* – in everyday exchanges of sociability – and cherished in individual hearts. Through these *moeurs*, subjects of the state in the seventeenth century could in fact often show more resistance to the crown and its institutions than through the laws on which citizens of free countries could base their opposition. Nations which have always been independent, as well as nations that have achieved independence, cannot grasp how such *moeurs* work. To prove this assertion, Tocqueville contrasted two forms of liberty. Aristocratic liberty that was individually won gave it a singularly extraordinary power. The modern democratic idea of liberty, which for Tocqueville was the right notion, was based on the conviction that all human beings, endowed with the natural intelligence to direct their own lives, bring with them from birth an equal and imprescriptible right to autonomy. Such a notion takes on power from the moment people believe that they have absolute control over their own lives. Then they will tend to believe that "the sovereign will" – the term Tocqueville employed – is only an emanation of the union of the wills of everyone.[30] Political obedience now becomes obedience to one's self and replaces the foundations of political morality in which aristocratic liberties gained their power from the institutions justifying inequalities. The first Napoleon's power he ascribed to the failure of democratic individualism to found viable political institutions ensuring liberty and a common goal. Tocqueville referred to the emergence of a general theory of democratic liberty, and, in the spirit of his very opening remarks on how traces of the ethos of one political culture may be found in transmuted form in another, he linked the new theory to the older but still vital sense of independence that was the patrimony of the few under the Old Régime.

---

[30] Ibid., p. 62.

Tocqueville easily discerned that the taste for this kind of liberty was disseminated in the literature of the day rather than through actions, by individual not collective efforts, by an opposition often immature and irrational, rarely, if ever, serious and systematic. In this way opinion was shaped. At this point, Tocqueville made a distinction between opinion's critical function and its uncritical reception. The ensuing confusion, which he implied plagued public perceptions, resulted from identifying the second with the first. Opinion was by turns strong and weak, all-powerful and elusive, but at all times disorderly, capricious, indefinable. It was "a body without organs; a shadow of popular sovereignty rather than of the sovereignty of the people itself." It could not have been otherwise in the absence of free institutions. And, doubtless thinking of the dangers to liberty in his own day, he spoke of the necessity of free institutions as a safeguard against the lassitude of populations, too complacent to ask if liberty could be lost by default.[31]

With his conclusion, Tocqueville left his English readers with a historical paradox that he was to take up again more trenchantly in the 1850s. For now, he was more aphoristic. However novel the Revolution appeared to be, it had introduced only new forms and had changed nothing in principle. "All the Revolution accomplished could have been achieved, I don't doubt, without it; it was only a violent and rapid process by which the political conditions were adapted to the social ones, the facts to ideas and the laws to *moeurs*."[32] The vital question was the future of liberty. All forms of government were, he told Reeve, more or less perfect means of satisfying humanity's need to have it (even if the species did not always know that without liberty it would cease to be fully human). He was a partisan neither of aristocracy nor of democracy. He had no political illusions. He did not hate nor love aristocracy and felt confident that he could judge it with some detachment. Democracy had not harmed him personally. He was, he felt, equally distant from the emotions each could generate to enable him to think about both with impartiality.[33]

From revolutionary equality to revolutionary despotism

One of his first thoughts in 1850, on completion of his *Souvenirs* and fourteen years after his 1836 schematic essay, was to avoid another story of the Revolution. A reinterpretation of the history of the First Empire seemed like a better point of departure:

[31] Ibid., p. 64.   [32] Ibid., pp. 65–66.
[33] Tocqueville to Reeve, March 22, 1837, *OC*, VI, pp. 37–38.

I had often thought of the Empire, that singular act of the drama, which has still not achieved its dénouement, that is called the French Revolution. But I had always been disheartened by the sight of insurmountable obstacles and especially by the thought that I would appear to be wishing to remake famous books. But, this time, the subject has appeared to me in a new form which seems to me to render it more accessible. I have thought it was not necessary to undertake the history of the Empire, but to seek to demonstrate and to make understandable the cause, the character, the compass of great events that formed the principal links of the chain of that period . . . The facts would be, as it were, only the solid and continuous foundation which would form a support *for all the ideas that I have kept in my head*, not only on that epoch but on the one that came before it and the one that followed it, [and the facts would also act as a support for understanding] the character, the extraordinary man, who filled that epoch, the direction he gave to the French Revolution, to the nation's fortune and to the destiny of all of Europe.[34]

He made a rough sketch of the themes for such a work at Sorrento.[35] Then at the end of 1851, more than a year after he left office, Louis-Napoleon's successful coup d'état rekindled Tocqueville's fascination with the first Napoleon. During 1852, he worked on the post-Thermidorian period trying to put his finger on the state of the French mind after the Terror and the failure of the Directory's efforts to establish legitimate roots for its authority. Only when this project was completed would it be possible, he concluded, to tackle the exact moments of Bonaparte's accession to power. What he knew from the beginning was that, though analogies could be drawn between the conditions of 1798–99 and 1848–51, the two Napoleons were hardly comparable. They were both extraordinary, but in very different ways. Tocqueville did not underestimate Louis-Napoleon's ambition, but it was not matched by genius. Louis-Napoleon was extraordinary "through the circumstances which had combined to raise his mediocrity to so high a level."[36] Left enveloped in mystery was how "the worst plays are those which succeed best. If Louis-Napoleon had been a wise man, or a man of genius, he would never have become president of the Republic."[37] The first Napoleon had both the ambition and the genius, Tocqueville had no doubt, and in addition produced a better play, but a play that nonetheless ended in disaster and tragedy. The first Napoleon attracted Tocqueville's grudging admiration; the second attracted his contempt.

The first Napoleon had, he noted in 1842, a mixed record as a military commander. His military exploits were less impressive than the appalling

---

[34] Tocqueville to Beaumont, December 26, 1850, *OC*, VIII, pt. 2, pp. 343–44 (my italics).
[35] *OC*, II, pt. 2, pp. 301–04.   [36] *OC*, XII, p. 229.   [37] Ibid., p. 212.

number of dead left on the battlefields of Europe,[38] and far less important than his consolidation of the centralized administrative state. The first indications that Tocqueville was thinking along these lines appeared earlier in *Democracy in America*, when he wrote about the ease with which Napoleon's genius not only brought to perfection the Convention's concentration of powers "to a single point," but also the longer-term tendencies in which "our *moeurs* and laws had always run together simultaneously toward the establishment of an intelligent and enlightened despotism."[39] Toward the end of the first volume of the *Democracy*, his notes include the striking idea that, if Napoleon had succeeded Louis XVI he would have found a strong royal power, but one upon which the restraints present in the *ancien régime* might have acted as a force against his will to gain unchallenged power. As representative of the people, the powers he could call on had become much more encompassing than any available to the governments of the Old Régime.[40] But there was no point in blaming or praising Napoleon. He simply inherited the administrative powers; he could not reject them once they had been expanded.[41]

Tocqueville found it difficult to reach a firm position on the might-have-beens or how to detach himself from his preferences when they did not coincide with historical forces. These problems deeply affected his *métier* as historian. The power of individuals in shaping events appeared to be greater, he said in the *Democracy*, in non-egalitarian societies; it was altogether much less visible in democracies. How should Napoleon be viewed? People can have their destinies modified or changed by the accidental influence of a powerful man, like Napoleon; or by a natural disaster; or by a military battle. It is possible to deny the influence of individuals and to believe in accidents. In democratic societies individual influences are infinitely less important than accidents, but the impact of accidents is common to both aristocratic and democratic societies. Commenting on what he believed to be the tendency in his own generation, he said that modern historians claimed that not only people, but accidents as well, have no power to disturb the chain of antecedent causes leading to the fall of societies. Tocqueville, siding uneasily with modern historians, nevertheless went behind the prevailing but facile distinction between the actions of individuals and accidents, and suggested that, if the term accident were to be taken at face value, the fact was that, as soon as the origins of accidents were sought, one was always driven back to individual actions. Most modern historians avoided the labyrinth they

---

[38] Tocqueville expressed his horror in notes for the inaugural address to the Académie française in 1842, "Discours de M. de Tocqueville," *OC*, XVI, p. 252, note 3.
[39] *Nolla edn.*, I, pp. 71–72.   [40] Ibid., p. 304.   [41] Ibid., II, pp. 246–47.

would have been forced to enter if they really bent their minds "to perceive clearly and to bring sufficiently to light the influence of individuals." They preferred instead to speak of race, nature or the spirit of civilization, "grand words that I cannot hear uttered without involuntarily recalling the horror of the void that was attributed to nature before the discovery of the weight of air." Tocqueville said that there was some inconsistency in their explanation, stemming from their practice of resorting to "grand words" to support badly conceived general reasons. "My comparison [nature's horror of a vacuum]" he wrote, "does not apply only to the latter [improperly thought-out general reasons], because the *weight of the air* is a general cause, as well as being *the abhorrence of a vacuum*."[42]

In 1842, when Tocqueville resumed these questions,[43] he placed Napoleon even more pointedly at their center. Napoleon appeared on the scene after the destructive work of a revolution which seemed to legitimize all the new laws. The tempest had produced conflicting results. It had first exhilarated, then exhausted, the people. A passion for liberty had been one of its starting points, but the object of that passion had turned to conquest. A new society had been created, even more effective and stronger than the society that had been destroyed, but few had grasped how that power had come into being and how long it would last. People wanted a stable social order to ensure their gains. Napoleon's genius lay in his instinct for discovering the sources of the deep social and psychological unease and finding in himself the resources to relieve it. But all these were accidental, not deep and permanent causes, Tocqueville added, of the movement of history. In the first place, he denied that despotism was a necessary outcome of the process he was describing: "*Necessary* despotism, I deny it. In a certain measure, *yes*. To the degree that it was [necessary] *no*. I am an enemy of immoral necessities."[44] Secondly, an explanation of despotism fell short if it failed to take account of its modern sources in the revolutionary mind. The eighteenth century and the Revolution had produced a taste for liberty, but had also disposed men toward obedience. How did this come about? He claimed that it was not necessary to show that the Revolution had moved people toward independence and anarchy – an indisputable facet of the Revolution – nor did he wish to deny the benefits of the Revolution (freedom of religion, legal equality, revisions to the penal code, forms of criminal justice and other changes).

Instead, the other side of the changes had to be demonstrated, as

---

[42] Ibid., pp. 83–84 and notes f and g. The emphasis is Tocqueville's.
[43] In his inaugural speech to the Académie française, *OC*, XVI, pp. 251–69.
[44] Ibid., p. 259, note a.

Tocqueville also made clear in his 1842 sketch. Despotism grew out of modern philosophy's stress on the power of the individual reasoning mind to act as its own arbiter with the consequence that it isolated rather than united individuals.[45] What was to be feared therefore was that "power would come to dominate all, not because it had its source in public opinion, but because public opinion did not exist."[46] What did he mean by this curious affirmation? By interpreting the Revolution as a confluence – "the idea of centralization and popular sovereignty were born on the same day" – he theorized the existence of a close and necessary fit between them.[47] Popular sovereignty came into existence with a revolution that had produced a society of equal individuals; but democratic sovereignty had not created a workable political society. Instead each particular interest prevailed over the general interest. Political sects multiplied, each an agglomeration of individual interests in defense of single goals. All tended to exploit their individual wishes to gain possession of the social power, "and to make of each citizen less than a man"[48] – the very antithesis of a civil society of free peoples. "Among free peoples, government is conducted only through [the agency] of parties, or rather government is the party which possesses power. Thus government is much more powerful, persevering, farsighted and strong when more compact and permanent parties exist within its bosom."[49] Tocqueville pointed an accusing finger at the defects of the representative system and the irresponsibility of the party system in the last years of the July Monarchy.

Individualism, as Tocqueville conceived it first in its democratic forms in the *Democracy*, produced the opposite results. The idea has decided Rousseauian resonances, and Tocqueville, without attributing it to Rousseau, may indeed have had him in mind when he stated, "I believe firmly that it lies with our contemporaries to be great as well as prosperous; but on condition of remaining free. Only a condition of liberty can elicit those powerful common emotions which can transport . . . human souls to places outside of themselves; only liberty can create variety in the midst of a uniformity of conditions and the monotony of our *moeurs*; only liberty can divert our minds from petty thoughts and elevate the goals of our desires."[50] In 1842, when he made these remarks, Tocqueville moved toward but stopped short of fully arguing one of the fundamental theses of *L'Ancien Régime*, namely, that the abstract ideas of the men of letters contained, as if in a chain, the embryo of despotism. For the time being,

---

[45] Ibid., pp. 259, 262–63. The idea echoes his strong condemnation of individualism in the *Democracy*, Nolla edn., II, pp. 96–98.   [46] *OC*, XVI, p. 260.   [47] Ibid., p. 262.
[48] Ibid.   [49] Ibid., p. 260.   [50] Ibid., pp. 266–67.

he saw Napoleon as the legitimate offspring of a conception of popular sovereignty that readily submitted to the requirements of an unreflective individualism.

What did Napoleon do with his prize? Tocqueville took this problem to heart in 1846 when he discussed the development of administrative centralization under the Empire at the Académie des Sciences Morales et Politiques.[51] While four years earlier the politics of the revolutionary impulse seemed of primary importance, he now took the view that the Constituent Assembly's administrative innovations, not the political institutions that it introduced, were truly audacious and original. It had created the model for a modern way of governing in a world rocked by revolution, whether initiated from above or below through the aegis of political ideas or more often under the cover of civil laws.[52] The influence of these administrative changes on French ideas, customs, actions and *moeurs* was more powerful than any political changes. What was radically new in the French Revolution therefore was the methodical order of an administrative machine presiding over the rigorous and logical chain of command uniting all of its parts in a single body. Napoleon inherited the innovations, but he transformed the original ideas that inspired them. Instead of executive councils, single agents dependent on, and responsible to, the central power were appointed; before Napoleon's revisions, the councils had been elected, but no longer. Even the absolute monarchs had not dared to codify such a practice as a general principle. "Napoleon succeeded in appropriating this vast machine that had been conceived and molded by liberty [to meet] the needs of absolute power."[53] The existence of councils, placed alongside the agents of the central power – whether prefects, subprefects or mayors – did not alter the substance of the administrative machine, since the center exercised control over all facets of life.

To a revolution so total must be given the credit for the work of the Constituent Assembly's administrative innovation. However ingenious the innovators proved to be, they would have achieved little if the ground had not been cleared for them in advance.[54] These sweeping changes were the surprising features of the Revolution. Tocqueville told the Académie that "the revolution . . . rendered all these things [the administrative changes] not only practicable, but easy and necessary; this unprecedented revolution . . . was able to reverse all the small or great powers that had existed up to that point; to abolish all individual rights,

[51] "Rapport fait à l'Académie des Sciences Morales et Politiques (1846) sur le livre de M. Macarel, intitulé: *Cours de droit administratif*," *OC*, XVI, pp. 185–98.   [52] Ibid., p. 196.
[53] Ibid., p. 188.   [54] Ibid., p. 189, note a.

all local freedoms, and all individual prerogatives; and to extinguish almost all the differences that had separated citizens and recognized the singularity of citizens so that one was forced to recreate with one fell swoop and according to one plan the entire system of public administration."[55] A uniform body of administrative law had come into being that touched the lives of everyone without exception. Tocqueville spoke about the beginnings of modern bureaucracy, more far-reaching, in his opinion, than the introduction of modern democracy. Such developments demanded the most serious attention, and could only be grasped if people who understood administrative law and those who wrote political treatises worked together to understand how these neighboring but distinct questions were related. Unless these questions were dealt with, liberty would continue to suffer irreparable blows.

When Louis-Napoleon assumed full power, changing the Constitution of the Second Republic to legitimize it, Tocqueville looked more closely at the immediate historical events culminating in Brumaire. In his notes on the event, Tocqueville made it clear that an inspection of the record would disclose the fact that Bonaparte did not gain his objectives with as much ease as he had previously believed, and that, in fact, the degree of despotism, as it took root, was not a foregone conclusion – a point previously made in the *Democracy* when he inveighed against the idea of despotism as the necessary sequel of the Revolution. Despite his military genius, Napoleon was unable to achieve the needed revisions to the Constitution of the Year III without the independent efforts of key republicans, such as Cabanis and Boulay de la Meurthe, to bestow greater powers on the executive arm of government. These were intended not only to reduce the reach of the legislative branch, but to curtail the popular will. Common to both transfers of power was the unpardonable sin of injuring liberty, already weakened by the Revolution.

Tocqueville chided Boulay de la Meurthe and Cabanis for not suspecting that the measures they supported contained the seeds that would germinate into a new kind of despotism.[56] Tocqueville had given much thought to the democratic forms of despotism in the second volume of the *Democracy*, where he enunciated what came to be for him a general law. "A nation that asks nothing of its government but the maintenance of order is already a slave at heart, the slave of its well-being, awaiting only the hand that will bind it."[57] The documents he consulted for information on the 1799 coup were, he judged, composed in a turgid and twisted style, *violent à froid*. The so-called radical Jacobin plot against the Republic was a transparent invention. The men who had seized power

---

[55] Ibid., pp. 195–96.   [56] *OC*, II, pt. 2, pp. 311–12.   [57] *Nolla edn.*, II, p. 128.

used one of the oldest tricks in the world: they justified their actions by claiming superior wisdom and benevolent intentions. What he had not known until he read the available records was that the deputies from both Councils, the lower and upper bodies of the legislature, set up by the Constitution of the Year III, had convinced themselves that they were not the victims of a forced dissolution, but the fortunate recipients of a timely restoration of order. He read Cabanis's first speech as the response of a man accustomed to, but weary of, living in an atmosphere of crisis. At the same time, he implied that Cabanis could not have known that military intervention would lead to the end of representative government. Again the law of unintended consequences was called on as an explanation of intersecting but conflicting agendas.

It is not entirely surprising that Tocqueville tempered his criticism of Cabanis. Though he defended his own positive response to the military suppression of the June 1848 insurgents on the grounds that France faced a threat to order from the combined efforts of reincarnated Jacobins and socialists of varying stripe, there were, in their actions, some things he could not take that seriously, as may be recalled from his characterization of them as pathetic and semi-comic actors with a political vision that mimicked the worst excesses of the first Revolution. It was only some time after the second Napoleon was firmly in power as head of the Second Empire that Tocqueville conceded that the new government was keeping alive the fear of a Jacobin and socialist menace to rally the middle classes and the better-off peasants.

Tocqueville turned toward Cabanis as a figure who, across the generations, may have appealed to him as an early proponent of liberal ideas. Tocqueville, as much as Cabanis, expressed deep uncertainties about the full exercise of the democratic will when it appeared to put liberty in jeopardy. However, Tocqueville tended to support democracy as the expression of an irrepressible power in the modern world. He was, we may infer, much testier about other parts of Cabanis's speech, especially those that failed to recognize the vitality during the *ancien régime* of local initiatives and regional liberties, or those that showed scant appreciation of the *parlements'* opposition to the crown. *L'Ancien Régime* would see a further development of the theme of the survival of liberties in the last decades of prerevolutionary France. What he saw, and felt that Cabanis had failed to appreciate, was that the coup of Brumaire in 1799 was a reenactment, though on a more terrifying scale, of the power of the servants of the modern despotic state to impose their will, and thus to limit liberty.

Cabanis's brief allusions in his Brumaire speech to the failure of the Greeks and Romans to preserve their freedom were taken up by

Tocqueville, who expected to make use of them in his analysis of the origins of the First Empire.[58] He distinguished between the conditions that gave rise to it and to the Roman Empire. The empire in Rome, he argued, preserved democratic language to conceal its plunge into despotism. "It retained names, while doing away with things," he said, anticipating modern critiques on the slipperiness of representation. In France, the initiation of an ostensibly more mature period in politics under the First Empire obscured the fact that it actually constituted the restoration of a historic attachment to arbitrary forms of government. Both the governments of the Napoleonic and the Roman régimes promoted some of the superficial and questionable practices of democratic equality, such as finding the means to satisfy popular envy, while concealing the extent to which they also sanctioned an equality of servitude. Anyone who had this shallow understanding of democracy was ignorant of the value of the words he was using or, even worse, cynically refused to give them any value. The language of the Revolution, Tocqueville said, might be studied in certain respects and in certain conditions as an instrument of deception.

The similarities between the founding and justification of the two empires were striking. In each, a society of isolated individuals faced the sovereign whose power was totally concentrated, not shared. The degraded people of France had achieved "equality under a master, [and it is] more precious [to them] than equality before the law . . . and [this kind of equality] allows permanent social inequalities to continue." He closed his notes on the analogies between the two earlier empires with a reference to a "learned" paper (received by the Académie) which he was reading in January 1853[59] (one month after the proclamation of the Second Empire). "When Roman liberty succumbed under the military force of the Emperors," Tocqueville said, "the forms of the Republic were conserved, and authority passed into imperial hands without subverting the former Constitution; in theory at least, the supreme power rested in the people." He added, "In fact, Ulpian and Gaius, by stating that the will of the prince is law, are pointing to the idea behind that law, which appears at the beginning of every new rule. By this law the Senate transferred to the prince every one of the rights of the people (*quum omne ius suum populus in principem transferat*)."[60]

---

[58] *OC*, II, pt. 2, pp. 320–22.

[59] At just that moment, as Beaumont was reading volumes 9 and 10 of Thiers's *L'Histoire du Consulat et l'Empire*, which had been published in 1851, he referred to Tocqueville's observations that the volumes were devoid of any general ideas whatever: Beaumont to Tocqueville, January 12, 1853, *OC*, VIII, pt. 3, p. 82.

[60] *OC*, II, pt. 2, p. 322 (italics in the Latin in the original). Tocqueville is referring firstly to Tacitus, *Annales*, I.2, and additionally to Tacitus, *Hist.*, IV.3.

We find in his other notes on the Revolution more reflections on the mystifications of revolutionary discourse. As he charted its progress from Thermidor to Brumaire and then to the founding of the Empire, Tocqueville told himself that the philosophical character of the Revolution was "its *principal* characteristic, though a *temporary* one." He pondered what was for him the astonishing survival of the "irreligious, Voltairian, Encyclopedist, impulse [which] still moves the writers and speakers, while it has already ceased among the masses, where a contrary movement is beginning. This is a frequent phenomenon during revolutions. Those who had helped to make the Revolution with their phraseology continue to write and speak in the same manner for a long time while the majority has already silently begun to change."[61]

Tocqueville had begun to speculate along these lines during the late summer of 1852, when he wrote on why, after Thermidor, the French people surrendered themselves to the more encompassing authority of a single ruler. While they gave up republican ideas, the people remained revolutionary in their sentiments. The discrepancies between the love affair with liberty in 1789 and the constraints and risks that the French had come to associate with it under the "agitated servitude"[62] of the Republic were not discerned by the politicians and writers, who had stumbled into a dream world. Tocqueville did not mean that they still believed that an imaginary society could be transformed into a real one. What he found striking was the persistence of the revolutionary discourse. By the end of the decade, words and realities had moved even further apart. Neologisms that were intended to create solidarities in friendship, conjugal love and family loyalties concealed the extent to which privacy had actually suffered invasion. The revolutionary party that exercised power after Thermidor retained all the rhetoric of the most critical, radical period of the Revolution. The "last thing a party abandons," Tocqueville observed, "is its language, because among political parties, as elsewhere, the common people make up the rules of its usages [fait le règle en matière de langage], and find it easier to give up ideas that have been handed down to them than to give up words they have acquired."[63]

Tocqueville seemed to give some scope to popular, self-conscious intentions. Frenchmen responded fearfully but, above all, cynically to the seductions and obfuscations of the new language, precisely because they sensed that its original associations with the Terror no longer carried real power and that it need not stand in the way of protecting whatever gains the Revolution had placed in their hands. Their great anxiety over the

[61] Ibid., pp. 239–40. [62] Ibid., p. 276. [63] Ibid., pp. 278–79.

possibility of loss made it all the easier for them to give up liberty, which the Revolution in its halcyon days had promised but had almost consistently suppressed. The most certain sign that liberty was endangered was the way the press inflated protestations of devotion to it. Tocqueville warned that the thing to watch was not what the press said but the way in which the public listened. Reception was the key to the shaping of language and the intentions of those who made a profession of crafting it. "The very vehemence of the press is sometimes a mark of its weakness and a forerunner of its demise; its clamor and its perils often have the same voice. It screams only because its audience is growing deaf, and the deafness of the public makes it safe to silence the press later."[64] French people at both ends of the language spectrum – the press and its readers – gave up what was the most precious of things for what was immediately available.

For Tocqueville, such rationalizations amounted to self-deception since what was immediately useful could prove to be harmful. The masking achieved through language by political leaders and their supporters – in this case, appeals to liberty made during the most enthusiastic and energetic periods of the Revolution – were no longer given credence during its most tired period. At that point, disenchantment and deception set in.[65] It was a time when people turned against themselves and their earlier beliefs. To conceal the enervation of the soul, a mutual process of deception facilitating the satisfaction of material needs becomes part of a decaying moral and political condition. It was in this way that words achieved their opacity and blinded people to what Tocqueville thought was their real need – the preservation of heroic devotion to great ideas. But French people were by turn more civilized and more savage than any other people, driven more by the sensations of the moment than by principles honoring the memory of the past and by a concern for the future. This fall into the commonplace was one of those "surprises,"[66] he concluded, for which no one was quite ready. As he said a few months later, when he was casting his eye on the institutions of pre-revolutionary France, what he "really" wanted to understand was the France of the *ancien régime* at the moment the Revolution surprised it.[67]

[64] Ibid., p. 279.   [65] Ibid., p. 276.   [66] Ibid., p. 281.
[67] Tocqueville to Beaumont, April 8, 1853, *OC*, VIII, pt. 2, p. 103.

6   Three faces of history in *Democracy in America*

Complete equality eludes the grasp of the people at the very moment when they think they have grasped it, and "flies," as Pascal says, "with an eternal flight"; the people are excited in the pursuit of an advantage, which is more precious because it is not sufficiently remote as to be unknown or sufficiently near as to be enjoyed.[1]

The full meaning of what drove Tocqueville's final assault on the "surprises" of the Revolution will be denied us unless we execute a last movement backward, from the 1850s, from 1848 and from 1836, to the period of Tocqueville's composition of the *Democracy*. By employing this strategy, we may pick up the threads – as we may imagine he retrieved them – of his fascination with the great changes in Western society that aroused his interest, and of how, in trying to account for those changes, his conception of history took on greater texture. He looked back on his evolution as a writer who, during a lifetime concerned with change, perceived his own intellectual changes. Intellectual growth, he said, is an emotional process in which "we . . . never stop bringing the ideas that we embrace into a struggle against those that we do not [embrace]; the ideas that we have had in our youth, with those suggested by the present condition of society and its opinions."[2] The *Democracy* may be seen as a youthful intellectual laboratory, but youthful only in the sense that Tocqueville was trying on his views of history that were to remain with him throughout his life even as he refined, elaborated and emended some of them. We have at our disposal not only the *Democracy* as a finished work and his correspondence in which he discussed his ideas less formally and, for that reason, perhaps more revealingly, but also his extensive notes and drafts for every section of the book. They reveal his preliminary, but just as often his fuller, thoughts.[3]

The *Democracy*'s unique critique of the institutions of the American

---

[1] *Nolla edn.*, I, p. 152.
[2] Tocqueville to Kergorlay, February 3, 1857, *OC*, XIII, pt. 2, p. 325.
[3] References to these notes have already been made as the *Nolla edn.*

democratic experience takes on a more contingent quality when viewed against Tocqueville's larger concerns with the unknown future of modern societies. Democracies were too often unmindful of how the conditions of, and rationale for, democratic political and legal practices, founded on an ideology of equality, might overwhelm liberty. Once we see that the kinds of historical questions he asked in the *Democracy* recurred in many of his later writings, a picture of how, over time, Tocqueville's mind embraced a vision of the historical truth that met his criteria of veracity and persuasive power will take on firmer contours.

In a little more than a year, from May 1852 to September 1853, he worked to clarify his purposes in reconstituting the distant sources of the eclipse of the *ancien régime*. The depth of Tocqueville's commitment to liberalism and how it might be preserved through his own efforts as a private man, no longer able to play an active role in politics, is evident in his watchfulness over the politics of his own time and in his views of how his rediscovery of the past could illuminate the sources of political passivity in France. But he was going into a kind of internal exile, which he feared:

I have always needed a certain kind of esteem from my fellow human beings, a certain confidence in them, to continue my passionate interest in those ideas treating the happiness and greatness of human societies. For the first time, this esteem, this confidence, at least insofar as our fellow citizens and contemporaries are concerned, are absolutely lacking. At no period in my life have I been more deeply convinced of the necessity and excellence of free institutions and at no time have I ever seen more clearly that, without them, people cannot have a true moral greatness; and never have I been more convinced that the defects either in our education, or in our natures, our misfortunes and our errors [are such as to] make us incapable and unworthy of enjoying them [the free institutions].[4]

But once he settled into the enforced solitude he needed to find the traces of the past, he announced his *métier* as a historian who wanted to leave his readers in no doubt about his loyalties and convictions. The best way to reach this objective was a rigorous avoidance of proselytism. "I believe that the books that have made men reflect most, and which have had the greatest influence on their opinions and their actions, are those in which the author has not sought dogmatically to tell them what is agreeable for them to be thinking, but those in which the author has directed their minds to the path which leads to truths and finds them, as if they had come upon them by their own efforts" [mais où il a mis leur esprit sur le chemin qui conduit aux vérités et leur a fait trouver celles-ci, comme d'eux-mêmes].[5]

---

[4] Tocqueville to Corcelle, May 13, 1852, *OC*, XV, pt. 2, pp. 54–55.
[5] Tocqueville to Corcelle, September 17, 1853, ibid., p. 81.

In fact, some considerable effort is required to perceive what lies at the bottom of Tocqueville's achievement in bringing America to Europe and in making Europeans – especially his countrymen – understand that the foundations of their society, while irrevocably shaken by the Revolution of 1789, could not escape an even larger historical past that was pointing ever more in the new direction of equality. The magnitude of his enterprise may best be captured by recognizing that Tocqueville started from the proposition that the ethos of a society subsists on unexamined codes, and that it begins to unravel once they are questioned both by those who live by them and by those who challenge them. This was a premise that Tocqueville wanted his audience to take seriously as a starting point for a journey to a historical epoch that was fading from memory. And he thought that this could not be accomplished without considering how the secular ideas of the eighteenth century weakened the old society. Tocqueville did not see the Enlightenment in total monochrome. He acknowledged, for example, as we shall see, that its skepticism did not absorb the whole of intellectual activity – that the century harbored strong religious and mystical elements – and that both were part of what he saw as a cosmopolitan movement cutting across national frontiers, expressing hope and belief in total, near-redemptive change. In the aftermath of this understanding both of the Enlightenment and of the Revolution, Tocqueville carried forward some of the issues they both raised into at least the first half of the nineteenth century, and tried to distinguish those that he felt deserved to be salvaged and given fresh meaning from those that had revealed intrinsic weakness and could safely be abandoned.

Tocqueville saw connections between the nature and dynamics of political authority, individualism and materialism in the democratic era, and the place of indeterminateness and probability in history. These were not always clear to himself, nor are they to modern readers. How he dealt with the perplexities may best be explored by looking at three faces of the *Democracy*. The first centers on Tocqueville's views on the origins of community, and the origins and explosive nature of modern democracy. This first section next considers the problem of the social dynamics of self-interest in a post-aristocratic society. A key and controversial concept in the debates of seventeenth-century moralists, it raised issues which were transformed by the discourse on commerce and virtue in which Montesquieu, Adam Smith and Rousseau were leading participants in the next century. Tocqueville in turn took the transformation a stage further when he worked on the relationship he perceived between liberty, commerce and virtue in America. An essential part of the dynamics of individualism hinged, as he saw it, on acknowledging how and why the comforts of material well-being not only intensified it, but weakened the spiritual lives of peoples committed overwhelmingly to egalitarian ideals.

The middle section of the chapter comprises his thoughts on religion and the role of providence in history. We have already seen how these questions informed his idea of history. They will be examined this time with a closer eye to a consideration of his lineage with Pascal[6] and also with Rousseau, for the latter's Pascalian bent also entered Tocqueville's field of vision. These affinities will perhaps not be immediately apparent.[7] Tocqueville's persistent doubts about the future of a democratic and industrial age in which moderns lived in a state of alienation from themselves and their fellow beings, and were not at home anywhere, not even a country their ancestors had once known,[8] recall Rousseau's antimodernism, but also both Rousseau's and Pascal's struggles with the foundations of religious belief. Admittedly, Tocqueville's connections with Pascal and Rousseau demand delicate treatment. He carried on, one might say, a silent "dialogue" with them, trying to control the questions, and indeed determine the answers.

The final section of the chapter, one which occupies the later spaces of the *Democracy*, takes us back to Tocqueville's earliest discussion of the aristocratic ethos. Tocqueville wanted to give strength to his conviction that even modern notions of self-worth must be seen within a continuum of notions of honor. He made the psychological and social manifestations of honor an important part of his scheme to measure the distance between its traditional resonances and the new forms that sublimated its origins, but which did not disappear from the sights of democratic peoples who sought to give it a defined place in the ideas and practices of identity and authority.

The moral culture of democratic equality

Tocqueville's reliance on, and departures from, Rousseau provide some of the contexts for the ways in which he wrestled with the changing

---

[6] Tocqueville's Pascalian bent has been studied by Luis Díez del Corral, *La mentalidad política de Tocqueville, con especial referencia a Pascal* (Madrid, 1965). See also Peter A. Lawler, "The Human Condition: Tocqueville's Debt to Rousseau and Pascal," in *Liberty, Equality, Democracy*, ed. Edouardo Nolla (New York and London, 1992), pp. 1–20.

[7] For fleeting glimpses of the relationship, see Pierre Manent, *Tocqueville et la nature de la démocratie* (Paris, 1982); Lamberti, *Tocqueville and the Two Democracies*; Marvin Zetterbaum, *Tocqueville and the Problem of Democracy* (Stanford, 1967); Hilail Gildin, *Rousseau's Social Contract: The Design of the Argument* (Chicago and London, 1983); Roger Boesche, *The Strange Liberalism of Alexis de Tocqueville* (Ithaca, 1987); Richard Vernon, *Citizenship and Order: Studies in French Political Thought* (Toronto, 1986), chap. 4.

[8] *Nolla edn.*, II, p. 265.

resonances of virtue and the disputed ground of goodness in an egalitarian and commercial society. His semi-Rousseauian ideas stand as a kind of overture to his comparisons between what he called the semi-savage and the enlightened human condition, that is, the stage leading from one to another by way of an age of belief. His own conviction that security and happiness were the driving social forces forced him to deal with what might be realistically expected from them as against what he preferred them to be. He adopted a qualified Rousseauian anthropology, and embraced, as well, a Rousseauian sensitivity to the sources of moral decay. Tocqueville's moralism hardly fell into the full Rousseauian mode. If the goal of well-being could be reached without injuring human morality unduly, civilization, as it was turning out, was worth the risk. Besides, the web of history, which for Rousseau did not mark out a privileged path to truth,[9] was an irrepressible reality for Tocqueville.

The survival of public virtue in a mutually strengthening relationship with a protective concern for liberty was almost as problematic, though not as refractory, as Rousseau came to believe. In his despair, Rousseau tried to escape from history. When Tocqueville at times surrendered to despair, it was because, when he imagined what new shapes liberty might assume over time, he experienced real difficulty in predicting how it might survive. Thus, by contrasting but not by opposing the moral and political spheres, Tocqueville considered how the two could meet without harming liberty. He saw the moral world as "classified, systematized and decided beforehand; in the political world everything is agitated, disputed and uncertain. In the one [the moral world] there is a passive though a voluntary obedience; in the other [the political world], an independence scornful of experience, and jealous of all authority."[10] These worlds, he suggested, need not pass by one another in complete ignorance of what each could offer the other. Religious sensibility tied the worlds together. "Religion perceives that civil liberty affords a noble exercise to the faculties of man and that the political world is a field prepared by the Creator for the efforts of mind."[11] He may well have had in mind Pascal's appeal to human grandeur and the courage to deal with misery by cultivating the capacity for thought.[12] But Tocqueville did not know where unaided rational thought would carry humanity. He did think that the rational elements of unitarianism, which he compared with deism, would, if embraced by the upper classes of America, "in the absence of all beliefs in another life . . . fall into the depths of the doctrine

---

[9] *OCR*, III, p. 144.   [10] *Nolla edn.*, I, p. 35.   [11] Ibid.

[12] Pascal, *Pensées*, p. 95: "Thus all our dignity consists in thought. It is on thought that we must depend for our recovery, not on space and time, which we could never fill. Let us then strive to think well; that is the basic principle of morality."

of interest"[13] – in other words, into a religion that merely served the purest of utilitarian ends.

The facts that he found during his American travels, he said from a distance of some five years, had been useful, but they had actually confirmed his own presuppositions.[14] Providence; the irresistibility of the democratic revolution; the finger of God: these are words that he used to describe the gathering force of equality.[15] They were almost exactly the words he used in a letter from Yonkers in 1831, when he wrote that he felt free to express "the beginnings of opinions without being afraid of interpretations."[16] The latter – his own and those of others – would, he implied, come in time:

We are moving toward an unbounded democracy . . . what I see in this country convinces me . . . that France arranges these matters badly; but we will be thrust there [toward democracy] by an irresistible force. All efforts made to arrest this movement will only bring about interruptions . . . In a word, democracy henceforth appears to me a fact that a government may have the pretension of *regulating*, but not *stopping* . . . the most rational government is not one in which all the interested parties take part, but one that is directed by the most enlightened and most moral classes in society.[17]

An entirely new and unsettling era in history was opening before the old civilizations of Europe. How it was to be understood and received entailed the question of determining how political decisions were to be made. The desirability of élites in a democracy, an idea which he expressed in 1831, was nearly the same as Rousseau's notion that people in a democracy fulfilled their responsibilities when they met, after due reflection, to pass on the ideas of their superiors, and reject those they felt to be in error.[18] But he confessed some unease in his notes to the first volume when he tackled the subject of participation.[19] How do individuals and societies alike correctly discern their own interests, and, most importantly, the conditions of their liberty? Just asking the question was proof, he said, that there was no secure answer, and that therefore there might not exist any absolute right to be actively engaged in the political life of a country. But, on the other hand, by the time a principle was laid down to establish the criteria that would establish measurable qualities of political discernment, the grounds for supporting participation of any kind might very well be eroded. From this laconic comment, he went on to make what for him was a more interesting point: since human discern-

[13] Tocqueville to Kergorlay, June 29, 1831, *OC*, XIII, pt. 1, p. 231.
[14] Tocqueville to Kergorlay, end of January 1835, ibid., p. 374.   [15] *Nolla edn.*, I, p. 8.
[16] Tocqueville to Kergorlay, June 29, 1831, *OC*, XIII, pt. 1, p. 225.
[17] Ibid., pp. 233–34. The emphasis is Tocqueville's.   [18] *OCR*, III, p. 439.
[19] *Nolla edn.*, I, p. 46, note e.

ment by definition leads to differing interpretations of what is best in the first place, it is hard to concede entirely the force of one argument without at the same time entirely refusing the strength of the other. The way out of the impasse was to distinguish, he concluded, the different spheres of intelligence and practical experience.[20] He thought he had solved the problem of political participation by shifting it from the abstract level of rational discourse to a more manageable level – the level of practice.

Before opening a discussion of the conditions of equality in colonial America, Tocqueville traced its rise in France[21] to the distribution of landed property to greater and greater numbers of people outside the *noblesse*; the growing availability of material goods produced by commerce and industry, leading to a redistribution of wealth and a uniformity of desires; the crown's monopolization of power tending to a leveling of all classes; and the dissemination of scientific and cultural products opening up the democratization of knowledge. These changes had the force of a river from which no banks were visible. Dikes to stem its flow would be powerless; it would be better to construct a holy arch to guide humanity along its flow. The revolution of equality conjured up the fall of the Roman Empire and the barbarian invasions.[22] Predictions about its demise and what might follow it had flourished at the time, but they were naive conjectures; no one was able to foresee, for example, the creation of the feudal system. Humanity fatefully and arrogantly discerns effects without taking account of causes, and judges what is without knowing what will be.

We can hear the voice of the historian determined to know the sources of this new revolution, the new deluge, as Tocqueville called it. But we can also hear the voice of a man with a taste for metaphysical questions. This predilection and his rhetorical powers are on full display much more in his notes than in the text, where they are relatively restrained. Modern societies are carried along by a force greater than the forces human beings can summon.[23] The force that makes everything work is invisible to human beings who are carried along with it "to a still unknown point in the universe." Tocqueville, dedicated to following the path of *true discernment*,

---

[20] Ibid.

[21] Tocqueville told Kergorlay in 1847 that, when he was composing the *Democracy*, France was constantly in his mind, and that his aim was not so much to offer a complete picture of the United States as to seek out the contrasts and resemblances between the two societies: Tocqueville to Kergorlay, October 18, 1847, *OC*, XIII, pt. 2, p. 209.

[22] In 1831, while still in America, Tocqueville wrote that he needed Guizot's works on Roman society and the Middle Ages to help him dissect American society. See Tocqueville to Chabrol, May 18, 1831, *BYT*, B.I.a (1–2).

[23] *Nolla edn.*, I, p. 7, note r. This citation and others that follow, as well as the arguments, are from this source.

knows that the modern world can travel the road either to despotism or to the republic. "In this century of liberty I fear for the future liberty of the human species. I am not drawing on the past when I speak of my fears . . . but on the very nature of man, who does not change."

What in humanity's unchangeable nature did Tocqueville fear? Its habitual blindness; its readiness to be deceived; but most of all its capacity for making wrong choices. Human beings will always be in a state of error. Thus knowledge of the past bears out the fact of human immutability. When the past is studied, it reveals, in addition to the changing conditions of humanity's material and intellectual evolution, the cardinal rule about the inalterability of the emotional and reasoning elements of human conduct. He was puzzled by the paradox that the passion for equality, which should, he thought, logically diminish as conditions became more equal, appeared instead to become more intense. The paradox illustrated a curious and bizarre aspect of human nature; there is a strong need in human beings to seek the path of error, the path of what he called least resistance. Living in slavery or under modern forms of despotism might appear to be much easier and deceptively more preferable. Under what situations? Human beings might well choose to live under conditions in which all would be equally deprived of rights rather than choose liberty. If such were the case, much more, he argued, must be demanded from humanity than the surrender to the pleasures of life that asks for nothing but happy, yet mindless, resignation. The conditions of modernity, taking flight in America and parts of western Europe, and the future of humankind everywhere, were, on the other hand, bringing the value of liberty into the consciousness of new historical actors.

Tocqueville, like Rousseau, carried forward the idea that the links and tensions between personal and political liberty could not be adequately explained by a totally individualistic notion of a self, free from the larger community. Both insisted that, while freedom was an almost primordial, natural force, it could yield its richest meanings only to human beings who perceive themselves as autonomous moral actors, engaged with each other in a common endeavor to stretch the boundaries of existing social and political orders. For Rousseau, this meant using the capacity for reflection and judgment, which make human beings the authors of their freedom.[24] In the introduction to the first volume of the *Democracy*, Tocqueville announced his purpose in terms evocative of Rousseau's concern to preserve the self as author of personal liberty, voluntarily accepting political authority, without being led astray by feelings of pride or servility:

[24] Jean-Jacques Rousseau, *Emile*, trans. Elizabeth Foxley (London, 1974), p. 292.

I can conceive of a society in which all men would feel an equal love and respect for the laws of which they consider themselves the authors; . . . in which the loyalty of the subject to the chief magistrate would not be a passion, but a quiet and rational persuasion. With every individual in possession of rights which he is sure to retain, a kind of manly confidence and reciprocal courtesy would arise between all classes, removed alike from pride and servility. The people, well acquainted with their own true interests, would understand that, in order to profit from the advantages of the state, it is necessary to satisfy its requirements. The voluntary association of the citizens might then take the place of the individual power of the nobles, and the state would be protected from tyranny and license.[25]

This credo was given an even firmer footing in his dismissal of people who thought that they could combine the passion "to be led and . . . the wish to be free." He condemned this "compromise between administrative despotism and the sovereignty of the people": "The nature of whom I am to obey signifies less to me than the fact of extorted obedience."[26] It is highly likely that he was affected by what Rousseau called the most important of all laws, embedded in the "hearts of the citizens; a law which creates the real constitution of the state . . . and prepares a people in the spirit of their institutions." In tracing the history of the American settlements, Tocqueville spoke of customs, manners and opinion in the Rousseauian sense of how they work together to substitute the "force of habit for that of authority."[27] Indeed, Rousseau and Tocqueville claimed, as did Montesquieu, that knowledge of society would have no power if, in Tocqueville's words, it neglected the "notions and opinions current among men and . . . the mass of those ideas which constitute their character of mind."[28]

The exercise of political power was legitimate only when, if not disregarding the power of those notions and opinions, it was based on obedience from individuals voluntarily uniting with their fellows and identifying with them in a perception of their common interests. Thus the law, evoked democratically, is the product of a people's own work.[29] The expression of the will of a whole people was, Tocqueville said, a prodigious phenomenon, and when it declared itself, it overwhelmed the imagination. The majority complies because it thinks of the whole will as a contract to which it is a party.[30] Common opinion has it that Tocqueville is the prophet of a society placed at the mercy of an unreflective and intolerant majority; that he was simply talking about the perils of majority will. When he said, however, that the majority could be in error, he had been anticipated by Rousseau. It is well to recall that

---

[25] *Nolla edn.*, I, p. 11.   [26] Ibid., II, p. 268.   [27] *OCR*, III, p. 394.
[28] *Nolla edn.*, I, p. 223.   [29] Ibid., p. 185.   [30] Ibid., p. 189.

Rousseau maintained that the moral qualities of sound politics lacked a "precise mode of measurement."[31] In Rousseau's theory, each expression of the general will constituted a moral transformation. Tocqueville believed that the *real* will could not be located in the process of counting heads. He dealt with his unease in much the same way as Rousseau. A legitimate "government . . . follows the real will of the people, and not of a government that simply commands in their name."[32] That *real* will for Tocqueville was embodied, not in "the sovereignty of the people," but in the "sovereignty of mankind," which rises above a simple majority. If people are willing to give full power to simple majorities, they surrender themselves to the "language of a slave."[33] He agreed with Rousseau that popular sovereignty could not be threatened as long as *government of the self* was exercised,[34] and that it embodied a *real* will, which had to be guarded against impostures.

It was easier to assert than to explain the *real* will. In Tocqueville's reckoning, the principle of popular sovereignty was simpler and less opaque than Rousseau's. Moreover, unlike Rousseau, who lived in an ancient monarchy with its associations of divine images, he did not endow sovereignty with a sacred character, which the prerevolutionary idea of the monarch as sovereign carried with it. Sovereignty was "more or less at the bottom of almost all human institutions"; and, in America, at least, it was "neither barren nor concealed," spreading "freely, and arriv[ing] without impediments at its most remote consequences."[35] Sovereignty had, in short, been demystified. Like most post-Rousseauians, including Madame de Staël who wrote a small admiring essay on Rousseau in 1788,[36] Tocqueville was spared the problem of applying his political ideas in a prerevolutionary age – in an age in which considerable thought was given to, many illusions were shattered by and much blood was spilled on the founding of a durable polity.[37]

Though conceptions of political order, like order in other domains, do not tell us everything that is to be known about Rousseau,[38] order *qua* order was deeply etched in his consciousness and was a significant part of his yearning for calm and harmony. Like Montesquieu, Rousseau envisaged change as a mark of degeneration and decay, the result of a regressive clash of forces in societies in which human beings were irremediably

---

[31] *OCR*, III, p. 419.   [32] *Nolla edn.*, I, p. 173.   [33] Ibid., I, p. 196.
[34] *OCR*, III, p. 439 (my emphasis).   [35] *Nolla edn.*, I, p. 45.
[36] Mme. de Staël, *Lettres sur les écrits et le caractère de J.-J. Rousseau* (1788), Vol. I, *Oeuvres complètes de Madame la baronne de Staël-Holstein* (Geneva, 1967).
[37] Cf. Hannah Arendt, *Between Past and Future* (Cleveland and New York, 1961), pp. 136–41, for her discussion on political foundations.
[38] Cf. Maurizio Viroli, *Jean-Jacques Rousseau and the Well-Ordered Society* (New York, 1988).

tied to customs and prejudices.[39] Their destruction through revolution, with the hope of creating a new and free society, was hence highly problematic. Except in the most glaring of tyrannical injustices, revolutions were dangerous and futile. Hence, Rousseau's answer to the prospect of breaking through the burdens of the past to the exercise of liberty was guarded.

Tocqueville was as much moved as Rousseau by the underlying order in the universe, but he left behind him any notions that change was bound to lead human beings away from themselves, or that the only acceptable change, as with Rousseau, was one ensuring the individual's return to his or her authentic self. The battle, he was sure, was not between the natural and the civilized self, as it was with Rousseau. Neither did Tocqueville feel called on to pronounce on the question of the self as an obdurate or insubstantial entity, but he did have a lively notion that individuals might be able to make happy adjustments, perhaps not as easily as they might make unhappy ones, to the changing conditions of society. Definitions of happiness drew on his irony. Since human beings appeared to prefer the less rocky road to it, they might indeed mistake that path for happiness. Of another phenomenon he was also certain. Change was as natural to human societies as it was intrinsic to the universe in which nothing stood still. Order was not identical with stasis, or, if a proper reading of stasis is taken, it was in its interstices that change was to be located. The crux of change was not change itself, but how the feeble efforts of human beings might control it. Tocqueville believed, as we have seen, that political disorder in Europe since 1789 was far from over, but, until the signs of breakdown became apparent to him in 1847, he thought that a *modus vivendi* could be accomplished that would contain revolutionary ferment within existing political institutions.

Lurking in the background of French political life, as well as in America, was the compulsion to impose uniformity and the growing impingement by public authority upon private areas of life. For Rousseau, long before these changes could be discerned as a pattern for political conduct in the future, personal distinctions were imposed by heredity, or were acquired very early in life, as he witnessed its manifestations through the artifices and conventions of a decadent society. Nonetheless, he was no partisan of a totally undifferentiated equality either. He expected neither perfection nor passionless human beings. Human beings without passions would be poor citizens; moreover, passions could be directed toward meritorious goals, such as respect for what lay beyond immediate interests.[40]

---

[39] *OCR*, III, p. 385. Cf. Starobinski, *Jean-Jacques Rousseau: La Transparence et l'obstacle*, p. 50.   [40] *OCR*, III, p. 259.

Diversity, for Tocqueville, was the precious source of the unexpected richness of life, and it was – he implied – constitutive of freedom. Yet, since there was no need any longer to distinguish between sovereignty and government – Rousseau's differentiation between the real source of political power and the instrumentalization of that power – Tocqueville was driven to the conclusion that a democratic government could manipulate the hunger for wholeness and purpose by dictating its substance and terms. Governments, especially democratic ones, might thus gain semi-divine powers of creation.[41] They were already becoming new idols:

> The unity, the ubiquity, the omnipotence of the supreme power, and the uniformity of its rules constitute the principal characteristics of all the political systems that have been put forward in our age. They recur even in the wildest visions of political regeneration; the human mind pursues them in its dreams.[42]

There were ways to mitigate the heavy hand of the majority, but Tocqueville's heart was not totally engaged in his discussion of how to strengthen American political institutions to avoid unchecked power. They were desirable, but palliatives all the same, for he knew that they were useful to the degree that the wills of democratic decision-makers remained clear. Just as important was his point that the will of the majority could be located in various forms of government, whether democratic or monarchical. But it was the tutelage that people willingly imposed on themselves that Tocqueville found most discouraging. He was not averse to – indeed, he spent some time discussing – various methods of restraining the full force of the popular will – not the general will dear to Rousseau's heart. What was to be avoided was the idea of placing full powers in a single representative assembly. "As it is simultaneously furnished with great material force and immense moral power, it alone possesses the right to speak its voice in the prevailing silence, alone can act in a context of universal weakness, it feels itself above all laws, is freed from all rules, and is immune from all resistance. It manipulates all wills, abolishes rights, alters or changes mores to serve itself. And if it so happens that it will be destroyed or even destroys itself, the habits of servility that it has created will survive."[43] A unitary state with a single omnipotent representative body – a fatal flaw in the Revolution – had been overcome by "the principle of the division of the legislative power . . . This theory, nearly unknown to the republics of antiquity, first introduced into the world almost by accident, like so many other great truths, and misunderstood by several modern nations, has at length become an axiom in the political science of the present age."[44]

---

[41] *Nolla edn.*, II, pp. 240–41.   [42] Ibid., p. 242.   [43] Ibid., p. 269, note t.
[44] Ibid., p. 67.

Other aspects of political obligation troubled Tocqueville more. If he deplored the propensity in America to call frequent elections; if he cited Jefferson and Hamilton to warn against poorly conceived and hastily passed laws from a boorish and badly informed House of Representatives; if he feared the political instability both could cause;[45] and if he stated that the two greatest dangers to democracies lay "in the total subjection of the legislature to the will of the electoral body, and the concentration of all the other powers of the government in the legislative branch,"[46] he had a larger point in mind. He was not questioning the value of representation in a centralized modern state. Hamilton's warnings, expressed in *The Federalist*, No. 71, impressed him. Though the people, Hamilton pointed out, "*intend* the PUBLIC GOOD," which is often the result of "their very errors," they also should, but do not always, know that they can be deceived by calculating manipulators of the popular will into thinking that they always "*reason right* about the *means* of promoting it."[47] Hamilton was referring to the ambitious, avaricious and desperate actions of men who exploit popular confidence and, in order to minimize those actions, he encouraged the practice of relying on the guardians of the people's interests to arrange matters in such a way as to give the people the opportunity for reflection before agreeing to rash decisions. Tocqueville issued his own warning that the "rare and brief exercise of their [the people's] free choice, however important it may be, will not prevent them from gradually losing the faculties of thinking, feeling and acting for themselves, and thus gradually falling below the level of humanity." In brief, all talk about the "different modes of election" was window-dressing. It could not attack the real problem that originated in "the constitution of the country," itself the paradoxical result of introducing freedom, while increasing the tendency toward administrative despotism.[48] Tocqueville argued that tyranny and arbitrary government could mask themselves successfully as legitimate majority rule. The *deceptions* in such situations were more important than the paradoxes that could be drawn from them.

Tocqueville was afraid that the new legitimacy would in fact become more overreaching than either the older forms of tyranny or arbitrary rule. In its concealed form, it threatened to become a source of unrestrained power, whether in the courts or in the legislature. This new face of authority was an open invitation to Europe's demagogues to substitute themselves for the people, and to tell them that they "know what is good"

---

[45] *Nolla edn.*, I, pp. 151–59.   [46] Ibid., p. 119.

[47] Ibid., p. 118, note 35. The emphasis is in the original. See Alexander Hamilton, John Jay and James Madison, *The Federalist: A Commentary on the Constitution of the United States* (New York, n.d.), pp. 464–65.   [48] Ibid., II, pp. 269–70.

for them and prevent them from gaining such knowledge by and for themselves. We may recall that Rousseau gave his Legislator the role of guide to, but never that of author of, the political will. Tocqueville confronted this problem indirectly, subsuming it under his observations of how the role of Legislator could be usurped. In his eyes, the perversion of the political will was "a discovery of modern days that there are such things as legitimate authority and holy injustice, provided they are exercised in the name of the people."[49] He expatiated on this to Mill, telling him that he refused a democracy in which people are forced to be happy on the authority of their rulers, but that he accepted one in which the people learned to discern all the conditions for their happiness. "You know," he said, "that I am not exaggerating the final consequence of the Democratic Revolution that is now taking place in the world; I am not looking at it as the Israelites did when they looked toward the promised land. But . . . I believe it useful and necessary and I walk toward it with resolution, without hesitation, without enthusiasm and, I hope, without weakness."[50] The right of the stronger, and submission to it, was already acquiring modern guises. He almost paraphrased Rousseau, for whom "the last term of inequality" constituted a return to "the sole law of the strongest." Rousseau's intention was to show how the "state of nature in its purity" had suffered from the "consequence of excessive corruption" by society.[51] Rousseau was speaking of the inequality, Tocqueville of the equality, of conditions that led to despotism. Tocqueville reversed the sources of the oppression; but he and Rousseau were equally sensitive to the human weaknesses that created them.

The originality of Tocqueville's theory of power and freedom is to be found in the distinction *in kind* that he perceived between aristocratic and democratic forms of oppression. The first he condemned less strenuously than the second. So awesome is the "kind of aristocratic refinement and . . . air of grandeur in the depravity of the great," that they have little need to engage in petty acts of corruption. The opposite is the case in democracies, where everyone, professing to believe in an equality of talent and virtue, explains economic, social or other kinds of superiority as proof of vice; and "an odious connection is thus formed between the idea of turpitude and power, unworthiness and success, utility and dishonor."[52]

It was by this route that Tocqueville was led to one of his great insights: the struggle within the democratic psyche between the desire for equality and individual achievement was relieved by the principle of "self-interest

---

[49] Ibid., I, p. 302. Cf. Melvin Richter, "Toward a Concept of Political Legitimacy," *Political Theory*, 10 (1982), pp. 185–214.

[50] Tocqueville to Mill, June 1835, *OC*, VI, pt. 1, p. 294.   [51] *OCR*, III, p. 191.

[52] *Nolla edn.*, I, p. 173.

rightly understood." This question, which I discussed in the preceding chapter as part of Tocqueville's attempt to deal with the survival of virtue in a modern society, must now be taken up once more to bring into even sharper focus the difficulties Tocqueville experienced in finding an equivalent for republican virtue in an age of equality. He shared with Montesquieu the idea that commerce prepared men for freedom. But Tocqueville lived at a time when liberty could no longer be defended by privileged groups, and had instead to find its guardians in the middle classes for whom the power of money and the grip of modern individualism turned them away from caring for liberty. He was thus not disinclined to see liberty and wealth in some of the ways the seventeenth-century French moralists did. His perception of the coming into being of political liberalism, which he did not, it is important to point out, equate with the liberal economic paradigm, must be looked at because of the dangers that he believed might be posed by the full implementation of economic liberalism. The commercialization of society was one of those historical movements in which peoples were losing the habit of respecting what they no longer knew, but had not yet learned to know what they ought to respect. In such a critical phase of historical transformation, people are tormented by a deep sickness, live in a state of agitation, find peace nowhere and are laid out on a bed of pain.[53]

For democratic man, the taint of moral corruptibility is removed by the belief that self-interest is driven and justified by the urge to improve one's social position: all are involved in acts of social emulation. In the process everyone is ready to condemn, but cannot be greatly tempted to escape from, the constraints of simple equality. The net result, thus, is to reinforce it constantly. By contrast, in England the aristocratic ethos and enlightened ideas go hand in hand. The democratic ethos encourages attention to the particular, while the aristocratic cultivates a taste for general ideas. Tocqueville called on Adam Smith to help him both to assess English ideas on wealth, and also to see whether Smith could furnish him with a foundation for dealing with the problematic future of moral sensibility and practice in a commercialized society.[54]

Smith did not have any place for equality within his frame of reference. Political power, other than in its jurisprudential context which Smith expected in time would furnish an impartial science of government sublimating and legitimizing the rawness of power, was not Tocqueville's primary concern either. Besides, power – like inequality – was one function of wealth or its absence, and needed no further explanation. Where Tocqueville and Smith may be said to meet is on the ground of the impact

[53] Ibid., p. 187, note t.　　[54] Ibid., II, p. 29 and note m.

of commerce on morals and politics. The rich, as Smith saw them, were more dedicated to the retention of their status and wealth, and the poor lacked the resources to overcome their stupor and greed to think of replacing their "natural" rulers. Emulation unintentionally drove the industrious middling ranks of society to improve the human species, and at the same time to create the conditions of a more extended civility. Their successful accumulation and their opulent life styles induced a state of awe in their social inferiors. "Our admiration of success," Smith declared, "is founded upon the same principle with our respect for wealth and greatness, and is equally necessary for establishing the ranks and order of society."[55] Yet he "could not abide 'vicious and offensive' displays of luxury and lust; he fled from them, as from an open invitation to libertinism, by pressing on his contemporaries a model of society that would preserve social and sexual proprieties in a world where the opportunities for the gratification of the senses had been so greatly expanded."[56] There was another side to the unremitting drives of the middling ranks of society: their propensity for self-love threatened to undermine industry, duty and reputation. But this was offset by the obligation to act according to justice. In turn, if such responsibilities were faced, the negative forces of the market and the sting of resentment would be removed. This solution would serve, Smith hoped, to conflate the market's impersonal and personal components, and to remove the suspicion that virtue was nothing but a mere expedient.[57]

Tocqueville's problem was not quite the same as Smith's, since emulation worked through different mechanisms in an equalitarian society where there was no readiness in the inferior ranks of society to regard their economic superiors as better than themselves. People aspired to wealth and status, but did not think that they were barred from them by a social gulf. Wealth, as Tocqueville recognized, did operate to some extent as the lubricant for social ascent in England, but social change was slow, appeared to be under control and proved a successful barrier against sudden convulsions. Yet he turned away from Nassau Senior's optimistic and, for him, limited notion that the division of labor was adding to the prosperity of the laboring classes. Wealth meant, Tocqueville conceded, not only more money in the hands of more people. It created "happiness,

[55] Smith, *Theory of Moral Sentiments*, VI.iii.3.28.
[56] Harvey Mitchell, "'The Mysterious Veil of Self-Delusion' in Adam Smith's *Theory of Moral Sentiments*," *Eighteenth-Century Studies*, 20 (1987), p. 419. Cf. Laurence Dickey, "Historicizing the 'Adam Smith Problem': Conceptual, Historiographical and Textual Issues," *Journal of Modern History*, 58 (1986), pp. 579–609.
[57] Cf. Michael Ignatieff, "John Millar and Individualism," in *Wealth and Virtue: The Shaping of Political Economy in the Scottish Enlightenment*, ed. Istvan Hont and Michael Ignatieff (Cambridge, 1983), p. 339.

personal consideration, political right, easy justice, intellectual enjoyments, and many other indirect sources of contentment."[58] But class antagonisms in England could not be overlooked, whatever expanding wealth appeared to promise to workers. New wealth would certainly expand human happiness, civility and knowledge, but the distribution of goods would become a problem unless policies were adopted to alleviate the condition of the larger and growing number of workers without access to these benefits. Past solutions were inadequate and counterproductive. Essential was a clear-sighted examination of how to balance the productive powers and consumption needs of society.[59]

American society was not without class conflict, but Tocqueville always thought that its social openness would continue to mute it. What Tocqueville found more interesting was the question of the *origins* of the market economy. Without presenting his argument step by step, his departure from Montesquieu's analysis of the links between commerce and liberty is significant. Tocqueville isolated liberty from its associations with the *moeurs*, laws, social habits and modes of thought of a specific society, and endowed it with the autonomous power to create the conditions for commercial development. Such reasoning might appear odd, but not if we keep in mind that he almost consistently conceived of liberty in the same spiritual terms he reserved for virtue. Virtue was nothing but the *free* choice of what is good.[60] As a modern with grave doubts about the future, trying to fashion a coherent account of the status of liberty, its moral dimensions and its social forms, he was worried that democratic politics and commercial institutions would dispense with virtue altogether. The "secret tendency" of democratic institutions promoted prosperity, "in spite of their [the citizens'] vices and mistakes; in aristocratic governments public men may frequently do harm without intending it; and in democratic states they bring about good results of which they have never thought."[61] This was baffling, but no more mysterious than the unintended miseries of life for many in aristocratic societies:

The world is a book entirely closed to man. Often there is in the very foundation of democratic institutions a hidden tendency which carries men toward the good, that is, to converge on general prosperity despite their vices and their errors, while in aristocratic institutions a secret propensity sometimes comes to light which, in spite of their talents and virtues, leads them to contribute to the miseries of the

---

[58] Tocqueville to Nassau Senior, February 21, 1835, *The Correspondence and Conversations of Alexis de Tocqueville with Nassau William Senior from 1834 to 1859*, ed. M. C. M. Simpson, 2 vols., 2nd edn. (London, 1872), I, p. 7.

[59] See Tocqueville's "Mémoire sur le paupérisme" (1835), in *OC*, XVI, pp. 117–39. His second memoir on pauperism appeared in 1837, ibid., pp. 140–57. For a full treatment of this question, see Seymour Drescher, *Tocqueville and England* (Cambridge, Mass., 1964).   [60] *OC*, V, pt. 2, pp. 90–92.   [61] *Nolla edn.*, I, p. 184.

greatest number of their fellow men. If a hidden force independent of men did not exist in democratic institutions, it would be impossible to give an adequate explanation for the peace and prosperity that reign at the very heart of certain democracies.[62]

Like Smith's invisible hand, Tocqueville's concept of the unintended consequences of pursuing self-interest was a clever adaptation of Montesquieu's principle of false honor in a monarchy. False honor was, Montesquieu said, "as useful to the public as true honor could possibly be to private persons," and he compared it to the "power of gravitation" to draw every individual "toward the public good, while he was thinking only of promoting his own interests."[63]

Tocqueville, whose thoughts on the changing contours of honor we have looked at and will examine once again later when we will see him returning to give it greater focus, saw additional consequences for the future of honor in modern societies that were ready to dispense with it by giving it a price tag. The transformation did not altogether displease him. "Commerce renders men independent of one another . . . gives them a lofty notion of their personal importance, leads them to seek to conduct their own affairs and teaches how to conduct them well; it therefore prepares men for freedom, but preserves them from revolution."[64] This eulogy of commerce was not full-hearted, because he saw commerce mainly as a defense against violent change; it served to defuse the passions of an aristocratic society. Because he also wanted to show that liberty had a *telos*, independent of concrete context, the praise was, in fact, less than fulsome. The higher purpose of liberty could not be realized if persons succumbed to the "cowardly love of present enjoyment," in which they would "lose sight of the interest of their future selves and those of their descendants and to prepare to glide along the easy current of life rather than to make, when it is necessary, a strong and sudden effort to a higher purpose."[65] The risk was that democratic societies, even if they carried within themselves powerful antidotes to violent revolutionary change, would create the same objects of desire for everyone and create a uniformity of tastes: a materialistic ethos, feeding ever-spiraling needs, was "a dangerous disease of the human mind."[66] Calling Plato's condemnation of professed materialists to mind, he hoped that people would find sources of spiritual strength[67] to overcome the mental strain of

---

[62] Ibid., I, p. 184, note m.

[63] Montesquieu, *De l'Esprit des lois*, in *Oeuvres complètes*, ed. André Masson, 3 vols. (Paris, 1950–55), I, pp. 33–34.

[64] *Nolla edn.*, II, p. 213. Cf. Albert O. Hirschman, *The Passions and the Interests: Political Arguments for Capitalism Before Its Triumph* (Princeton, 1977), pp. 123–25.

[65] *Nolla edn.*, II, p. 219.   [66] Ibid., p. 130.   [67] Ibid., pp. 131–32.

living in a democratic world of intense joys and equally intense dis-appointments.[68] "The sentiment of envy gains its greatest energy only among equals. That is why it is so common and passionate in democratic centuries."[69] The fear of the effects of materialism haunted Tocqueville, but he did not transform his fear into a total rejection of the modern world.

What did he find acceptable and why? Many of the problems he raised dated from the drafts to the first volume of the *Democracy*. In a revealing passage, he asked himself how Montesquieu's reasoning on the place of virtue in republics might apply to the modern American experience:

Americans do not constitute a virtuous people, yet they are free. This does not constitute a decisive refutation of Montesquieu's belief that virtue is essential to the existence of republics. There is no need to interpret Montesquieu's idea in a narrow sense. What that great man wished to assert was that republics may be sustained only through the operation of society upon itself. What he meant by "virtue" is that moral power which each individual exercises upon himself, and which keeps him from violating the right of others. In the eyes of the moralist, there is nothing virtuous about such a triumph of a man over temptation if it should be the case either that temptation is slight, or that the decision is made as the result of calculating the agent's personal interest. But Montesquieu was concerned more with the result than with the cause. In America, it is not that virtue is great, but that temptation is small, which comes down to the same point. It is not disinterestedness that is great, but it is interest, properly understood, which again comes to almost the same thing. Montesquieu, then, was right, although he discussed virtue in the ancient world, and what he said in connection with the Greeks and Romans still applies to the Americans.[70]

The original way in which Tocqueville dealt with the problem of motivation and consequence should not be obscured by his argument that resistance to great temptation is a *sine qua non* for the exercise of virtue, or that interest properly understood in contemporary American society obviates the question of disinterestedness. Raymond Aron caught some, but not all, of Tocqueville's intentions, by suggesting that he meant to find elements in common between interest and virtue.[71] What is more important is that, by reintroducing cause (motivation) as the significant determinant of virtue, Tocqueville was taking issue with Montesquieu. It was the absence of the will to be virtuous in American democratic society that caused Tocqueville to ponder what might take its place, or whether the "hidden tendency," as he called it, that carried men to do good in democratic societies answered the question of the sources of virtue. Much had to

---

[68] Ibid., pp. 125–26.   [69] Ibid., p. 125, note h.   [70] Ibid., I, p. 243, note a.
[71] Raymond Aron, *Main Currents in Sociological Thought*, trans. Richard Howard and Helen Weaver (New York, 1968), p. 259.

rest on that elusive tendency to call unreservedly upon the action of self-interest in the modern age. There would be no need to call on utilitarian arguments only if morals and ideas of justice were powerful.[72] They had not been necessary in classical times. So he had said in 1831:

The sacrifice of individual interest to the general good was the principle of the ancient republics. In this sense, it may be said that they were *virtuous*. The enfolding of individual interest in the general interest appears to me to constitute the principle of virtue. A kind of refined and intelligent egoism seems to be the pivot upon which the whole machine turned. The people of our times are not embarrassed to ask themselves how virtue is to be understood as a good, but they do claim to prove that it is useful. If this last point is true as I think it is in part, this [American society] can pass as an enlightened, but not a virtuous, one.[73]

The question that Tocqueville uneasily left open in 1831 was how and to what degree the two principles – those of the individual good and of the general good – could be melded in modern societies. Only the future, he observed, would reveal if conscience, or reflection, or calculation, could master political passions which had not yet been, but which would surely be born.[74]

It was to Plato that Tocqueville looked in the first place to consider the claims of the classical past upon the present. At first he was inclined to say that Plato was of little consequence for moderns. He thought him "infantile," a better philosopher than a political thinker, which summed up Tocqueville's impatience with utopian schemes. In the *Democracy*, his distance from the primitive republicanism of the ancients led to an unflattering comparison between them and the modern era's achievements:

When I compare the Greek and Roman republics with these American states; the manuscript libraries of the former, and their rude population, with the innumerable journals and enlightened people of the latter; when I remember all the attempts that are made to judge the modern republics by the aid of those of antiquity, and to infer what will happen in our time from what took place two thousand years ago, I am tempted to burn my books in order to apply none but novel ideas to so novel a condition of society.[75]

But he did not burn his classics. He read and absorbed their ideas. Though he said that he felt quite removed from their history and myths, they captivated him.[76] The Golden Age was a metaphorical construct that made a powerful claim on his imagination. The classical concentration on the nature of virtue, justice and beauty he found deeply appealing. What disturbed him about modern times was not so much that people were

---

[72] *Nolla edn.*, I, p. 188, note u.   [73] *OC*, V, pt. 1, pp. 234–35.   [74] Ibid.
[75] *Nolla edn.*, I, p. 235.
[76] Tocqueville to Royer-Collard, August 25, 1836, *OC*, XI, p. 19.

drowning themselves in petty things, as that they were failing as "theorists" to imagine great deeds.[77] He cited Plutarch to show that, by equating "*virtus* [with] the name of virtue itself . . . that *virtue* in Latin was as much as to say *valor*," the Romans had given virtue a very narrow meaning.[78] Its ancient connotations could not carry the weight of modern man's needs and aspirations. From his study of ancient civilizations, Tocqueville concluded that, while the tyranny of small states might be more galling in its invasion of the private lives of citizens, tyrannical government was unlikely to have flourished in them. Indeed, the ancient republics "had been the cradle of political liberty."[79] Liberty was in fact subject to greater risk in large democratic ones. But he accepted the dangers as a historical reality; and he added that there was nothing in the past, nor any certain signs to the future, that would preclude boldness and intellectual genius in large states.[80]

Morals and politics had been seen rightly as essential to one another in ancient times; their divorce under modern conditions might prove to be calamitous to both.[81] The great task of modern moral philosophers was to show democratic peoples that self-interest properly understood, or a morality based on self-interest rightly understood, was "their chief remaining security against themselves."[82] The psychological mechanism by means of which they could be bound to existing rules of morality was part of that task. There was no question that such self-interest would produce great acts of self-sacrifice, but by "disciplin[ing] a number of persons in habits of regularity, moderation, foresight, self-command," it would lead them to virtue, if not of the extraordinary, then of the commonplace, kind. In compensation, the general level of conduct would be raised, and general depravity would become less common.[83]

The "daily acts of self-denial" which Tocqueville saw as the personal articulation of the principle of self-interest rightly understood was in some measure anticipated by Rousseau and by Smith, to whom we now return. Smith's theory of moral sentiments encompassed a view of self-interest that rested on a determination by human beings to earn true merit to meet their own sense of self-worth. The theory rested on the assumption that others were also motivated by the psychological satisfactions of performing meritorious acts, with the consequence that the interests of all were served. He qualified this principle by showing that, even if

---

[77] Tocqueville to Corcelle, March 19, 1838, *OC*, XV, pt. 1, pp. 96–99; Tocqueville to Royer-Collard, April 6, 1838, *OC*, XI, pp. 60–61.
[78] *Nolla edn.*, II, p. 196 (italics in the original).   [79] Ibid., I, p. 122.
[80] Ibid., pp. 122–23.
[81] Tocqueville to Kergorlay, August 8, 1838, *OC*, XIII, pt. 2, pp. 40–41.
[82] *Nolla edn.*, II, p. 115.   [83] Ibid.

self-command was an ideal that was rarely met, it was the moral idiom within which members of society carried out their social interactions. He also, however, invoked self-deception as an important and indispensable element in the constitution of modern morality. Of this Rousseau would have no part; and it was his refusal that led Adam Smith and those who followed him to thrust Rousseau's deep antipathy to modernity aside as a harmful vestige of a more innocent time. Self-denial and delayed gratification played their socially positive role through mechanisms of self-deception, as Smith theorized about their purposes and effects. As Rousseau conceived the problem, a heightened self-consciousness – in the sense of knowing the self's true destination – was the necessary condition for human beings willingly to seek the subordination of individual wills to the general will, under conditions acceptable to all. Only then was it possible to end deception. Only then would human actions be virtuous. Man had the capacity to perceive that it was in his true interest, *intérêt bien entendu*, to "clarify his reason with new understandings, warm his heart with new sentiments, [so] that he may learn how to apply his being and his felicity in dividing them with his fellowmen."[84] Human beings have an interest in being just by finding the reasons for justice in their own hearts. Once they did, they would be led to cultivate it in harmony with the common interest. Since Rousseau claimed that they had an interest in *willing* a state of self-command, only a matter of degree separated him from Tocqueville. Both recognized the great power that habit exercised on the will. Will, thus reinforced, had the force to improve human happiness, as Rousseau said, and to give human beings the "peace, security and inner balance" they truly sought[85] or, as Tocqueville thought, to create the conditions of their inner security.

Just as, if not more, important was the view of human society that Tocqueville made his own. No person, acting in the name of a false belief in a full "independence" of intellect, could fail to become subject to a futile servitude, ending in powerlessness. There is a difference between that servitude, which forbids any of us to decide on matters vital to ourselves, and the "salutary servitude," the willingness to trust many opinions without discussion "which allows [us] to make a good use of freedom."[86] The belief in the unboundedness of the individual mind is a dream. Thus, when Tocqueville opines that it is important to find where authority resides in an age of democracy, "and by what standard it is to be measured," he says that it is to be found in an authority already in

---

[84] *OCR*, III, pp. 288–89.

[85] Cf. Judith N. Shklar, *Men and Citizens: A Study of Rousseau's Social Theory* (Cambridge, 1985), p. 55.   [86] *Nolla edn.*, II, p. 20.

existence. For him, authority in a democratic period of history resides in the opinions held by the greatest number, not in the will of all, nor in the general will. The democratic majority carries greater weight than individual judgments. In a society governed by an egalitarian ethos, people tend to belittle their own views, because they feel that they are no better and no worse than those held by every other member of society. Hence they seek security in the superiority of collective judgment and endow it with a kind of religious aura.[87] Thus, democratic society, like all others, possesses a common stock of beliefs which give it cohesion. Without it and the common action it generates, "there . . . is no social body."[88]

A fair equivalence exists between Rousseau's negative view of *amour-propre* and Tocqueville's unqualified objection to *égoïsme*. Each may be regarded as the victory – for Rousseau, of the *moi humain* over the *moi commun*; for Tocqueville, of the individual good over the general good. "How small, cold, and sad life would become if," he told Kergorlay, "beside this everyday world so full of egoism and cowardice, the human spirit could not construct another in which disinterestedness, courage, in a word, virtue, could breathe at last."[89] But individualism was subtly different from the *égoïsme* in traditional societies that Tocqueville spoke about; *égoïsme* and *amour-propre*, which may be thought of as the same, were to be distinguished from modern individualism. Democratic individualism arose from erroneous judgment and emotional perversity; it drew men away from society and froze the virtues of public life, and deceptively encouraged isolation as a kind of healthy complacency. It was in fact worse than *égoïsme* because, being of democratic origin, it could start with the desiccation of public, and end with the destruction of private, virtue. Modern individualism arose from but paradoxically undermined equality;[90] it was not embedded, as was Rousseau's *amour-propre*, in the very structures of inequality.

The major point to be made is that Rousseau believed that equality would enhance the chances for the social development of *amour de soi*, while Tocqueville feared that equality would achieve the very opposite. One of his major and most profound ideas about the leveling features of equality is that it creates great unease. To escape from it, democratic people embrace individualism, but then find themselves trapped between its demands and the rituals and realities of equality. They can never know rest, and lose sight of the urgency of developing liberty as a practical reality. Individualism makes democratic man both "independent and

---

[87] Ibid., p. 24.   [88] Ibid., p. 20.
[89] Tocqueville to Kergorlay, July 6, 1835, *OC*, XIII, pt. 1, p. 376.
[90] *Nolla edn.*, II, pp. 96–98.

powerless." It forces him into a social void, from which he tries to escape by surrendering to the imposing power of the state.[91] Buffeted by the winds of equality and individualism, he becomes a victim of the state and knows nothing but his isolated self. In such conditions, what can liberty do for him except to heighten his sense of fragmentation?

Economic expansion speeded up opportunities for actions that Rousseau categorized as the expression of *amour-propre*. The antithesis he saw between wealth and virtue, and between wealth and liberty, may be grasped more firmly if we keep in mind that the pursuit of wealth in modern society represented for him a search for distinction and was, *ipso facto*, immoral. The point he wanted to make was more subtle and, at bottom, Pascalian. The primary source of moral corruption is luxury's concupiscent origins and goals: "the superfluous awakens lust; the more one gets, the more one desires."[92] Thus luxury, which is "either the effect of wealth or renders it necessary . . . corrupts both the rich and the poor, the former by possession, the latter by covetousness."[93] This induced a fatal circuit of acute anxiety and prompted the rich to exploit the poor.[94] Everything becomes purchasable; the objects of lust can be bought and sold: "there are those who aspire to authority by selling its uses to the rich, and enrich themselves in this way; others – the greatest number – directly aim to gain wealth with which they can one day be sure of possessing the power either to buy authority or those who are its repositories."[95]

Generations later, Tocqueville worried about the potential clash between the owners of wealth and workers. But the past could not be recovered; the mores of other societies could not be replicated in changed conditions. The determination to be modern does not detract from his anguish over some of the same disturbing questions Rousseau raised, particularly the fate of human beings living in a society without guides to moral conduct and without signposts giving them some palpable sense of how they might determine their private and public selves. The multiplication of needs, unfulfilled desire and psychic fatigue were already changing lives. Nothing was to be gained from futile conflicts of opinion that divided people into two groups: those who built their lives

---

[91] Ibid.
[92] *OCR*, III, p. 612. Cf. J. C. O'Neal, "Rousseau's Theory of Wealth," *History of European Ideas*, 7 (1986), pp. 453–67. Mandeville, the most relentless exponent of a naturalistic and non-providential doctrine of self-interest as the basis of economic improvement, which at the same time rigorously eschewed the question of morality as a species of hypocrisy, evoked Rousseau's ire, as well as Smith's. For a lucid examination of these and related questions, see Edward J. Hundert, *The Enlightenment's "Fable": Bernard Mandeville and the Discovery of Society* (Cambridge, 1994).   [93] *OCR*, III, p. 405.
[94] Ibid., pp. 177–78.   [95] Ibid., p. 939.

around morality, religion and order, and those who claimed to give priority to liberty and equality under the law. Few thought of combining these concepts of the good life to work for "political and moral grandeur," with a keen and reasoned taste for liberty.[96] In this, as in his thoughts on commerce and virtue, he searched for the saving midpoint. The meaning of his quest may be deciphered as a longing for grand moral gestures. Informed by religion, protected by the rule of law, guided by respect for liberty, human beings could do more to take responsibility for themselves as political persons. People need not condemn themselves to live under petty tyrannies, to be content with passing interests, or to endure daily miseries. Tocqueville recalled the tempestuous times of the Revolution and shuddered to think that the high hopes of its actors had probably been lost forever and would prove as ephemeral as, and no different from, the petty disputes of his own time.[97]

Tocqueville was sensitive to the corruption of elected members, but most of all to their power, which was its source. Did he concur with Constant who wished and predicted that politics would matter less and less to modern peoples? He admitted that there were indeed many areas of life that politics need not touch directly; and he was grateful that people could indeed find refuge and retain their integrity in some small corners of oppressive modern states. He was worried, however, that the corners would be spied out in time. So, if he was prepared, as Constant was, "to reject the conceit that modern politics should become the whole of life," he did so only by urging, as Constant also did, that politics must remain a "crucial and indispensable element in social life."[98] The individual would, moreover, likely find that retreat from public life would make his private space an insalubrious and unsafe locus of human action. The realm of political action, mediated by liberty, was the only way to negotiate the treacherous path between public and private virtue. There was another sense in which he thought of *virtus*. There was a link between *virtuosity* and liberty. "The great object in our time," is "to raise the faculties of men, not to complete their prostration." Looking back to the debates in the colonial assemblies during the American Revolution, he praised the "great orator debating great questions of state in a democratic assembly . . . expand[ing] his thoughts, and heighten[ing] his powers of language . . . [and drawing] on the general truths derived from human nature to solve the particular questions under discussion."[99] He took no

[96] Tocqueville to E. Stoffels, February 21, 1835, *Beaumont edn.*, V, pp. 426–28.
[97] Tocqueville to Royer-Collard, August 20, 1837, *OC*, XI, pp. 39–42.
[98] Stephen Holmes, *Benjamin Constant and the Making of Modern Liberalism* (New Haven, 1984), p. 192.   [99] *Nolla edn.*, II, pp. 85, 89.

comfort from Kergorlay's predictions that every society would in time produce varieties of ambition[100] sufficient to raise them above mediocrity, or that it was beside the point to think of men as superior beings.[101] He was ready to admit that there were "few . . . who can ever attain to that . . . state of rational and independent conviction which true knowledge can produce out of the midst of doubt."[102] The liberal belief in rationality is clearly affirmed, but so is a neo-Pascalian sentiment that arose from his interest in questions of indeterminacy. Moreover, he found that, both in the natural and social sciences, thinkers were having trouble with those questions.[103]

In light of Tocqueville's regret that the excesses of the Revolution had travestied liberty, his great concern was to fortify it in the future. The development of constitutionalism, which owed much to Constant and to Royer-Collard, and to some of the achievements of bourgeois culture, was accorded some minimal value for its promotion of public life. The prospect of a de-moralized liberty was almost as unacceptable for him as it was for Rousseau, but he was willing to gamble on future political skills to revitalize the association between freedom and morality. He could never have imagined, as Rousseau did, the remorseless physical and mental torture that powerful men could impose on their victims. Tocqueville's vision was not that dark. Modern democracy, in its despotic forms, would be tolerable, because no one would remember what liberty was once he or she had voluntarily given it up:

Under the absolute sway of one man [the monarch] the body was attacked in order to subdue the soul; but the soul escaped the blows which were directed against it and rose proudly superior. Such is not the course adopted by tyranny in democratic republics; there the body is left free, and the soul is enslaved.[104]

Against such a possibility, Tocqueville made a strong appeal, on the one hand, to the moralist in societies where democracy and irreligion coexist, to teach citizens the need to resist "a thousand petty selfish passions of the hour [so] that the general and unquenchable passion for happiness can be satisfied"; and, on the other hand, to those in power to "practically teach the community day by day (without saying so) that wealth, fame and power are the rewards of labor."[105] The functions of moralist and legislator were thus blended.

[100] Kergorlay to Tocqueville, February 6, 1838, *OC*, XIII, pt. 2, pp. 14–18.
[101] Tocqueville to Kergorlay, March 2, 1838, ibid., pp. 19–24.   [102] *Nolla edn.*, I, p. 145.
[103] Ibid., pp. 145, 222, 242.   [104] Ibid., p. 200.   [105] Ibid., II, p. 134.

Cosmic and historical contingency: the metaphysical and religious foundations of liberty

Some of the linguistic flourishes in the *Democracy* do not meet Tocqueville's later, more sober, promise to himself. At this stage in his life, he was carried away by the exhilarating prospect of penetrating the depths of a social and political phenomenon that had eluded even the most perspicuous of observers, past and present. Guizot's lectures and books had prepared him to appreciate it in the long perspective of the uneven development of feudalism and the political consequences of feudalism's breakup in the different parts of Europe. Montesquieu's comparative approach strengthened his feelings of awe at time's sweeping indifference to the fate of once-powerful and seemingly indestructible civilizations. He was thus prepared to witness in America, not only the indecipherable signs, but concrete instances of a new civilization in the making. The study in the nineteenth century of past civilizations included many of the troubling questions that agitated eighteenth-century thinkers. Montesquieu's intellectual universe was, as with many of his contemporaries, deeply indebted to, but often struggling to free itself from, competing classical conceptions of rightful authority and the good. This is evident in his movement toward historical relativism in his taxonomy of political cultures. Some of the eighteenth century's contexts of those ideas, particularly as Montesquieu framed them, made a firm impression on Tocqueville before he left for America.[106]

In addition, some of the power of Pascal's vision of the nature of conscience and deception reached Tocqueville in diffused and altered form through Rousseau who, as we have just seen, was much concerned with these very same problems in modern society.[107] Together, the fideism of the one and the theism of the other helped to form Tocqueville's moral and religious reflections and beliefs. Pascal tried to stifle doubt and skepticism under a willing surrender to Christian belief, but just as significantly he placed on human beings the duty "to seek [for answers] in their

---

[106] Tocqueville to C. Stoffels, April 21, 1830, *Nolla edn.*, II, pp. 322–24. The best guide to Tocqueville's debt to Montesquieu is Melvin Richter. See, *inter alia*, "The Uses of Theory: Tocqueville's Adaptation of Montesquieu," in *Essays in Theory and History: An Approach to the Social Sciences*, ed. Richter (Cambridge, 1970), pp. 74–102; Richter, "Modernity and its Distinctive Threats to Liberty: Montesquieu and Tocqueville on New Forms of Illegitimate Domination," in *Alexis de Tocqueville – Zur Politik in Demokratie*, ed. Michael Hereth and J. Höffken (Baden-Baden, 1981), pp. 61–80.

[107] On the affinities and differences between Pascal and Rousseau, see Harvey Mitchell, "Reclaiming the Self: The Pascal-Rousseau Connection," *Journal of the History of Ideas*, 54 (1993), pp. 637–58.

doubt."[108] The doubt that Pascal spoke about appeared in Tocqueville's self-questioning over uncertainty. For him, however, Christian faith could not fully assuage it. Rousseau resolutely distinguished his theism from deism. That theism was not far from some of Tocqueville's thoughts on religion as a kind of natural force that satisfied human longings for the ineffable. From them both, Tocqueville learned about dissimulation. He also was an uneasy legatee of their deep aversion for the enthusiasms for material well-being that deflected human beings from examining nature. Human beings are both flesh and spirit, but the angel is not overwhelmed by the beast:

I adore the angel and . . . I would like to see it in ascendancy at any price. I am thus exercising my brain at all times to discover if, between these two extremes, there isn't a middle way for humanity . . . leading neither to Heliogabalus nor to Saint Jerome . . . I am therefore not as shocked as you [Kergorlay] when you complain so bitterly about *honest materialism*. Not that it doesn't excite my contempt as much as yours. But I envisage it from a practical perspective, and I ask myself if something, if not similar, at least analogous is still not the best . . . not for any individual man, but for our poor species in general.[109]

His views on infinity may also be extracted from his notes on immortality – "the love of the infinite, lofty aspirations, and a love of pleasures not of earth."[110] He set aside what he believed were professions of materialism by Plato's predecessors and contemporaries as a gross diminution of the psychological needs of human beings throughout the ages, and to make his point, he adduced the strong spiritual elements that suffused all good literature.[111] In defense of the spiritual, he wondered, within an ingenuous circularity that sometimes affected his logic, whether it might even not be inappropriate to think of the soul as a kind of organ analogous to bodily organs:

The need for the *infinite* and the bleak experience of the *finite* that we meet at every turn, sometimes torments me, but does not distress me. I see in it [the infinite] one of the greatest proofs of the existence of another world and of the immortality of the soul. According to everything we know about God's works, we know that he does not do anything without having in mind either an immediate or a distant goal. This is so true that in the physical world all we need is to be presented with an organ to conclude with some certainty that the animal that possesses it uses it in such and such a way, and experience proves this. Reasoning by analogy, I cannot believe that God has endowed our souls with an *organ* for [comprehending] infinity, if I may express myself in that way,

---

[108] Pascal, *Pensées*, pp. 157, 275. See also A. J. Krailsheimer, *Studies in Self-Interest: From Descartes to La Bruyère* (Oxford, 1962).

[109] Tocqueville to Kergorlay, August 5, 1836, *OC*, XIII, pt. 1, p. 389. The emphasis is Tocqueville's. The same point is made in the notes to the *Democracy*, Nolla edn., II, p. 131, note k.   [110] *Nolla edn.*, II, p. 130.   [111] Ibid., p. 131.

simply to free himself for eternity from the *finite*, and that he would not have given the soul, the *organ* of hope, for a future life if there were not a future life.[112]

These questions stayed with him throughout the composition of the *Democracy*, particularly its second part. He was, it is also plain to see, immune from the anti-Christian legacies of the eighteenth century. Religion was important to Tocqueville on three grounds. First, he regarded it as the fountainhead, since the Reformation, of modern notions of political liberty. He never relinquished the conviction that, once the essence of religious sensibilities was submerged in the relentless movement toward greater and greater equality, one of – perhaps, the principal – sources and mainstays of liberty might drop away and take liberty along with it. Second, he saw religion as a good beyond the satisfaction of material goods. As a modern, but very much the Romantic, he never expressed this in a more convincing way than when he speculated that for moderns the poetic imagination alone was capable of arousing feelings for the divine. He dismissed the force of premodern beliefs in mythical divinities, personifications of passions and visible agents of the divine as "operatic machines," freezing spectators into submission. Religion had to appeal on aesthetic grounds – though he confessed that he had to find practical proof of his contention.[113] Third, he wanted to relate religion to an understanding of the meaning of providence. He tended not to accept Christianity's claim to have a direct route to providence which Christianity equated with itself. But it is not always clear that he consistently maintained the separation. Sorting this out appeared to be less important than his conviction that a secular revolt against the metaphysical constituted an amputation of an important part of human existence. The appeal to the metaphysical did not warrant a politics founded on the political pretension of the French Catholic Church. He found aggressive political religiosity repugnant: it offended both religion and politics. The search for political solutions was not distasteful. Preferably the quest should recognize how religion, when not tied to a repressive secular arm of the state, or when successful in opposing theocratic notions, could nurture the conditions for civil and political liberty. Tocqueville transformed his metaphysical impulse into a sociological analysis of the function of religious belief in history.

Belief in a pure Pascalian transcendence was, for a modern like Tocqueville, out of the question. Alive in him, however, was a lasting and aching hope that modern democratic life need not be inimical to religious feeling. Without

---

[112] Ibid., p. 131, note h (Tocqueville's emphasis).
[113] Ibid., p. 76, note s. His notes indicate that he was probably discussing these ideas with Charles Stoffels on April 22, 1837.

its religious foundations, liberty was likely to diminish in the modern world. In time, history, under whose indifference to human wishes equality was taking confident strides into the future, might well bury religion or transform it beyond recognition. Ironically the shadow of uncertainty under which Tocqueville lived had almost the same purchase on the future as certainty. Fideism suspended skepticism, but did not promise certain salvation. The movement toward equality was a historical force, but a full-blown and limit-less equality was a doubtful benefit. If history pointed to the strengthening of equality, it seemed conversely to point in no definitive direction for liberty. Humanity could, nevertheless, take steps to temper equality so that it need not necessarily impinge on liberty. To drive away his doubts Tocqueville embraced a voluntaristic view of the individual and collective selves. A tute-lary, paternalistic power was, he said, circumnavigating the life of a people and infantilizing them. It deadened thought and the pain of living:

There are people who have no wish to distinguish themselves from their fellows; there are others who, on the contrary, have an unquenchable will and continue to do so. Finally, there are others who make only the most minuscule efforts to rise above the earth and who just as soon sink back toward it. These last are the most unfortunate of all, because they have [to endure] the troubles ambition brings, without having any of its doubtful pleasures. The whole of man is in will. His entire future is hidden in it as in a germ that comes to life with the first ray of good luck.[114]

Thus the uncertainty that plagued Tocqueville had this double edge. It could, if seen positively, be used as a weapon against the propensity to make confident predictions or sanction arrogant prophecies mapping out an absolutely certain kind of future. If viewed as a negative force, it evoked a kind of resignation – a position that Tocqueville found intoler-able. Thus, although he detested his doubts and decried his inability to solve the dilemmas posed by uncertainty, he actually made them work to give him strength. He wanted to escape from dealing with ontological questions, for they always led him back to the blankness of the obscurities facing him in his encounters with doubt.[115]

How he found a workable compromise may have very well been due to Kergorlay. Tocqueville wrote to him at length while he was working on the most difficult parts of the *Democracy*. He took Kergorlay's ideas on doubt and uncertainty with utmost seriousness, and he regarded him as his equal in intellectual matters.[116] It was almost as if Tocqueville were

---

[114] Ibid., p. 266, note m.

[115] Ibid., p. 77, note v. In an early letter (November 19, 1831) to Ernest de Chabrol, cited by Nolla, Tocqueville spoke about the "veil" that concealed the true contours of earthly objects. He found living in this "perpetual half-light" fatiguing and despairing.

[116] Tocqueville to Kergorlay, September 4, 1837, *OC*, XIII, pt. 1, p. 472. See also Tocqueville to Kergorlay, September 17, 1838, *OC*, XIII, pt. 2, pp. 43–44.

awaiting answers to questions which had been troubling both friends for years. "I don't myself feel, as you do," Kergorlay told Tocqueville, "the impossibility of living with doubts."[117] What was clear to Kergorlay was that complete certainty was out of the question. Doubt and enlightenment had the same source: an irrepressible movement from stages of darkness to enlightenment. Doubt stands at the point where enlightenment falls into obscurity. Thus they exist side by side. At each step more truth is discovered, and more errors are cast aside, except that truth and error are not sharply separated. Absolute certitude is thus not accessible: truth and error do not lie on either side of a well-marked boundary. What can take the place of certitude is probability. Though admittedly it is an expedient, it is a great advance over total doubt. Kergorlay urged Tocqueville to give up the idea that men were condemned to live under the blanket of absolute doubt forever.[118]

Tocqueville seems to have been calmed by Kergorlay's assurances – at least for a time. He told himself in his notes to the *Democracy* that he would like "to dare to speak somewhere about Louis's [Kergorlay's] idea – that there is a difference between absolute affirmation [certitude] and pyrrhonism; that the theory of probabilities is the only true, the only *human* system, provided that probability is capable of making people act as energetically as [a belief in] certitude. All this is very badly put, but the germ [of the idea] is there."[119] Daily experience, he wrote Royer-Collard, told him that he would have to be content with probabilities and approximations of truth, but that he could not suppress his "unbridled and unreasonable passion for certitude" and the need for a feeling of completion.[120] Tocqueville reluctantly accepted that probabilities, rather

---

[117] Kergorlay to Tocqueville, March 2, 1838, *OC*, XIII, pt. 2, p. 19. The entire letter is to be found on pp. 19–24. The letter is a reply to a letter written by Tocqueville between February 2 and March 2. The letter, to which Kergorlay refers as having been written "two days ago" (either January 31 or February 1), is missing from the published correspondence.   [118] Ibid., p. 20.

[119] *Nolla edn.*, II, p. 280, note e. The emphasis is Tocqueville's.

[120] Tocqueville to Royer-Collard, April 6, 1838, *OC*, XI, p. 59. Neither Kergorlay nor Tocqueville appeared to be aware of, or they make no allusions to, the works on probability by Siméon-D. Poisson, among them, *Recherches sur la probabilité des jugements en matière criminelle et en matière civile, précédées des règles générales du calcul des probabilités* (Paris, 1837), or A.-A. Cournot, *Exposition de la théorie des chances et des probabilités* (Paris, 1843). One of Poisson's studies, "Recherches sur la probabilité des jugements principalement en matière criminelle," appeared in *Comptes rendus hebdomadaires des séances de l'Académie des Sciences*, I (1835). Both Poisson and Cournot are discussed in Ian Hacking, *The Taming of Chance* (Cambridge, 1990). Cournot wrote admiringly of Tocqueville's notions of honor. See his references to the *Democracy* in his *Essai sur les fondements de nos connaissances et sur les caractères de la critique philosophique* (first published in two volumes in Paris, in 1851). See the new edition of this volume, *Oeuvres complètes*, ed. Jean-Claude Pariente (Paris, 1975), pp. 212–13.

than certitude, existed in the realm of the human, and that in this life the truth of the divine could at best only be dimly apprehended. But he remained anxious all his life about his need for certain signs of divine truth.

Tocqueville stands on the other side of thinkers, like Hegel, who believed that history has a final goal. Tocqueville asked humanity to take responsibility for itself. Human beings might perhaps seize hold of fragments of the truth, but no more. Historical moments may be instantiations of the truth, but never the truth itself, which can never be reduced to a mere instance. Thus any one foolish enough to profess a complete or absolute system purporting to reveal truth is perpetrating a falsehood or committing an error. Such a person should be considered *ipso facto* a tyrant and an enemy of humanity.[121] The taste for general ideas is, however, natural to humankind. It is an emanation from the divine, the greatest "generalizer" in the universe. The human psyche feels restrained by the constant contemplation of the particular, and breaks away from it to enunciate general laws.[122]

Similarly, the tendency of modern historians to deny both the importance of individuals and accidents in modifying history, based on the supposition that there is a "chain of causes" that cannot be breached, stems from their failure to perceive that accidents find their origin in individual actions; and that these cannot be disregarded.[123] Americans in particular live as if providence had chosen them. They believe that they have reached a certain point in history, and assert further that it was necessarily bound to have followed the path that led them there. Tocqueville's sardonic comment was that this was an explanation that followed the path of least resistance.[124] But we have another view in his notes. "It seems that providence, having traced the diverse paths that nations must traverse, and fixed the final end point of their journeys, leaves to individuals the trouble of relaxing or expediting humanity's march that they know neither how to deflect or suspend."[125] When he added that people living in democratic times think that they have grasped destiny to their bosoms and can in consequence control it, he was ridiculing the presumption as the ultimate demonstration of democratic solipsism. Democratic egalitarianism in fact encouraged people to think in the most shallow way about their connections with their ancestors and their descendants, and to invest all in present-mindedness.[126] Tocqueville deplored the prospect that they would lose a sense of the past and of time, and of how past

---

[121] *Nolla edn.*, I, p. 20, note f.
[122] Ibid., II, p. 26, note b. Tocqueville, as we saw in the *Souvenirs*, moved from particulars to the enunciation of general historical laws.   [123] Ibid., p. 83, note f.
[124] Ibid., p. 85.   [125] Ibid., p. 96, note g.   [126] Ibid., p. 98.

peoples lived and what values they had, as well as how the different forms of authority operated to give them a sense of temporal and spiritual order. What do these reflections amount to? Equality in Tocqueville's scheme is a stage that Western peoples will experience. It is also a scheme that rejects the idea that nothing lies beyond the stage of the coming of democratic equality, and that, once it is achieved, history is destined to end.

It is best, Tocqueville seems to be saying, to regard the enunciation of general laws of history and the workings of providence as an expression of the instinctive desire of human beings to seek meaning, but that such meaning as human beings are capable of achieving would be incomplete without the admission of the contingent. On an everyday level, democratic societies are best advised to test general laws against practical problems – a salutary check against the extravagances of theory.[127] The fortuitous, contingent and unpredictable have causes, but they are not law-determined. Others, like Antoine Cournot, might have said that chance, like order, may be thought of as embedded in the nature of things.[128] Tocqueville left this question in suspense. While human beings cannot resist the formulation of general laws and theories, they must remind themselves that they are subject to error in this and in other workings of the mind, and that they are best advised not to forget that human beings are only one of the many things among the many millions of entities which God uses in the government and order of the universe.[129]

Thus Tocqueville gave enormous but finite scope to human intelligence. It is capable first of perceiving that, however mysterious are the processes by which order is reached, order is in God's design. Once human beings know this, they will gain a better understanding of the provisionality of general historical laws and how the refractory actions of human beings may be fitted into and explained by them. Tocqueville took into account the advances of theoretical scientific inquiry, and certainly did not intend to minimize its importance, but he was less inclined to extend the ordinary meaning of science to the study of history, politics and morals. Nevertheless, in those realms too, human beings would also be enabled to know, again imperfectly, where to locate their true interest.[130] Tocqueville considered ways to discuss the question of how to reconcile and transform the links between interest and morals in their modern setting – a problem that he felt was being neglected by moral philosophers.[131] A proper understanding of the doctrine of interest would free it from false notions of gross egoism that submit fellow human beings

---

[127] Ibid., p. 31.
[128] See Cournot, *Essai sur les fondements de nos connaissances et sur les caractères de la critique philosophique*. See note 120 in this chapter.   [129] *Nolla edn.*, II, p. 32, note d.
[130] Ibid., p. 116, note n.   [131] Ibid., p. 115.

to one's will; on the other hand, it was not, he maintained, to be confused with utility. He had no difficulty locating and containing the doctrine of interest in the useful, but the useful, he maintained, was only one part of the doctrine. It should be possible, he said, to work out a defensible philosophical position recognizing that interest demanded the sacrifice of immediate for longer-term concerns.

In the original Christian doctrine, the belief that a sense of duty underlies action demanded a simple adoration of God. It was the condition of achieving eternal life. True interest, thus conceived, was located in the other world and drew human beings away from the "cloaca of human and material interests."[132] The doctrine of interest well-understood in today's world, by contrast, can make honest human beings. But only the love of God can make them virtuous. "The one [the first] teaches men how to live, the other [the second] teaches men how to die, and how can one make men who do not wish to die live well for long?"[133] Modern democratic peoples prefer the first because of their expectations of achieving more of this world's goods than peoples living in aristocratic ages when such hopes were unrealistic, and who were for that reason driven to seek consolation in the promise of life after death. Both modern and religious doctrines place interest at their core, but modern and premodern human beings behave differently. As we have seen, he had no illusions about the workings of the inner spirit in aristocratic societies. He was interested in isolating the driving psychosocial force that underlay them, and he was intent on distinguishing the power of the new democratic dynamic. At the same time, he was driven by his belief in the disparities between human intelligence and human weakness to reaffirm that transcendent principles counted even in the modern world. Hence he rejected a strict utilitarianism.

Tocqueville clearly intended the *Democracy* to be read as an impartial and "theoretical judgment" of two societies, one losing its *ethos*, the other newly creating one.[134] He had made similar observations to Royer-Collard, to whom he also wrote that the problem of measuring the impact of equality on human sentiments and opinions was more philosophical than political, and that he was buffeted by the fear of going on forever and of falling into an abyss of gross generalizations.[135] Speaking about the reception accorded the *Democracy*, after the second volume appeared, he wrote wearily that his audience would have had no problems with it if he had written about France and America as if each were a totally discrete

---

[132] Ibid., p. 116, note n.   [133] Ibid.
[134] Tocqueville to Reeve, November 15, 1839, *OC*, VI, pt. 1, p. 48.
[135] Tocqueville to Royer-Collard, August 15, 1838, *OC*, XI, p. 67.

society. But that had not been his purpose. He wanted to look for the general characteristics of democratic societies for which there were no existing models. Only people very skilled in seeking "general and speculative truths" would be able, he said not very hopefully, to grasp the thrust of his work.[136]

The fate of caste, honor and shame under democratic equality

In focusing on inequality in the 1836 *Essai*, Tocqueville seemed to reverse the stress he had placed on the advent of equality in the first volume of the *Democracy*, as if in preparation – still some years away – for his history of the decline and end of the *ancien régime*. The time was ripe for a mirror image of the rise of the totally new phenomenon of modern democracy in the Western world. Only in the second volume did he sharpen the two images, as he described one in contrast with the other. It was as if with each brush stroke of his right hand taking us into the depths of the social dynamics of inequality, he brushed in with his left hand the social dynamics of its opposite; but also with a sense of how the values of the new transformed, yet emerged in some sense from, the old. The continuities are there, not simply because of the objective presence of traces from the past, but because the human mind is not totally shaped by the realities of the world it perceives. Sometimes it apprehends realities that are yet to come. This is not always apparent; indeed, it is often obscured by the contrasting images Tocqueville evoked, as he measured the failures of the old society by the successes of the other. The process of decay was not wholly discernible; it lay partly concealed. The ambiguities of change are another important feature of how Tocqueville saw the problem. The new is not successful in any obvious way; neither can its success be regarded so. The new is successful to the extent that it struggles to find the more or less proximate modes for feelings that must find expression in any society, even if they can only be dimly made out. The discussion of the aristocratic ethos and of the democratic ethos is therefore as much a description of similitudes as it is of differences. Neither can be understood without the other.

The strategies of contrast, according to Tocqueville, would lose their purpose if they were to be interpreted straightforwardly as an analysis of how a society and its values lose their rationale. The contrasts are present to convince us that, though time covers successive waves of social relations in dust, it does not bury humanity's deepest urges, for good or for

---

[136] Tocqueville to Mill, December 18, 1840, ibid., p. 330.

bad. Hence the other purpose in Tocqueville's strategy of contrasts is to bring us closer to what he saw as a more lasting but intractable problem: the tension between the social construction of good and evil and the autonomous, ahistorical existence of both, namely, the existence of good and evil independent of the human species itself.[137] He asked whether good and evil were external or internal to humanity. The metaphysical Tocqueville was profoundly disturbed by the question. He endeavored to particularize it by calling on human experience. Killing was contrary to the "universal and permanent interest of the human species." Put this way, killing appeared to be evil. Was it evil in all cases? One answer was to look at the reasons given for justifiable homicide. Tocqueville took up the problem from a social angle. A particular and momentary interest of a nation or class may see killing as excusable or even honorable. He thus acknowledged that he was relativizing and taking the sting out of murder. How was that social reality and retention in a belief in absolute values to be dealt with? The question fatigued him. He confessed that, "I am too tired at this moment to see clearly . . ."[138] but added that he expected to return to the questions when he felt fresher. The question kept cropping up, but he dealt with it in a less than systematic way.

Opinion, a strictly social construct, was conceptually and empirically easier to deal with. Tocqueville took another step toward a theory of dysfunctionality or impasse, and this time round he found that he needed to support it by looking at the psychosocial mechanisms – which were themselves epiphenomena of hypothetically basic traits of human nature – that once made the aristocratic social system work. The question of caste remained for Tocqueville far from a simple matter, but whether he understood its mechanism fully in prerevolutionary France must now be considered at the point where he took it up again in the *Democracy*. The purity of blood lines, ensured in large part through the preservation of patriarchy and primogeniture, was relatively unthreatened when everyone in the stratified society of aristocratic France knew their place and felt no urge to rise, since it was unthinkable that they could be toppled from the heights from which they commanded their inferiors. The fear of the pollution of pure blood lines – the threat to the purity inherent in bodily constitutions through contact with bloods of inferior substances – was not so great or so rigid in France to prevent castes, not only from experiencing, but imagining how they might experience, the admission of inferiors into their ranks. The mixture of bodily fluids was not unthinkable, and how it became thinkable is described by Tocqueville in the context of

---

[137] *Nolla edn.*, II, p. 193, note e. The discussion and the citations in the following two paragraphs rest on the questions Tocqueville raises in this note.   [138] Ibid.

the kinship network of the caste and its power to determine marriage patterns in the families that made it up.

It is not strange that caste plays an ambiguous role in Tocqueville's conception; however much caste might operate in other societies, it was not without its ambiguities there as well. Body/soul images may differ as between, say, Eastern and Western societies, and are complicated further by notions of caste, but whether they are unreservedly dualistic or non-dualistic – a highly contentious matter[139] – it must be said in favor of Tocqueville's interpretation that he more than implied that it was both the body and the soul, however societies related them, that would be involved in any threat to the integrity of caste. Unlike other societies where castes seemed to be permanently in place so that the sources of their permanence became the problem demanding answers,[140] the aristocratic society of France that Tocqueville described appeared to be more permeable. His problem resides in the calculation of its strengths and fragilities. From the time of the origins of aristocracy, it already had many of the characteristics of a caste, then lost a few of them under economic pressures, but retained enough of them to make it a hybrid, unable to make up its mind about the fullness of its commitment to its older self-image, or its readiness to drop it.

How far did he carry his analysis of the question in the *Democracy*? He contrasted, as he did in the 1836 *Essai*, aristocracies of birth and of wealth. Once the first breach in the ranks of an aristocracy of blood was made, its members were caught in a labyrinth of confusion, no longer knowing their own minds, no longer able to resist fresh temptations to succumb to social intrusion. Where this happened, as in England, aristocratic pride was on its guard. It shifted its ground for self-esteem from birth to money, but struggled mightily to absorb it rather than be absorbed by it. Tocqueville detected a politics of liminality at work in the shaping of social relations.[141] If, as was the case in England, money was not seen as intrinsically injurious to its ethos, but rather as a means of remaining at the social apex, the aristocracy had a good chance of surviving, but not with its pristine values intact. A second way, that of the French aristocracy, pursued neither policy consistently. The French

---

[139] For two classic discussions of caste, see Marcel Mauss, "Les techniques du corps," *Sociologie et anthropologie* (Paris, [1936], 1960) and Louis Dumont, *Homo Hierarchicus*, trans. Mark Sainsbury, Louis Dumont and Basia Gulati, rev. edn. (Chicago, 1980).

[140] As Tocqueville likely discovered when, in the summer of 1843, he read the abbé J.-A. Dubois's study, first published in English, *Description of the Character, Manners and Customs of the People of India; and of Their Institutions, Religious and Civil*, trans. Henry K. Beauchamp (London, 1817). It was published in French under the title *Moeurs, institutions et cérémonies des peuples de l'Inde* (Paris, 1825). Tocqueville's notes on the book may be read in *Pléiade edn.*, I, pp. 1019–56.   [141] *Nolla edn.*, II, pt. 3, chap. 2, pp. 149–50.

aristocracy's attempt to retain itself as an impenetrable caste was pursued in a haze of self-deception. The attempts were real, but fringed with exceptions which were not always acknowledged. In this territory of ambiguities, Tocqueville picked up some of the trails of social gain and psychic loss.[142] Since belief, pretended or genuine, in providential privilege was the animating force of caste, in periods of change often the smallest privileges were most jealously guarded – a certain proof of a defensive mentality despite all the apparent signs of power. A caste that was fissured by jealousies and uncertainties originated in the concessions to ranks below it, and by the anti-aristocratic agenda of the crown. He found these jealousies and vanities comparable to the same feelings brought to the surface in democratic societies, where rapid social mobility highlighted both the opportunities and the precariousness of individual lives.

The difference was that in democratic societies, members thought not only of themselves in their private concerns, but of their nation. The same could not be said of a privileged aristocracy that identified itself with no one but itself. This failure to see beyond its immediate interests would have revolutionary consequences, but at this point in his ideas Tocqueville did not expand on the insight. He stressed instead the ironies revealed by aristocratic societies in decline. Modernity and homogeneity were converging as the differences of caste, profession and family were vanishing. No longer were human beings separated by distinctions; they imitated one another – but even without imitating one another they became more and more alike. No longer would human beings living in particular societies be the subject of inquiry. "All the nations which take, not any particular man, but Man himself as the object of their researches and their imitations are tending in the end to a similar state of society . . ."[143]

The emotional resonances of honor, as it arose in feudal aristocratic society, were the best way, Tocqueville thought, to grasp the different manner in which societies express the universal need for self-esteem and the feelings released when it is not satisfied.[144] The origins of honor launched him on one of his most difficult ventures. As if in anticipation of its perils, he confided to himself that honor is born in human fantasies.[145] Discussion of honor at the highest abstract level, however, did not appeal to him. He chose to look at how, in aristocratic society, the homage paid to honor reached its most extensive forms. Where honor reigned, the need for magnificence and glory, pride and domination, were unquestionably taken as expressions of virtuous conduct, so much so that the

---

[142] Ibid., pt. 3, chap. 16, pp. 188–89.   [143] Ibid., p. 192.   [144] Ibid., pt. 3, chap. 18.
[145] Ibid., p. 192, note b.

"natural order of conscience"[146] was subdued and even perceived as obstructive.

The feelings of shame associated with the loss of honor were more complex. Any relaxation of the codes of honor was seen as the harbinger of shame. Those who lived by the codes could invoke shame as the ultimate injury to self-esteem. Honor preserved could be identified with virtue, but could shame inflicted be identified with vice? Honor was essentially active. A person bound by its codes actively worked to have it at all times. Thus the active preservation of honor in various circumstances was where one would, in a caste society, locate and name it and identify it with virtue. The unintended consequences of actively working for it, but not achieving it, could result in shame. But the passive acceptance of slights would be even more devastating. Yet could either the first action, or the second non-action, be called vice according to the existing codes of honor? Only if – and then much more problematically – failure led to the disintegration of character, through the loss of reputation, affecting not only the person whose honor was at stake, but the network of family and kinship dependent on him. In that case, Tocqueville reasoned that the discussion would have to shift to another level altogether: to universal qualities of virtue and vice; and if that route were taken, the abstractions that he feared might reappear. Honor or shame would end, not as being acquired through acculturation, but as intrinsic qualities of human conduct located transculturally. In the end, Tocqueville refused to fit the preservation of honor or the shame of losing it into moral categories of virtue and vice.

Tocqueville touched on the confusions that emerged from discussions of honor. Rules of honor were very numerous and punctiliously followed in caste societies. The meaning to be attached to them over time and space, especially as aristocratic time passed over into democratic time, was hard to determine. Public opinion had much to do with presumed recognitions, rather than definitions, of honor, because opinion had no solid rock upon which to make its judgments, with the result that it made only the most tenuous contact with honor, and left it much more fluid in democratic society.[147] Still, he asked, was opinion consequence or cause?[148] Montesquieu, Tocqueville noted, referred to "our honor" and not to honor itself; and this is what Tocqueville also did, but he was plainly not happy with an absolute distinction. His father asked why honor imposed duties that "reason, nature and virtue" condemned.[149] All three might be restored, his father told him, by accepting an overarching

---

[146] Ibid., p. 194.   [147] Ibid., p. 200, note u.   [148] Ibid., p. 202, note w.
[149] Hervé de Tocqueville to Tocqueville, January 17, 1838, ibid., pp. 200–01, note v.

thesis of utility such as, he believed, David Hume had suggested, but would that make the problem a non-issue? Tocqueville's father did not think so, since time changed notions of the useful. Even within the time frame of French aristocratic society, the applications of honor differed among various social groups. The duel, universally regarded by the nobility, with its warrior traditions, as the supreme method of repairing honor, was cast aside by the magistrate for whom the duel would have been dishonorable, since his honor consisted in probity, decency and a retired life, while a merchant located his honor in his integrity, fidelity, warranties and correct calculations.

Slowly, but ineluctably, honor was losing its older significations. Tocqueville thought he could find his exit from this "genuine intellectual cul-de-sac"[150] by stepping beyond the limits imposed by a caste society, which was losing its raison d'être, to the widest interests of a more homogeneous society where differing notions of honor would begin to disappear as loyalties to society at large took their place. All people would then be bound by the compulsions to be as like one another as possible, despite real inequalities, and would hence share in a common or universal morality with commonly accepted ideas of self-worth. This could only be because, as Tocqueville clearly intended to say, the ideas of justice were prior to the idea of the human species itself, the same point he made when he promised to return to the question of good and evil as entities transcending the human species. Again he strayed from metaphysics to sociology. When "all the races of mankind should be commingled," he noted, "and . . . all the nations of earth should have the same interests, the same wants, undistinguished from each other by any characteristic peculiarities, no conventional value whatever would then be attached to men's actions . . . The simple and general notions of right and wrong would then be recognized in the world."[151]

Among the sources leading to the disruption of older loyalties was the appearance of new attitudes toward labor and new patterns in the division of labor. Ostensibly in aristocratic society, work, when prompted by ambition or pride, was not tainted by a desire for profit. But the reality was that aristocratic attitudes did not show an indifference to money. There were pretenses that money was of secondary interest, and these pretensions settled into traditions. The dissonances were manageable as long as other factors did not intrude, but they surely would, as Tocqueville suggested in his analysis of the several factors leading to the dissolution of the aristocratic value system. In its place, work came to be

---

[150] Tocqueville to Beaumont, January 18, 1838, *OC*, VIII, pt. 1, p. 279.
[151] *Nolla edn.*, II, p. 202.

valued as a measure of the human personality, and money became the universal measure. There was nothing intrinsically degrading about any kind of work, as there was about most kinds in a society based on caste.[152] Money then was the great liberator of human labor from its associations with sordidness and lowliness of character. However, if a new caste based on money in a developing manufacturing economy arose, it did so on the backs of workmen, who became more and more separated from their masters; and inequality became a feature of the new society. Tocqueville saw this not as a normal part of such a society, but rather as "an exception, a monstrosity, within the general social condition."[153]

Tocqueville suggested that the economic fluidity created by money established new norms, and would serve as a barrier against castes based on permanent agglomerations of great wealth. The implied strength of individualism was a powerful antidote against the creation of a corporate body uniting all industrialists and manufacturers. In addition, as has been noted already, the democratic conditions of sociability worked against aristocratic notions of responsibility for servants. Women were also related to labor in a new way, exercising their own judgment on all matters, including sexual morality, before they entered marriage, and then appeared willingly to accept a subordinate role under the eye of their husbands.[154] The deference was part of the commercial spirit of American democracy in which all persons, women as well as men, put work above all other values. Women shared their husbands' rise to and fall from fortune "with calm and unquenchable energy; it would seem that their desires contract as easily as they expand with their fortunes."[155] In other ways, the principle of equality between men and women was reinforced by the principle of political economy, which "carefully divid[es] the duties of man from those of woman in order that the great work of society may be the better carried on."[156] The division of labor, however, did not extend into the more fundamental acceptance of men and women as beings of equal value.

On the question of command and obedience, the master–servant relationship in aristocratic society rested on a gradation of ranks both as between superordinates and subordinates, and within each of the two groups. The ranking structure remained acceptable to all provided that there were no internal and external sources to disrupt commonly held notions of right and wrong. Masters and servants interiorized notions of command and servility; both regarded it as natural. "The two conditions are always distinct and always in propinquity; the tie that connects them is

---

[152] Ibid., pt. 2, chap. 18.   [153] Ibid., p. 141.   [154] *Nolla edn.*, II, pt. 3, chap. 9.
[155] Ibid., p. 173.   [156] Ibid., p. 179.

as lasting as they are themselves."[157] It was by making up an "imaginary personality" – that is, by the pretense of borrowing his sense of self from his master's greatness – that the servant found it possible to surrender his obedience. The same mental adjustments were at work within the ranks of the subordinate. In sum, a complementarity existed between the social hierarchy and the emotive responses that supported it. In an egalitarian society, a ranking system still tied masters and servants, but configured their relations differently. "A species of imaginary equality between them" was now at work, "in spite of the real inequality of their conditions."[158] Tocqueville's point was that the practices of command and obedience were part of every social fabric. But these "ideal types" took on their true significance, and were revealed in their nakedness in periods of revolutionary change. In those conditions, attention focused on the mentality of classes caught between the interstices of one ethos, losing its mandate, and another not yet fully born, and searching for one. In periods of revolution, the ordering of ranks was disturbed and the cement that joined masters and servants in close harmony began to loosen. It was then that the accepted forms of obedience were illegitimized, for they were seen as "subjection" unjustly wrested from the subordinate elements in society on the basis of their presumed permanent inferiority bolstered by notions of divine obligation, and now resented as such. These were dangerous times, for neither those who searched to command, nor those who were looking for direction, could find their compass either as private individuals or as citizens:

> Then it is that the dwelling of every citizen offers a spectacle somewhat analogous to the gloomy aspect of political society. A secret and internal warfare is going on there between powers ever rivals and suspicious of one another . . . The reins of domestic administration dangle between them [masters and servants], to be snatched at by one or the other. The lines that divide authority from oppression, liberty from license and right from might are to their eyes so jumbled together and confused that no one knows exactly what he is or what he may be or what he ought to be. Such a condition is not democracy, but revolution.[159]

The period of preparation for the breakdown of the aristocratic ethos was symmetrical with the period of waiting, during revolution, for the appearance of a legitimate authority to which people in their private and public roles could confide their obedience. Finding the harbingers of revolution, Tocqueville stated, was as important as the changing material conditions of the economy with its rules of land ownership patterns, consecrated by long usages in rents of all kinds. Minds were as much the key

---

[157] See for this and what follows the chapter on masters and servants, ibid., pt. 3, chap. 5.
[158] Ibid., p. 157.   [159] Ibid., p. 159.

to social stability and instability as the changing conditions of land ownership and cultivation. It was in the "depths of consciousness" that one had
to seek the cumulative effects of exactions callously executed, trust
eroded and hatreds festering. Only then could the origins of the questioning of the legal foundations of an existing society be fully understood.
Mental and material disturbances acted as one; neither one was the
simple cause or consequence of the other. The initiation of new modes of
contractual relationships, in which money replaced traditional transac-
tions, upsetting family and wider kinship networks, led not only to a
chronic state of social instability, but to the unsettling of the "human
heart." Democratic times, with their new forms of partible inheritance,
engendered democratic emotions. Once the new forms of property relationships were pushed through by revolution, the question was how long
it would take to achieve the stability in which the human heart would find
some peace with itself. For Tocqueville, democratic times were inherently
unstable, "but most unstable of all is the human heart."[160] What was true
for the population living on the land was also true, if not truer, for the
manufacturing classes, whether property-owning or working, since,
"when the greater number of men are opening new paths to fortune, *it is
no less difficult to make the few support in peace their wants and their desires.*"[161]

The final version of his polarization of social systems based on caste
and equality left out his distinction between democratic social conditions
and democratic political institutions, attributing to the first stability, and
to the second a propensity to revolution.[162] He may have been thinking of
the classical democratic, but unstable, *polis.* In any case, he dropped the
distinction for the moment, probably because he wanted to concentrate
on mentalities as a more productive way of perceiving why human beings
take the steps away from loyalty to the prevailing patterns of authority and
deference. He referred to the mental somnolence induced by a caste
system and the psychic but isolated restlessness of individuals living
under equal social conditions. In neither of these would human beings be
able to mobilize their mental energies for great innovations. They might,
however, in more fluid situations:

But between these two extremes of the history of nations is an intermediate
period, a period of glory as well as of ferment, when the conditions of men are not
sufficiently settled for the mind to be filled in torpor, when they are sufficiently
unequal for men to exercise a vast power on the minds of one another, and when
some few may modify the convictions of all. It is at such times that great reformers
arise and new ideas suddenly change the face of the world.[163]

---

[160] Discussion of these issues is in ibid., pt. 3, chap. 6.   [161] Ibid., p. 164 (my emphasis).
[162] Ibid., p. 216, note r.   [163] Ibid., p. 217.

He had at this point not articulated his fullest views on how to recognize these great turning points in history in advance of their occurrence, but there is no doubt that he contemplated the renewal of revolutionary situations with reluctant excitement mingled with apprehension. There is no doubt either that, in thinking about the end of aristocratic society, it was the breakdown of morality – as in the increasing departures from its norms in the realms of family integrity and marriage – that intrigued him. Even in the most "righteous and necessary kinds of revolutions," moderate or virtuous personalities were unlikely to be at the helm. Such a turn of events seemed to him an inevitable consequence of a rotting social system, which tried to keep its privileges, while lacking real power and showing how no vestige of loyalty to its former values remained. The defenders of the past surrender to vices "which cling about it like worms upon a carcass."[164]

[164] Ibid., p. 177.

IV

Historian of the breakdown of the old society

7   Tocqueville on the general laws of revolution

In other words, you cannot observe a wave without bearing in mind the complex features that concur in shaping it and the other, equally complex ones that the wave itself originates. These aspects vary constantly, so each wave is different from another wave, even if not immediately adjacent or successive; in other words, there are some forms and sequences that are repeated, though irregularly distributed in space and time. Since what Mr. Palomar means to do at this moment is simply *see* a wave – that is, to perceive all its simultaneous components without overlooking any of them – his gaze will dwell on the movement of the wave that strikes the shore until it can record aspects not previously perceived; as soon as he notices that the images are being repeated, he will know that he has seen everything he wanted to see and he will be able to stop . . . Only if he manages to bear all the aspects in mind at once can he begin the second phase of the operation: extending this knowledge to the entire universe.[1]

From the particular to the general in historical explanation

Tocqueville disclaimed that he was laying down an unassailable maxim when he wrote in the second volume of the *Democracy* that the social conditions of democracy were unlikely to be conducive to revolution. "It is obvious that, if I present as an absolute truth that equality destroys ambition and prevents revolutions, I would be contradicting a large part of my own ideas that I had previously expressed."[2] If revolutions were not peculiar to aristocratic societies alone – though he wondered for a while if threat of revolution were in fact the chronic natural state of democracies – it was their outbreak in aristocratic societies that he had in mind more than the possibility of revolution in democracies. He left the question in abeyance, even as he reached rather firm conclusions – in contradistinction to Aristotle's view – about the improbability of revolutions in societies

[1] Italo Calvino, *Mr. Palomar*, trans. William Weaver (Toronto, 1985), pp. 4–8.
[2] *Nolla edn.*, II, p. 203, note f.

based on an egalitarian ethos. He was far from regretting what he thought might very well be the passing of great revolutions, but he also hoped that the cultivation of pride would serve as an antidote to the democratic diminution of great ambition. Even if pride might be counted a vice, it was preferable to the dead hand of mediocrity and could quite possibly give modern human beings "a more enlarged idea of themselves."[3]

Turning to revolutions in aristocratic societies, he tried his hand at a morphology. He noted first what for him was an empirical fact: the repressed ambitions of those aiming to overthrow the existing order appeared to attract ever-widening coteries of revolutionaries. Secondly, revolutionary enthusiasm and ambition were paradoxically nourished by aristocratic mores, including not only the passions peculiar to aristocracy, but also its notions of ambition. Third, and once this early phase of revolution was over, the extraordinary events etched themselves in memory and remembrance. Why? Principally because of the larger-than-life gestures and exploits of extraordinary revolutionary leaders. "Our civil turmoils," Tocqueville mused, "have brought to light men who, because of the immensity of their genius and their crimes, have remained in our tableaux of the past like misshapen but gigantic and massive bodies that never cease to attract the fullest plaudits of the crowds." He proceeded to comment ironically but sadly that, while there had been one Mirabeau, there might now be lurking in the background many petty Mirabeaus who could only reproduce his vices, never his genius.[4] The unflattering comparison may be indicative of his admiration for the glories of 1789 and his abhorrence of the Terror, and, as well, his fear of future disorders in French society under the Orléanist régime.

The introduction in the *Democracy* of problems and incidents from the Great Revolution, and the allusions to the politics of the July Revolution as well, show that Tocqueville strove to understand and enunciate the conditions for, and the outcomes of, revolution in the form of general laws. In his speculations on the conditions leading toward highly centralized forms of government, he wanted to keep in mind the particularities of the societies he was comparing so that any elaboration of a "theorem" would not lose in strength so long as it kept counterexamples in sight. One of his earliest, illuminating attempts to single out the general features of revolution had less to do with centralization than with the differences he discerned within the broad spectrum of aristocratic societies. As usual, he took the English aristocratic experience as the best example of how revolution might take a route different from the one followed in France.

---

[3] Ibid., p. 207. See the additional remarks that Tocqueville thought he might combine with the arguments in his chapter on ambition.   [4] Ibid., p. 204, note h.

In one of his concise statements about the elements that taken together constitute a revolution, he singled out as indispensable a total change in legal foundations, a total social transformation and a total substitution of one regulating societal principle for another. All of these conditions were to be found in England in 1833, where the aristocratic principle of the constitution was losing its *élan*.

Yet in England large-scale protest was contained. The "secondary aristocracy" and the aspiring middle classes were determined to ensure the maintenance of order and, moreover, had no desire to challenge the inheritance laws that ensured primogeniture, and were satisfied to work through the prevailing conditions of social mobility that permitted access to the upper ranks of society. Still, the situation in 1833 had been fluid enough, largely due to the mounting voice of the *proletariat*, for the unexpected to take command and for the entire social edifice to plunge into the abyss of revolution.[5] To the contrast he made between the French and English aristocracies, he added another closer to home. When he looked at the action of the English and Anglo-Irish aristocracies, he attributed to the first a calm and wise concern for the conditions that ensured the longevity of institutions, and to the second he assigned a total lack of apprehension for its future, driven as it was by the spirit of faction, religious intolerance and the sheer desire to oppress.[6]

Older aristocracies, such as in Florence, were unable to block revolutionary challenges or to bring revolutions to a close. Tocqueville came to this conclusion upon a reading of *The Prince*. The tenor of the book Tocqueville found superficial and detestable, because of its assumption that the world is Godless, but even more damaging to Machiavelli, in Tocqueville's words, was that he was "the grandfather of Thiers."[7] His aversion did not prevent him from acknowledging Machiavelli's acuity. Florence was more prone to internal conflict during the ascendancy of its aristocracy than after its destruction. From this comparison, Tocqueville surmised that, after the demise of the Florentine aristocracy, revolutions were due to its republican form of government and not to its democratic constitution.[8] In his notes to the *Democracy*, he had more to say about Machiavelli, who, he conceded, had accidentally stumbled on the smaller and secondary, but not the general causes of revolution and war. Tocqueville accepted the Florentine's argument that a conqueror had more to fear from conquering a state ruled by a prince and aristocrats than from one in which the prince ruled alone over the populace. In the

---

[5] *Pléiade edn.*, I, "Voyage en Angleterre en 1833," pp. 449–57. The term *proletariat* is Tocqueville's.   [6] Ibid., "Voyage en Angleterre et en Irlande de 1835," pp. 554–56.

[7] Tocqueville to Kergorlay, April 5, 1836, *OC*, XIII, pt. 1, p. 390.

[8] "Machiavel (1836)," in *OC*, XVI, pp. 537–50, esp. p. 549.

first case, the surviving aristocrats could appeal to the populace and drive out the conqueror. In the second case, that is, in the absence of an aristocracy, the conqueror had nothing to fear, since he could easily subdue the populace. The first set of conditions obtained in the attempt to conquer France. Tocqueville contended that Machiavelli had not grasped the possibility of two general conclusions. Democratic states exert every effort to defend themselves from attack, but once beaten they have fewer resources to regain their strength; by contrast, aristocratic societies can muster them and work to reverse the conquest. Democratic societies, in addition, do not have the stamina to engage in long civil wars. Tocqueville read a classic treatise in political theory and extracted a general law about the sources and consequences of revolution. Democratic societies lend themselves less easily to revolution, but more readily to authoritarian rule in the absence of intermediary bodies such as an aristocracy. Civil conflict in democratic societies is resolved by surrender to the forces that promise a return to order in the person of a leader.[9] Machiavelli seemed to offer retrospective proof for the tendency to surrender to despots in societies riven by civil disorder and foreign wars, as in France after 1794.

For Tocqueville, a formulation of the general laws of revolution was inseparable from the question of state centralization. The question of the origins of modern despotism came into sharper focus in chapter 4 of the last part of the *Democracy*. "If all democratic nations are instinctively led to the centralization of government, they tend to produce this result in an unequal manner. This depends on the particular circumstances which may promote or prevent the natural consequences of that state of society, circumstances which are exceedingly numerous, but of which I shall mention only a few."[10] As for the concrete details of different social conditions, he had already broached them in the distinction he made between the movement toward *centralized* administration in France and *legislative* centralization in England. Each was the result of competing concepts of social cohesion. The first, prevailing in France, asked society to guarantee the well-being of its members, while that which obtained in places like England and America assumed that individuals were best served if society gave them the means, but did not undertake, to ensure their own well-being. The first means of achieving social cohesion was simpler and led to uniformity; the second was more complicated but was the only one truly compatible with political liberty. What stood in the way of the second was the mania favoring centralization that was monopolizing the democratic ethos both in England and America.[11] But it was not only a democratic

---

[9] *Nolla edn.*, II, p. 233, note e.   [10] Ibid., p. 246.
[11] *Pléiade edn.*, I, "Voyage en Angleterre et en Irlande de 1835," p. 492.

phenomenon. The regulatory mania – a mania for power – was a human one. That it took different forms was again for Tocqueville a salutary phenomenon insofar as its least abusive manifestations could be used as a countervailing example and force against its most egregious expressions. Indeed, England, despite certain defects in its ways of ordering things, was more apt to combine order and prosperity than France, because of its ability to establish general principles applicable to all members of society through parliament, while at the same time permitting a devolution of local administrative and judicial powers to blunt the full force of the state.[12]

The larger issue that Tocqueville took up in the *Democracy* was that the revolutionary destruction of aristocratic societies produced conditions of equality without enhancing the taste for liberty which was the only barrier against the accumulation of the sources of power at the center. The opposite was likely to be true in democracies with traditions of aristocratic liberty, and that would consequently probably gain, as in America,[13] equality without experiencing revolution to free themselves from the onerous burdens of a privileged caste. The characteristics of full-blown revolutions, such as those which marked France, were missing in the American War of Independence, for the principals were not engaged in ending or defending the privileges of a non-existent aristocratic society. America also had the advantage of a favorable conjuncture of conditions that preserved it from the consequences of an excessive concentration of powers. Thus, giving due attention to the emergence of democratic social conditions with or in the absence of revolutionary upheaval, Tocqueville concentrated on the outcome of revolution, that is, on the outcome in France, and also in the rest of Western Europe when it too would succumb, he expected, to the thrust of egalitarianism.

For Tocqueville, the central criterion for measuring revolutionary situations and outcomes was the question of how conditions of inequality were transformed into conditions of equality. America and France had moved toward equality from opposite directions and with different momentums, one "pass[ing] through no revolution, the second through revolution." Thus among the Americans "it is freedom that is old; equality is of comparatively modern date."[14] In Europe, monarchs had pursued policies designed to create a general subservience – a kind of *negative equality*.[15] The prerevolutionary state apparatus was the engine that

---

[12] Ibid., pp. 505–06.
[13] Cf. *OC*, V, pt. 2, p. 203, where, in his American traveling notes in 1831, Tocqueville wrote that America presented the most perfect image, good and bad, of the special character of the English. All that was brilliant, generous, great and sumptuous in the British character was aristocratic and not English.   [14] *Nolla edn.*, II, pp. 247, 246.
[15] The phrase is mine.

determined the *moeurs*, manners, habits, order (and orders) of society. The continued reduction by the French eighteenth-century monarchical state of the intermediary bodies to impotence changed the outer face of state power, that is, the constituted bodies through which the administration worked. The inner life and dynamic of the state remained intact, in spite of the changes in political culture that called into question existing political forms, exposing them to inspection, discussion and change, according to differing conceptions of political order. Eclipsed temporarily by the 1789 Revolution's promise of a new political culture that would curtail the powers of the centralized state, it survived those attempts almost immediately, in fact as early as September 1789. The major revolutionary political factions never dreamt of dispensing with it, or setting it up on new foundations. Instead their central aim was to capture the power of the state and make it their servant. It was viewed, as before 1789, as the organizing force of the new society. And, after the vicissitudes of the Revolution were endured, and the popular elements that tried to commandeer the state for its own purposes were defeated, the administrative apparatus was taken over, in the first place, by a well-placed or a luckily placed personality (Bonaparte); and, in the second place as the revolution drew to its close, by the remnants of the aristocracy who transferred "the management of all affairs to the state."[16]

The state, then, as Tocqueville conceived it, possesses a duality, but this truth is not seen clearly by those who try to command its power. Various classes try to, and believe they can, use it against their enemies. But it is an autonomous force. State power is not simply an instrument of a class; it rises above all classes; and, for that reason, it can impose its will on each and every one of them. "Men who live in the ages of equality are naturally fond of central power and are willing to extend its privileges; but if it happens that this same power faithfully represents their own interests and exactly copies their own inclinations, the confidence they place in it knows no bounds, and they think that whatever they bestow upon it is bestowed upon themselves."[17] As far as one may speak of revolutionary outcomes, an element of futility may be detected in the Tocquevillian thesis of the state's staying power. To combat that curious perversity, he stated that, whatever the strength of the state to command talents in a century of mediocre intellectual capacity, a democratic society, such as America's, alive to the presence within it of the countervailing forces nurtured by traditions of liberty may have the resources to challenge the power of state subordination and centralization.

What is constant in Tocqueville's incipient general model of revolution

[16] Ibid., p. 247.   [17] Ibid., p. 250.

is that the state plays a role in the aristocratic societies of France and Europe that the democratic society of America denies it. The state had a special significance in France and Europe because it was lodged in an aristocratic society; and it was in the fissures in that society, in part the unintended consequence of the state's actions, that the roots of revolution were located. In America, the state, before and after the War of Independence, was weak and, most important, distant, and liberty was strong. There the state had a kind of phantom existence. Indeed, so much so that Tocqueville was astonished and perplexed during his stay in America to find so few visible signs of government emanating from the center. How did things get done? Each locality governed itself; power seemed to flow upwards rather than the other way round. The disadvantage was that there seemed to be no way for government to impart a sense of character and stability to the separate parts making up political society.[18] Nor could government do anything, for example, to exercise some control over and give direction to education.[19] The absence of such authority would not long endure, he said, the moment America found the need for a permanent army, the surest condition for the concentration of power.[20] America appeared nevertheless to function, though somewhat strangely. How much better off France would be, Tocqueville added, if the Bourbons, instead of fearing communal organization, had sought gradually during the Restoration to transfer some power to the localities.[21] No one seemed to be aware of the state's actions in America and what it was supposed to do. America seemed to be a society made up of individuals following their own wills.[22] He also informed his father that an understanding of American political institutions was not possible without having some point of comparison, notably, what was meant by and how centralization expressed itself in France. He was very much aware, he said, that in France the government meddled in everything. But by what mechanisms was it able to do so?[23]

He was able to penetrate, with the help of his American informants, but probably more so by a reading of Nos. 15 and 23 of *The Federalist*, the unusual conditions that prepared the United States for laying down what he said appeared to be a stable foundation for a federal government. It had been able to do so because it paid attention to the need for a fine balance between the individual states and the federal government in

---

[18] Tocqueville to Chabrol, July 16, 1831, *BYT*, B.I.a (1–2).

[19] Note on "Centralization," November 3, 1831, *Pléiade edn.*, I, p. 233.

[20] Tocqueville to Chabrol, July 16, 1831, *BYT*, B.I.a (1–2).

[21] Tocqueville to Hervé de Tocqueville, July 4, 1831, ibid.

[22] Tocqueville to Chabrol, October 7, 1831, ibid.

[23] Tocqueville to Hervé de Tocqueville, October 7, 1831, ibid.

which each did not encroach on the other's power. The process had been facilitated by the fact that the newly independent states, before a federal constitution binding them together came into being, had had little time to develop pride and the national prejudices that made old societies reluctant to give up their sovereignty. Neither the ancient Greek federations, nor the United Netherlands and the Swiss Confederation, had been able to create a united people. They had created a repository of power but not a central sovereignty – Tocqueville meant presumably a sovereignty that distributed powers on a rational basis – with the inevitable consequence of civil war and anarchy. None had been able to perceive that the key to a successful federation lay in perceiving the dangers to its existence that only an adjustment of its laws could correct – laws based on a familiarity with representative forms which in America had 150 years of experience behind them, and consequently were used to forge a firm foundation for the support of a strong but limited central government.[24]

When Tocqueville gave the question further thought, he traced the American attitude toward the state to the experience of the American colonies' rupture with Britain. The state's omnipresence was felt only when it was viewed as acting against the rights of the colonists who thought of themselves as freeborn Englishmen. He captured the idea in a succinct formula: "The Revolution in the United States was caused by a mature and thoughtful taste for freedom, not by some vague, undefined instinct for independence. No disorderly passions drove it; on the contrary, it proceeded hand in hand with a love of order and legality."[25] This analysis only makes sense, however, if we accept Tocqueville's insistence on the countervailing power of free institutions at almost every level to challenge the metropole. It was, Tocqueville postulated, as if, after the rupture with Britain, the last thing desired or needed in the newly independent states was the consolidation of state power at the center. Together with his wonder that the various states of the future union took a rather long time to come together to achieve it, and his admiration for the men who organized the American federal polity, he granted the American Revolution a unique quality, setting it apart from what happened in France.

Tocqueville, to be sure, interpreted the break with Britain as a challenge to its authority, but he appeared to consider it as nothing more than walking away from state power as it existed in the metropole. The Americans did not have to capture the state; they had to fashion one. Then Tocqueville reiterated his general thesis that the state would

---

[24] Note on "Union, Gouvernement Central," December 28 and 29, 1831, *Pléiade edn.*, I, pp. 264–67.   [25] *Nolla edn.*, I, p. 57.

become stronger in America as well as everywhere else, creating the framework in which equality became the single norm by which to measure legitimacy. The difference he wished to draw out was that a society, like that of France, which achieved equality through revolution, can reorder itself or find its equilibrium only by recognizing the injuries to public and private life inherent in the power of the state and introducing safeguards to escape its full impact. American society, by contrast, had a very different relationship to the action of the state, and therefore was not so dependent on it. What is more, at the time of the successful break with Britain there was in America nothing like the French experience of falling into an illusion of politics; hence the links holding society together were not obliterated. On the contrary, these social links retained their primacy. When a revolution of such a devastating nature as it assumed in France was absent, the dominance of civic social relations, which Tocqueville equated with traditional warrants given to liberty, did not come under threat:

No one in the United States has pretended that, in a free country, a man has the right to do everything; on the contrary, more varied social obligations have been imposed on him than elsewhere; no one thought to attack the very basis of social power or contest its rights; the object was only to divide up the right to exercise it. By this means it was hoped that authority would be made great, but officials small, so that the state could be well regulated and remain free.[26]

When he turned back to France, as he did soon after he completed the first volume of the *Democracy*, he provided one of the best encapsulations of his creed as a liberal with a firm commitment to the forging of constitutional checks against the power of the state to override civil society. He was to flesh it out in his early years as a legislator when, as we shall see, he had to face the practical problems of supporting all steps toward the securing of a stable régime. What did he lay down as the necessary ingredients of liberalism? He did not take the simple line that there was no need for an energetic central government. Indeed, more than in an aristocracy, such a stabilizing force was needed in a democratic society where, instead of being concentrated, there was no single source of power under the dominance of one class. The dispersal of this power over several classes and groups demanded direction, but a restricted one. The central government should not have the kind of power that would permit it to neglect public opinion and the legislative power representing it. Such a central power, moreover, need not be incompatible with local liberties. Distribution of powers of this kind would permit citizens to move freely and with assurance, concerned with their own private lives and their own

---

[26] Ibid.

initiatives, yet mindful of their direct and indirect exercise of extensive political rights. These were the fundamentals of liberal political principles. The practical means to achieve them needed to be sedulously and slowly cultivated, and preferably approached along two fronts: on the one side, from the government itself preparing a vital public culture; on the other, from a citizenry enlarged in size as its *capacités* expanded.[27]

Thus in 1840, with the completion of his second volume of the *Democracy*, Tocqueville was, if not completely, fairly confident in his analysis of the trajectory of democratic revolution. Still, when he plotted it in general terms as a succession of psychosocial stages, France, rather than America, was more on his mind. In its first stage, enormous energies fueled by boundless ambition are released, bringing to dizzying heights of power groups of men competing with one another and inspiring others waiting in the wings to profit from the general confusion caused by changes in laws and customs. The power shifts continue for some time during the self-consuming aberrations of the Revolution, and take place in an atmosphere in which people cannot respond outside their former contexts of behavior. The second stage is a compound of recollection and a sense of instability, each stimulating further ambitions, while opportunities for satisfying them diminish rapidly. The last stage is reached with the complete disappearance of the privileged class of the aristocracy, the onset of political amnesia (the selective blotting out of the memory of the general and specific political struggles), and the restoration of order when the adaptation of desires to available means is reasserted. Then "the needs, the ideas and the feelings of men cohere once again: men achieve a new stable level in society, and democratic society is finally established."[28]

Both the search for general laws on the sources of revolution and the nature of centralization consumed much of Tocqueville's attention during his membership of the Orléanist Chamber. The first of these was glimpsed in chapter 3, where I introduced Tocqueville's early belief that revolutions in France were improbable. The particular context of French politics in the last ten years of the July Monarchy gave him an opportunity to deepen his analysis of how revolution and centralization were related. From it, he emerged with an analysis of the sources of revolutionary discontent and action.[29] He argued that there was little in the political and social situation to feed fears of revolutionary action. The challenges from republicans and Legitimists were ephemeral and easily contained. There had to be something more at work to produce a revolutionary situation

---

[27] Tocqueville to E. Stoffels, October 5, 1836, *Beaumont edn.*, V, pp. 433–36.

[28] *Nolla edn.*, II, pp. 203–04.

[29] The full analysis is to be found in six articles he wrote for *Le Siècle* in January 1843. See *OC*, III, pt. 2, pp. 104–06.

and process. As always, his nodal point was the Revolution of 1789, which exemplified a set of general laws based on observation of revolutions that had taken place in the past. He began with the principle that a party that represents only the superior class or inferior class of the population never makes a successful revolution. The former lacks material force and often lacks spirit as well; the second lacks education, wisdom and knowledge. Revolutions are achieved when at least a portion of the inferior class puts its muscle and passions at the disposal of the superior and well-to-do class, or when a portion of the superior class shares in the release of popular emotions and allows itself to be propelled by them. Revolutions attempted by only one of these classes are always aborted. In the case of 1789, agreement between the bourgeoisie and the people made the Revolution. A similar accord came into being in 1830 when the middle class and the people joined forces. The combined energy of the people and the ardor of the middle class created the conditions for the successful revolutionary challenge to the Bourbon government's July Ordinances that precipitated the revolutionary events of July. Tocqueville, however, wanted to put his finger on the decisive pressure point of the crisis. For him, it was the last Bourbon government in 1830 that took the fatal steps leading to the momentary alliance between those who wanted only to modify the Constitution and those who wanted to destroy it. The first served as the head of the Revolution; the second as its body. But there was, after the initial destruction of the Restoration monarchy, no radical repudiation of its Constitution, and no prolonged popular violence. The republicans, left to themselves, had no following in the country after the July Revolution. They continued to set off minor disturbances. That was all, and the chance that they would leave a permanent mark on the popular consciousness was not increased by the new government that did not adopt measures so extreme as to swell republican ranks. Tocqueville obviously had in mind the government's relatively calm approach to the presence of opposition from both extremes, the right as well as the left.

New revolutions in the future were not out of the question. The most likely source of discontent leading to revolutionary action was to be found in the working class and the growing part of the economy controlled by industrial property owners. The antagonisms energized by these two classes were a source of unease. While, to be sure, equality was increasing its sway over people, it seemed to be losing the battle in the industrial world where a new aristocracy of wealth was emerging. One aspect of the new equality was the infinite division of capital, leading to a constantly shifting number of new proprietors, each eager to participate in a share of the profits. The other aspect was a consolidation of capital in the hands of an exclusive class creating utter dependency among the workers. The vast disproportion between profits and wages was indicative of the depth of the social division. Such shocking disparities could not last for long. Eventually, but not immediately, a new outbreak of revolution would occur unless policies to reduce the growing gap were introduced. The industrial workers would be the next revolutionary shock troops, not only in France, but throughout the civilized world. When Tocqueville wrote these words in 1843, he singled out the workers in the new industries, but he underestimated the possibilities of a union of forces between them, the republicans and those legitimately constituted groups in the *pays légal* who were not averse to the abandonment of constitutional forms should the government lose its nerve and its control over the forces of order.

The maddening fact for Tocqueville was that, according to his observations, the French middle class experienced doubt about its capacity to lay down a peaceful order.[30] Nearly every group or party daring to question the legitimacy of the new régime the bourgeoisie feared as revolutionary, not only in intent, but in reality. When Tocqueville spoke about stability as the terminus of a successful democratic revolution, America was principally in his mind. France, by contrast, carried particular legacies within its ancient bosom that acted as obstacles to a full resolution of the revolutionary drama. The chief of these was the 1830 Revolution itself. While it was espoused by its supporters as the last stage of the earlier revolution, the event itself raised questions about its origins and outcome. Tocqueville liked to think of it as a last stage of a longer revolutionary process, when he said that the French could count as valuable some awareness and knowledge of how revolutions broke existing régimes apart. The experience of revolution alone, upon whose foundations new thoughts could initiate the appropriate forms of political and social culture, would be enough to dissipate chimerical fears about the future. Tocqueville asked the French political community to avoid the error of confusing the machinery of state under the *ancien régime*, when obedience was unflinching and mute, with the conditions of the July Monarchy, when it could be fairly said that sovereignty was shared and public opinion was a force that could and did question the exercise of state power. Politics now subsisted in an environment of relatively free challenges to power. The still fragile politics of a society with painful memories of revolution had, however, created their own new context, vastly different from the politics of two generations ago. It was time for the French administration to trust the majority of its citizens instead of seeing dissent as the gateway to disorder. Admittedly, there were unfortunate

---

[30] The next part of the analysis is in ibid., pp. 106–19.

signs that the administration was moving to enhance its powers, reducing them at the local level and transferring them to the center, from which point the government could more easily win support for its actions through systematic corruption of the entire political body.

Equally misguided was the opposition's decision to act as standard bearer of a fuller democratic franchise. Not only, in Tocqueville's suspicious eyes, was such a move disingenuous. The political strategy, like the government's centralizing moves, which were prompted by fear and constituted a serious blunder, was a confession of something even more disturbing. Political principles were seen by the two chief parties as meaningless, but nevertheless each ostensibly invoked them – lending them an air of seriousness – to purchase power. Politics had dropped all pretenses and become nothing but a cynical game. Both government and opposition really believed that corruption was a natural and necessary part of political life. It was the politically corrupting power of the competing party brokers that mattered, not the principles they espoused. The government stressed that centralizing the administration was the only way it could gain the power to resist revolutionary struggles; the opposition called on public opinion to combat that notion, but in fact it had no intention of building its power on different assumptions. Tocqueville did not include in his description of the new political culture a full analysis of popular perceptions. The public liked what he called generosity and honesty. But he did not take the next step in trying to explain the alienation by informed and disaffected sections of the population from the corrupt politics of the régime. If he had, he might have given greater weight somewhat sooner to the paradoxes of a political culture that subsisted on a tacit as well as an unscrupulous acceptance of corruption, and how a political constituency, denied participatory rights, possessed an instinctive grasp of the direction of politics, and quite correctly perceived and opposed it.

What he did instead was to recall what he regarded as the permanent distinguishing features of the 1789 Revolution. It was an event that he said again and again transcended class, party, special interest groups and particular opinions. All, without regard to rank, income and birth, and motivated only by honest work and by virtuous feelings, believed they would share in power and wealth; and that they would, through a powerful effort of the will, raise the common level of humanity. But the cost was enormous. The violence through which the Revolution moved had left its mark. It indelibly stained thoughts and passions, especially as each struggle for a new constitution and new laws led to series of reversals and increased the propensity to believe that force could always be called on at times of crisis to destroy all resistance. The revolutionary spirit fed on the firmly anchored delusion that political disputes were not a question of rational resolution. If any of the Revolution's true importance for humanity were to be preserved, its noble and glorious principles had to be freed from contamination by this pernicious revolutionary spirit.

That France was embarked on a unique political journey was even more firmly entrenched in Tocqueville's analysis by his comparisons with other political traditions. The contrasts, as we saw, highlighted differences more than similarities. An accurate description of his own political culture, he maintained, required comparative study.[31] From America and England, he extended his gaze to Prussia. Having elaborated why in America democracy was more likely to escape the state's most stifling interventions, he turned once again in the 1840s to the concrete problems that were besetting the French experiment to create a stable relationship between the immovable fact of administrative centralization, the experiment with representative government and the concrete constitutional framework for the safeguards that political liberty required. The French parliamentary régime, sharing certain similarities with the English, possessed a centralized administration "a thousand times"[32] more elaborate and complex than Prussia's. There, in the absence of a political constituency to which it had no need to make concessions, the power of the state was direct and unimpeded, but not susceptible to the mundane aspects of corruption. There was no need, for example, to win the support of a non-existent body of representatives owing much of their power to an enfranchised body of electors. In England, as he had argued before, there was an absence of a highly centralized corps of public servants and a wider distribution of powers to local grandees and their servants. Together these two features of English political institutions greatly reduced the government's power to corrupt, not that its disposal of egregious favors and patronage was absent from the political machinery.

What, he asked, might be expected from the uneasy coexistence in France of so novel a combination of representative government and administrative centralization? As he saw it, the central administration was solidly lodged in the very social life of the French nation. Every collective and individual aspect of life bore the imprint of the administration, from the most private to the most public, from the smallest locality to the grandest bureaucratic entity. He might have been echoing a number of

---

[31] See chap. 2 for Tocqueville's interest in comparative analysis, and my comments on "the language of perspicuous contrast," an idea taken from Charles Taylor, "Understanding and Ethnocentricity," in *Philosophy and the Human Sciences*, ed. Taylor, II, p. 125.

[32] The citation is from Tocqueville's article, "La centralisation administrative et le système représentatif," *Le Commerce*, November 24, 1844, *OC*, III, pt. 2, pp. 129–32, from which his additional arguments are taken.

observers of the French state, no more so than Royer-Collard who gave his Restoration colleagues his version of the political patterns that were established following the Revolution:

From a society left in dust there came forth centralization. Its origins need not be sought elsewhere. Centralization did not arrive, as did so many other doctrines, no less pernicious, with its brow held high, with the authority of any principle. Its penetration was unpretentious to say the least, as if it were a necessary consequence. Indeed, all that does not fall into the domain of individuals falls into the public sphere – the concern of the State.[33]

The point was not hard to grasp in the terms that Tocqueville believed reflected French political reality. The same men who, as ministers, deploy the engines of the administration to achieve their goals, themselves act as administrators; but in a parliamentary régime they cannot do so without submitting their actions to the scrutiny of the deputies. Hence France gazed at the strange and egregious spectacle of ministers-administrators, who enjoyed, as Tocqueville put it, more prerogatives than were ever in the pockets of the greatest despots. They found themselves in theory at least, and in practice at times, at the mercy of the Chamber, but just as, if not more, often, he added, of one man. Perhaps the latter was a veiled reference to Louis-Philippe who retained considerable constitutional powers to impose his will.

The French polity, as he saw it in the 1840s, practically ensured that the ministers-administrators would abuse the system at the top to free themselves from such powers of review as the Chamber possessed. To give weight to his observations, Tocqueville argued that the movement of the system in this direction fed into and was fed by the unique French social and economic structure. It differed from structures in other countries. The polarities of wealth in France were not so pronounced, for example. As he might have put it in a twentieth-century setting, there was not enough wealth to trickle down and, without it, the state was expected to step in, not to meet real needs, but to respond to unrealistic material desires. It was only too ready to do so in order to extend its powers and to accustom recipients of government handouts to look at it as one, if not the only permanent, source of well-being. The political and administrative structures conspired to create a distorted view of politics. No one saw through it, not least the parliamentary opposition that asked that new powers be given the government while at the same time reproaching it with corruption. Unless full public discussion – by which Tocqueville meant a plurality of views expressed by groups divided by tastes, self-

---

[33] Speech in the Chamber of Deputies, January 2, 1822, cited in Pierre Rosanvallon, *L'Etat en France de 1789 à nos jours* (Paris, 1990), p. 112.

interest, money, position and opposing moral stances – disclosed the contradictions inherent in the opposition's hypocrisy, "moral misery" of a kind experienced almost nowhere in the Western world would descend on France. With that phrase Tocqueville predicted the de-moralization alike of the public and private spheres. Both could suffer erosion. The dynamics and salubrious effects of civic public life would be usurped by administrative powers, visible only in their effects, not in their processes, since the techniques to render them unobtrusive were not really so difficult to cultivate. The realm of the private would also lose its sharp definitions wherein the habits of the heart, mind and senses would gain some security against the individualism that democratic peoples were all too ready to substitute for them. An undifferentiated society, a society without boundaries between private and public, a society heeding the dictates of an unreflective equality, would consign everyone to anonymity.[34] Such an illusory sense of what the personal and political good amounted to could only issue forth from the double assault of a seemingly benign administration and an impoverished concept of a vibrant public life.

One other safeguard might work to put a brake on the full development of a conflated and inflated ministerial-administrative corps. But he was of two minds about this startling aspect of French parliamentary life. He raised it more than once.[35] What gains and losses might be expected from the eligibility of public servants for membership in the Chamber? On the one hand, they constituted a highly qualified group, capable of acting against the democratic ethos of the Chamber. On the other hand, if their sole aim in seeking election was to advance their careers in the public service, measures had to be adopted to resist them. The Chamber should, he said, be considered as a political body, not the normal route to the fulfillment of administrative ambitions. Moreover, under a constitution that lodged greater power in the executive than in a fragile legislature, importance should be given to strengthening the latter.

Tocqueville appeared to think that the mere presence of public servants might counteract volatility in the Chamber and stimulate the practical

[34] Cf. Hannah Arendt, *The Human Condition* (Chicago, 1958), pt. 2, pp. 22–78, who discusses the relationships between the private and public spheres.

[35] See his speech in the Chamber on February 7, 1840, *OC*, III, pt. 2, pp. 237–41, on a proposal to exclude or to retire from the Chamber all public servants. He had no doubts about their *capacités*, but he also felt that their exclusion could be dangerous to the political life of the nation. He was not totally clear on where the real danger lay. He expressed the general fear that they might come to constitute a solid group capable of using their considerable resources to strengthen the executive power more directly, whether inside or outside the Chamber. Another occasion to expand these opinions came in February 1842 when he prepared his notes for an intervention in another debate on the place of public servants in the Chamber (ibid., pp. 246–49). On neither occasion did he present a really satisfactory argument for or against the inclusion or exclusion of public servants.

need to seek majorities. All weapons – even the presence of public servants acting as legislators – were to be considered for their pragmatic
effectiveness in the struggle against the exercise of overwhelming executive power. In private notes to himself,[36] he declared that his real interest
was the creation of a stable relationship between political liberty and the
law, as well as the restoration of some of the rights which the July
Monarchy had curtailed or restricted, such as freedom of the press,
refusal to have public servants answerable to the courts and the failure to
guarantee citizen security.

Together with the limitations arbitrarily imposed on freedom of
association and elections freed from corruption and fraud, the achievement of these goods were his major concerns as a liberal. He declared
himself the determined foe of the kind of democracy found in and defined
by gross forms of legislative demagoguery that gained power from
exploiting the disordered, violent, unenlightened and irreligious actions
of the masses. He belonged, he said in a self-congratulatory mood,
neither to a revolutionary nor to a conservative group. If forced to choose,
he felt more inclined to support the latter than the first. He preferred, he
said, the methods, but not the goals, of the conservatives, and he dis-
approved of both the methods and goals of the revolutionaries. This
species of liberalism is contained in his tortured search for a *via media*. He
saw in the July régime the elements that might give life to this middle
course. He had no plans to bring to French political institutions the very
different experience of American democracy. Nor had he any ideas about
combining in a single theory his prediction that democracy in America
might tend to a new despotism resting on the uninhibited desires of a restless citizenry, and the particularities of the French political process that
showed many signs of succumbing to the close links between centralization and electoral corruption, both of which sprang from the establishment of equality by the Revolution of 1789.

His more complete theory of the structural continuity in France's
development as a modern state lay in his future work as a historian of pre-
revolutionary France. At this point in his life, he analyzed the pervasive-
ness of centralized administration in the social and economic life of
France in the years of the July Monarchy. What he saw was the precarious
nature of a régime that might blunder into revolution, because of its
incapacity to modulate the variables of centralization, representative
institutions and the pressures from within and without the *pays légal* to
introduce ever fuller measures of equality. The single thing common to
the political structures of the *ancien régime* and those of post-1830 France

---

[36] Ibid., p. 87.

was the ambiguous position of liberty. Even so, the sources of its ambiguity were not the same over this span of time. Liberty's status and survival before 1789 was dependent on a struggle waged between the *parlements* and the crown. Each had its own political program in which utilitarian purposes were uppermost in deciding the role liberty was to be given in any *modus vivendi* the parties in the struggle might have reached. The other variables leading to 1789 did not have quite the same weight either, even if appearances might suggest otherwise. In the earlier epoch, equality was yet to be pronounced an unequivocal good and a necessary quality of individual and social life. Representative institutions were still in their incipient and uncertain state; and much of the outer shell of the institutions of the state remained intact and would undergo a large transformation in order to make them a more efficient instrument of control.

Tocqueville did not stipulate that the variables he had isolated were related in a direct and uncomplicated way to the events leading to and from 1789. He had no agenda that included the forging of a connection between the political failure to perceive that the effects of centralized administration in the lives of the French might end in the disintegration of political stability in the 1840s, and the evolution of the 1789 Revolution incorporating, as one of its major achievements, a powerful state edifice. The French political structure made the modern state assume a form distinguishing it from others – the English, American and Prussian. There was thus no symmetry, necessary or accidental, between the pre-1789 and post-1789 French political structures. If there were, it would be necessary to consign Tocqueville's assertions about the uniqueness of the Revolution to a realm of the purest rhetoric – as a mere moment in the passage of relentless time. That instant, as much as the large-scale processes and cultural frameworks of the Revolution, awaited explanation.

Toward a theory of revolutionary rupture

The expected move toward the *via media* in the 1840s was caught in the toils of political conflict that expressed the internal contradictions of the political constitution of the 1830s. To render them innocuous demanded probity and political will. Contrary to these expectations, the turmoil of 1848 erupted through the thin carapace of order. Tocqueville had supposed that the bourgeois revolution of 1830, consciously invoking the principle of enlightened self-interest, would show itself capable of restraining its most outrageous exhibitions of commercial greed, limiting corruption within acceptable bounds, and conceding a minimum, sometimes more than a minimum, of recognition to the wishes and needs of the parties without representation – parties on the democratic center and left. The scenario took another turn. From this personal and political crisis, Tocqueville emerged shaken and distressed by the political ruptures that appeared to have become a permanent part of French life, showing every sign of burying the Great Revolution's hopes of regeneration. He had now to rethink his previous views on the general laws of revolution, and it was this goal that drew him back to the sources of the breakdown of the *ancien régime*. It also returned him to the epistemology of historical inquiry.

By turns, the prospect of throwing himself into historical questions energized him and threw him into a disconsolate mood. To Beaumont he opened his heart. With a recurrent feeling of helplessness, he was losing himself in what he called an "ocean" of research as important as the subject he had chosen with which to culminate his life's work. It was not only discouragement with himself but with human beings in general. Seen from the long perspective of time, there was not much that could be learned about their "perplexities, their incessant repetition of new words over three thousand years of human history; and finally about the insignificance of our species, our world and our destiny, and about what we call our great revolutions and our great concerns."[37]

Work was the sole balm. The archives of the *généralité* of Tours excited but distressed him. He tried to sketch out a plan of attack, but he could not settle on one. Instead he moved from one part of the landscape to another, finding questions wherever he turned. He thought the Tours archives might have the documentation to demonstrate the extent of the material benefits gained by various social strata during the Revolution: how the true monetary value of the confiscated lands could be established; what feudal rights had been abolished; and what debt load and rents were extinguished with inflated assignats.[38] He anticipated that whatever he discovered about the changes in landholding patterns would not lessen his sense of deep resignation to the course taken by the Revolution. The Tours archives revealed a thousand reasons to hate the *ancien régime*, but few to like the Revolution. Why? He was ambivalent. The *ancien régime* collapsed quickly under the weight of time, imperceptible changes in ideas and the political and intellectual condition of the people. Perhaps with a little more patience and good will it might have been transformed by distinguishing what was detestable from what was good about it. We should remember the weight Tocqueville had given to the possible routes open to the participants in the revolutionary turmoil

---

[37] Tocqueville to Beaumont, March 23, 1853, *OC*, VIII, pt. 3, pp. 95–96.
[38] Tocqueville to Kergorlay, July 22, 1852, *OC*, XIII, pt. 2, p. 244.

of 1848 and 1849. Other possible endings were never far from Tocqueville's way of assessing past and present. But, once he removed his glance from the specificities of a living situation, the rediscovery of those of two generations ago proved too daunting. It is not surprising that he took the longer and less personal view. Between 1750 and 1780 the government had undergone, he noted, a sea change. On the surface the same laws, regulations and principles were all in place. But deeper down, other ways of doing things, other habits and another cast of mind were waiting to break through the surface. Rulers and ruled had changed beyond recognition:

> The fall into revolution was not due to an excess of sickness, but to progress. Having reached the middle of the staircase, you throw yourself through the window to reach the bottom more quickly. Besides, this is almost always the way of the world. It is almost never when conditions are most detestable that they are smashed, but rather when, as things begin to improve, people are given a chance to breathe, to think, to exchange views and to measure the extent of the rights they have achieved against the grievances they still feel. Although the burdens are actually fewer, they appear to become unbearable.[39]

Tocqueville feared that he would be overwhelmed by the problem of finding explanations for, and meaning from, the apparently sudden eruption of a revolutionary mentality. Premonitions of a hypothesis of the futility of a belief in the possibility of total change are unmistakable. They were to recur in his final reflections. The evocation of the sickness metaphor, which he almost immediately displaced with a seemingly detached analysis of the meaning of progress, we might take as a bit of irony, but the analysis lacks the customary ironic resonances. The sequential juxtaposition of sickness and progress convey a feeling of deep resignation: people have no real way of knowing what they are doing when they embark on new journeys, but they do, on the other hand, act as if or believe they do know, finding, or perhaps stumbling on, when the older principles of order come to be questioned, the opportunities for discovering or rationalizing a commonality of thought and expectations. He could not resist the thought some weeks later that "the greatest revolutions do not change people as much as has been claimed, and what people fundamentally are is at all times what they have been."[40]

That any new understanding of the Revolution in France was possible thus depended on the bringing together of a number of conclusions from the *Democracy* and the *Souvenirs*, from his extensive and concentrated

---

[39] Tocqueville to Freslon, September 25, 1853, *Beaumont edn.*, VI, pp. 233–34.

[40] Tocqueville to Lavergne, October 31, 1853, ibid., VII, p. 305. See also Tocqueville to Mme. Phillimore, June 20, 1852, ibid., pp. 282–83, and Tocqueville to Edouard de Tocqueville, September 17, 1852, ibid., p. 291.

excursions into the public domain, including his years as a legislator, and, as well, from his more academic writings. He did not conceive the problem as a question of origins in the sense of an unbroken chain, so much as a problem of how ideas and practices in one period take on new forms in another. He pondered the mystery of how historical time flows on through change and around it, though not in the sense of a naive interest in origins lending credit to the theme of continuity predicated on a simple view of plotting cause and effect.[41] The past was a continuous whole, to be sure, but it was not without its discontinuous events. Tocqueville had already argued against historical linearity in one of his last letters to Royer-Collard:

> National destinies do not resemble a straight and continuous line which moves either from top to bottom or from the bottom to the top, but resemble rather the opposite: curves dipping and rising a great many times before people finally disappear from the face of the earth. The conquest of the entire world by the European race which is taking place in our time, the increasingly complete power of humanity to impose its power on the secrets and forces of nature – is this prodigious activity, though badly ordered – especially so by our contemporaries – a certain sign marking the beginning of an orderly epoch of decadence?[42]

Yet when he wrote that the Revolution of 1789 was "the great transformation of the whole of European society, achieved through violence, but prepared and necessarily heralded by the work of centuries,"[43] he showed that he did not want to be brushed by the winds of a future thick with darkness. His preference instead was to deal with the changes closer to his own time that had been rocking the old order for only a few generations. He wished to be true to two ideas that were fundamental to his thought. The first, enunciated many times before, took its inspiration from his uninterrupted interest in cross-Channel institutions: if the English experience of revolution would in some distant time, in the broadest sense, be continuous with the European revolution, it had undeniably in the past taken its own route and would in the future again assume particular forms.[44] The second was that nowhere but in France had the late eighteenth-century revolution been of such moment. But he still quite consciously measured it against a more modest time frame than that in which he spoke about the rise and fall of civilizations. In light of all that had already flowed from it, and all that still lay submerged, waiting to come to the surface of human consciousness, his eye remained on the

---

[41] Cf. Roger Chartier, *The Cultural Origins of the French Revolution*, trans. Lydia G. Cochrane (Durham, N. C., and London, 1991), pp. 4–7, who speaks of the "chimera of origins."   [42] Tocqueville to Royer-Collard, September 15, 1843, *OC*, XI, pp. 114–16.

[43] Tocqueville to Ampère, October 21, 1856, ibid., p. 351.

[44] Tocqueville to Beaumont, November 15, 1835, *OC*, VIII, pt. 1, p. 157.

comparatively near historical horizon calculated in centuries rather than eons. The horizon was as far as the human eye could reach, but as it receded under the force of time, it became an even more wavering, and a less fixed, phenomenon.

More than most of his contemporaries, Tocqueville saw the advantages of historical detachment, but at the same time he wanted to avoid a false distance that would dry up the wells of meaning and judgment.[45] He was not, however, a presentist,[46] in the sense of seeing the past as simply an anticipation of the *now* – the *now* that some people living in it might mistake as the embodiment of the rightness of past decisions, and who believe in addition, quite wrongly, that history is a linear narrative of the lives of historical actors who emerge from the messiness of the past and claim, as their successors also do, to be on the winning side. Information about and knowledge of the present – the empirical evidence and the reflective bent which Tocqueville lent it – was a fairly firm part of the focus of many of his inquiries, and was even more important, as he said, for the rediscovery of the past. Essential to his life as a public writer was the responsibility he felt not only to discover and dissect the *idées mères*, best translated as the mother lode of the crucial ideas that move persons and groups alike, and the obligation to educate his audience to the demands of modern public life. It was wrong-headed, while evaluating why people in the past took up and were influenced by certain arguments and why they rejected others, to conclude that the arguments had value for them alone. It was preferable to ask if the arguments possessed some intrinsic value outside their immediate context. Rediscovering the intentions of past actors was an inquiry meant to explain how significant features of a society's past, passing through the *now*, might point to intentions in the future, as yet not apparent. At the same time, people who were cognizant of the power of impersonal forces were in a better position to distinguish real from false choices, and had some chance to give shape to their intentions and the worlds they wanted to make.

Tocqueville laid out both the forces and choices in stadial fashion. Once such a procedural analysis discerns revolution in the first place as a

[45] Among others who have considered the nature of Tocqueville's detachment, see Edward T. Gargan, "Tocqueville and the Problem of Historical Prognosis," *American Historical Review*, 68 (1963), pp. 332–45, and Gargan's older work, *Alexis de Tocqueville: The Critical Years, 1848–51* (Washington, D.C., 1955); Salomon, *In Praise of Enlightenment;* Jack Lively, *The Social and Political Thought of Alexis de Tocqueville* (Oxford, 1962); Pierre Birnbaum, *Sociologie de Tocqueville* (Paris, 1970); Hugh Brogan, *Tocqueville* (London, 1973); Saguiv A. Hadari, *Theory in Practice: Tocqueville's New Science of Politics* (Stanford, 1989).
[46] For a discussion of "presentism," see David Hull, "In Defence of Presentism," *History and Theory*, 18 (1979), pp. 1–15.

challenge to the ordering of reality in an existing culture, it moves to the next stage, going beyond the presentation of the rupture as a surprising disturbance that momentarily conceals the sources of crisis that precedes it. Revolution next comes to be seen as a *point of departure*, a headlong pursuit into the new and unknown. But the need people have to explore the evidence or to appeal to the transcendental to orient their lives is not far behind: not unexpectedly contemporaries confess perplexity and reach out for explanations. Thus are revealed the powerful fears generated by the disorder, followed by the hesitant, because unknown, steps taken to escape from it. Such are the preoccupations of contemporaries of the event. For the historian, there remained the additional problem of understanding what lay on either side of the event itself. How might the event be seen either as a bridge linking the before and after; or perhaps even more epistemologically demanding, how might the event be thought of as containing in itself both cause and effect?

Tocqueville was not at all disposed to discount as inconsequential the precise moment when events take a particular turn, or when individuals act in an unexpected way. It is only in retrospect, as soon as the unexpected is experienced and thought about in the present, that individuals are mocked by reminders from the past. Yet, because the reminders are neither opaque nor transparent, reflection leads to the notion that the past does not totally shape the present in any obvious way. Of course, the fantasy that persons or collectivities could start wholly afresh in utopian fashion would always be hard to dispel, even if they kept in mind the realities of their previous psychological stances and moral systems. But if Tocqueville was wary of utopian visions, expressed either before the rupture of order, or after by revolutionaries groping toward ideal solutions, he was far from unreceptive to taking up the question of free choice. His mind was not set on a simple condemnation of the past as an incubus on the present. He wanted to understand the role of human diversity in shaping it in order to avoid illusions about the future. Thus for Tocqueville the French Revolution had heavy paradoxical meanings. They were structured in humankind itself. The analogs of self and society could, he believed, capture civic reality; but that was not the same as claiming that it could be caught by reducing the complexities of civic reality to personal biography.

What was more or less well formed in his mind, as he felt his way to his "archival" study of the weaknesses of the *ancien régime*, were the social structures of the aristocracy, in particular its caste-like features. This interest dated from his earliest exposure to Guizot's lectures, and remained a constant thread in his analysis. In the second place, the acute analysis of the appearance of a modern state apparatus, whose distinguishing feature was its autonomous power to impose itself on the citizenry quite unknown in monarchical-aristocratic societies, reached its fullest flowering in his last work. Also of importance was his attempt to integrate into his interpretation how eighteenth-century and earlier perceptions of human nature, and competing theories of social organization, opened up spaces for public discourse through which the flow of ideas in pre-democratic society spilled over into and shaped the ideologies of the Revolution. He introduced into the discussion of the breakdown of the *ancien régime* a hitherto neglected aspect of a society's multiple self-images, which furnished a critical armory by means of which to question it. The movement into the distant reaches of prerevolutionary France brought out for him the subterranean signs leading to the ruptures that tore both the old and the new France apart. All of these questions marked his attempt to rediscover how the past led to his present. They also gave him his last opportunity to think about and refine his ideas on the general laws of revolution.

8   The aristocratic ethos on the defensive

Communities have existed which were aristocratic from their earliest origin, owing to circumstances anterior to that event, and which became more democratic in each succeeding age. Such was the lot of the Romans, and of the barbarians after them. But a people, having taken its rise in civilization and democracy, which should gradually establish inequality of conditions, until it arrived at inviolable privileges and exclusive castes, would be a novelty in the world; and nothing indicates that America is likely to be the first to furnish such an example.[1]

By looking at the *ancien régime qua* régime, Tocqueville was intent on capturing as nearly as possible the fullest range of collective fears, frustrations, aspirations, other feelings and emotions, and intellectual precepts that might reveal its deepest tensions. He did not systematically take up the question of how individuals, rather than groups, having introjected those tensions, sought release from them. He tended very much to see the old society as a pathology, and he also pathologized many crucial aspects of the revolutionary attempts to end it. If pathology, it nevertheless grew out of a lengthy process of breakdown in the complex social and political framework of European feudalism, from which an ethos of individualism emerged. The origins of that individualism he ascribed to Bacon, Descartes and Luther, who had in common the conviction that individual selves, by casting their gaze on the world, exercising their own reason and forming judgments solely on such foundations, altered the way authority was perceived and justified. Tocqueville wanted to know why the philosophical questions which animated these thinkers became the common coin of politics in the eighteenth century.[2] It was the epistemological revolution occurring within the declining vigor of aristocratic feudal society that attracted his attention, more than the study of feudalism as the crucible from which capitalism emerged.

In *L'Ancien Régime*, Tocqueville directed his lens of vision to structures

[1] *Nolla edn.*, I, p. 304.   [2] Ibid., II, p. 16.

and their voices. Therein lies a shift, yet by no means a definitive one, in his perception of the historical process. He continued to be uncomfortable with fatalism or determinism of all schools. Nor did he give up his conviction that human beings can make their own history, though not in conditions of their own choosing. We saw that Tocqueville treated both historical actors and historians who believed that there was no difference between what people were doing and what they thought they were doing as persons indulging in a kind of self-delusion. He did not take the unequivocal view that the historical process could itself be considered as, or reduced to, a mental construct, removed from phenomenal reality. People do not simply free their own identities as collective beings from the communities into which they are born. Making their own history meant working within those communities, but with a consciousness of real or supposed alternative courses of action that might reinforce, adjust or repudiate their various solidarities. They possess some consciousness of their own pasts, of the generations preceding them, some notion of the links joining both, but their perceptions are inescapably – here the term *irresistibly* is justified – fragmented. Such being the case, continuities seen, not as a series of simple sequences, but inclusive of ruptures, whether deep or shallow, cannot be dismissed. Tocqueville found the idea of institutional determinateness unacceptable, and he voiced his defiance by saying that the emotional and ideological ingredients of societies are structured before they assume the protective and solemn coloring of the laws that keep them in place. He built these assumptions into his analysis of the *ancien régime*, but he rarely permitted himself, or he found it too difficult to work out, an analysis meshing the actions of historical personages with and within the larger structural modes he was attempting to delineate in *L'Ancien Régime*. Instead he embodied the substance of their beings as persons in the collective units that gave voice to the tensions between and within them. The stance he took was thus the very opposite to that which he found so suited to his purposes in the *Souvenirs*. *L'Ancien Régime* gave priority to the search for the laws governing human conduct *en masse*. If he tended to set to one side the search for reasons for individual action, it was not because he thought them unimportant. He did not intend his striving for an all-encompassing vision to injure the realities of what was going on at the levels of the individual psyche.

Reconsidering centralization: the key to breakdown?

His intense interest in the plotting of the processes of administrative centralization in his own political experience prepares us for the significant role he accords centralization in *L'Ancien Régime*. As a deeply embedded part of the old society, it appears in the book to stretch out to achieve even greater plenitude, breaking away from the legacies of older institutional restraints curbing its full powers. Tocqueville's analysis of this part of the breakdown of Old Régime France seems to swamp the attention he gave to its social and ideological tensions. Without a close inspection of the way he constructed his argument, it would be premature to say that he either succeeded in, or was completely satisfied with, his attempts to create a picture of networks in which the mores and actions of the *noblesse* and the maneuvers of the centralized state reinforced each other's weaknesses and led to the disintegration of the old society. It is not always clear whether Tocqueville tried to achieve his purpose by using one as the causal and effective agent of the other, or whether he did so by seeing them as changing places in the causal link. At times it appears as if he accords primacy to the one; at other times, he reverses the order. Despite the fluctuations in his reflections and some of his more definitive statements, he never fully embraced a unidirectional causal interpretation, nor a wholly political one. For him, there were more interesting and productive ways – though he never felt quite fully satisfied with them – of perceiving what effectively brought an end to the old society.

Tocqueville's sense of what these were came to him from a profound belief that all societies possess and are driven by a vital force that suffers enervation and depletion over time.[3] Creative adjustments or responses can prevent a full-blown crisis and sudden, because unexpected, collapse into a revolutionary situation. But there were other instances, most notably the experience of the French Revolution in which what came into being was a new vital principle. Tocqueville treated this transformation paradoxically. He saw the new principle taking embryonic shape in the old society that was losing its vitality, carrying with it a good deal of the debris of the old society, feeding off it long after it left its womb. In Tocqueville's scheme, the longer-term effects of revolutions had also to be distinguished from the trauma of short-term change. What appears as cataclysmic – Tocqueville never minimized the reality of the Revolution's surprises – was in fact only a manifest reality, since, as Barnave said before him, the Revolution had not only long been in preparation, but could be understood only, as Tocqueville also strongly maintained, by looking at the breakup of feudal institutions that were common but not everywhere the same in Europe. "The Revolution was the inevitable outcome of a long period of gestation, the abrupt and

---

[3] *OC*, II, pt. 1, p. 145.

violent conclusion of a process in which six generations had played an intermittent part."[4]

On the side of the French state's centralizing tendencies as the long-term source overwhelming the particularism of local self-rule that threw the old society off balance, Tocqueville's final version of *L'Ancien Régime*, together with his preparatory notes and afterthoughts, attest to the time he spent poring over the documentary details of the centuries-old and cumulative surges of monarchical power. Much of this ground Tocqueville had already traversed as early as 1836, and whenever he felt it necessary to advert to the lessons of the Revolution. Now, as he worked on these same questions, he conscientiously reviewed and sought more proofs for his earliest contention that the accretion of state power at the expense of the presumably greater representativeness of local assemblies, albeit they were shot through with inequalities, could hardly be contained within the existing institutional constraints of the Old Régime. Up to this point, much of the basis for his contention was the unmistakable legacy of the Napoleonic state structure, and his theoretical speculations that were supported by his first-hand observation as a deputy of how the French state bore down on its citizens. This time, as he bent himself to the task of the historian, intent on an exhaustive search of the sources, he started a closer examination of how the German states exerted their power. He wanted to know if the French state's aggrandizement of power, and hence its path to the modern nation-state, was unique. By the same token, he used this comparative approach to continue his search for general laws of revolution. More pointedly, he was determined to understand why France was unable to break loose from the old society without revolution.

The question that intrigued Tocqueville was the specificity of the symbiotic relationship that took shape between crown and aristocracy in all of Europe as it emerged from the "pure" forms of feudalism. The first volume's comparative view is almost wholly devoted to Franco-English contrasts, with fewer telling allusions to, or illustrations from, the wider European scene. In this respect, he sharpened but did not basically alter the way in which he had previously distinguished the English and French exercise of power. The English, and later the British, monarchy increased

---

[4] Ibid., p. 96. Bérenger de la Drôme's *Oeuvres de Barnave*, 4 vols. (Paris, 1843), was, as far as I can make out, not consulted by Tocqueville. This omission is curious and surprising. There is a similarity in their concepts of revolution and the processes of historical change. The significance of their similar approaches lies in the fact that two insightful and prescient minds, though separated by more than a generation, shared certain ideas born in an intellectual culture of which Guizot and others, who looked at France's past, were also part.

the power of the state without emasculating the power of the aristocracy, which continued to express its wishes with much freedom and to maintain its powers without abasing itself before the center. Why? Principally because the idea of political liberty was deeply entrenched and had never been extinguished. This was one of Tocqueville's earliest convictions, dating from his travels in England in the early and mid-1830s. He continually came back to this point. His thoughts on reading a 1788 work in September 1853, for instance, form one more example of his claim that the crucial point was the presence or absence of political liberty. The vices of human nature, he said, derived naturally from this general condition. If the English were able to escape from them, it was not because they had better sense, were more humane or more patriotic, but because they did not live in a society dominated by a caste mentality which cut off the landed nobles so sharply from other groups in society, despite the presence of various processes and forms that actually brought them together. The English were not prey to that natural and irresistible temptation to isolate themselves and to give in to their egoism.[5]

Reading Blackstone gave him an opportunity to solidify his argument. He turned to Blackstone, not for his profundity – indeed he did not think that well of him[6] – but to bolster, for him, an important argument about the nature of the English legal process. He did not dissent from Blackstone's analysis of the English system, using it to develop his own way of distinguishing it from the French. No country in the world had achieved the great goals of justice as well as England. There the courts secured each person's property, liberty and life. That did not mean, he said, that the vices of the judicial system served justice. Like all organized systems of justice, the English had secondary and principal vices. The first, easily perceived by the masses, obstructed but did not destroy justice. The second set was hidden, but not from those learned in the law. Depending on the political organization of society, the two sets of vices could change places. For example, in aristocratic times, when inequalities and privileges tended to prevent the protection of the weak against the strong and failed to ensure impartial justice, the system's principal vices were disclosed, but these began to diminish in importance as the political conditions of the people changed. Without adducing evidence for his

---

[5] *AT*, 43A, Dossier J, "La France avant la Révolution. Miscellanés." He was reading Jean-François Gaultier-Biauzat, *Doléances sur les surcharges que les gens du peuple supportent en toute espèce d'impôts, avec des observations historiques et politiques sur l'origine et les accroissemens de la taille, sur l'assujettissement du tiers état . . .* (no place, 1788).

[6] He first read Blackstone in 1833. Twenty years later, he thought him "an inferior writer, without liberality of mind or depth of judgment; in short, a commentator and a lawyer, not what *we* understand by the words *jurisconsulte* and *publiciste*." See *Correspondence and Conversations of Alexis de Tocqueville with Nassau William Senior*, II, p. 44.

theory, he said that under these circumstances, the vices of the legal system became obstructive, rather than destructive. Viewed from this angle, the defects of the English system actually prevented the strong from overwhelming the weak. The state was thus inhibited from oppressing persons, to the point of safeguarding them from the most common and most dangerous sort of venality and partiality characteristic of democratic epochs when the pressures of public power made the courts its servile agents.

The inner workings of the English law therefore were to be found in a spirit pervading all parts of English legislation – a spirit that was the very soul of the system. It would not be found by seeking it in isolated or detached, specific or particular, signs of legislation. Tocqueville clearly meant by legislation the positive law, but he also saw it imbricated in normative law. Both converged to guarantee individual rights and their free defense against oppression, whatever its source. The harmony existing between the foundation and form of the administrative and other laws stemmed from this convergence. The mind of Montesquieu is apparent in Tocqueville's gloss of Blackstone, and becomes even more evident as he urged that a detailed examination of English laws and usages, rather than a consideration of political institutions, would reveal the nature of liberty, how it was achieved and why it remained durable in England. Montesquieu's point that England had taken the best advantage of religion, commerce and freedom to forge a reasonably equitable legal and political system impressed itself on Tocqueville.[7]

It would be absurd, Tocqueville suggested, to believe that English society had two faces – self-government, public disclosure and guarantees, being one; the other being its secrecy, arbitrariness and the absence of all forms of protection of the weak against the strong. To give in to this illusion would be to succumb to an incoherent belief that no contradiction existed between political laws conceived in the republican spirit and administrative laws understood in the spirit of an absolute monarchy. In a classical sense, the English legal and political system embodied the republican spirit. For all these reasons, Tocqueville concluded that the English system was superior to the existing French one.[8] It seemed to matter less to him that the people might in fact not perceive the inner spirit of justice than that it protected them. This was not too high a price to pay to ensure liberty, and Tocqueville's approval reflects a loyalty to the idea that something might be preserved from the aristocratic ethos,

---

[7] De l'Esprit des lois, in Oeuvres complètes de Montesquieu, ed. Masson, I, Book 20, chap. 7.

[8] AT, 43B, Dossier L, "Etudes sur l'Angleterre. (Notes tirées de Blackstone.)" For the published notes on Blackstone, see OC, II, pt. 2, pp. 356–59.

specifically its encouragement of individual excellence, and its respect for liberty, however unequally it was distributed. In the course of its development in England, the ethos had proved able to lose its exclusivity and was responsible for producing a system of justice that was certainly less injurious than a system in which democracy, if carried to extremes, as it threatened to do so in the post-1848 atmosphere in France, could impose its will through a democratic despot to the extent of obscuring and obstructing the protections every human being requires to be free. The absence in the *ancien régime* of a judicial system infused by the republican spirit of liberty made possible the plethora of departures from the justice to be found in the courts and their appropriation by the state's centralizing administrative units.

In one of his notes, Tocqueville remarked that despotism in a "society like ours" is "an accident. Anarchy naturally engendered a despot; a moderate political liberty is the natural condition"; and he intimated that he would be giving some thought to "the reasons."[9] Tocqueville did not offer at this point any proof of why human beings "naturally" aspired to political liberty, a distinctly non-Aristotelian thought. The search for reasons for this putatively common human goal that he promised for some future agenda may be some mark of his dissatisfaction with the apriorism that underlies most of his appeals to liberty, and a reminder to himself that liberty is always under threat, although less so, to be sure, in certain political régimes like England's than in others. It may also be that, as he studied the differences between past and existing political cultures more closely, his imperatives changed slightly, not in the direction of a bland commitment to cultural relativism, but to a deeper understanding of all human societies. While displaying a great diversity of *moeurs*, societies of whatever stripe need not be trapped by them.

But while his newest study inspired him to seek deeper and deeper explanations, his earlier, not incautious discussion of republicanism in America – which was, he said the likeliest of all to endure – is reminiscent of how much attention he had already given to why he thought the mores in that new society lent themselves to the consolidation of republican liberty. "In the United States, religion, too, is republican, for the truths of the other world are held subject to private judgment, just as in politics the care for men's temporal interests is left to the good sense of all. Each man is allowed to choose freely the path that will lead him to heaven, just as the law recognizes each citizen's right to choose his own government." Still, the *consensus universalis* upon which republicanism rested could be compromised by too many changes in the law, leading to instability – the

[9] *OC*, II, pt. 2, p. 343.

anarchy Tocqueville refers to – with the risk of the nation falling into despotism. But he thought such a development improbable, since, in the first place, human beings have sought throughout history to enlarge their liberty, as in the movement from aristocracy to democracy, and, in the second place, because no nation which, like America, started "from a basis of civilization and democracy, should . . . arrive at inviolable privileges and exclusive castes." These were the characteristics of aristocracies achieving power through conquest, demanding from subjects subjection, which is "nothing more contrary to nature."[10] What he faced now, as he looked back at the administrative structures of the French monarchy, almost two decades after making these observations in the *Democracy*, is the question of why their development seemed to favor their survival beyond 1789, in spite of the countercurrents against them, which came to light in 1787, and which lasted perhaps even as late as 1792.

England and America had moved furthest in entrusting their political and judicial bodies with the power to diminish the state's capacity to extend its dominance over the lives of their citizens. Where did the German states, as they struggled to enter the modern world, stand in regard to this question?[11] In the summer of 1854, Tocqueville traveled to Germany with this question in mind. He almost at once described the Germans in Bonn, where he took up residence, as pleasant but unprepared for public life. But then, he said, what people could be said to be ready anywhere in continental Europe, where free institutions had been dead for over two centuries, and where civilization, instead of preparing men to live in liberty, simply adorned and legitimated servitude?[12] The absence of political institutions in central Europe, shaped as they were by generations of absolute government, sixty years of centralization and a period of administrative dependence that could lead either to servitude or revolution,[13] was unquestionably related, Tocqueville wrote, to the more fundamental question of how and to what extent the slow or rapid breakdown of feudalism over centuries had altered the balance between the nobles and the state apparatus in the various German principalities and kingdoms. How these structures were held together and then fell apart was far from clear. Tocqueville wrote to his friend, Circourt, that to reduce the relics of the different feudal customs in all parts of the country to a single and general overriding principle was an intricate assignment.[14] But he tried to unravel it.

---

[10] *Nolla edn.*, I, pp. 300–05.
[11] A brief account of his German inquiries may be found in Françoise Mélonio and Lise Queffélec, "Tocqueville et l'Europe," *OC*, VI, pp. 271–75.
[12] Tocqueville to Sedgwick, July 17, 1854, *OC*, VII, pp. 156–57.
[13] Tocqueville to Sedgwick, August 14, 1854, ibid., pp. 158–59.
[14] Tocqueville to Circourt, June 30, 1854, *OC*, XVIII, pp. 179–81.

The people with whom Tocqueville discussed these issues and the general surveys he consulted throw some light on his queries.[15] There was, for example, disagreement over the persistence and ubiquity of serfdom. From Hälschner, professor of German law at Bonn, he learned that serfdom still existed in the eighteenth century, though it had been greatly weakened. Walter, another of his informants, did not dissent from this view, but expanded it to affirm that in some areas the local nobles controlled the administrative structures, while in others, royal officials called the tune. Specifically, Bavaria and the Rhenish provinces remained closer in spirit to the old society than Prussia. Many of the same sources for the diversity of conditions were to be found in Germany as in France. War and the semi-ruin of the nobles in both areas had also decisively enhanced state power in Prussia. Concluding that there had been several systems in the various Germanic states, he turned to Ludwig Häusser's *Deutsche Geschichte*[16] for additional concrete instances. In most of Prussia and Austria, according to Häusser, local assemblies were no longer meeting. Only in Württemberg and Mecklenburg did they possess some semblance of authority. Their disappearance was on the whole not regretted, for they were recognized as having served special interests. The population turned to absolutism, because it sought to destroy serfdom. Indeed, where the princes were conscientious, their efforts unified the state, created order, provided protection, improved the well-being of bourgeois and peasant and raised the general level of public education. Even ecclesiastical states, such as Cologne, Münster and Trèves, had initiated such improvements.

Tocqueville found the German picture similar in a "thousand details" to the French. He was impressed by signs of the same anxieties, vague feelings of discontent and hatred of the past that were evident in pre-revolutionary France. Lessing and Herder were among the men of letters who, in the absence of practical political life, made, as did their French counterparts, abstract literary politics the focus of change. He had noted earlier that the real difference between eighteenth-century French and German philosophers was that, while both condemned the present and were moved by a desire for change, the French wanted to abolish the present by adopting a new plan, while the Germans wanted to rebuild without destroying the ancient foundations.[17] When it came to

---

[15] On Tocqueville's German inquiries, see *AT*, 43B, Dossier Q, "Allemagne." These ideas should be read in conjunction with the notes in *OC*, II, pt. 1, pp. 265–72.

[16] Ludwig Häusser, *Deutsche Geschichte. Vom Tode Friedrichs des Grossen bis zur Gründung des deutschen Bundes*, 4 vols. (Berlin, 1861–63). The first volume, which Tocqueville consulted, ends at 1795. Häusser wrote his own history of the Revolution, *Geschichte der französischen Revolution, 1789–1799, herausgegeben von Wilhelm Onken* (Berlin, 1867). A reference to Tocqueville's *L'Ancien Régime* may be found on p. 14.

[17] Tocqueville to Circourt, June 14, 1852, *OC*, XVIII, p. 76.

centralization, Tocqueville was fascinated by Prussian developments. Just as he found Blackstone an aid to illuminate his understanding of England, he felt that Prussia's movement to state consolidation, first under Frederick and later under his successors, offered the most interesting points of contrast, and sometimes points of contact, with France's efforts. In eighteenth-century Prussia, centralization could be seen, he said, in embryo, but it was still far from being as complete and as concrete as in France before the Revolution. The *Mittelstand*, highly placed public officials whose interests set them apart from ecclesiastical, professorial or commercial bourgeois groups, occupied a unique place in the state. They were also unique in all of Europe, Tocqueville concluded. Because they were forbidden to purchase noble property and could not obtain the highest posts in the civil service, yet were important to the administrative functions of the state, their incipient antagonism to the nobles erupted in a more open defiance once the Revolution in France was in progress, and once they saw themselves increasingly essential to the state's power, and especially as they compared their own administrative competence with the aristocracy's unearned privileges. Frederick's code, the *Allgemeine Gesetzbuch für die Prüssische Staaten* was promulgated in 1795, long after his death, but, while it approved the principles of a limited monarchy, they were never applied. The code inspired no firm approval.

Tocqueville found the earlier attempt at codification, the *Corpus Iuris Fredericianum*, which was the work of chancellor Samuel von Cocceji in the mid-1740s, potentially more revealing. Though Frederick set this older code aside in favor of the later one, for Tocqueville the first promised to throw more light on the nature of Prussian administrative practices and the Roman law that inspired them. From a political viewpoint study of the Roman law was crucial. It introduced both democracy and servitude into the modern world. It did much to disorganize and finally destroy the old society, create the conditions for centralization and replace a disordered liberty. What Roman law achieved in Germany, it also achieved to a smaller degree elsewhere, except in England. It degraded political society. General symptoms of the death of the old society were to be found everywhere in Europe. Though nuanced, they were unmistakable. These were stray, rather than organized thoughts. Tocqueville gave no reasons for his assertions about the key importance of the Roman law, except, as we shall presently see, by implicitly contrasting it with the common law that was protective of liberty.

In his notes, Tocqueville wondered instead about the death of old and the birth of new societies – this problem was indeed part of his subject.[18]

---

[18] See *AT*, 43B, Dossier Q, "Allemagne."

The notes contain his first ideas that every society is animated by a vital principle. Bodily organization has its political analog – an idea that was hardly new. The aging of societies proceeds unabated, irrespective of their intrinsic vices or virtues. The same institutions that produce life cause death; what creates prosperity also causes ruin. From this reflection an interpellation is needed to fill in the gaps of his argument. And it is not hard to see, given his constant binding of sameness and difference, that Tocqueville thought not only about the death of institutions as a general principle, not only about the aging process as *sui generis*, but about the different outcomes of aging and death. What role, if any, did liberty play in the process? When associated with medieval institutions, liberty was capable of preserving its special characteristics, but it was unable to produce devotion, great civic virtues and prosperity. Instead, in the long run it was overwhelmed by the administrative and democratic despotism visible in continental Europe. This modern double-headed despotism came into being when aristocracy had lost its utility, while sterility and venality might be the only features of democracy to survive. Each of the two forms of government, aristocratic and democratic, contributed to modern despotism. It absorbed into itself the power of coteries, nepotism, blind obstinacy and egoism, characteristic of aristocracies, and the corruptions and intrigues peculiar to democracies.

In this kind of despotism, healthy democratic institutions were not likely to grow. What was alive in both France and Prussia alike, despite their differences, was a new species of administration that placed itself above and beyond all the older institutions. In the older cultures of Europe, thus, the choice was between England, for whose aristocracy he continued to express his uncritical esteem, and the rest. England's aristocracy was vigorous because of its respect for a liberty which cultivated new forms of the common law, representation of all classes, equality before the law and distinctions based on wealth and talent, not on birth. It was a liberty that was based on new principles more or less continuous with its past. Tocqueville, as always, set America apart, because it did not have an aristocratic feudal past, only some remnants of aristocratic liberty in transmuted form.

Another problem nettled Tocqueville. If it were necessary to have a revolution to destroy the old society and introduce a new one, how was it possible that Prussia escaped revolution? It was one thing to know, as Tocqueville claimed to know, the reasons for England's more-or-less orderly transition. The Prussians owed their invulnerability to violence to the French Revolution for quite other reasons. The *Allgemeine Prüssisches Landrecht* (1794), to be sure, had already accomplished much to ensure an orderly transition. It destroyed nothing, it was moderate in its impact and it was a regulating and limiting force. But would it have been able to assume its moderate and non-violent stance if the French had not, by the very fact of their revolution, served as a warning and as a challenge to introduce the changes needed to become a modern state? Tocqueville did not, as he promised himself, take up this thought again.

He turned to the more tantalizing question of what, beyond the more obvious constituents of centralization, might be thought of as its essence. His reasoning shows that he was uneasy about where the emphasis of his analysis should lie. He also seems to reverse himself as he proceeded to its end. He gave the edge in the first place – on other occasions, as we saw, he attributed equal or greater power to the autonomy of ideas – to the argument that institutions derive their vital principle more from the *moeurs* of a people than from any ideas they might have. How else can we explain the fact that, while the future revolutionaries in 1788 and 1789 were totally hostile to centralization and favorable to local life, centralization was reestablished?[19] As he put it, centralization is itself not an institution. It is ultimately a trait of character, perhaps of French national character. French people are fearful of being alone in their views, of finding themselves isolated from one another. Hence they are unable to resist the urge to join the crowd.[20] They look to it for protection. Centralization thus serves to alleviate the psychological stress of exercising autonomous and individual judgment.

Tocqueville did not seem to have had in mind his earliest firm judgments about the powerful urges in Americans to drift from their unquestioned ethos of individualism into a smug conformism. A centralized administration was not, he had written, the source of their need to gain strength by losing themselves in the mass. This time, Tocqueville affirmed that he was ready to give "the last word . . . to centralization," which "grows and deepens in strength, even if it seems to diminish superficially, because the work of society [le travail social], the *individualization*, and the isolation of social elements is still going on . . ."[21] Tocqueville appeared at this point to be coupling centralization and the modernizing forces leading to social uniformity, and gave lesser weight in the end both to the force of *moeurs* and of ideas, and more gravity to passions. His allusions to *moeurs* as a reality and as a conceptual tool sometimes look like an echo from a more distant analytical period of his life. He held on to it, but it seemed to carry less of the burden his arguments required for mounting a comparison of the different ways in which societies moved from the

[19] *OC*, II, pt. 2, p. 200.   [20] Ibid., p. 332.

[21] Ibid., p. 343 (Tocqueville's emphasis). As far as I can discern, this is the first time he uses the neologism. I could not find it in the *Democracy*.

particular nature of local loyalties and the struggles of feudal life to the conditions of modern life.

Tocqueville did not abandon his focus on the nature of the centralizing process in France as the long-term source and consequence of the Revolution – "the same conditions which had precipitated the fall of the monarchy made for the absolutism of its successors."[22] Still, he felt it an error to regard that process as an irreducible force. There are many indications that he was ready to modify the grand manner in which he couched what he called his "diatribe"[23] against the *ancien régime* and centralization, at least in its prerevolutionary forms. Readers of Tocqueville are so accustomed to agreeing with the general tenor of his statements on the gradual expansion of the centralized administration during the *ancien régime* that they tend to overlook the extent to which he was not always sure about its centrality. Because he had chosen as his subject the ultimate sources of the death of the old society, he was conscious that he tended to stress its evils. Such a perspective could blind him, he admitted, to the realities of its authentic physiognomy. This perception is a demonstration of Tocqueville's ability to make important distinctions. He was engaged, in other words, in two reciprocal inquiries. One was an analysis of how the old society worked and might be seen as standing on its own before its collapse. The focus of such an inquiry could be distorted if special care were not taken to block out as far as possible the notion that there was an old society doomed to extinction. Postmortems invariably looked for causes of death. The focus was determined by the knowledge that the old society faltered, fell prey to disorder and was swept aside.

It is curious therefore to encounter the word "abrupt" to describe the "immense remodeling of all the rules and of all the administrative practices."[24] It may be that he chose to characterize the remodeling in this way to describe the last efforts of the crown to reform the administration, entailing, as it turned out, a program that made some allowance for provincial assemblies, but that in fact was intended, he argued, to revitalize and enhance the centralizing organs of the government at the expense of local bodies. Such a reading is plausible if the citation is rendered fully. The remodeling, he wrote, "preceded the political revolution" and "had already caused one of the greatest upheavals that had ever taken place in the life of a great nation." The first revolution – Tocqueville meant the remodeling to be seen as a revolution – had an incommensurable influence on the second and, indeed, caused "it to differ entirely from all revolutions the world had known before or has witnessed during the last

---

[22] *OC*, II, pt. 1, p. 243.   [23] *OC*, II, pt. 2, p. 368.   [24] *OC*, II, pt. 1, p. 242.

half century."[25] The projected renovation triumphed over all efforts to counter it, and only temporarily collapsed when it encountered strong sentiments favoring a redistribution of powers suggested by the various political strands of opposition. Arguments in this vein were introduced bit by bit in the finished volume of *L'Ancien Régime* and reached the climax on which he wanted to end it. The wreckage of the absolute government and its plans did not in fact end France's history of centralization. Its institutions were not incompatible with equality and were revived and "centralization was built up anew."[26]

The coherence of the argument reverberates if the qualifications he intended to introduce for his projected second volume are taken up. They show that Tocqueville was adding a significant subtext that underscored his attempt to see why France had to endure or might have escaped revolution. In its judgments on the nature of the struggle between the legally constituted bodies and the central monarchy, Tocqueville's first volume was more dogmatic than his afterthoughts. Its chief points were stated elegantly but with a finality that Tocqueville later believed needed greater shading. What were his original points?[27] The central monarchy was not entirely free to do as it wished, but the power of a proud aristocracy to oppose it had been effectively excised. The existence of forms of liberty and the expression of opposition to the government were present in the old society through judicial debate and appeal, and these were "incompatible with the concept of a servile state."

Almost against his will, Tocqueville found himself full of admiration for the intrinsically valuable aspects of the old society. It fostered values, such as the heroism that can make people true citizens, instead of morally correct and well-behaved people with a "craving for material well-being which leads the way to servitude." The phrase "the discreet, well-regulated sensualism which prevails today" – a condition that militates against the obligations of citizenship in a society based on an ethos of equality – takes us back to the pages of the *Democracy*. So, why were the liberties associated with the hodgepodge nature of the old society, which "prepared the French for the great task of overthrowing despotism, [making] them by the same token less qualified than perhaps any other nation to replace it by stable government and a healthy freedom under the sovereignty of law"?

In his post-1856 reconsiderations,[28] Tocqueville fleshed out the defects of the Old Régime constitution. Even after the destruction of the Estates

---

[25] Ibid.   [26] Ibid., p. 248.
[27] They are set out in, and the citations in this and the following paragraph come from, *OC*, II, pt. 1, pp. 168–77, specifically pp. 175–76.   [28] *OC*, II, pt. 2, pp. 363–64.

General in the seventeenth century, the monarchy was not absolute. Languedoc was a good example of a *pays d'état* that retained its autonomies despite the central government's attempts for generations to curtail them.[29] As for municipal government, "civic rights were constantly bestowed, taken away, restored, increased, diminished, modified in a thousand ways, and unceasingly. No better indication of the contempt into which all local liberties had fallen can be found than these eternal changes of laws which no one seemed to notice."[30] Perhaps no more telling feature of the nature of the central administration under the monarchy was the political uncertainty it generated. Though *ancien régime* political society was in large degree incoherent, civil society managed to have a coherence of its own. Individuals in the different classes continued to acknowledge some of the ties that held them together uneasily. For example, the links between *seigneurs* and people were also not totally sundered; and, at some levels, political structures were influenced by connections of this kind. For, however unorganized they were, their very presence constituted an affront to government.[31] But the counterweights and the guarantees protecting freedoms were cumbersome, more often than not injuring the public good, without really ensuring individual security.

Tocqueville could find no predictable and regular procedures and structures in which liberty could be consistently articulated and exercised. Judicial bodies assumed the responsibilities of surveillance and opposition. By their very nature, the courts encouraged the qualities needed to render acceptable and responsible judgments that found no easy place in the political life of society. The habits of adhering to forms and rules were qualities, Tocqueville stated, that did not serve the process nor the goal of the government. The result was that, when the *parlements* assumed a political role, they called into question not only the defects but the useful parts of the monarchy as well. The monarchy used arbitrary force to obscure from the popular gaze the vices of the *parlements* when

---

[29] See the Appendix in *OC*, II, pt. 1, pp. 253–65. Cf. these remarks with his notes on *Mémoires des intendants dressés par ordre du duc de Bourgogne (1698) par le comte de Boulainvilliers (août 1853)*, in *AT*, 43A, Dossier J, "La France avant la Révolution. Miscellanés." At his request, his friend, Adolphe de Circourt, sent him some information on the composition and procedures of the Etats of Languedoc, where the *noblesse* had less power than the upper clergy and the syndics of the bigger towns. Circourt wrote, "All in all, this body had a reputation in the province and maintained some sense of national life there." See Tocqueville to Circourt, May 17, 1855, and Circourt to Tocqueville, May 18, 1855, *OC*, XVIII, pp. 244–46.   [30] *OC*, II, pt. 1, p. 283.

[31] Ibid., pp. 301–02. The last sentence of this note sums up Tocqueville's interpretation of the sources and results of the Revolution: "The Revolution burst these ties, and substituted no political bonds in their stead; it thus paved the way for both equality and servitude."

they acted as political bodies. When the monarchy took such action, these quasi-judicial bodies turned themselves almost unwittingly into objects of popular acclaim. At a more profound but not immediately transparent level, the monarchy's policy really had the effect of depriving them of a sense of what they could legitimately accomplish as political bodies: by taking on a political role that judicial bodies could not fulfill, they were not fulfilling the single role of which such bodies are capable. The judicial bodies had become hybrid entities, inspiring ambiguities and, in addition, unrobing their inner ambivalence. This was not to say that judicial bodies could not possess a political function. In a balanced monarchy, they checked the administration, and acted as an intermediary between the sovereign and the people. France was not such a monarchy. Though Tocqueville did not invoke the names of Blackstone and Montesquieu, there is no question that he had them in mind when he spoke of a balanced monarchy with a sense of how the separate judicial and legislative spheres, when properly related, acted to safeguard the spirit of an enlightened public authority.

Tocqueville weighted the various elements of the French administration, and found that they did not add up to a complete system of centralization which neatly dovetailed into the politics of an absolute monarchy. He was aware not only of the exceptions to the general drift toward centralization, but also of how, in perhaps the most important instance, these exceptions were the result of the processes of *anoblissement*, which placed power in the hands of lawyers who bought offices and constituted the *noblesse de robe* that spearheaded the opposition to the crown. The way in which they climbed to power had the effect of injuring their moral power to act as the spokesmen of a disinterested public voice. He did not deny the fact of their being suborned as well by other processes that made them the servants of the crown. The effect of this development was to reduce their ability to assume a role of durable opposition. What they abdicated was not an administrative role in the state. Indeed, over time, they became its agents. To compensate for their loss of genuine independence, they multiplied and made the most of factitious social distinctions to keep themselves apart. Neither those distinctions, nor their judicial opposition to the centralizing power, nor still their participation at local levels of administration, could conceal the fact that they showed minimal concern for political liberty as a countervailing authority to the evolution of state power. The contrasts between the two judicial systems of France and England revolved around this distinction between an independent judiciary and a hobbled one.

Tocqueville worked over his proofs and revised the text of the first volume, trying to get his main theses right. The absence of *lex loci* in

France, and the dissimilarity of laws and customs of the different provinces, were not alone in contributing to the collapse of the old institutions. Truer was the theory that absolutism had gone a long way in France, and that, because of the concentration of power in Paris, the local power to resist the latter was limited. Indeed, "the centralization of France under the old Monarchy, though not so complete as its Democratic and Imperial tyrants afterwards made it, was great."[32] Tocqueville did not misread the system of the Old Régime, nor did he present a monolithic picture of it.

Of the two lines of inquiry, the first, the isolation of the weaknesses of the *ancien régime*, was emphasized in the finished volume; the second, with its reemphasis of the régime's "true" features, could not of course be conducted without reference to the other. Tocqueville not only described the specific developments of French centralization, he also saw it as an expression of the evolution of modern state power, a process that was common across Western, and, to a lesser extent, other parts of Europe. On reading the memoirs of the Napoleonic comte Mollien in August 1853,[33] he was struck by the sheer growth of state power as it became the principal consumer and greatest spender, as well as the greatest stimulus to industry.[34] By the same token, those who were tied to government as its creditors, contractors and suppliers of capital for its shipyards and road construction in fact did not possess any guarantees from the state for their capital outlays. State power thus increased, but it did not really succeed in assuring investors that those who managed the state's finances could underwrite its financial stability, nor deal with the growing burden of debt. Finances were in disorder, on the one hand; economic growth, on the other, was stimulating the needs of a consumer society which for Tocqueville also led to the proliferation of puerile ideas and theories and a host of violent sentiments. These two movements – fiscal disorder and economic growth – were rapidly moving toward a collision, leaving in their wake enflamed feelings directed against the government.

Though Tocqueville did not carry this idea a further step, he was implying, in harmony with one of his chief theories, that state power has a

[32] Nassau Senior's conversation with Tocqueville, May 18, 1856, *OC*, VI, pt. 2, pp. 44–45.
[33] *AT*, 43A, Dossier J, "La France avant la Révolution. Miscellanés." François-Nicolas, comte Mollien, born in Normandy in 1758 into a commercial family, entered the Ministry of Finances while still in his teen years, and worked on the complexities of the farmers-generals' taxing powers and privileges. He left the ministry in 1790 or 1791, but was recalled by Napoleon in 1800. Tocqueville was consulting François-Nicolas Mollien's *Mémoires d'un ministre du trésor public, 1780–1815*, 4 vols. (Paris, 1845), I, p. 130.
[34] Cf. in chap. 6 Tocqueville's observations in the *Democracy* on how in the advanced economies of the United States and Europe, the state, as he saw it, was moving to control the most dynamic parts of economic life.

momentum of its own, but that in order to maintain its forward motion, it must look to political will for its major support. In France, the discovery of such a will had become more and more problematic. Still, in the end, Tocqueville was unwilling to concede that the will toward centralization was incompatible with a fresh political realignment. It followed that the vices of centralization were not incorrigible. Revolution was not, he believed, needed to deal with them. He had said as much in his 1836 *Essai*. If corrections had been initiated to ensure minimal public prosperity, and if a prudent form of national representation had been made part of it, the centralized administration could have been changed peacefully. In that event, a sound groundwork might have been laid for a modern state to come into being, unencumbered by the vast drain of the country's resources necessitated by juggling the relics of a feudal past, frozen in grotesque manifestations of *gentilhommière*.[35]

The conditions for revolution were ripe for other than the usually adduced reasons. It was made, he said firmly, not to change the administrative rules, but to change the condition of humanity.[36] By this he surely meant the multiple and complex ways in which human beings relate to one another in their private lives both as individuals and in their community associations and in their public lives vis-à-vis the state and its myriad officials. If he now conceived the goal of the Revolution in this way, he had moved some distance from the position that "the Revolution sought to increase the power and jurisdiction of the central authority."[37] This was how he put it in the chapter of *L'Ancien Régime* in which he discussed what the Revolution accomplished. He conflated aims and consequences. His argument that the Revolution was the instrument that brought the modern state into being remains intact only if it is expanded to take account of his revised interpretation. In his rethinking of the question, he argued that the *failure* to reform the government, along the lines that he believed were possible, proved to be the *precondition* for a much more advanced centralized administration with infinitely greater powers than those available to the monarchy. Along the way, the policies of successive revolutionary régimes, stimulated by internal crises and external war, solidified the state's power.

An incomplete theory of class and caste

If, then, in Tocqueville's view, the overwhelming urge to change the human condition was what drove the French to use violence to break up

---

[35] The locution is to be found in Tocqueville's comments on Gaultier-Biauzat's work in *AT*, 43A, Dossier J, "La France avant la Révolution. Miscellanés."
[36] *OC*, II, pt. 2, pp. 375–76.   [37] *OC*, II, pt. 1, p. 96.

the old order, rather than the impulse to transform the administrative rules, we must return to consider how Tocqueville understood the divisions in *ancien régime* society, sections of which found the instruments to articulate dissent. The deep alienation was not so much a response to the ideals of an aristocratic ethos, as a reaction incorporating felt degrees of alienation from the existence of glaring inequalities in the form of privileges which caught everyone in their net either as beneficiaries or as victims. The origins and development of class divisions in the old society are part of Tocqueville's study of the tensions in the social fabric. The aristocratic ethos, as it came to be professed in France, represented in his scheme a subversion of its original values and a reason for questioning its social and political self-image as well as the image other classes carried in their heads about it. The moment the ethos was reducible to the overriding imperatives of birth, it crystallized a fatal flaw from which, at least in Europe, a caste would find it hard to escape. Tocqueville was uttering his final pronouncements on this subject. As he had said many times before, the caste structure was not absolutely impermeable,[38] but because the barriers were nonetheless real, the task of identifying its mechanisms in order to breach them created a climate of profound social ambiguity. Tocqueville identified the social rigidities and the escape routes from them as one of the major stress points in the old society. Together with the caste's failure to retain, let alone strengthen, its governing role, the strains that it transmitted down through the social ranks conspired to bring France to a critical turning point – to the point when it moved from trying to find a means of negotiating a peaceful transition to a more equitable society, to a mental condition demanding a clean break through violence.

Bourgeoisie and nobility were becoming more alike, yet the gap between them was widening. These apparently opposing developments reinforced one another and were proof of the strains induced by the spirit, if not always by the letter, of class separation. In turn, though full-fledged individualism did not yet exist, what Tocqueville called a kind of collective or group individualism, encapsulating the separate interests of distinctive social groups, sharpened differences and antagonisms. The distinctions were thus not only class-based. They were also expressed in the myriad corporate groups that had sprung into existence to promote special goals. Premodern France was a class society in some respects, but also a society in which the separate corporate groups looked inward, looking askance at and showing suspicion of a government that challenged the exclusivity of the jurisdictions, commercial, municipal and so

---

[38] Cf. Ernest Gellner on the open question of the permeability of the English aristocracy in his *Plough, Sword and Book: The Structure of Human History* (London, 1988), p. 160.

on, over which they exercised a precarious sovereignty.[39] Tocqueville rightfully did not identify the practices and attitudes of these groups as categories of caste. France was, apart from the aristocracy which had taken on most of the features of a caste, as much, if not more, a society divided along class lines. France was not a society of castes rigidly defined to locate and punish segments of the population that transgressed social, economic and mental boundaries. Social anxiety existed only for those who lived as far as they were able, in a society undergoing change, on the premise that their superiority bestowed by birth entitled them to privileges. France was, then, socially and psychologically divided along three points of an axis: caste, collective individualism and class. Exclusivity, but not in the most rigid sense, was the source of division.

Tocqueville's analysis did not always fully observe the distinctions he drew. When writing about the mutual alienation of landowners and peasants, he firmly asserted that, of course, individual exceptions of empathy between them existed, but that his major concern was "with classes as a whole, in my mind the historian's proper study."[40] Thus for him a class analysis appeared to be paramount. To carry out his intentions, at times he subsumed the other sources of distinction under the general rubric of class. "The segregation of classes, which was the crime of the late monarchy, became at a later stage a justification for [its actions], since, when all the wealthy and enlightened elements of the population were no longer able to act in concert and take part in the government, the country became, to all intents and purposes, incapable of administering itself and it was necessary for a master to step in."[41] He pursued the point by comparing the isolation of classes in the Old Régime with the absence of class distinctions in his own day, adding that only their traces remained visible in jealousies and antipathies[42] – a curious utterance in view of his designation of 1848 as a class war. Tocqueville's discussion of class could have been more acute had he expanded his inspired but spare remark that the middle class showed enough energy to make of itself "a pseudo-aristocracy that on occasion displayed the spirit of resistance of a true aristocracy."[43] It possessed the resources, as holders of public offices, to show itself independent of the central government, and it was conscious of its privileges and prestige, which it defended against concessions to the central power. Indeed, it too possessed privileges and a thousand defenses against the abuse of power, not available to the remainder of the population. But it could not carry the opposition beyond a certain limit, even if the government, which could place obstacles in the path of the

---

[39] *OC*, II, pt. 1, pp. 157–58.   [40] Ibid., p. 179.   [41] Ibid., p. 166.   [42] Ibid., p. 167.
[43] Ibid., p. 173.

middle class, indeed in the path of "the enlightened and comfortable classes," paradoxically could not really do the things that were properly in its jurisdiction.[44]

But the middle class had neither a judicial nor a political voice to breach the boundaries which blunted its ambitions, sentiments and actions. This point is slightly obscured in Tocqueville's discussion. He moved without pause to locate the resistance. It came, he said, from within the judicial system. As we have seen, its best and its worst features were on constant display, resulting in a sterile, because ultimately disastrous, collision between the government and the *parlements*, which discredited both. The paradox was that the ancient aristocracy, by taking refuge in and acting as a caste, acted aggressively *qua* caste, when it found itself on the defensive in the late 1780s, spurred on by memories of its defiance earlier in the century. Caste therefore dictated the terms of the final confrontation with the central government, exposing, in the process, the impotence of the *noblesse*. Their failure brought the middle class to center stage, for which it was preparing itself by fashioning a political program that gave voice to the ideology of class. It asserted its class ambitions, keeping its distance from what Tocqueville called the superior classes, matching the determination of the latter to maintain themselves apart. Both failed in the process to understand the immensity of the coming Revolution.[45]

To differentiate itself further, the middle class also showed scant regard for the peasantry from which it scrupulously held itself aloof. Caste and class were in conflict, until, almost by default, caste gave way to class as the determining voice in the future political configuration of the nation. Tocqueville presciently saw and applauded the union of the "isolated units in the social system"[46] as one of the distinguishing and generous features of the pre-Revolution and of the Revolution.[47] But he did not press the more decisive point that the middle class as class tried to take the commanding lead. That it did not achieve complete success may be gathered from what he said in 1848 about the period from 1789 to 1830. As he saw the problem, a long and violent struggle between the ancient feudal aristocracy and the middle class took place before the latter came into possession of its full powers with the establishment of the Orléanist

---

[44] *OC*, II, pt. 2, p. 362.   [45] Ibid., p. 108.   [46] *OC*, II, pt. 1, p. 167.

[47] Cf. his remarks in his speech in the Constituent Assembly on September 12, 1848, "The French Revolution . . . had never had the idea of dividing the citizens . . . into property holders and proletariats, you will never find these words that are so charged with hatred . . . in any of the great documents of the Revolution. The Revolution wanted politically a condition in which there would be no classes; the Restoration [and] the July Monarchy wanted the contrary. We ought to want what our fathers wanted." See *OC*, III, pt. 3, p. 179.

monarchy.[48] In *L'Ancien Régime*, he gave the matter more thought than he had in 1848, and he was ready to say that from August 8, 1788, when the decision was made to convoke the Estates General, the focus of the crisis shifted from the resistance of the *parlements* to the state, and that "the authentic mother passion [la véritable passion mère] of the Revolution, the passion of class that the *parlement* was not representing, took precedence over the question of the struggle for power with the monarchy that others were going to represent more effectively." What the *parlement* ironically represented for Tocqueville was an impotent form of liberalism, a false liberalism, he called it, since it could not take hold in a rapidly changing political culture that no longer saw any need to support the old society's discredited and suspect guardians of liberty.[49] That the *parlementaires* were fostering an inauthentic liberty is surely the way Tocqueville would have dealt with the objection that, by focusing on the "virile virtues," "healthy self-respect" and the nurturing of "many outstanding personalities," he was attempting to rescue liberty from the ashes of the Old Régime.[50] As he categorically affirmed again and again, and more emphatically in a letter to Beaumont, as he was putting the finishing touches to *L'Ancien Régime*, the distinguishing feature of the old society was the "absence of all political liberty,"[51] the revitalization of which was the crucial reason for supporting a conservative republic in 1848 and 1849.

Tocqueville always maintained that the French aristocracy gave up its rights to be considered an authentic one when, instead of carrying on as a governing class in the spirit of the English aristocracy, it invoked the principle of bloodlines as its sole identifying mark, and acted as a caste, thereby losing its voice as a counterweight to the central government. There is a problem embodied in this formulation, revolving around a perplexing question that Tocqueville's analysis raises, but leaves partially unanswered. The question is important, for it goes straight to the ultimate sources of the final political breakdown. Did the *noblesse* willingly, once it assumed the characteristics of a caste, succumb to the blandishments of the central power and seek and gain, as compensation for its losses as a governing élite, additional but other kinds of privileges to strengthen itself as a caste; or did it try, from a weakened political position, which was both self-inflicted and inflicted by an external force, to

---

[48] "Question financière: Note de Tocqueville: Je retrouve ceci aujourd'hui [novembre 1848]," *OC*, III, pt. 2, p. 735. The extract is taken from notes that Tocqueville made in 1848. He found them prophetic because of his admonition that the middle class must take care to act as a responsible political class to avoid the dangers of increasing the popularity of socialist doctrines.   [49] *OC*, II, pt. 2, pp. 100–01.
[50] Ibid., chap. 11.   [51] Tocqueville to Beaumont, April 24, 1856, *OC*, VIII, pt. 3, p. 395.

hinder the central administration, but was unable to fully apprehend the long-term consequences of its challenges; or was it simply over the long run battered into submission? Tocqueville took up portions of the question by saying that it was because of the transformation of the aristocracy into a caste that, at its upper reaches, society ended up composed of a head and a body increasingly separated from each other, tending, as civilization progressed, to render the head weaker and the body stronger. The body metaphors were obviously meant to represent the caste-like aristocracy and the monied middle class. To gain advantage from this development, the monarchy used one part of the social body against the other, enabling it to achieve absolute power. The monarchy had no other choice. Following its nature, it expanded its power.[52] It took up the instruments of power when the caste-like *noblesse* gave them up. Tocqueville's critique of the caste system of aristocracy appears to lean toward assigning it a good deal of the responsibility for the failure to resist centralization. He did not unreservedly place his bets on that side of the equation. His critique of the aristocracy was almost matched by his scathing assessment of the crown's equally myopic thirst for vengeance against it. When both sides revealed their incapacity to grant legitimacy to one another's claims, deadlock ensued. To end it, the monarchy blundered politically in separating the two issues of doubling the third and voting in common. To that extent, the crown's initiative proved disastrous. So it did have the upper hand but it played it badly. Had voting in common been granted, a revolution would have followed, but it would have been a revolution permitting the "élite" classes to salvage something.[53]

If Tocqueville had taken his own admonitions seriously to use class as a principal category of his analysis, he might have been able to offer an even more powerful reading of a society riven along the different lines he delineated. He would then have given greater force to his proposition that the *noblesse* had failed in its responsibilities as a class; that the *noblesse* as a caste was oblivious of its long-term interests; and that only as a class could the *noblesse* have been able to see what these truly were. That indeed they did not strengthens such a theory. Tocqueville certainly was aware that the caste's understanding of its self-interest was determined by the trade-offs it received in the form of great material and social advantages. On the question of what made up the social and political elements of that self-interest, the aristocracy ultimately deceived itself. He called the self-deception a "singular imbecility of those who made it [the Revolution] happen without wanting it."[54] And for this failure to know

<hr />

[52] *OC*, II, pt. 2, pp. 358–59.   [53] Ibid., pp. 112–14.   [54] Ibid., p. 115.

what that self-interest was – how, in Tocqueville's belief, the "passions and interests" could accommodate one another in producing the general good as well as in uniting in a common cause – he condemned the aristocracy on moral as well as on political grounds. A bit of practical experience would have changed the political landscape. It might have united all the wonderful sentiments and a willingness for sacrifices which came from all quarters.

The importance of Tocqueville's critique cannot be overestimated. It is odd at first, in view of his scornful gaze at the caste-like aristocracy, to see him attribute to it a disinterested belief in reform and a feeling for humanity.[55] What he meant was that, like all sections of enlightened opinion, it naively appealed to abstract notions of the general will and natural equality, but really lacked the political and commercial experience to think constructively about how to preserve the people from the oppression of tyranny and revolutionary misery.[56] He contemplated regretfully but not nostalgically the wounds of an enfeebled élite, and he did not take false solace from a detached view of human frailties. When he looked back at the shortcomings of the putative leaders of Old Régime society, he could not have failed to have in mind the failures and defects of his contemporaries who had also deceived themselves before 1848 and were continuing to do so. They had no inkling that liberty entailed the necessity of cultivating political responsibility of the highest order, including, as one of its desirable features, the more memorable and enduring qualities, such as independence of mind and a sense of honor, that made the original aristocratic ethos admirable. There is a symmetry in this reasoning. For, in reviewing the failures of the aristocracy in France, and the spurious reenactments of the 1789 Revolution in 1848, Tocqueville concluded that it was the absence of a mature liberty that was common to both epochs.

One group deserved to be taken seriously as reformers of the old society. The physiocrats, "while never losing sight of theory, paid . . . heed to practical politics." When Tocqueville wrote about their reform proposals, as well as about the Old Régime administrators, he commended them for policies that rested on scientific methods as "they became more and more positive and more certain." Turgot drew most of his praise, but it was tinged with criticism for his unquestioning belief that the state had the right to determine the spirit of the nation and its people. On the one hand, Turgot's beliefs earned Tocqueville's heavily guarded and ambivalent respect as the embodiment of "everything [that was] false or right about the Revolution"; on the other, he indignantly dismissed his "profound ignorance of man, his needs, passions, vices, inherent weaknesses –

---

[55] OC, II, pt. 1, p. 231.   [56] OC, II, pt. 2, p. 109.

an ignorance which is all the more striking in a century of science and philosophy; for the study of man was the great study of the epoch."[57]

The physiocratic taste for intellectual symmetry invaded their liberal vision – so much so that, while they espoused the rights of property, individual liberty and the supremacy of the natural law, they were ready to bend human wills. Their reverence for the commands of a benign natural law stemmed from a logic that deduced individual interests from their supposed conformity with reason, which, they falsely reasoned, itself disclosed the direction of the natural law. Tocqueville thought this circularity amounted to a deformation of natural law. It was this kind of intellectual arrogance that prepared the ground for the creation of the modern state through revolutionary means. It was to the physiocrats that modern democratic despotism[58] and, indeed, socialism owed its origins.[59] They "carried their theories to fanatical lengths," forfeited their claim to judge society's needs and solutions and ceased to be "conscientious public servants or able administrators."[60] Because they were no longer personally popular by 1789, their real power in shaping the Revolution had not been perceived.[61] Turgot and "his whole school . . . are the true precursors [of the Second Empire]" and, as Tocqueville told his friend, Corcelle, they "best represented the true spirit of the Revolution and foresaw most clearly how the equality of conditions could lead to the centralization of power."[62]

Of Le Trosne, another physiocrat, and an excellent magistrate, who was a friend of order, justice and religion, and guardian of acquired rights, Tocqueville lamented his failure to understand that the reforms he advocated totally ignored the claims of proponents of representative assemblies to share in the work of reform, and instead thought that, once they got their hands on the sovereign power, they would simply impose change from above. Trust in the state incarnated an authentic revolutionary temperament. Experienced administrators like Le Trosne had no idea that the reforms they were tracing marked a revolution, totally overshadowing the stumbling attempts by a moribund administration to extricate itself from its problems.[63]

---

[57] Ibid., pp. 418, 426.   [58] *OC*, II, pt. 1, chap. 3.   [59] Ibid., p. 213.
[60] Ibid., pp. 209–10.   [61] *OC*, II, pt. 2, pp. 369–73.
[62] Tocqueville to Corcelle, December 31, 1853, *OC*, XV, pt. 2, pp. 88–89.
[63] *AT*, 43A, Dossier D, "Economistes." Le Trosne was the author of *Administration provinciale* (Basle, 1779).

9   Ideas and public opinion: the formation of a new ethos

There can hardly be a stranger commodity in the world than books. Printed by people who don't understand them; sold by people who don't understand them; bound, criticized and read by people who don't understand them; and now even written by people who don't understand them.[1]

Questioning the general and returning to the particular

The arousal of public awareness touched off the Revolution, but the creation of a critical body of opinion long preceded it. So Mrs. Grote recorded Tocqueville as saying in 1854. "Alexis thinks that the writers of the period antecedent to the revolution of 1789 were quite as much *thrown up by* the condition of public sentiment as they were the exciters of it."[2] By the very nature of its subject, the *Democracy* had some years before elicited Tocqueville's running commentary on the power of democratic opinion. When he later surveyed the deteriorating political situation in 1847, he remarked that indifference to the importance of public opinion was suicidal in free states, though not so, he added strangely, in absolute monarchies which could dispense with it.[3] When he reviewed the genesis of public opinion in prerevolutionary times, he admitted that he was not sure how its power was manifested, because France in that period could not be said to have been an absolute monarchy by any classic definition, and that therefore public opinion presumably was of no small importance. He found, as he read the books and documents on the discontent in France, that the Swiss financier, Jacques Necker, who was in charge of finances twice before the Revolution, had been aware of how opinion was taken very seriously indeed by the French monarchy, and indeed was beginning to assume a significant voice in helping to enlighten its institutions.

[1] Andre Lichtenberg, in J. P. Stern, *Lichtenberg: A Doctrine of Scattered Opinions* (Bloomington, 1959), p. 299.
[2] Mrs. Grote's notes of February 13, 1854, *OC*, VI, pt. 2, p. 407 (emphasis in original).
[3] "Notes de Tocqueville, 1847 [?]," *OC*, III, pt. 2, p. 724.

Necker's conclusions were rather different from Tocqueville's.[4] He welcomed Necker's perception of opinion as an invisible force that insinuated itself into every part of the nation's consciousness.[5] He agreed fully that one of the great sources of its force is a general inclination individuals have to impose limits on their own views, because it is psychologically too taxing to absorb and tolerate a diversity of opinions. Consequently, individual opinions are forced on the defensive, clearing the way for the opinion of the majority to carry all before it. In Tocqueville's interpretation of this point, individuals fear being isolated by relying on their own beliefs more than they dread lending themselves to what might be an error – a reaffirmation of his view that the authority of the majority displaced the authority of transmitted tradition. For Necker the merging of opinions was salutary, since it nourished "a love of true glory, stimulated the performance of great deeds through honor and praise [and] . . . kept men from engaging in evil and cowardly actions through fear of evoking contempt and shame." Public opinion served most of all to restrain the arbitrary exercise of public power. Necker also pointed out, but did not linger on, the rather different role of public opinion in true republics, where Tocqueville claimed its true essence was to be found in the cultivation of liberty, which inspired individuals to trust their own judgments, and not fall victim to majority pressure.

But Tocqueville did not delve deeply into the differing functions of opinion in republics and monarchies. He was much more drawn to furnishing a greater psychological edge to the point he had made in the *Democracy*. In democracies, the crowd provides security, while individual ideas are vulnerable.[6] Because this is how opinion is formed, its grandest and most generous expressions are only such in appearance. In fact, when the crowd believes it is acting as one, it acts out an illusion. Once it senses this, it abandons one common course of action in favor of another. But what really happens is that it slips irrecoverably out of one illusion and into another. Public opinion may be said to have an invisible quality. Hence its force. For that reason it must be feared or treated with caution.

---

[4] See Tocqueville's notes on the 1784 edition of Necker's *De l'administration des finances*, 3 vols. (Paris, 1784), in *AT*, 43A, Dossier J, "La France avant la Révolution. Miscellanés." The references to public opinion are to be found in Necker, I, pp. xxxii–xxxix.

[5] In his *Introduction à la Révolution française*, ed. Fernand Rude (Paris, 1960), p. 23, Barnave's description of the emergence of public opinion in a wealthy and enlightened society as a "spirituous substance . . . born and developed by a fermentation in a large gathering of men" is very much like Necker's view of it.

[6] *Nolla edn.*, II, p. 22: "In times of equality men, being so like each other, have no confidence in others, but this same likeness leads them to place almost unlimited confidence in the judgment of the public. For they think it not unreasonable that, all having the same means of knowledge, truth will be found on the side of the majority."

Because of its instability, the objects of its desires may be equally illusory. Necker, by contrast, wrote about the power of enlightened opinion before the impact of democratic opinion was seen as a normal, yet still largely incomprehensible, presence. Tocqueville's long interest in how opinion served to create a mass society impatient with diversity explains why he found Necker's analysis useful for his own analysis of opinion on the eve of the Revolution. Different as prerevolutionary opinion was from its later democratic manifestations, some of the very roots of this predemocratic opinion were to be found in the last years of the monarchy.[7]

The great speed with which the body of opinion was radicalized, reaching all levels of society, Tocqueville told himself, had to be traced to an understanding of how revolutions occur. And it is in the attempt to rediscover these aspects of the Revolution that his own language becomes most alive. Though he did not neglect the question in *L'Ancien Régime*, almost as soon as it was published he planned to turn his attention to the next phase of his project. He had stopped his study of the end of the old society, he said in an urgent note to himself, before taking into his vision how class passions were "formless, latent, aimless . . . still drugged by the prevailing state of social and political immobility."[8] It was in 1787 that the opposition assumed a definite form. Because his goal was to describe the sentiments and ideas that successively produced the events of the Revolution, he searched for journals, brochures, private letters and administrative correspondence from which he hoped

---

[7] Jürgen Habermas, *The Structural Transformation of the Public Sphere: An Inquiry into a Category of Bourgeois Society*, trans. Thomas Burger (Cambridge, Mass., 1989), and Reinhart Koselleck, *Critique and Crisis: Enlightenment and the Pathogenesis of Modern Society* (Cambridge, Mass., 1988), set the tone for the great number of studies of the changing nature of opinion from the early modern period to the present. For a sampling of the research on the decisive yet often intangible power of the printed word during the Revolution, see Emmet Kennedy, *A Cultural History of the French Revolution* (New Haven and London, 1989); *The Press in the French Revolution*, ed. Harvey Chisick (with Hana Zinguer and Ouzi Elyada), The Voltaire Foundation, CCLXXXVII (Oxford, 1991); and the essay by Anthony J. La Vopa, "Conceiving a Public: Ideas and Society in Eighteenth-Century Europe," *Journal of Modern History*, 64 (1992), pp. 79–116. It should be noted that Habermas particularly singled out Tocqueville's insights. Hannah Arendt also perceived Tocqueville's seminal contribution to the question. In *On Revolution* (New York, 1963), pp. 227–30, Arendt, quite obviously following Tocqueville, writes that opinion was discovered in the American and French Revolutions. In France, however, no stable political institutions existed through which opinion could pass. The result was that opinion remained in more or less pristine form, and took firm shape expressive of conflicting mass sentiments in emergency situations. From them, a dictatorial régime was born in which undifferentiated public opinion became essential to its power. In the process of consolidating this power, all opinions were deadened. See also Keith M. Baker, "Politics and Public Opinion under the Old Regime: Some Reflections," in *Press and Politics in Pre-Revolutionary France*, ed. Jack R. Censer and Jeremy D. Popkin (Berkeley, Los Angeles and London, 1987), pp. 204–46.

[8] *OC*, II, pt. 2, p. 135.

to reconstitute the state of public opinion.[9] Only then could the full picture of the emotional intensity of the opening days of the Revolution – when people, filled with ardor and hope, thought the skies were opening – be glimpsed. "But who would dare to say in the presence of such a model, 'Anche io son pittor' [I too am a painter]!"[10] He began in 1857 to gather information on the temper of the different sections of the population and the political programs that were being presented to the public. He also searched for further proofs of his belief that the abstract politics of the men of letters fatally compromised a practical approach to the problems France was facing. He gathered fuel to reply to some of the criticism his evaluation of the men of letters had aroused among his friends.[11]

Five years before, in his April 1852 address to the Academy of Moral and Political Sciences,[12] only a few months following Louis-Napoleon's coup of December 1851, Tocqueville had expanded the distinction he had previously made in *Democracy in America* between the natural and human sciences, in the course of which he offered his concept of politics. Both questions bore on his thoughts on the relationship between knowledge, opinion and politics. His sketch places the last and its problematic status as a science at the center of his address. Through the insights of philosophy and history we may see, Tocqueville told his audience, how human needs, while constant in themselves, are capable of changing the objects of their desires over time. There is a "permanent condition of humanity," and laws explaining it must be assumed to exist. They are, moreover, discoverable; but they are theories about practices. In this respect, Tocqueville spoke of government as an art that was concerned with the evaluation and management of practical problems arising from interactions in daily life. Political theory and government were therefore distinct, but each was meaningless without the other. Theorists who confined their inquiries to ideas, enveloping themselves in "thick clouds of learning," had none of the qualities needed for practical affairs. Any presumption on their part that they had a privileged place in politics was a great source of disquiet for Tocqueville, and contributed to his critique of the intellectuals in the eighteenth-century Revolution. He refused to give

---

[9] Tocqueville to G. C. Lewis, October 6, 1856, *Beaumont edn.*, VII, p. 410.
[10] Tocqueville to Freslon, October 8, 1856, *BYT*, D.III.a.
[11] The criticism came, for example, from Beaumont, while Tocqueville was in the last stages of revising *L'Ancien Régime*. Beaumont took the view that Tocqueville was right to correct some contemporary misconceptions of Enlightenment political theory, but he thought that "the political edifice, which emerged in 1790 and 1791 from the philosophical and literary theories of the time, had some serious chance of survival." See Beaumont to Tocqueville, April 22, 1856, *OC*, VIII, pt. 3, p. 392.
[12] *Beaumont edn.*, VI, pp. 116–23.

political theory the status that theory possessed in the natural sciences; but he did not deny its value so long as social theorists did not lose sight of the fact that political theory by itself had no meaning apart from actual human practices, which is the object of the theory and not comparable to a natural phenomenon whose regularities the natural sciences were capable of disclosing.

As a science, politics gave birth to general concepts from which it was possible to grasp the facts of human existence. Upon the basis of these facts politicians went on to devise policies and formulate action. An appeal to the historical record was needed to deal with the particular and unusual circumstances of the crises of the old society, when an inchoate public opinion came into being from which numerous factions drew their sustenance and tried to create a new public culture. Tocqueville wondered how the findings of responsible theorists and the actions of knowledgeable and experienced politicians might have worked to prevent or at least to mitigate the destructive effects of revolution, both in the last century and in his own. His exposition of these questions makes clear his belief that the politics of the new régime had been distorted by philosophers and men of letters who tended to think about government as a mechanism that could be quickly changed on the basis of untested principles, particularly theories about human nature and a trust in the capacity of human beings to live according to the dictates of reason. It was not that they were unable to reason, but reason seen as ineffable was a notion Tocqueville found hard to accept.

The limits of the rational and abstract mind were incorporated in Tocqueville's further interpretation in the years following the 1852 address of how the contradictions of the French absolutist state distorted the debate on the nature of politics. In fact, the state closed off opportunities for meaningful political dialogue except within boundaries narrowly defined by its defenders and apologists. As philosophers and men of letters found themselves locked into its parameters, their theories about the nature of politics tended to extravagance. Moreover, as the bureaucracy shifted the limits within which it permitted criticism, writers of all kinds but, for the most part, authors of political treatises, found themselves on a seesaw of tolerance and repression. Because of the state's arbitrary guidelines, or perhaps more accurately, because of the lack of clear ones, a practical countervision of a reformed politics was never satisfactorily elaborated. As a result, when the old society began to stumble from one crisis to another, the political debate tended to focus on grand notions of politics that owed their origins to a generation or more of abstract speculation on the nature of political obligation, the place of free choice within it and non-absolutist notions of natural law;[13] or, from the opposite perspective, how the government could further empower itself by eliminating administrative irregularities ostensibly in the name of a prudential equity. The fragile forms of liberty that Tocqueville admired were mangled by politicians and populace with a naive and intolerant optimism, and this led to feverish and homicidal bids for power. More immediate and identifiable class needs and hatreds pushed liberty out of the way, and a clear-sighted and heroic defense of it failed to materialize. Thus Tocqueville conceived of the Revolution as a process that resulted in the burial of freedom by politicians and people who drew their inspiration for an ideal future from a chaotic marketplace of ideas.

In all civilized countries, Tocqueville firmly believed, writers were the progenitors of revolution. He momentarily even suggested that all upheavals shared in the general absorption by a receptive audience of the most abstract ideas suggested by intellectuals; but, as we know, he reserved this distrust of abstract ideas for the French experience alone, exempting earlier modern revolutionary changes from the fault line of intellectual abstraction. The caveat, however, does not detract from nor lessen the importance of his more fundamental and general point that revolutions find their origins in ideas, for it shows how much Tocqueville was committed to an idealistic conception of historical change. It was in the mind that all revolutions that are achieved by actions are prepared.[14] In December 1857, he rendered this thought more subtle. "It is not the flaws in firm ideas in regard to the reforms that lost the nation in 1789. It is the absence of firm, clear, fair and reasonable ideas without [the promise] of revolution that did. What characterizes this moment in our history is both the precision of ideas and [political] inexperience. [There were] few [opportunities] for trial and error; not even that half-light that brings out the obstacles that cannot be foreseen."[15] In short, the ideas, though abstract, were at the same time too directive, so that their logic overwhelmed the need to test them against the hard realities of the quotidian.

For all his wisdom, Tocqueville did not always clearly reveal the whole range of the critique of the Old Régime. His distinctions between the great theorists and the widely different ideas expressed by men of letters with divergent views were few, and he often gave the impression that they were identical. It was easy enough to single out Montesquieu, Voltaire and Rousseau. Rousseau had, as we saw, no inconsiderable influence on

---

[13] See *OC*, II, pt. 2, p. 121, for example, Tocqueville's impatience with Lacretelle's pamphlet on the convocation of the Estates General: "All the arguments [for the establishment of a government] are drawn from natural law, the rights of man, metaphysics."

[14] *AT*, 43B, Dossier K, "Idées diverses."   [15] *OC*, II, pt. 2, p. 198.

Tocqueville's ideas about a just polity, including the unsettled question of determining the nature of free political choice commensurate with self-esteem and self-preservation. Without saying precisely how Rousseau's *Contrat social* led to the disastrous actions of the revolutionaries, Tocqueville saw in the movement toward locating full powers in a single National Assembly a legacy of Rousseau's radical version of how to implement the idea of an incontrovertible general will. He had no doubt that, if those of Montesquieu's views that were free of his metaphysics had prevailed in the public debate of the last months and days of the final crisis, rather than Rousseau's, the Revolution would have taken a different turn, not only because the moderation of the first would have checked the radical applications of the second, but most of all because, as a political theorist, Rousseau was the most popular utopian dreamer and served a less responsible political agenda.

As for Voltaire, Tocqueville did not regard him as a political thinker of the first rank. His politics erred on the side of locating power in those who could wield it fearlessly and skillfully against the *canaille* whom he feared. Voltaire's importance lay elsewhere, as the writer who had done more than anyone else to ridicule the past and all its institutions, its ideas and feelings, exposing, through his sense of the absurd, all laws which he believed were more or less contrary to what he called reason. The very foundation on which the society in which he lived – inequality – he condemned as no less opposed to good sense and equity. He had indeed prepared much of the ground for legitimizing a revolutionary mentality.[16]

But there was no French or European conspiracy, as the abbé Barruel had tried to convince the credulous in his attack on key thinkers, among them Voltaire, whose correspondence with the monarchs of Europe ostensibly worked subterraneously to undermine the old society. Circourt directed Tocqueville in 1852 and again in 1857 not only to Barruel but to the remonstrances of the *parlement* of Paris in 1771, which he believed "were full of teachings which were at the time prophetic, and now hermeneutic, because they explain the [preparatory] work that was carried out subterraneously [to change] human minds."[17] He also listed a number of writers who were part of the questioning spirit of the early and later Enlightenment. The first were weightier thinkers and more accessible insofar as they were as much political as philosophical. These included d'Argenson, Condorcet, Helvétius, Raynal, Diderot, Mably, Servan and Mallet du Pan. The second were moved less

[16] Tocqueville to Lewis, August 15, 1856, *Beaumont edn.*, VII, pp. 404–05.
[17] Circourt to Tocqueville, May 21, 1852, *OC*, XVIII, p. 72, but for the full range of his comments, see the entire letter, pp. 69–75.

by the imperative of Enlightenment rationalism than by a rather different kind of impulse, ascribing error not to the absence of reason, but as a necessary process of achieving truth. Such was Saint-Martin's *Des erreurs et de la vérité*, which after its publication in 1775 attracted a sect of Martinists, whose main preoccupation was not his philosophy but a mysticism which they prised out of his writings.[18] There were in addition the Freemasons, Illuminati, Swedenborgians, Rosicrucians and Mesmerists.

Tocqueville's mind was as resistant to conspiracy theories in 1857 as it was five years earlier. In 1852, he told Circourt that secret societies were a symptom of the old society's disease and not the disease itself: its effects, not its causes.[19] In 1857 he recalled his aversion to these theories and said that Leopold von Ranke, who had replied to Circourt's queries on Tocqueville's behalf, had misunderstood his interests: "I have never believed that the Illuminati had an appreciable influence on the coming of the French Revolution."[20] His fascination with them was as a group that symbolized one of the numerous symptoms that characterized the psychological condition of the time. His interest and knowledge extended to Ernst Brandes, who had read Burke, and to Georg Forster, who had lived briefly in Paris during the Revolution, and whose letters revealed how some Germans were infatuated with the idea of change and renewal.[21] What he now found astonishing was the curious coexistence of a scientific conception of the world and a world subject to faith. The first claimed to be on the threshold of mastering the laws of nature; the second sought a new basis for a mystical and spiritual vision of the world. The origins of the new intellectual outlook could be traced, he said, to the sixteenth and seventeenth centuries. Indeed, the inquiring spirit and the appeal to individual reason were not new; all societies shared these faculties and could not exist without them. Liberty of thought on certain matters coexisted with authoritative pronouncements on belief. In the ancient classical epoch, the individual, by force of the period's spirit and *moeurs*, had been secretive about attributing to himself the right to be his own judge in matters of belief. The propensity to act as one's own judge therefore was not accomplished without regret, sometimes with a sense of terror and by a kind of invincible necessity.

---

[18] For this conception of error, I rely on David Bates, "Variations of Error in Late Enlightenment France," Ph.D. dissertation, University of Chicago, 1994. The Martinists originally formed themselves around Martines de Pasqually, by origin a Portuguese Jew, whose cabalistic ideas attracted disciples in Paris and southern France.
[19] Tocqueville to Circourt, June 14, 1852, *OC*, XVIII, pp. 75–76.
[20] Tocqueville to Circourt, February 2, 1857, ibid., p. 379.
[21] Tocqueville to Circourt, March 11, 1857, ibid., p. 385. Brandes (1758–1810) was also a great influence on Stein. Forster's *Briefwechsel. Nebst einigen Nachrichten von seinem Leben* in 2 vols. was published in Leipzig, in 1828–29.

What then was the distinctive intellectual physiognomy of the eighteenth century? Two things, he said. First, as he already said in the *Democracy*, the subjection of everything to the power of individual examination; second, its elevation to the status of an abstract, absolute and general principle on all questions and making everyone subject to it. No other period had demanded such dogmatic, indeed religious, adherence to the idea that individual reason should be the sole arbiter of truth, ignoring the difficult question of further judgment.[22] What Tocqueville's inquiries revealed for him was that, though reason as the ultimate test of truth was a hallmark of the eighteenth century, other currents of thought, challenging it as the sole criterion of truth, existed alongside it, with the result that the eighteenth century could not be viewed so confidently as an unqualified century of reason. Still, the end point was the same for those who adhered to the dogmatism of reason and for those who adopted a mystical vision of truth. Making visible the invisible in the sense of ultimate revelation was common to both. The longing was universal, as was the hunger for change, though no one had any real notion of how either could be accomplished. "All of Europe presented the spectacle of an immense mass tottering at the precipice."[23]

Condorcet's *Esquisse* was not on Tocqueville's reading list; neither was d'Argenson's *Considérations sur le gouvernement de la France*, though his *Mémoires* were glanced at for prophecies of revolution, and Fénelon's earlier predictions were also consulted.[24] As for Morellet's *Code de la Nature*, Tocqueville reviewed its main points, found them repulsive in their comprehensive dismissal of individual choice, down to its prohibition of any belief in the soul's immortality. The absolute and crushing equality, the uniformity in all things, the mechanical equality of every movement of the social body, the prescribed tyranny – Morellet said it all.[25] The treatment of the men of letters was at times monolithic, but it cannot be denied that some of them – not only Montesquieu – had some appreciation of some of the differences between theory and practice, even if they believed, as Tocqueville could not with as much certainty, that almost nothing durable could be built on the insubstantial vestiges of the ancient freedoms. Most of all for Tocqueville, the thinkers of the Enlightenment did not qualify for the role of political theorists. And upon their shoulders, he placed responsibility for the revolutionary search for the ideal *polis* as a journey into *la société imaginaire*, in which "everything

---

[22] This characterization of the eighteenth century may be seen in notes Tocqueville made for his acceptance speech at the Académie française in 1842: *Pléiade edn.*, I, p. 1644.
[23] *OC*, II, pt. 2, p. 46, but see all of pp. 33–46.
[24] See *AT*, 43A, Dossier J, "La France avant la Révolution."
[25] See *AT*, 43B, Dossier R, "Analyse du code de la nature par Morelly. Section première."

appeared simple and coordinated, uniform, equitable and in conformity with reason" – a society with the power to substitute itself for an actual society, displacing the complexities of the latter's confusions, irregularities, diversities, contradictions, hierarchies and inequalities.[26] He wanted to show how intellectuals and modern despots could unintentionally act in collusion, especially when, as in his own age, there were thinkers who had no trouble in stifling their doubts – if indeed they had any – and prided themselves in their ability to find perfect solutions for the complexities of life. As a historian, his "cause" was to identify "liberty and human dignity," not only when writing about it but also while "being entangled by [human affairs]."[27]

From the start, the language of discontent was widely diffused.[28] Without being fully conscious of the effects of their actions, the *parlements* contributed to the power of the new opinion:

The inflated sentiments, the exaggerated expressions, the incoherence and the ungainly images, those constant citations from antiquity which were to be characteristic of the language of the Revolution were already habitual at this time. Tranquillity or moderation was completely absent. The overwhelming inclinations of all minds were to commonplaces; nor was it permissible to express anything simply; it was necessary that the expression should overflow beyond the original idea or sentiment.[29]

Understanding what finally brought about the Revolution meant trying to rediscover how ideas came to be dressed in such garb, how it might be possible to plumb to the essence of opinions.[30] They were the hardest to capture. And Tocqueville felt he would never succeed, either in assessing how they worked to bring about the conflagration or how they persisted in new forms during the Revolution's successive changes. "Till now, I have found only one way, and that is in some way to live each moment of the Revolution with its contemporaries by reading, not what one has said about them or what they said about themselves later, but what they themselves said, and, as much as possible, what they really thought."[31]

This had been his wish from the beginning, when he expected that his achievement of a proper distance from his subjects could give him the gift of knowing them better than they knew themselves.[32] But the veil covering them remained. However much had been explained, there was still

[26] *OC*, II, pt. 1, p. 199.
[27] Tocqueville to Kergorlay, December 15, 1850, *OC*, XIII, pt. 2, p. 233.
[28] See Mrs. Grote's transcriptions of conversations with Tocqueville at St. Cyr, February 13, 1854, *Correspondence and Conversations of Alexis de Tocqueville with Nassau Senior*, ed. Simpson, II, pp. 48, 52.   [29] *OC*, II, pt. 2, p. 80.   [30] Ibid., p. 117.
[31] Tocqueville to Kergorlay, May 16, 1858, *OC*, XIII, pt. 2, p. 337.
[32] *OC*, II, pt. 1, p. 71.

something unknown about the Revolution and all revolutionary manifestations since 1789. There was no doubt that it had let loose in the world a revolutionary race of men who renewed themselves ceaselessly. Only the theater of action changed. Great schools for revolution could open themselves in the public arena and appeal to violent and wandering men in any part of the world.[33] These sentiments were consonant with his warnings during the 1840s when he urged his fellow deputies to make the parliamentary régime work. The subject was seemingly intractable, but he was not deterred from returning to it again and again. He introduced the metaphor of a *mal révolutionnaire*, at least as early as 1853, tracing it to the permanent social conditions, habits, ideas and enduring *moeurs* founded by the Revolution. But as if to give the idea greater importance, he thought of the *mal* as an autonomous force with the character, as he put it, of a doctrine. It is not only a tendency of minds and hearts. It is a theory, a philosophy, supported by democratic ideas contemptuous of stability, tradition and individual rights, and in the end embedding itself as a permanent feature of modern life.[34] Five years later he spoke of it as a "virus," belonging to a new and unknown species. Revolutions in the past had not bred such a phenomenon. "The immoderate, violent, radical, desperate and audacious, almost insane, yet powerful character of these revolutionaries has no precedents . . . in the great social agitations of past centuries."[35] It was a specific kind of illness. Its symptoms could be located in an abhorrence for the rules of propriety, in a love of risk-taking, in a surrender to errors, vices, miasmas similar to the fevers engendered in hospitals where the illness takes on its specificity, although its birth is the result of a thousand different previous diseases.[36] Images of disease, sickness, defective organs and the need to dissect them to locate causes were meant to expose the sources of the old society's defects, even its evils. Metaphors of unsettled and "unnatural" states of body and mind were commonplace in the period leading up to the Revolution and after,[37] but his originality lay in using them, not only as signs of a body politic nearing its end, but to describe political and social actions subversive of existing society.

From the context with which he surrounded the revolutionary illness, it is safe to say that he meant the successively more violent stages of the Revolution itself as well. *Le mal révolutionnaire*, he seemed to be arguing,

---

[33] *OC*, II, pt. 2, p. 338.   [34] Ibid., p. 348.

[35] Tocqueville to Kergorlay, May 16, 1858, *OC*, XIII, pt. 2, pp. 337–38.

[36] See this description in *AT*, 43B, Dossier K, "Idées diverses."

[37] For an absorbing study of the metaphors of disease employed in brochures by lesser and more important figures, such as Mirabeau and Sieyès, see Antoine de Baecque, *Le corps de l'histoire. Métaphores et politique (1770–1800)* (Paris, 1993).

in time became synonymous with the revolutionary government, which was illegitimate, although he did not say how, except by suggesting that it was due to the excesses of democracy itself. The newness of democratic equality led to scenes of brutality and inhumanity. The violence, which he contrasted with the benign nature of democratic theory, grew out of the very texture of the lives of oppressed people and need not therefore be surprising. Here his conclusion that the Revolution was a cry for changing the human condition may be recalled. We cannot know whether he thought the *mal révolutionnaire* was a fall or an original flaw, since he seemed to have been unable to choose between these two explanations. Thus he could scarcely have found it a simple matter to speak of individual responsibility, and he retreated to the notion that, if anything, the *mal* manifested itself and could best be represented as an example of a profound break with the past, which, in its turn, descended into incoherence and error.[38]

The development of such incoherence – the revolutionary disease – may have been given its impetus and rationale, he suggested, by the pamphleteers who were especially prominent in 1788–89, as well as in the views expressed in the *cahiers*. His notes reveal the importance he ascribed to a fairly close inspection of how the ideas that were to seize the revolutionary imagination came to the top, obscuring the earlier, more moderate ones. The raw and not so raw feelings of indignation, resentment and vengefulness, shown by a people who as yet played no part in politics, and hence could not be said to have been capable of creating a public opinion, were embodied in the abstract language of the men of letters. By their monopolizing of opinion, Tocqueville saw them and their acolytes, most significantly the political class of the old society and the politicians and publicists of the Revolution itself, as the self-proclaimed defenders of the truth that was waiting to be born. Little by little, the discontent was linguistically transformed into a power ostensibly bearing a single political truth.[39]

The most interesting illumination Tocqueville gained from his reading of the 1787 pamphlets was that the conditions for revolution were already discernible in appeals to a social contract, the ultimate authority of the

---

[38] For a discussion of "error," see Georges Canguilhem, *On the Normal and the Pathological*, trans. Carolyn R. Fawcett (Dordrecht, Boston and London, 1978), pp. 171–75. Another perspective is to be found in Jon Elster's theory that illusions or imaginaries occur when "both the external situation and the internal processing . . . come into play . . . [O]ne could also speculate, though I would be more skeptical as to the value of the outcome, that differences in social origin generate differences in the internal apparatus and thus in the liability to illusions (keeping the external situation constant)." See Jon Elster, "Belief, Bias and Ideology," in *Relativity and Relativism*, ed. Martin Hollis and Steven Lukes (Cambridge, Mass., 1982), p. 137.   [39] *OC*, II, pt. 1, p. 195.

"nation" and even equality of taxation. Some, still imbued with a liberal, not a democratic, spirit, bore an unmistakable tonality of revolutionary violence. It was already imprinted in the minds of the disputants, though the goal of the revolution was still concealed. Violent expressions of love for liberty marked at least one of the pamphlets. None of this kind of rhetoric had been invoked less than twenty years earlier against the abbé Terray's arbitrary policies as controller-general. The situation had changed radically in the intervening period. In more peaceful times, such as during Terray's administration, the government needed only to look for and gain support from various social groups mindful only of their own particular interests. Or the way to deal with any hint of common resistance was to single out its parts and destroy them. In the face of a great public passion, when everyone marched to the same tune, such policies no longer worked. The new language some twenty years later reflected a changed mood, a strident set of expectations that reached down to the deepest parts of the human soul, now ready to be set ablaze, in Tocqueville's words, like molten metal that awaits only one last spark to devastate all in its path.[40] As startling was the fact that the *parlements* used the same bombastic language, which Tocqueville called a harbinger of the democratic hyperbole that was to come. The defiance of the Paris *parlement* came after the enforced registration in August 6, 1787, of the crown's tax proposals and the subsequent exile of the magistrates to Troyes. In fact, Brienne's measures, as head of the Council of Finances, were designed to win support by serving popular interests, but they were not perceived that way in an atmosphere in which the *parlement* was temporarily given the benefit of the doubt because of its assumption of the role of guardian of the nation's interests.

The irony of the situation gave Tocqueville pause. The intrinsic value of any measure was less important than the circumstances in which it was launched into the public arena. Possibly recalling his 1852 address on the nature of politics, Tocqueville remarked that, in the light of the crown's failure, politics could not be considered either as a science or as an art – an unmistakable allusion to his 1852 talk to the Academy of Moral and Political Sciences. There are no fixed rules in politics, not even the putative rule that in order to please the public it is necessary to do what will please it. All that could be said was that, when the totality of circum-

---

[40] *AT*, Dossier 45B, 9, Liasse BB, "1787. Travaux divers sur cette année." The pamphlets in question from which Tocqueville gathered these impressions were: [Anonyme], "Les vrais principes de la monarchie française"; [No author mentioned by Tocqueville], "Supplément aux Rémonstrances du Parlement du 24 août 1787"; [Anonyme], "Fragment d'une correspondance"; [Anonyme], "Conférence entre un ministre et un conseiller."

stances renders the exercise of power popular, people will willingly endure the evils that are an inevitable part of it. Such an option was no longer in the government's grasp; nor did it even know that the option was closed to it. The other conclusion Tocqueville drew was that the *parlement* did not perceive fully what was going on either. Its symbols of resistance, coming as they did from a distant past, carried no political weight at all. It no longer had the power to win the support of public opinion which had outdistanced it. The *parlement*, he continued, imagined that its fortune rested on the ancient privileges that it had once enjoyed, while it turned out that the force, which was accidentally bestowed upon it by the state of public opinion, was not only not supportive but was positively hostile, as it was to all the old institutions.[41] By August 27 the Toulouse *parlement*'s language had become incredibly overwrought and openly breathed revolutionary defiance of the government. The violence of the language now struck Tocqueville less than the incapacity, so late in the day, of the political institutions – both those that supported and those that opposed the government – of the old society to absorb the mutual reproaches without feeling threatened by them.

Tocqueville laid down as a general law that all revolutions, not only the French, owed their force to the cumulative effect of public opinion. Neither the government nor its legally constituted opposition could control its pressure, for it was truly running its own course. How could it indeed be resisted? Tocqueville thought it could not. He reversed the question and he also focused his gaze on the government, temporarily removing his focus from the *parlement*. Not enough thought, he said, had been given to the failure of governments to deal with the forces of resistance to their power. When the magnitude of the resistance became universal, its power became so great as to become invisible and hence irresistible. Invisible, because its presence was not fully discernible, it was nevertheless felt over the whole body politic, inducing a sense of inertia in the government from which it could not recover. For Tocqueville, the evidence was clear: the government was descending into impotence.

But before the government reached the nadir of its power, it followed two strategies. First, it reproached the *noblesse* for wishing to fortify their own position at the expense of the crown; secondly, toward the end of the reciprocal challenges, it totally denied whatever rights remained to them. Whatever truth or legitimacy these rights might have once had were therefore also denied.[42] Tocqueville was nevertheless convinced that the

---

[41] These remarks on the consequences of the August 6, 1787, *lit de justice* appear to follow the observations he made about the language of the Toulouse *parlement* on August 27, also in *AT*, Dossier 45B, 9, Liasse BB, "1787. Travaux divers sur cette année."

[42] *OC*, II, pt. 2, p. 108.

final achievement of stasis had not totally silenced all voices of compromise. He discerned it in the persistence of liberal and prudent ideas in a pamphlet said to be written by Brissot and Condorcet, who were convinced that the founding of an authentic political liberty was not impossible.[43] Before the final dismissal of Montesquieu as a thinker from whom the parties to the crisis could learn to forge a new and legitimate political system, that is, before opposition turned into revolution, "Montesquieu was the oracle, Rousseau still remained the sublime dreamer."[44] Soon no one was taking Montesquieu's ideas seriously, not even those who in times past had paid serious attention to them, so that the principles, interests and influences that were once considered important vanished from the agenda. Instead, Rousseau's ideas were in full floodtide and were submerging calm reason and the genuine study of the human sciences.[45]

Roederer's pamphlet, "De la députation aux Etats généraux," published late in 1788, was a good example, Tocqueville believed, of how quickly Rousseau's ideas had become the guiding light of revolutionary hopes. In the pamphlet's acceptance of the social contract, its rejection of Turgot's physiocratic project to ensure special representation to the landed proprietors, but above all in the dismissal of Montesquieu's idea of the acknowledgment of a connection between principles of government and the kind of legislation they produced, Tocqueville saw the negation of principles essential to a balanced monarchy. To alleviate the crisis, there had to be a realistic, not a fanciful, expectation of the practical advantages that the state would derive from pursuing such ideas. If the nature of practical politics were not treated seriously, principles would indeed be reduced to the level of abstraction, and the idea of a common liberty would simply be a new name for slavery. The pleas for a single assembly, moreover, would be an opportunity – and Roederer, Tocqueville tells us, was not unaware of such an eventuality – for the rich who were to be found in all three orders to act as a counterweight to the "people."[46] Tocqueville wanted to demonstrate the incoherence of Roederer's views by arguing that a legitimate division of powers ruled out the creation of a single legislative body with powers greater than those

[43] *AT*, Dossier 45B, Liasse CC, "1788. Travaux divers sur cette année." The pamphlet in question is entitled "La destruction des anciennes libertés municipales reconnues."

[44] Ibid. These notes, Tocqueville tells us, were based on a variety of sources. His remarks follow his précis of a lengthy book published in 1787, *De la constitution française* (Amsterdam). It claimed that France had a constitution, a body of fundamental institutions, from which departures had been made, but which must now be revived, and in the name of which the struggle against the government would gain firm legitimation.

[45] *OC*, II, pt. 2, p. 121; cf. *AT*, 45B, Liasse CC, "1788. Travaux divers sur cette année." Tocqueville composed these notes on the pamphlet attributed to Condorcet and Brissot, "La destruction des anciennes libertés reconnues."   [46] Ibid.

granted to the executive. At the same time, Tocqueville believed that the direct and rapacious exploitation of the poor by the rich, in the name of an ostensible common goal to ensure equality, was deplorable.

In the demands for change that came rolling off the presses, all the familiar grid points were rapidly superseded. Not only were privileges seen as unjustifiable; so too were individual rights. The very idea of a temperate and measured government, a government in which different classes formed society, reflecting the different interests into which it was divided, capable of generating countervailing policies, a society in which men thought not only as a common unit, but calculated their interests with regard to the general good – all these considerations soon disappeared from the most moderate minds and were replaced by the idea of a crowd composed of similar interchangeable elements, whose deputies were ideally imagined as being representative of numbers, not of interests, nor of persons. Tocqueville did not cast a wholly negative eye on these ideas. They in fact spelled out an alternative notion of society and government, even a peaceful and disinterested one. To give them their due, Tocqueville recognized that they were in fact rooted in the depths of all minds and were not solely the product of passions, although passions came to their aid and gave birth to them and were capable of producing violent effects. Always, he insisted, the dissection of what constituted opinion supposed a prior analysis of the meshing of interests and passions.[47] It was always curious, he added, to see how theory rationalized both.[48]

Sieyès's "Qu'est ce que le Tiers-Etat?" was the key revolutionary pamphlet. It was not a mere work of theory. It was a veritable *cri de guerre*, Tocqueville marveled, "a specimen of the violence and radicalism of opinion, [appearing] even before the struggles that are said to have provoked violence and radicalism." It was the germinal expression of the Revolution [le plus congénital de la Révolution]. Tocqueville reacted to the manifesto's call for full-scale war against the ancient and legal structures of France and Sieyès's appeal for the unqualified and absolute acceptance of his theories, without regard for their practical consequences, with a profound note, first of outrage, then of wonder at the breathtaking presumption that the cultural and political past of an ancient civilization could be so totally ignored.[49]

---

[47] Ibid. Tocqueville was commenting on a pamphlet with the title "Pétition des citoyens domiciliés à Paris, décembre 1788." Tocqueville saw this as a general law of revolution and noted this four years earlier, in 1853. See *AT*, 43B, Dossier K.

[48] *AT*, 45B, Liasse CC, "1788. Travaux divers sur cette année." Tocqueville was reading a pamphlet he identified as "Examen du pouvoir des Etats généraux."

[49] *OC*, II, pt. 2, pp. 139–47.

Two crucial points emerge from Tocqueville's analysis of Sieyès's powerful and decisive pamphlet, to which he gave added emphasis in his evaluation of pamphlets written by Mounier,[50] Barnave,[51] Brissot,[52] Rabaud-Saint-Etienne[53] and Pétion.[54] The first was the overwhelming evidence for the existence of general approval of a political program warning against the idea of united action by all the existing legal orders and social ranks to deal with the constitutional problems facing the nation. The national will, Mounier found, was now being spoken of as a single will that could not be legitimately expressed by any assembly of the three orders. If in opposition to a single national will, arguments were trotted out to preserve the integrity of the existing orders, there would be, the new arguments went, three representations – ending in the creation or recreation of a fragmented political will. According to the pamphleteers, there would ensue the illogical spectacle of three "nations" formulating a simulacrum of a single nation and a single representation, culminating in fact in the strangling at birth of a purer and undifferentiated common will. Sieyès proclaimed that any appeal to the British bicameral system would amount to a travesty of true political principles. Tocqueville questioned Sieyès's late dating of the beginning of the aristocracy's slide into its caste-like immobility, and he deeply regretted the removal of an aristocratic element from the polity that was coming into being.[55] The second point to arise from Tocqueville's analysis of these political views was his observation, made many times over, but now clinched by the presence of almost total public unanimity, that Montesquieu's constitutionalism was quickly being cast aside. The radicals, who were responsible for this eclipse, were too blinded by their aversion for the old society to grasp the benefits of a gradual readjustment of the balance of political forces in the monarchy.

Mounier's great error was to allow himself to be carried away by the

---

[50] I am following the editors of *OC*, II, in the citation of Jean-Joseph Mounier's work, consulted by Tocqueville, "Nouvelles observations sur les Etats généraux de France" (1789). This will also be the case for the succeeding citations of the pamphlets discussed in the present section.

[51] The editors do not provide a reference to Antoine Barnave's brochure. Tocqueville's own notes refer to its title as "Contre les édits du 8 mai et le rétablissement des parlements" (1788).

[52] Jacques-Pierre Brissot de Warville, "Plan de conduite pour les députés aux Etats généraux de 1789" (1789).

[53] Rabaud-Saint-Etienne, "Considération sur les intérêts du tiers état par un propriétaire foncier" (1788).

[54] Péthion, "Avis aux Français sur le salut de la patrie" (1788). I have retained Tocqueville's original spelling here, but I use Pétion, which is the proper spelling, in the text.

[55] These points in the Sieyès pamphlet are given special stress in Tocqueville's analysis, *OC*, II, pt. 2, pp. 141–45.

bizarre notion that a bicameral assembly was to be avoided because only a unicameral one could effect the changes France required. Only after they were introduced did Mounier say that he felt secure enough to entrust the nation to a divided assembly. Such a formula, which placed the political future of the nation at the mercy of a single class or a single party, Tocqueville complained, was "excellent indeed for making a revolution, but hardly the one to bring it to an end at the right time." The obliteration of all the features of an orderly society in these circumstances degraded liberty, and equality, left on its own, simply became another name for servitude.[56] Such a turn of events in Tocqueville's eyes was a striking demonstration of how the powers of centralization were strengthened. Mounier's precise aim, he charged, was not to show support for centralization, but he nonetheless did not object to the steps leading to it.[57] This instance of unintentional consequences was once more the reward of false premises.

Barnave, too, had originally spoken out against political innovation when the monarchy dared to invade the rights of the magistrates in 1788. He did so, Tocqueville observed with approval, in the spirit of Montesquieu's detestation and fear of despotism. Tocqueville marveled at Barnave's youthful appeals for a union of all classes and interests, his praise of the "illustrious families" of France that protected the monarchy with their blood, and his "sincere" appeals to natural equality and democracy; and although Tocqueville supported the prospects of a permanent union of all the existing political forces against a despotic state, he conceded more readily than before that such a union had reached the limits of the possible.[58]

Thus, though he kept coming back to the theme of united action, noting that the future Girondin, Brissot, had appealed for caution, conciliation and harmony, he acknowledged that Brissot's opposition to the exclusivity of the first two orders was his major and most decisive argument. As a result of his stay in the United States, Brissot had become convinced that a Convention was a necessary stage in the remaking of the political map of France. For Tocqueville this was a truly revolutionary idea. Whether or not Brissot's text justifies Tocqueville's reading of it, Tocqueville derived a certain pleasure from, and accorded his respect for, his understanding of the conservative nature of the American political experience. As proof, Tocqueville mentioned the American decision to adopt a bicameral legislature. He may also have been recalling his praise of the makers of the American Constitution. Recognition of the utility of American practices was much more desirable in Tocqueville's opinion than the views of the

[56] Ibid., pp. 150–51.   [57] Ibid., p. 148.   [58] Ibid., pp. 153–54.

"worst imitators" who had "taken from the United States the abstract principles of their constitution without having felt the need to apply them conservatively which had been achieved in America."[59]

From Brissot Tocqueville went on to consider Rabaud-Saint-Etienne who, he dryly observed, took four years to discover that he was tired of acting the part of the tyrant and was executed for admitting that he was mistaken for thinking that the régime of privileges was more to be feared than royal power. Rabaud's sudden insight, Tocqueville could not resist adding, was a good case of human intelligence knowing too late that it was liberty that needed support; instead, Rabaud's mind had mistakenly turned its energies to a defense of equality, come what may.[60]

There was more in Tocqueville's interpretation of the desire shown by all the pamphleteers to move swiftly against any political maneuvers to retain any relic of traditional forms of representation. The question of choice hardly entered into the situation. In their desire to end privilege, these pamphleteers could not think clearly about the possible advantages of adopting the English political model to reduce and limit, rather than abolish what, he conceded, had to be ended.[61] Similarly his notes on a pamphlet attributed to Pétion show how he remained convinced that the revolutionary discourse was moving further and further away from Montesquieu's ideas and that, although liberty was not forsaken, the "final word of the Revolution" came to be "let us try to be free by becoming equal, but [that] it is a hundred times better to cease to be free than to remain or to become unequal."[62]

Tocqueville again returned to the theme of equality. Hunger for it had become so great that it was elevated above and displaced for all practical purposes everything else that the actors of 1789 were bringing to political consciousness in their desire to regenerate France. Those who were responsible for the deflection were not, however, "new beings," nor "the isolated and ephemeral creation of a single moment, destined to disappear with it . . . They were already here when we were born, and they are still with us."[63]

Tocqueville had already given his verdict in the *Democracy* on the semi-utopian and Rousseauian idea that liberty was the other side of equality's coin:

It is possible to imagine an extreme point at which freedom and equality would meet and blend.
Let us suppose that all the citizens take a part in the government and that each of them has an equal right to do so.

[59] Ibid., pp. 155–57. Cf. *Nolla edn.*, I, pp. 155–56.   [60] *OC*, II, pt. 2, p. 160.
[61] Ibid., pp. 158–63.   [62] Ibid., pp. 168–69.   [63] *OC*, II, pt. 1, p. 208.

Then, no man is different from his fellows, and nobody can wield tyrannical power; men will be perfectly equal because they are entirely free. Democratic people are tending toward that ideal.[64]

To be sure, political liberty could threaten disorder and even lives when carried to excess, but its transgressions were more easily perceived and therefore controlled than were the excesses of equality. Though democratic people have, he allowed, a natural taste for liberty and even cherish it, their passion for equality is stronger, and its extravagances are the more easily accepted and even justified. When he expressed himself in this way in the *Democracy*, he granted that "freedom cannot be established without it [equality], and despotism itself cannot reign without its support." On the surface, as he knew from classical theory, equality was the common feature of both a despotic polity as well as of a democratic one. The second, though, had few chances of healthy growth, if men gave themselves up to an imaginary society in which liberty and equality were thought to be perfectly compatible, or if they failed to exert their skills to reduce the tendency to an unreflective and total defense of an overriding equality, itself a form of tyranny, or transformed into such by a modern tyrant. This danger could be traced, Tocqueville found, to Rousseau's ideas, which set the tone for the remaking of France. But we may also say that Tocqueville would have welcomed the idea that, to avoid modern tyranny, the exponents of equality would have to leave ample room in a democratic polity for all citizens to exercise their political liberty within the limits of a shared moral environment to determine the nature of their society and politics. We know how much Tocqueville's social theory rested on a concept of the decisive, because deeply rooted, role of *moeurs*, not only in structuring a society but also its political forms.

He was puzzled by what some of the *cahiers* of the Third Estate seemed to be saying, especially on the question of transferring privileges from individuals to an intermediary body, and not to the state. Could it be that there was no overpowering sentiment in the *cahiers* for giving power directly to the state? Yes, he said in one place.[65] No, he said in another: there was little difference in the *cahiers* of all three orders in their belief that the state had to be the source of all that was permissible, and of all that was to be forbidden.[66] But the Revolution was not made because of a desire to enhance the state's power. Rather the state was viewed in France as the normal instrument for effecting change, and the power willingly

---

[64] *Nolla edn.*, II, p. 94. For the rest of Tocqueville's thoughts on the question, see pp. 94–96.
[65] *AT*, 45B, 2e chemise, "La liasse 1789. Depuis le 1er janvier jusqu'à la réunion des Etats généraux." Tocqueville was reading "La Régénération de la France ou essai sur la réforme que les Etats généraux ont à faire." Tocqueville does not name the author of this pamphlet.   [66] *OC*, II, pt. 2, p. 367.

handed to the state was one of the Revolution's decisive outcomes. No less important in grasping its nature was the extraordinary power of the lawyers, a point he had made in 1836. The lawyers who had been part of a judicial system that had its contradictions exposed under stress took a leading part in the revolutionary changes. Their knowledge and experience made them the logical heirs of the Revolution. So it was not surprising that the restructuring of the general principles, administrative details and secondary rules of the judicial system was the Revolution's most complete triumph.[67]

That the current of history ran so powerfully toward one destination and swept all in its flow was a symptom, Tocqueville regretfully concluded, of the disarray and disorder of political ideas, which had been left to drift in bizarre directions in an unstable régime.[68] Only by puzzling out the predicaments facing historical actors, and the problems facing historians could he shake off the feelings of extreme discomfort at the thought that nothing could halt the trajectory of an event, however small, let alone one fraught with enormous significance. Do the actors even pause to ask whether they can alter the trajectory? The question lies at the bottom of Tocqueville's decision to canvass the options that he thought might have been available to, and perhaps even considered by, some of the leading actors during the revolutionary crisis. He adopted a speculative-empirical approach as a way of rethinking what practical alternatives were available to the actors. The example he chose was one of the most crucial tests of the government's besieged mentality, namely, the decision taken on December 27, 1788, when Jacques Necker caved in to the arguments advanced by spokesmen of the Third Estate that it represented the national will.

Necker's greatest error, compounded by Louis XVI's decision to accept his advice, was to generate hope for voting by head, but then the steps needed to authorize it were avoided out of neglect, shortsightedness or mental fatigue. If the king had ordered voting by head, it would have been hard, so Tocqueville speculated, for the privileged orders to struggle against the current of approval that such a decision would have created in the public mind. Alternatively, had the king from the start refused the demand, the Third Estate would have found it very difficult to press for it. In both instances, the failure of an unequivocal decision itself helped

---

[67] *AT*, 43B, Dossier C, "Analyse des cahiers. Etudes faites en 1856 sur les cahiers originaux aux archives. Documents de dates diverses: Travail sur les cahiers faits vers 1836." Tocqueville is commenting on the *cahier* of the Third Estate at Rennes.

[68] *AT*, Dossier 45B, Liasse CC, "1788. Travaux divers sur cette année." Tocqueville is reflecting on "La Voix d'un citoyen" by Pierre d'Olivier and [Anonyme], "Réflexions impartiales."

determine the outcome. Tocqueville's purpose in this bit of counter-factual thinking was not to question the avoidability of the Revolution. The Revolution was inescapable, but it might have been achieved with a greater chance of peace and tranquillity of mind.[69]

In pursuing these questions, Tocqueville let his mind wander over the terrain of the nature of political error. Why do such errors arise? He approvingly cited what he thought was G.-J.-P. Target's novel insight that the truly great errors in politics were a consequence of the inadvertent confrontation of the *moeurs* of one period with the emergent principles of another set of *moeurs* in another era.[70] Errors, Tocqueville distinguished from mere mistakes, which were the result of a misunderstanding or ignorance of existing rules. The point Target made, and which Tocqueville accepted, was that the rules were no longer taken seriously, because they had lost their legitimacy; and, as Tocqueville said in another place, this happened when the ruling class, vitiated by egoism, indifference and other vices, no longer possessed the moral authority to govern.[71] From the disregard for the rules, another error, equally grave but of a different nature, was committed by the revolutionaries. Their unflinching and arrogant pride in their own unaided powers was a kind of hubris, but one which was, all the same, the only way a people could show itself capable of more than servitude.[72] Such a conception of error helped Tocqueville explain the destructive and creative aspects of historical change. The decay of one régime and the error it spawned created an opportunity for historical actors to see the world as if in a totally decontextualized present. Tocqueville likened this mentality to a new religion, carrying its acolytes toward an unknown destination.

Tocqueville was determined not to indulge in a nostalgic evocation of a dead past, nor to pretend a sympathy for an unqualified democratic equality that he could not summon. His purpose was to see why the one lost its dynamic and how the dynamic of the other had changed and would further change the face of Western culture. He sought evidence that might show how the actors of the time did not simply rationalize their actions retrospectively, but perhaps would show that they acknowledged

---

[69] *AT*, Dossier 45B, 2e chemise, "La liasse 1789. Depuis le 1er janvier jusqu'à la réunion des Etats généraux." The pamphlet which prompted these opinions, by an unknown author, was entitled "Observations sur le rapport fait au Roi par M. Necker le 27 décembre 1788."

[70] Ibid. Tocqueville's notes indicate that he found Target's idea in a piece called "Les Etats généraux convoqués par Louis XVI." Tocqueville was uncertain about the authorship of the pamphlet. Target later took an active part in the Constituent Assembly's debates on the range of executive power.

[71] In his speech to the Chamber on January 27, 1848, *OC*, III, pt. 2, pp. 756–57.

[72] *OC*, II, pt. 1, pp. 207–08.

some awareness of why they acted as they had. He found Joseph Mounier's memoir and later reflections on the Revolution particularly revealing.[73] Mounier took the position that the Revolution was avoidable even after the Tennis Court Oath, and that the final irruption was reached only after the fall of the Bastille. If the National Assembly had wanted to remain in possession of itself after July 14, Mounier thought it should have promptly declared that all the laws and courts would be continued in place, and it should have asked the king to use force to defend the existing legal institutions. But something new had been imparted to the situation – new interests, new passions, new positions – making France look something like the Roman world in the final stages of the republic, when that vast empire could do nothing but follow in the footsteps of a single city. The total novelty of the situation ruled out any other outcome. With this judgment Tocqueville agreed. "All assemblies remained true to the goals which give them birth" was his comment. The Constituent Assembly of 1789 had been set up to combat aristocracy and despotism. It was not psychologically prepared to deal with the anarchy of the July days, nor the even more chaotic events of the following October.

The final movement toward revolution had to be sought, as we recall from one of his earlier pronouncements, in the desire to change the conditions of men's lives. So another question altogether, he felt, had to be posed. Why did political principles and theories, which were common to the United States and France, lead to a change in the government in the first and a total subversion of society in the second? Because the forms that aristocracy and inequality took in France were absolutely insupportable and of such a nature as to push minds toward the most excessive doctrines and displays of demagoguery.[74] It was in the trust shown the state and in the view that the state was destined to carry out the wishes of a single assembly of equal men that equality assumed its peculiar French complexion. To underline his point, he not only showed his preference for the American Federalist party's suspicion of unqualified equality. He also expressed envy for the way in which the English upper classes had made their revolution in 1688 and carefully controlled it by ensuring that it did not pass into the hands of the people. Not so the National Assembly. Not satisfied with being the custodian of the nation's will, whatever practical

---

[73] Ibid., pp. 192–94, 210–12. The works in question are first, Mounier, "Exposé de la conduite de M. Mounier dans l'Assemblée national, et des motifs de son retour en Dauphiné" (1789), written almost immediately after he gave up his seat in the Constituent Assembly. The other, more theoretical, study was *De l'influence attribuée aux philosophes, aux francs-maçons, aux illuminés sur la Révolution de France* (Tübingen, 1801).

[74] *AT*, 45B, 2e chemise, "La liasse 1789. Depuis le 1er janvier jusqu'à la réunion des Etats généraux." Tocqueville based his argument on the information in a pamphlet, "Avis salutaire au Tiers Etat par un jurisconsulte Allobroge."

refinements might yet be introduced, the Assembly failed to pass Lally-Tollendal's "timid" motion of July 22, 1789, urging popular moderation. It thus transferred sovereignty to the people of Paris.[75]

We may thus see that some two decades after the intense thought that had gone into the *Democracy*, Tocqueville looked at the effects of a dedication to equality. In France it had created an inhumane revolution, blighting humanitarianism and generosity, two of the noblest features of the Enlightenment.[76] *Le mal révolutionnaire* had produced murderous effects and was always ready to be summoned up from the depths of human experience. On what grounds was he making these ominous claims? In part, he was calling on Burke's outrage at the revolutionary suspicion of all established opinion. But he was more interested in exposing the origins and consequences of public opinion. He did so delicately but devastatingly. He was far from denying the connection between ideas and actual events; but he refused to extend to the extreme actions of Year II a footing in solid ideas. At best, those actions and the ideology inspiring them constituted the revolutionary degradation of political ideas and conduct. Thus he did not suggest that Rousseau was responsible for the actions of the revolutionary dictatorship of the Year II. The humanitarians who were trying to transform political culture had no way of controlling a mass audience that had its own dreams of political transformation. In the Revolution, books were used by the populace, including the peasants, to satisfy their "lust for revenge." This led to the inevitable deterioration of opinion, as it descended downward to the people from the literary figures and self-styled philosophers.[77] Tocqueville's intention was to make the link between his earliest beliefs that the ubiquitous nature of public opinion in democratic nations stifled the critical mind and his later belief that nothing could resist its tyranny in revolutionary times, once it entered the open public arena of a polity that invoked a democratic parentage to support its legitimacy.

His general remarks on the Terror were couched in language he consistently used. But in trying to capture the Revolution's uniqueness, he gave a new twist to the term majority. In America, equality of conditions gave rise to the threats of tyrannical majorities to critical opinion and individual liberty. The majority in the French Revolution did not willingly acquiesce in the loss of its rights to tyrannical minorities, whose notion of a virtuous democracy meant the exclusion of more and more social enemies. Until his own time, Tocqueville had noted in the *Democracy*, despotism was thought to be odious, whatever its forms. But his detailed study of the Revolution made visible the political phenomenon

---

[75] *OC*, II, pt. 2, p. 188.   [76] *OC*, II, pt. 1, p. 246.   [77] Ibid., p. 196.

of "legitimate tyrannies" – those "exercised for but not by the people." In perhaps his only direct reference to Robespierre, he set aside the idea that his unique personality, rather than the system of government, was responsible for the aberration of the Terror.[78]

What had to be painted, Tocqueville promised in his notes for *L'Ancien Régime*, was the state of the revolutionary mind by means of which the majority rendered the tyranny of the minority possible. He admired Mallet du Pan's *Mémoires* for adverting to an explanation of the Terror that bordered on his own concerns. It was a powerful force that he said came close to organizing disorganization and uniting the forces of despotism and anarchy. The appearance of these forces, he agreed with Mallet, was not a singularly French but actually a European phenomenon, one of the most "active and contagious diseases of the human mind."[79] In the *Democracy*, he had already presciently observed that any legislative body, such as the French Convention, which had usurped the role of government, was destined to self-destruction, because, while its power was always subject to shifts in the popular will, it tyrannized society in the name of that will, by claiming a false identity with it. Its vigor was thus an artifice, subject to imminent collapse.[80] The insight is reminiscent of Montesquieu's analysis of the operations and ultimate impotence of despotism.[81] Something like the overthrow of the despotism of the legislative power, Tocqueville intimated, must have been begun but was not completed at Thermidor. By the end of his life, he was satisfied that he had discerned the contours of the new democratic despotism. He had shifted his concerns from the powers concentrated in the legislative body to those in the clenched fist of the executive power.[82] What he saw as the Revolution's inflation of the *illusion* of the popular will strengthened his belief that it was the key to popular subjection.

Tocqueville saw in the democratic revolution a single but agonistic event that tore its principal actors apart. For him it was indeed the specter haunting Europe, but it was also the creator of a new society. He may have departed from the full import of his original assertion that democratic peoples must "secure the new benefits which equality may offer them . . . [and] to strive to achieve that species of greatness and happiness which is our own."[83] But he did not doubt even then that, were the fall of democracy into democratic despotism to become more and more irreversible, it would be because human beings were willing to satisfy their inclination to simplify rather than diversify the means to

---

[78] *Nolla edn.*, I, p. 302 and note c.   [79] *OC*, II, pt. 2, pp. 227–28.
[80] *Nolla edn.*, I, p. 73.
[81] Montesquieu, *De l'Esprit des lois*, in *Oeuvres complètes*, ed. Caillois, I, pp. 396–407.
[82] *OC*, II, pt. 2, pp. 320–22.   [83] *Nolla edn.*, II, pp. 280–81.

reach their greatness.[84] His pessimism was, it should also be said, not that deep. He contrasted the "illness" of the revolutionary belief in total self-transformation with the "illness" of the postrevolutionary belief in the futility of political will and virtue, and rejected both the false expectations of the first and the self-indulgent nihilism of the second.[85]

---

[84] *OC*, I, pt. 2, p. 347.
[85] Tocqueville to Gobineau, December 20, 1853, *OC*, IX, pp. 201–04.

V

Epilogue

10   Further reflections

> A man on the point of making a decisive choice resembles a calculator
> doing a long addition. The one counts the figures, the other calculates
> the reasons. The man without resolution begins his addition again and
> again. The man of decision is pleased with the total sum, and proceeds
> on the soundness of his first calculation.[1]

In this book, I have asked my readers to follow me along an indirect path
to the birth of Tocqueville's conviction that the study of history would
release answers to the past and future of Western civilization. To plot the
critical points that lead to Tocqueville's final gesture as a historian in
L'Ancien Régime, I wove together several strands of Tocqueville's complex
and rich themes. As I reach the end of my efforts, readers will doubtless
discover that I have said both more and less than I intended.

Almost from the beginning of Tocqueville's work as an observer of how
rapidly Europe was experiencing change at many levels and on many fronts,
many but not all of his contemporaries singled him out as an unusually
gifted thinker. Many works on America were popular, but no other inquiry
into the mechanisms of the new society across the Atlantic fascinated so
many educated Europeans, who held up a mirror to his study of American
democracy and found in it an image, however imperfect, of their own
future. Many members of the upper classes recoiled from it, while others,
thinking about their own experience with revolution and war, began to recognize that European civilization might not be immune from further
change, even democratic change. Tocqueville was instrumental in alerting
some minds to the kinds and gravity of the changes that lay ahead. In the
several generations that followed his death, the reception accorded him,
especially in France, was transformed from minor enthusiasm and a kindly
tolerance into a kind of perplexed yet benign neglect. Just before the outbreak of war in 1939, J. P. Mayer published his study with its prophetic title.[2]

---

[1] "Notes et idées," [undated], *OC*, XVI, p. 572.
[2] J. P. Mayer, *Prophet of the Mass Age: A Study of Alexis de Tocqueville*, trans. M. M. Bozman
and C. Hahn (London, 1939).

Not until the 1970s and 1980s, when a younger group of French thinkers began to search for the weaknesses of French liberalism, was serious interest in Tocqueville renewed. They began the project of finding a place for him within the panoply of liberal thinkers – de Staël, Benjamin Constant, Royer-Collard and Guizot – who struggled, each in his or her own way, to lodge political liberty and rights within a secure constitution.[3]

Larry Siedentop's recent study relates briefly how Tocqueville anticipated figures as diverse as Frederick le Play, Ferdinand Tonnies, Henry Maine, Emile Durkheim and even Marx, Nietzsche and Weber.[4] Indeed it seems that there is a growing consensus, not only among French intellectuals, but also among scholars around the world, that Tocqueville was, if not the greatest political philosopher of the nineteenth century, certainly one of its leading political thinkers. Jon Elster supports this judgment, but not on the grounds that Tocqueville drove his ideas with consistent and coherent force to the production of an impressive range of theories. Elster is fascinated by a thinker whom he calls confused and confusing, contradictory and autistic, irresponsible, undisciplined, mad and spoilt, but who deserves paradoxically to be studied for his depiction of the psychological mechanisms to describe social institutions and change.[5] Elster rests his harsh, almost surrealistic, judgment mainly on a reading of the *Democracy*. My focus in this study, unlike Elster's, and unlike the focus of several other new studies, was not fixed on only one of his works. Tocqueville was a thinker whose gifts for the precise details of human conduct, even when they were offset by ambiguities, reflect the deep presence of these nearly identical qualities in the institutions and the lives of the people and social groups he studied in all his works. What he understood and sometimes accepted was not only the rational, irrational and rationalized springs of human conduct, but also and just as often its unpredictability. Of course, no study of Tocqueville can neglect his contradictions nor the incompleteness of some of his ideas.

But unlike Elster, who feels that Tocqueville's thought can only be

---

[3] For the reception given Tocqueville in France both in and outside academic circles, see Françoise Mélonio, *Tocqueville et les français*. Among several studies dealing with the distinct nature and fate of French liberalism and Tocqueville's contribution to it, see Pierre Manent, *An Intellectual History of Liberalism*, trans. Rebecca Balinski (Princeton, 1994). Of special interest for readers who wish to grasp the reasons for French intellectual infatuation with the power of the state, see Tony Judt, *Past Imperfect: French Intellectuals, 1944–1956* (Berkeley, Los Angeles and Oxford, 1992). Sunil Khilnani, *Arguing Revolution: The Intellectual Left in Postwar France* (New Haven and London, 1993), continues the story to the present. Tony Judt offers a more extended treatment of the French concept of rights in "Rights in France: Reflections on the Etiolation of a Political Language," *La Revue Tocqueville/Tocqueville Review*, 14 (1993), pp. 67–108.

[4] Larry Siedentop, *Tocqueville* (Oxford, 1993), pp. 138–47.

[5] Elster, *Political Psychology*, pp. 125–26, 131–35, 140–41, 191.

rescued from all these failures by an excessively heavy exegesis to show how often he slipped from one position to another, my judgment of him was governed not only by the existence of aporias or inconsistencies. They cannot be denied, but by themselves they do not constitute a decisive test of the unity and durability of an individual's ideas. What these are in Tocqueville's case I think may be located in Tocqueville's understanding and uses of history. But I did not want to confine myself, nor start with, his seminal work on the Revolution. No one needs to be persuaded that *L'Ancien Régime* remains a major intellectual challenge and a constant reference point for scholars, even for those who have expressed opposition to some of Tocqueville's predilections, tastes, prejudices and intellectual strategies. I believe I may have expanded the perspective from which to view this work. But historical philosophy or philosophy of history? These are not usually thought of as the theoretical frameworks which can accommodate Tocqueville's major concerns.

When I laid out the reasons for taking a contrary view and proposed that he has a legitimate, if special, place as such a thinker, one of my major contentions was that Tocqueville has been in large part misunderstood as a thinker who pulled away from metahistorical questions to embrace a proto-ethnographical outlook based on empirical findings. In fact, much of his stance as an objective observer of social dynamics is balanced by a highly deductive method. Concentration on his empiricism or his apriorism severely minimizes and more often marginalizes his consistent interest in metahistorical matters. They penetrated his powers of historical explanation and figured prominently in this book. Tocqueville placed the psychosocial elements in history against a constant background of first principles. For all their different cultural manifestations, a clear statement about them was necessary to dispel false notions of how to interpret them.

Neither a thought experiment, nor a conjectural history, nor a conjectural anthropology, was on Tocqueville's agenda. Even though he showed an interest in non-Western societies, for example those of Algeria, China, Persia and India, the universal features of human nature,[6] as he conceived them, were largely confined to Western aristocratic and democratic societies he used as contrasting models of how human beings order their worlds. In both of them could be found the need for approval or esteem from one's self and from others, as well as fellow-feeling and resentment; the need to command and to obey; the instinct for order and the discomfort caused by disorder; the instinct for religious experience without

---

[6] Ibid., p. 140. Elster denies Tocqueville's universals, but immediately lets them come in through a back entrance by saying that "they consist of permanent possibilities."

which people felt spiritually impoverished; the tendency for human beings to seek a match between their wishes and convictions and their capacities or means to satisfy them; the existence of complex body-images and how these are related to family and kinship networks; the division of labor, including that between the sexes; and the body/soul problem. How all these aspects of human actions were negotiated were matters, he thought, for social observers and historians. What was capital for him was what human beings found worthy of praise or blame. He applied this maxim by excavating the sources of human activity over time.

Of major importance, I contended, was his sense both of the particular and the general, and of the unknown nature of chance as human beings seemingly plotted rational solutions to their problems. Raising this question, as he did, brought to the center the role of contingency in human affairs. He felt uncomfortable with it, but he argued that it was an inextinguishable presence in human affairs and that it was necessary to incorporate it in the search for the meaning of change. He believed that no one could escape or avoid the wager every human being makes with life, in the fabric of which there is an irreducible contingency and ambiguity. The acceptance of the wager did not rule out legitimate questions. The suggestion that intentionality, choice and ambition might be futile was, for example, an idea to which he gave considerable thought in balancing the long revolutionary account extending from 1789 to his own day. It contained two problems for him. The first is itself in two parts. Does the historian, once he has canvassed the human capacity to sort out the reasons for choices made, rejected, or overlooked in times of crisis, feel that his task has been completed, or does he go on to declare that the enunciation of general historical laws must also figure in the task? Contingency, in fact, seems to have achieved a new lease on life. Mona Ozouf, for instance, notes how the Braudelian images of French identity, making up a deterministic model of explanation, may be in the process of being replaced by a focus on the way history is constructed by the actors themselves, "even though this construction is," she says "a kind of obscure need rather than a clear thought."[7]

By choosing Tocqueville's intensely personal recollections as a launching point, I wanted to stress the doubleness of being in the world and trying to know it by observing it. Through the process of acting and observing, of experiencing at one and the same time the spectator and

---

[7] See her article in *Magazine littéraire*, 307 (1993), p. 23. Compare also the recent introduction to a special issue of *Representations*, 4 (September 1994), devoted to "National Cultures Before Nationalism," in which the editors, Carla Hesse and Thomas Lacqueur, say that "we hope to restore to this history [of national identity] its contingency and particularity."

player roles, Tocqueville, the individual, became a historian who called on his permanent interest in metaphysical and metahistorical questions, already adumbrated in his constant reference to them in the *Democracy*. They were to carry much more weight the further away he got from his study of American culture, as if time had to pass before he could gain a fuller consciousness of them. The experience of capturing the events of 1848 prepared him for the even more ambitious task of completing his history of the specific strains and collapse of the Old Régime. Thus Tocqueville engaged his energies on two kinds of historical inquiry. While different, he never felt that they were ultimately opposed, because choice and structure, as he already revealed in the *Souvenirs*, could not be torn apart in any historical reckoning. Nevertheless the stress in the narrative discursive mode that he applied in each of the inquiries was different, so one might say that he found that different methodologies to elicit the veridicality of each proved to be the way of broaching the problem of how to recover the different units of historical time.

How historians and others have approached the question of "total" history cannot be raised here. I suspect that attempts to integrate *la longue durée* and *histoire événementielle* might turn out to be contrived. Neither is the problem resolved by seeing events and persons as emblematic of structures. Tocqueville, it seems to me, was on the right epistemological track by recognizing their differences. As I have argued, Tocqueville uses narrative in the *Souvenirs*, and hence may be said to have been practicing *histoire événementielle*, to grasp the perspective of historical actors, including his own. He knew, as well as Arthur Danto more than a century later, that there can be no ideal and complete narrative of events[8] if only because there will always be future descriptions which will be informed by different perspectives. Tocqueville was additionally aware of the open-endedness of narrative even if he transgressed some of its conventions in his *Souvenirs*. He was determined to discover law-like generalizations, particularly about the conditions governing revolutionary change. The comparative mode, with its promise to draw distinctions, held out for him a promise of broadening the basis for general historical laws. He found it useful to see how the articulation of the aristocratic ethos in European society differed from society to society. After all, it was the earth-shattering and unique French Revolution that was so startling, but he insisted that, in its largest context, it had to be understood as "a European event,"[9] and that, if it were, the conditions leading to revolutionary acts might take on a pattern. Still he continued to affirm that the unexpected

[8] Arthur Danto, *Narration and Knowledge* (New York, 1985).
[9] Tocqueville to Monnard, October 15, 1856, *OC*, VII, p. 354.

and the contingent confirmed the existence of choice, and he adamantly refused to subsume it permanently under the weight of structures. His reasons for taking this stand, as I have argued, were intimately related to his metaphysics. Its Christian elements emphasize that, while they have choice, human beings have only a limited power to establish law-like patterns in history. The isolation of the initial conditions of change, the starting points – the "points of departure," as Tocqueville calls them – demanded, he often felt, a near-omniscience not given to human beings.

But he also felt torn both when he apportioned blame and praise to individuals and communities for their responses to the demands of change, and when he apportioned weight between the moral consequences of their actions and the long-term outcomes for the generations that followed them. Behind this question was another: the coming into being of a society in which liberty might no longer be the animating force in human destiny. Tocqueville dealt with this inner crisis by drawing a distinction between choice and liberty, which were far from identical for him. Human beings, he said, often preferred, and were likely to prefer others to make choices for them. In short, the mentality of obedience was a powerful instinct kept alive by the promises and compensations of security, whether of an older kind as in an aristocratic society before it decayed and that he tended sometimes to idealize; or of the newer democratic kind where obedience was not only a social mechanism relying on depersonalized forms of benign authority, but, more than in any previous society, reinforced by the ideas and practices of excessive self-concern and the crudest forms of equality that negated the force of independent critical choice.

In facing these developments in Western civilization, Tocqueville called on his sense of the ironic and tragic and characteristically exposed the paradoxes in human conduct to support his explanations for the movements of history. Once he left this confessional mode of the *Souvenirs*, he told himself that it was achievement enough to know that, hovering above all personal weaknesses, was the fact that the mind feebly seeks unity, retreats from disorder and longs for coherence; and that – and this was no trivial matter for him, as we saw – the epistemological and existential foundations of historical inquiry could not be set aside as inconsequential. As he said, human action often ruled out logic, but not in writing where it could be factitiously introduced. "A man finds it almost as difficult to be inconsistent in his language as to be consistent in his conduct."[10] He adopted an uneasy agnostic or skeptical posture on the question of consistency and coherence. All that he could say was that the

---

[10] *OC*, I, pt. 1, pp. 13–14.

mysteries of the unknown could be borne by a faith in human power sometimes to sense the good. And this was the way in which he felt the Revolution had to be judged. The Revolution and its continuing ramifications he saw as a struggle between modern impersonal forces and liberty. Consequently he dismissed as presumptuous any idea of a final coherent narrative of the Revolution claiming to be a representation of reality. Coherence of this kind was illusory.

He tried to catch the shimmering reflections of the past, overcoming, he hoped, his own blindness in penetrating history's shadows. For it was his conviction that recognition of fallibility in one's self was the key to knowing the weaknesses of past generations. How close could he get to the objects of inquiry? Not by concentrating on institutions alone. He told Corcelle in 1853, when he had already started his research for his book, that "political societies are not what their laws make them, but what they are prepared in advance to be by the feelings, beliefs, habits of heart and mind of the men who compose them, and what native disposition and education made these men to be."[11] When he was in sight of the book's end, he was still not convinced that he was burrowing deeply enough into the past's underground passages. Since the "cataclysm of our revolution has left only debris covered by a new soil," it had to be removed to rediscover what he momentarily called a world that had been destroyed forever. In these words to Mrs. Grote,[12] he let himself forget what he believed was closer to the truth. The debris of the past in fact contained at least some of the particles that composed the new. The debris was the manifestation of people's thoughts and actions over time, as instantly forgotten as they were conceived and executed. Tocqueville was not immune from the feeling that the piling up of time created a never-ending and chaotic detritus, but he also felt the need to find the historical realities buried there.

Tocqueville saw the problem of the French Revolution as exposing the tensions between determinateness and choice, and continuity and change, not only within each of these pairs but between them. He perceived the two dualities as the principal variants of human history in which they dovetailed, informed and bore upon each other, but were not easily, because they were not self-evidently, reconcilable. He wanted to convince readers that the best lesson history could offer was that it never repeats itself despite the propensity human beings have to repeat themselves. The Great Revolution had to be saved from the burlesque into which many of its heirs and enemies had dragged it. Its real nature could

---

[11] Tocqueville to Corcelle, September 17, 1853, *OC*, XV, pt. 2, pp. 80–81.
[12] Tocqueville to Mrs. Grote, November 22, 1855, *Beaumont edn.*, VI, pp. 241–45.

not be revealed by fashioning a discourse of mutilation – cutting the Revolution from its roots in the *ancien régime*. If Tocqueville had been an advocate of stark continuity, his commitment to political liberty in a democratic age would have been a species of play-acting more perverse than the political acting he deplored. To be sure, fissures and faults lying deep in the human past were always at work, but if they shifted from time to time it was not without the help of human agency. A reverse theory of discontinuity, with implications of radically new directions, would have trivialized his sense of the past, since exercising liberty would have been as effortless as wearing clothes.

The problem of understanding the past was thus not reducible to a discussion of the relative merits of continuity and discontinuity as instruments of historical explanation. The Great Revolution had to be seen rather as an epicenter from which shocks continued to radiate. In it inhered, as it were, continuity with the past. At the same time, it was itself the very source of the change subverting the past, with determinateness and choice engaged in a ceaseless dialectic, extending from 1789 or even earlier to his own day. Tocqueville played on a subtle but vital difference when he spoke of the 1848 revolutionaries acting out the 1789 Revolution, rather than continuing its earliest promises. In such a framework, politics was locked into a repetitive mode; its actors continued to play the same scenario. From it no exit and no end to revolutions were possible. The makers of the 1789 Revolution had worked for, but failed to achieve, equal access to public office for all citizens – the goal that Tocqueville believed was its most impressive aspiration.

Tocqueville's opening remarks in *L'Ancien Régime* on the ironies of unintended consequences bear out the sense of loss bequeathed by the Revolution's unrealized hopes. He transformed the idea into a powerful image focused on the blindness of politicians. In their mutual challenges for place and power, they actually thought that intentions and results were unambiguously related. The end of action is not, he said, found in its intention. The net effect of the Revolution is to be sought as much in the unexpected tensions that create it as those that it creates. Unintended consequences are proof of the tricks played by history, and constitute the paradox that the revolutionaries used the debris of the old society to construct the new.[13] This can be taken as a silent rebuke, but also an endorsement of Edmund Burke, whom Tocqueville elsewhere criticized as blind to the abuses of the *ancien régime*, and blinder still to the grandeur of the revolutionary images of renewal. Tocqueville might appear to side with those who see change as mere froth on the tides of an implacable history.

[13] *OC*, II, pt. 1, p. 69.

Unlike Burke, however, who tended to see change as an inversion or perversion of a universal natural order, Tocqueville tried to remove himself
from those remnants of an older theodicy, and, as well, from the seductions of utilitarianism, both of which were present in uneasy opposition in
Burke's thought. Nor did he, like Joseph de Maistre, see the Revolution as
the manifestation of a divinely designated order, hidden in the mysteries
of providence, working through human beings who are cut off from divine
power, but privileged from time to time to glimpse, as if in a dream, the
divine plan.[14] Neither did he follow Louis de Bonald in identifying God's
will with the monarch, the supreme bodily presence of love, thought and
action, any deflection from which distorted secular, natural and divine
power.[15] Tocqueville used, as I have shown, some elements of the vocabu-
lary associated with theories of providence, but he drained them of their
conventional religious referents, and substituted for them a far more
detached and unknown divine presence, which almost amounted, in his
eschatology, to a divine absence from human affairs. He therefore ultimately deprived providence of consequentialism, which is its marrow.

The Revolution revealed for Tocqueville, as if in the smallest fraction of
time, an opening toward a wholly new order, after which there had come
a kind of fall. But was finality to be conceptualized and argued? After all,
buying into the idea of finality assumed taking on either the perspective of
God, or adopting a mechanistic and reductive philosophy and prizing it
as an ontological principle. There was no such finality for Tocqueville; no
end to the historical process; no final comforts to be found in Christian
theology – only the imperative to live in and make one's way through the
gnawing feelings of cosmological and historical incertitude. Tocqueville
would have found the current talk about the end of history not altogether
foreign, but he would have resisted its implications. He did not transform
his fear that the flatness of affect, the danger to art and philosophy pur-
suant to a loss of individual liberty, and the possibility that the Revolution
was the last great expression of human striving, into the end-of-
history position that Lutz Niethammer has explored, held especially
among thinkers on the right and left in the twentieth century, each of
whom had their own reasons for disillusionment with modernity.[16] In the
many allusions to and explanations of Tocqueville's dread of doubt and

[14] Joseph de Maistre, *Considérations sur la France* (1797), I, in *Oeuvres*, ed. Jean-Louis
Darcel (Geneva, 1980), p. 95.
[15] Louis de Bonald, *Théorie du pouvoir politique et religieux*, in *Oeuvres complètes de Louis de
Bonald*, 3 vols. (Paris, n.d.), pp. 149–51.
[16] For some of the more interesting discussions of this question, see Lutz Niethammer (in
collaboration with Dirk van Laak), *Posthistoire*, trans. Patrick Camiller (London, 1992),
and Perry Anderson, "The Ends of History," in *A Zone of Engagement*, ed. Anderson
(London and New York, 1992), pp. 279–375.

uncertainty about the coming of the bourgeois and democratic world, which he felt might subject everyone to the same forces of existence, I tried to show that they could be combated by enlisting hope. For hope was essential both to his modern sensibility and, also, a principle of history since it lifted human beings from a sense of repetitive catastrophe. Agnes Heller has expressed similar sentiments following a century of catastrophes undreamt of by thinkers of the middle of the nineteenth century, yet even so she can speak of hope as the historian's weapon against incertitude – Tocqueville's existential nightmare.[17] So, while his was a vision that admitted irony, despair and disillusionment, it had little if anything in it of predictions of an after-time in which the curtain would be dropped on all theories of origins and general laws, foundationalism and transcendence, but most of all on the promise of the freedom of the human species. Neither feelings of incertitude nor his occasional slip into a sense of futility[18] induced Tocqueville, who believed in some minimal tests of rationality and the mysteries of indeterminateness, ever to say that nothing can be said to matter.

As far as Tocqueville could see, there had to be a major historical contradiction in the hope that one's values could be restored by schemes to revive an unrecoverable past in order to meet the danger points of modern society. Hope was forward- not backward-looking. There was some hope in looking to what modern life might itself positively engender and hence nurture to counteract its worst tendencies. There need not be any fatalistic surrender to mechanistic determinism, a position which my book argues was antithetical to both Tocqueville's temperament and intellect. Likewise metaphysical freedom could be a chimera, once it was removed from the historical parameters in which it must be practically located. But within those parameters, intentions, choices and responsible acts might be navigated between technological mastery for its own sake and spiritual well-being in the absence of which being human lost its meaning. That was the crisis of freedom in modern society: its contingent and endangered condition – the freedom from self-deception. Tocqueville's suggestions for dealing with it were empirically and histori-cally grounded. He wanted moderns to face up to their ignorance of what he believed they needed most, freedom. He chastised them for not feeling anxious about losing it.

The dilemma facing the modern democratic world he saw in terms of spiritual emptiness. Charles Taylor, who has a close affinity for

[17] Agnes Heller, *A Philosophy of History in Fragments* (Oxford, 1993), pp. 49–51.
[18] For the argument that Tocqueville's work is an illustration of the futility thesis in history, see Albert O. Hirschman, *The Rhetoric of Reason: Perversity, Futility and Jeopardy* (Cambridge, Mass., and London, 1991), pp. 49–50, 138–39.

Tocqueville, uses his prediction as a leitmotif for analyzing the problem of, and suggesting some of the means to overcome, the modern condition of what I called the hyperindividualism that Tocqueville was convinced posed the greatest threat to a responsible political life, the essential source of public and individual freedom. Taylor also added, as if in confirmation of Tocqueville's other prediction, that moderns would "have to live with them (the bureaucratic state and the market) forever."[19] The two are linked by a concern for the ideal of being true to one's identity and submitting it to rational reflection in public discourse. Tocqueville, though expressing doubt about the future of liberty in democracy, was not the intellectual source of the disillusionment with either, which led thinkers, starting with Nietzsche in the last century and continuing with intellectuals on the right and the left in the interwar period and for some decades after 1945, to decry and attack both.

A good deal of Tocqueville's prognosis of the future can be traced to his uneasy relationship with the legacy of the Enlightenment. Much as he found the philosophers of the Enlightenment guilty of intellectual arrogance, and, sometimes primly, but more often with an astonishing cold cruelty, derided the men of letters of his own time, he appropriated and approved of the more moderate aspirations of the Enlightenment project, especially as Montesquieu gave voice to them. His response to Rousseau, though negative, was not unambiguous. So Tocqueville's attitude toward modern equalitarian society was colored by the legacies in his thought of an older morality and eschatology, just as both figured prominently in his reception of economic materialism. But, however much he may have been pulled by traditional morality, he could not follow it consistently. He had, despite his apprehensions about the modern world as he saw it emerging, plunged too far into it to think that the past could be or should be regained.

Tocqueville judged that there was a parasitic relationship between democratic ideology and materialistic culture detrimental to a vital civic and political life. Was the individualism he condemned of the kind that undermined social sociability and a healthy political culture? My interpretation of his idea of rightly understood self-interest suggested that the conflict within the democratic psyche between the need and the wish to be equal and to retain confidence in individual judgment was resolved by acts of social emulation that theoretically and often in practice promoted social mobility. In Tocqueville's scheme, a democratic people, driven by

---

[19] Charles Taylor, *The Malaise of Modernity* (Concord, Ontario, 1991), pp. 4, 9–10, 111. Also see Taylor's *Sources of the Self* (Cambridge, Mass., 1989), pp. 500, 502, 505. For an assessment, see Harvey Mitchell, "Charles Taylor on the Self, Its Languages and Its History," *History of Political Thought*, 12 (1991), pp. 335–58.

the ethos of individualism which pathologized the anxieties of getting ahead and not falling behind, reinforced the social side of the sociability by reaffirming equality. He did not idealize equality – he always spoke of it within a historical context – in the same way as he decontextualized and idealized liberty. Tocqueville asked his readers to infer rather than to consider the argument, namely, that democracies might be able to achieve practical and useful equality only by the exercise of liberty that respected the autonomous self's thought and the thought of autonomous others. Only then might there be a viable basis for democratic social sociability.

But how good were the chances for the success of a democratic political culture? Tocqueville was among the first to know that, especially in democracy, rulers and citizens cannot do without each other. They form a whole body, as do other political bodies, but in a wholly new and modern way. Tocqueville tried to dispel the confusion caused by the abuses to which he said such terms as *"democracy, democratic institutions and democratic government"* were subjected by people who feed the crowd with illusions. Such reductive spirits could not explain the complexity of these concepts because they failed to grasp that even a society under absolute rule may parade as democracy, because its ruler takes pains to govern by the laws that favor the people's welfare.[20] False democracy was this form of government. Democracy can subsist on varying degrees of participation, although, under ideal conditions preferably, but not necessarily, with the full enfranchisement of the adult population. The questions of gender and race, though hardly disregarded in America by early feminists and abolitionists, did not, however, engage Tocqueville's full sympathies. Nor did, after 1848, the working classes. For him, a viable and fair democracy always came down to the exercise of political liberty. Without it democracy was illusory. Democracy would remain in an inchoate state if another condition were not met, preeminently, the constitutional entrenchment of rights as the means to curb the powers of the majority. The point of democracy was not to produce a political body of absolute equals. It meant far more to ensure that no servile citizenry might join in an unconsciously complicit alliance with its governors to diminish it.

How, also, was political liberty to be protected to ensure that the grip that rulers and ruled exerted over one another was not so powerful as to exhaust them both and imperil creativity? Tocqueville faced these dilemmas only partly in his appeals to the creative spirits in society. In them the force of political liberty itself would, he tentatively thought, seemingly be kept alive. They would presumably be sensitive to and avoid the subjectivism that democratic individualism was breeding. And, by the same

---

[20] *OC*, II, pt. 2, pp. 198–99 (Tocqueville's italics).

token, they would be a potent force against revolutionary disturbances. He did not think through the practical implications of his admission that, in their ideal forms, liberty and equality needed one another, nor did he speak in later years as often as he had in the *Democracy* of the "greatness and beauty" to be found in the justice of equality.[21]

His arguments in praise of civil associations in democracies as paving the way for political ones, so that their reciprocal actions created a counterweight to the centralized state, must be balanced against another point that he made even more forcefully. The democratic state encouraged civil associations to turn their attention inward on themselves as a safety valve that discouraged revolutionary ideas and actions; but, in its attitude to political associations, it concluded unthinkingly that their independence was a dangerous, instead of a stabilizing, force. Again, he distinguished between the political cultures of the United States and France. In the first, where there was universal male white suffrage, political associations were free to exert their efforts to gain a majority, but never to assume that they could possess it permanently. In the second, where the state had scant experience of political associations and where most could never hope to gain a majority from a restricted electorate, they were regarded as dangerous. For these reasons, Tocqueville tended before 1848 to link revolution and democracy in France, but not in America.

Tocqueville may have been too quick to assign the major threats to liberty to the ever-expanding powers of the centralized state. His hostility can be explained by his experience of situations in which the state became the object of desire by competing groups as in the years leading up to 1830 and 1848, and he vicariously experienced, through his analysis of the collapse of the Old Régime, the reciprocal challenges that the pre-revolutionary state and the *parlementaires* hurled at each other. The result was to blind him partially to the ways in which the state might in fact not always exercise its tutelary powers and deprive citizens of their liberties and rights, but instead actually entrust the citizenry, through refinements in constitutional provisions and political representation, with the responsibility of ensuring and expanding them. But Tocqueville's right to be thought of as a sharp critic of the modern state legitimately marks him as a precursor of the more developed theories of bureaucratic power in the works of Weber, Pareto and Michels.

It was in fact not at all an easy matter to determine if the state existed as an entity independent of those who controlled it and those who tried to change the terms of control; and so it is not all that surprising that he did not see the linkage between government and groups within civil society as

---

[21] *Nolla edn.*, II, p. 280.

a form of reciprocal exchange in which the state and economic forces in particular helped one another and could thereby overawe relatively powerless sections of the citizenry. He did not approach the problem in that proto-Marxist, Gramscian way. In his analysis of the power of the new manufacturing classes, he showed an awareness of their burgeoning power, but his grasp of that problem was not that profound. He took the position that, because they depended so much on the state for assistance of all kinds, their economic growth actually tended to enhance the power of the state, perhaps even more than they increased their own. On balance, he tended to think that no matter how powerful certain sections in democracies proved to be, the state had the ultimate power to exercise its will and overcome any opposing wills. His prognosis has proven, as the last few generations have shown, to be more germane to non-democratic societies than to the bureaucratic state systems of liberal-democratic societies.

Centralized state institutions, on the other hand, Tocqueville also believed, could be partly held in check – he was talking about the United States – by the deep sense of the importance of defending liberty that several generations of the free exercise of religion had encouraged in the new world. In other words, he posited the beneficent effect of religion on political and individual liberty. Ideally, religious sects worked out their own notions of the good, but it was still a good firmly set in Christian precepts. He was aware of the religious, especially the Puritan, sources of the abolitionist movement to end slavery and counted it a good thing so long as it did not rule out political compromise. He took it very much as a given that the impulse that led to religious freedom at the time of the Reformation and the proliferation of religious sects, each guarding its notions of the good as its own truth, would remain unchanged. At the same time, it is necessary to keep in mind, first, that Tocqueville's positive linking of liberty and religion was inspired almost equally by the functional and the intrinsic value of religion. On the grounds of functionality, Tocqueville argued that Christianity was so widespread in the United States that it was almost indistinguishable from and therefore served to bind the mores and reason of the American people. On the grounds of its intrinsic value, we are reminded of a basic element in Tocqueville's psyche, to which much in this study has been devoted. While he insisted on the separation of church and state, and opposed the intervention of the clerisy in French politics, he did not think that the state should adopt a neutral stance in regard to religion, for without it human beings would lose something of their humanity and wander in an eternally unsettling state of perplexity. Skepticism was the absolute antithesis of all forms of spiritual life. Were skepticism to spread, the individual's withdrawal into a self-contained universe would in addition prove detrimental to political participation. Religion, as a binding force, kept human beings focused on sociability and political activity. In the absence of beliefs, a legitimate underpinning for authority in the moral and intellectual world would vanish only to have armies and prisons take its place.[22]

Tocqueville wagered that the sociability of innumerable and competing religious groups would act in favor of political liberty. Perhaps too optimistically, he thought that Christian sects, intent on preserving their freedom, would not threaten the freedom of their rivals. More important, he differentiated between knowing the truth and sensing the good of things. If human beings could not judge the truth, they at least had the God-given power to sense the good. Tocqueville's universalist ethic stood on a generalized notion of Christianity, the only bastion against Spinozism, deism and pantheism. Consequently, his position cannot be identified with the contemporary liberal neutralist stance that refuses to give privilege to a single conception of the moral good, which remains a focal point for discussion among such political philosophers as John Rawls,[23] who favors a position of neutrality against such critics as Alasdair MacIntyre who finds its implications an affront to a coherent moral system.[24] Tocqueville's liberalism is not, however, without some significance in this and other controversies in modern liberalism. Among them may be found Martha Nussbaum's warnings that giving in to our communal preferences can lead to ethical confusion; Michael Sandel's critique of the notion that individuals can stand aside and make plausible judgments apart from who they are; and Stephen Holmes's reservations about the superiority of communitarian liberal arguments.[25]

I close with a few final remarks on Tocqueville's uncertain state of mind about the Revolution's long-term meaning. As he put it to Henry Reeve, the Revolution will achieve its work in a future that might reveal what its work truly was, divulge the nature of the new society that emerged from its violent labors and disclose what the new society had left behind and

---

[22] "Idées de discours (octobre 1844)," *OC*, III, pt. 2, p. 551.

[23] John Rawls's *Political Liberalism* (New York, 1993) not only restates his oldest ideas. He revises some of them and adds others as well, while taking into account a number of writers who are critically sympathetic.

[24] The need to restore a notion of a universal good is identified largely, but not exclusively, with Alasdair MacIntyre, *Whose Justice? Whose Rationality?* (Notre Dame, Ind., 1988).

[25] All are related in important ways to Rawls and MacIntyre. See Martha Nussbaum, "Virtue Revived," *Times Literary Supplement* (July 3, 1992), pp. 9–11; Michael Sandel, *Liberalism and the Limits of Justice* (Cambridge, 1982); Stephen Holmes, "The Permanent Structures of Antiliberal Thought," in *Liberalism and the Moral Life*, ed. Nancy Rosenblum (Cambridge, Mass., 1989), p. 231.

what it retained from the past.[26] In this unknown future, if a vigorous political liberty were to survive at all, it needed to be founded, as he first enunciated its principles in the *Democracy*, on the prior existence of the natural trust people have for one another's opinions, since no one by themselves can possibly verify the whole of human knowledge. In turn, the channels of public opinion had to be kept open, but the kind of public opinion that drew on the citizen's critical sense, not the opinion that smothered it to gain a presumed consensus. Continuing the French Revolution meant a renewal of the ideal of liberty that it had failed to honor.[27] For that reason, as long as liberty faced direct or subtle threats, the Revolution, either as event or as a legacy, could not be over. But he was adamant that liberty would not be advanced by further rounds of revolution. François Furet's argument that the Revolution had "entered port" by 1880 calls to mind Tocqueville's image of a never-ending sea voyage during which the shores of deliverance seemed to be receding more and more.[28] In the middle and late 1850s, he expressed apprehensions that an impending civil war over the future of slavery might do irreparable harm to American democracy.[29] There is no question that the signs of civil war he detected would be one and the same as a revolution "caused by the presence of blacks upon American soil."[30] And he was pessimistic about the situation in France, where he saw little to choose "between despotism and a band of assassins," both of whom he held in contempt. There was "no solid terrain on which to establish a liberal and non-demagogic party."[31]

The sole means of counteracting disaster and chronic defeatism was to keep open the channels of communication. Such an outlook clearly implied keeping open its most enlightened side, at least in ensuring the civil liberty to seek to be educated freely and the right to self-expression, two of Tocqueville's cardinal principles of liberalism.[32] He might have found much to cheer in Hannah Arendt's view that the democratic body politic had no claim to pronounce on the nature of truth, and that the only way to safeguard the liberty to speak the truth was to ensure the

---

[26] Tocqueville to Reeve, February 6, 1856, *OC*, VI, pt. 1, p. 161.

[27] *Nolla edn.*, II, pp. 20, 24.

[28] François Furet, "Une Révolution sans révolution?" (interview), *Le Nouvel Observateur*, February 28, 1986, pp. 90–93. The reference to the end of the voyage is in *La Révolution 1770–1880* (Paris, 1988), p. 517. In "Histoire de l'idée révolutionnaire" (interview), *Magazine littéraire*, 258 (1988), pp. 18–20, Furet chose the 1980s as the time of closure.

[29] See, for example, Tocqueville to E. V. Childe, April 2, 1857; Tocqueville to T. Sedgwick, April 13, 1857, *OC*, VII, pp. 192–93, 195–98. In 1856, the abolitionist paper, *The Liberty Bell*, published Tocqueville's manifesto against slavery: ibid., pp. 163–64.

[30] *Nolla edn.*, II, p. 214.

[31] Tocqueville to E. V. Childe, January 23, 1858, *OC*, VII, p. 223.

[32] *Le Commerce*, December 11, 1844, *OC*, III, pt. 2, p. 584.

freedom to express one's opinion.[33] The stir Tocqueville wanted to make as a historian was to convince his readers that his interpretation of the past might succeed in telling them that whatever traces of human dignity might be found in the past were inseparable from the uses humanity made of liberty.[34]

---

[33] Arendt to Jaspers, July 9, 1946, in *Hannah Arendt–Karl Jaspers Correspondence 1926–1969*, ed. Lotte Kohler and Hans Saner, trans. Robert Kimber and Rita Kimber (New York, 1992), p. 49.

[34] Tocqueville to Gobineau, January 24, 1857, *OC*, IX, p. 280.

Select bibliography

Note: Tocqueville's works are listed under Abbreviations, p. xiii.

Anderson, Perry. "The Ends of History," in *A Zone of Engagement*, ed. Anderson (London and New York, 1992), pp. 279–375.

Arendt, Hannah. "Understanding and Politics," *Partisan Review*, 20 (1953), pp. 377–92.

The Human Condition (Chicago, 1958).

Between Past and Future (Cleveland and New York, 1961).

On Revolution (New York, 1963).

Aron, Raymond. *Introduction to the Philosophy of History*, trans. G. J. Irvin (London, 1961).

Main Currents in Sociological Thought, trans. Richard Howard and Helen Weaver (New York, 1968).

History, Truth, Liberty, ed. Franciszek Draus (Chicago and London, 1985).

Baker, Keith M. "Politics and Public Opinion under the Old Regime: Some Reflections," in *Press and Politics in Pre-Revolutionary France*, ed. Jack R. Censer and Jeremy D. Popkin (Berkeley, Los Angeles and London, 1987), pp. 204–46.

Inventing the French Revolution: Essays on French Political Culture in the Eighteenth Century (Cambridge, 1990).

Bakhtin, M. M. *Speech Genres and Other Late Essays*, ed. Caryl Emerson and Michael Holquist, trans. Vern W. McGee (Austin, 1986).

Barnave, Antoine-P.-J.-Marie. *Oeuvres de Barnave*, ed. Alphonse-Marc-M.-T. Bérenger de la Drôme, 4 vols. (Paris, 1843).

Introduction à la Révolution française, ed. Fernand Rude (Paris, 1960).

Bates, David. "Variations of Error in Late Enlightenment France," Ph.D. dissertation, University of Chicago, 1994.

Benjamin, Walter. *Illuminations*, ed. Hannah Arendt, trans. Harry Zohn (New York, 1969).

Birnbaum, Pierre. *Sociologie de Tocqueville* (Paris, 1970).

Boesche, Roger. *The Strange Liberalism of Alexis de Tocqueville* (Ithaca, 1987).

Boesche, Roger (with James Taupin), ed. and trans. *Alexis de Tocqueville: Selected Letters on Politics and Society* (Berkeley, Los Angeles and London, 1985).

Bonald, Louis de. *Théorie du pouvoir politique et religieux*, in *Oeuvres complètes de Louis de Bonald*, 3 vols. (Paris, n.d.).

Brogan, Hugh. *Tocqueville* (London, 1973).

Burke, Edmund. *Reflections on the Revolution in France*, ed. Conor Cruise O'Brien (Harmondsworth, 1968).

Calvino, Italo. *Mr. Palomar*, trans. William Weaver (Toronto, 1985).

Canguilhem, Georges. *On the Normal and the Pathological*, trans. Carolyn R. Fawcett (Dordrecht, Boston and London, 1978).

Carr, David. *Time, Narrative and History* (Bloomington, 1986).

Chartier, Roger. *The Cultural Origins of the French Revolution*, trans. Lydia G. Cochrane (Durham, N. C., and London, 1991).

Chisick, Harvey (with Hana Zinguer and Ouzi Elyada), ed. *The Press in the French Revolution*, The Voltaire Foundation, Vol. CCLXXXVII (Oxford, 1991).

Cobban, Alfred. *Aspects of the French Revolution* (London, 1968).

Collingwood, R. G. *The Idea of History* (Oxford, 1946).

The New Leviathan, ed. David Boucher, rev. edn. (Oxford, 1992).

Corral, Luis Dîez del. *La mentalidad política de Tocqueville, con especial referencia a Pascal* (Madrid, 1965).

Cournot, A.-A. *Exposition de la théorie des chances et des probabilités* (Paris, 1843).

Essai sur les fondements de nos connaissances et sur les caractères de la critique philosophique, in *Oeuvres complètes*, ed. Jean-Claude Pariente (Paris, 1975).

Danto, Arthur. *Narration and Knowledge* (New York, 1985).

de Baecque, Antoine. *Le corps de l'histoire. Métaphores et politique 1770–1800* (Paris, 1993).

Dickey, Laurence. "Historicizing the 'Adam Smith Problem': Conceptual, Historiographical and Textual Issues," *Journal of Modern History*, 58 (1986), pp. 579–609.

Drescher, Seymour. *Tocqueville and England* (Cambridge, Mass., 1964).

Dilemmas of Democracy: Tocqueville and Modernization (Pittsburgh, 1968).

"Why Great Revolutions Will Become Rare: Tocqueville's Most Neglected Prognosis," *Journal of Modern History*, 64 (1992), pp. 429–54.

Dubois, abbé J.-A. *Moeurs, institutions et cérémonies des peuples de l'Inde* (Paris, 1825). (First published in English as *Description of the Character, Manners and Customs of the People of India; and of Their Institutions, Religious and Civil*, trans. Henry K. Beauchamp [London, 1817].)

Duchet, Michèle. *Anthropologie et histoire au siècle des Lumières* (Paris, 1977).

Dumont, Louis. *Homo Hierarchicus*, trans. Mark Sainsbury, Louis Dumont and Basia Gulati, rev. edn. (Chicago, 1980).

Elster, Jon. "Belief, Bias and Ideology," in *Relativity and Relativism*, ed. Martin Hollis and Steven Lukes (Cambridge, Mass., 1982), pp. 123–48.

Ulysses and the Sirens: Studies in Rationality and Irrationality (Cambridge, 1984).

Political Psychology (Cambridge, 1993).

Ermarth, Michael. "Intellectual History as Philosophical Anthropology: Bernard Groethuysen's Transformation of Traditional *Geistesgeschichte*," *Journal of Modern History*, 65 (1993), pp. 673–705.

Féher, Ferenc, ed. *The French Revolution and the Birth of Modernity* (Berkeley, Los Angeles and Oxford, 1990).

Ferry, Luc. *The System of Philosophies of History*, Vol. II, *Political Philosophy*, trans. Franklin Philip (Chicago and London, 1992).

Furet, François. *Interpreting the French Revolution*, trans. Elborg Forster (Cambridge and Paris, 1981).

The Workshop of History, trans. Jonathan Mandelbaum (Chicago and London, 1984).

"Naissance d'un paradigme: Tocqueville et le voyage en Amérique (1825–1831)," *Annales, E.S.C.*, 39 (March–April 1984), pp. 225–39.

"Une Révolution sans révolution?," (interview), *Le Nouvel Observateur*, February 28, 1986, pp. 90–93.

La Révolution 1770–1880 (Paris, 1988).

"Histoire de l'idée révolutionnaire," (interview), *Magazine littéraire*, 258 (1988), pp. 18–20.

Gargan, Edward T. *Alexis de Tocqueville: The Critical Years, 1848–51* (Washington, D. C., 1955).

"Tocqueville and the Problem of Historical Prognosis," *American Historical Review*, 68 (1963), pp. 332–45.

Gellner, Ernest. *Plough, Sword and Book: The Structure of Human History* (London, 1988).

Gildin, Hilail. *Rousseau's Social Contract: The Design of the Argument* (Chicago and London, 1983).

Ginsburg, Carlo. "Microhistory: Two or Three Things That I Know about It," *Critical Inquiry*, 20 (1993), pp. 10–35.

Goldstein, Doris S. *Trial of Faith: Religion and Politics in Tocqueville's Thought* (New York, 1975).

Gruner, Shirley M. "Political Historiography in Restoration France," *History and Theory*, 7 (1969), pp. 346–65.

Guizot, François. *Cours d'histoire moderne: Histoire de la civilisation en France depuis la chute de l'empire romain jusqu'en 1789*, 5 vols. (Paris, 1829–32).

Habermas, Jürgen. *The Structural Transformation of the Public Sphere: An Inquiry into a Category of Bourgeois Society*, trans. Thomas Burger (Cambridge, Mass., 1989).

Hacking, Ian. *The Taming of Chance* (Cambridge, 1990).

Hadari, Saguiv A. *Theory in Practice: Tocqueville's New Science of Politics* (Stanford, 1989).

Halphen, Louis. *L'Histoire en France depuis cent ans* (Paris, 1914).

Hamilton, Alexander, John Jay and James Madison, *The Federalist: A Commentary on the Constitution of the United States* (New York, n.d.).

Häusser, Ludwig. *Deutsche Geschichte. Vom Tode Friedrichs des Grossen bis zur Gründung des deutschen Bundes*, 4 vols. (Berlin, 1861–63).

Geschichte der französischen Revolution, 1789–1799, herausgegeben von Wilhelm Onken (Berlin, 1867).

Hawthorne, Geoffrey. *Plausible Worlds: Possibility and Understanding in History and the Social Sciences* (Cambridge, 1991).

Heller, Agnes. *A Philosophy of History in Fragments* (Oxford, 1993).

Hereth, Michael. *Alexis de Tocqueville, Threats to Freedom in Democracy*, trans. G. Bogardus (Durham, N. C., 1986).

Herr, Richard. *Tocqueville and the Old Regime* (Princeton, 1962).

Hesse, Carla, and Thomas Lacqueur. "Introduction: National Cultures Before Nationalism," *Representations*, 4 (September 1994), pp. 1–12.

Hintikka, Jaako. *The Intentions of Intentionality and Other New Models of Modalities* (Dordrecht, 1975).

Hirschman, Albert O. *The Passions and the Interests: Political Arguments for Capitalism Before Its Triumph* (Princeton, 1977).

The Rhetoric of Reason: Perversity, Futility and Jeopardy (Cambridge, Mass., and London, 1991).

Holmes, Stephen. *Benjamin Constant and the Making of Modern Liberalism* (New Haven, 1984).

"The Permanent Structures of Antiliberal Thought," in *Liberalism and the Moral Life*, ed. Nancy Rosenblum (Cambridge, Mass., 1989), pp. 228–41.

Hull, David. "In Defence of Presentism," *History and Theory*, 18 (1979), pp. 1–15.

Hundert, Edward J. *The Enlightenment's "Fable": Bernard Mandeville and the Discovery of Society* (Cambridge, 1994).

Hunt, Lynn. *Politics, Culture and Class in the French Revolution* (Berkeley, Los Angeles and London, 1984).

Ignatieff, Michael. "John Millar and Individualism," in *Wealth and Virtue: The Shaping of Political Economy in the Scottish Enlightenment*, ed. Istvan Hont and Michael Ignatieff (Cambridge, 1983), pp. 317–43.

Jardin, André. *Alexis de Tocqueville, 1805–1859* (Paris, 1984).

Jaspers, Karl. *Nietzsche: An Introduction to the Understanding of His Philosophical Activity*, trans. Charles F. Wallraff and Frederick J. Schmitz (Tucson, 1965).

Johnson, Douglas. *Guizot: Aspects of French History 1787–1874* (London and Toronto, 1963).

Jouffroy, Théodore. *Mélanges philosophiques*, 3rd edn. (Paris, 1860).

Correspondance de Théodore Jouffroy, publiée avec une Etude sur Jouffroy par Adolphe Lair (Paris, 1901).

Judt, Tony. *Past Imperfect: French Intellectuals, 1944–1956* (Berkeley, Los Angeles and Oxford, 1992).

"Rights in France: Reflections on the Etiolation of a Political Language," *La Revue Tocqueville/Tocqueville Review*, 14 (1993), pp. 67–108.

Kahan, Alan S. "Tocqueville's Two Revolutions," *Journal of the History of Ideas*, 46 (1985), pp. 585–96.

Kelley, Donald. *Foundations of Modern Historical Scholarship: Language, Law and History in the French Renaissance* (New York, 1970).

Kelly, George Armstrong. *The Humane Comedy: Constant, Tocqueville, and French Liberalism* (Cambridge, 1992).

Kennedy, Emmet. *A Cultural History of the French Revolution* (New Haven and London, 1989).

Khilnani, Sunil. *Arguing Revolution: The Intellectual Left in Postwar France* (New Haven and London, 1993).

Kierkegaard, Søren A. *Stages on Life's Way*, ed. and trans. H. V. Hong and E. H. Hong (Princeton, 1988).

Knibiehler, Yvonne. *Naissance des sciences humaines: Mignet et l'histoire philosophique au XIXe siècle* (Paris, 1973).

Kohler, Lotte and Hans Saner, eds. *Hannah Arendt–Karl Jaspers Correspondence 1926–1969*, trans. Robert Kimber and Rita Kimber (New York, 1992).

Koselleck, Reinhart. *Futures Past: On the Semantics of Historical Time*, trans. Keith Tribe (Cambridge, Mass., and London, 1985).

Critique and Crisis: Enlightenment and the Pathogenesis of Modern Society (Cambridge, Mass., 1988).

Krailsheimer, A. J. *Studies in Self-Interest: From Descartes to La Bruyère* (Oxford, 1962).

La Vopa, Anthony J. "Conceiving a Public: Ideas and Society in Eighteenth-Century Europe," *Journal of Modern History*, 64 (1992), pp. 79–116.

Lamberti, Jean-Claude. *Tocqueville and the Two Democracies*, trans. Arthur Goldhammer (Cambridge, Mass., and London, 1989).

Lawler, Peter A. "The Human Condition: Tocqueville's Debt to Rousseau and Pascal," in *Liberty, Equality, Democracy*, ed. Edouardo Nolla (New York and London, 1992), pp. 1–20.

Lively, Jack. *The Social and Political Thought of Alexis de Tocqueville* (Oxford, 1962).

Lotman, Iuri M. "The Decembrist in Daily Life (Everyday Behavior as a Historical-Psychological Category)," in *The Semiotics of Russian Cultural History: Essays by I. M. Lotman, L. Ia. Ginsburg and B. A. Uspenski*, ed. A. D. Nakhimovsky and A. S. Nakhimovsky (New York, 1985), pp. 95–149.

Machiavelli, Niccolò. *The Prince*, ed. Quentin Skinner and Russell Price (Cambridge, 1988).

MacIntyre, Alasdair. "Epistemological Crises, Dramatic Narrative and the Philosophy of Science," *Monist*, 60 (1977), pp. 453–72.

Whose Justice? Whose Rationality? (Notre Dame, Ind., 1988).

Maistre, Joseph de. *Considérations sur la France* (1797), Vol. I, *Oeuvres*, ed. Jean-Louis Darcel (Geneva, 1980).

Manent, Pierre. *Tocqueville et la nature de la démocratie* (Paris, 1982).

An Intellectual History of Liberalism, trans. Rebecca Balinski (Princeton, 1994).

Marquard, Odo. *In Defence of the Accidental: Philosophical Studies*, trans. Robert M. Wallace (New York and Oxford, 1991).

Mauss, Marcel. *Sociologie et anthropologie* (Paris, [1936], 1960).

Mayer, J. P. *Prophet of the Mass Age: A Study of Alexis de Tocqueville*, trans. M. M. Bozman and C. Hahn (London, 1939).

Meek, Ronald. *Social Science and the Ignoble Savage* (Cambridge, 1976).

Mellon, Stanley. *The Political Uses of History: A Study of French Historians in the French Restoration* (Stanford, 1958).

Mélonio, Françoise. "Tocqueville: aux origines de la démocratie française," in *The Transformation of Political Culture*, Vol. III, *The French Revolution and the Creation of Modern Political Culture*, ed. François Furet and Mona Ozouf (Paris, 1989), pp. 595–611.

Tocqueville et les français (Paris, 1993).

Mignet, François A. *Histoire de la Révolution française de 1789 jusqu'en 1814*, 2 vols. (Paris, 1824).

Mill, John Stuart. "De Tocqueville on Democracy in America," *London and Westminster Review*, 30 (1835), pp. 85–129.

"De la Démocratie en Amérique," *Edinburgh Review*, 72 (1840), pp. 1–25.

A System of Logic, Ratiocinative and Inductive. Being a Connected View of the Principles of Evidence and the Method of Scientific Investigation, 8th edn. (New York, 1881).

Autobiography and Literary Essays, ed. John M. Robson and Jack Stillinger (Toronto and Buffalo, 1981), Vol. I in *Collected Works of John Stuart Mill*, ed. John M. Robson (Toronto and Buffalo, 1963–).

Essays on French History and Historians, ed. John M. Robson, with an introduction by John C. Cairns (Toronto and Buffalo, 1985), Vol. XX in *Collected Works of John Stuart Mill*, ed. John M. Robson (Toronto and Buffalo, 1963–).

Mink, Louis. *Historical Understanding*, ed. Brian Fay, Eugene O. Golob and Richard T. Vann (New York, 1987).

Mitchell, Harvey. "'The Mysterious Veil of Self-Delusion' in Adam Smith's *Theory of Moral Sentiments*," *Eighteenth-Century Studies*, 20 (1987), pp. 405–21.

"Charles Taylor on the Self, Its Languages and Its History," *History of Political Thought*, 12 (1991), pp. 335–58.

"Reclaiming the Self: The Pascal–Rousseau Connection," *Journal of the History of Ideas*, 54 (1993), pp. 637–58.

Mollien, François-Nicolas. *Mémoires d'un ministre du trésor public, 1780–1815*, 4 vols. (Paris, 1845).

Montesquieu, Charles-Louis de Secondat, baron de. *Oeuvres complètes*, ed. Roger Caillois, 2 vols. (Paris, 1949–51).

Oeuvres complètes, ed. André Masson, 3 vols. (Paris, 1950–55).

Considérations sur les causes de la grandeur des Romains et de leur décadence, ed. H. Barckhausen (Paris, 1900), and ed. Gonzague Truc (Paris, 1954).

Necker, Jacques. *De l'administration des finances*, 3 vols. (Paris, 1784).

Niethammer, Lutz (in collaboration with Dirk van Laak). *Posthistoire*, trans. Patrick Camiller (London, 1992).

Nietzsche, Friedrich. *The Use and Abuse of History*, rev. edn., trans. Julius Kraft (Indianapolis and New York, 1957).

Nussbaum, Martha. *Love's Knowledge: Essays on Philosophy and Literature* (New York and London, 1990).

"Virtue Revived," *Times Literary Supplement*, July 3, 1992, pp. 9–11.

Oakeshott, Michael. *Rationalism in Politics and Other Essays*, new and expanded edn. (Indianapolis, 1991).

O'Neal, J. C. "Rousseau's Theory of Wealth," *History of European Ideas*, 7 (1986), pp. 453–67.

Orr, Linda. "Tocqueville et l'histoire incompréhensible: L'Ancien Régime et la Révolution française," *Poétique*, 49 (February 1982), pp. 51–70.

Palmer, Robert R. *The Two Tocquevilles, Father and Son: Hervé and Alexis de Tocqueville on the Coming of the French Revolution* (Princeton, 1987).

Pascal, Blaise. *Pensées*, ed. A. J. Krailsheimer (Harmondsworth, 1965).

Peyre, Henri. *Literature and Sincerity* (New Haven and London, 1963).

Pierson, George W. *Tocqueville and Beaumont in America* (New York, 1938).

Poisson, Siméon-D. *Recherches sur la probabilité des jugements en matière criminelle et en matière civile, précédées des règles générales du calcul des probabilités* (Paris, 1837).

Rawls, John. *Political Liberalism* (New York, 1993).

Reisch, George A. "Chaos, History and Narrative," *History and Theory*, 30 (1991), pp. 1–20.

Rémusat, Charles de. *Mémoires de ma vie*, ed. Charles H. Pouthas, 5 vols. (Paris, 1958–67).

Richter, Melvin. "The Uses of Theory: Tocqueville's Adaptation of Montesquieu," in *Essays in Theory and History: An Approach to the Social Sciences*, ed. Richter (Cambridge, 1970), pp. 74–102.

The Political Theory of Montesquieu (Cambridge, 1977).

"Modernity and Its Distinctive Threats to Liberty: Montesquieu and Tocqueville on New Forms of Illegitimate Domination," in *Alexis de Tocqueville – Zur Politik in Demokratie*, ed. Michael Hereth and J. Höffken (Baden-Baden, 1981), pp. 61–80.

"Toward a Concept of Political Legitimacy," *Political Theory*, 10 (1982), pp. 185–214.

Ricoeur, Paul. *Hermeneutics and the Human Sciences*, ed. and trans. John B. Thompson (Cambridge, 1981).

Ripley, George, ed. *Specimens of Foreign Standard Literature*, 2 vols. (Boston, 1838).

Rosanvallon, Pierre. *L'Etat en France de 1789 à nos jours* (Paris, 1990).

Rousseau, Jean-Jacques. *Emile*, trans. Elizabeth Foxley (London, 1974).

Sacks, Kenneth. *Polybius on the Writing of History* (Berkeley, Los Angeles and London, 1981).

Saint-René Taillandier, René-G.-E. *Etudes sur la Révolution en Allemagne* (Paris, 1853).

Salomon, Albert. *In Praise of Enlightenment* (Cleveland and New York, 1962).

Sandel, Michael. *Liberalism and the Limits of Justice* (Cambridge, 1982).

Schleifer, James T. *The Making of Tocqueville's "Democracy in America"* (Chapel Hill, 1980).

Shiner, Larry E. *The Secret Mirror: Literary Form and History in Tocqueville's "Recollections"* (Ithaca and London, 1988).

Shklar, Judith N. *Men and Citizens: A Study of Rousseau's Social Theory* (Cambridge, 1985).

Siedentop, Larry. *Tocqueville* (Oxford, 1993).

Simpson, M. C. M., ed. *The Correspondence and Conversations of Alexis de Tocqueville with Nassau William Senior from 1834 to 1859*, 2 vols., 2nd edn. (London, 1872).

Skocpol, Theda. *States and Social Revolutions: A Comparative Analysis of France, Russia and China* (Cambridge and New York, 1979).

Skocpol, Theda, and Meyer Kestenbaum. "Mars Unshackled: The French Revolution in World-Historical Perspective," in *The French Revolution and the Birth of Modernity*, ed. Ferenc Féher (Berkeley, Los Angeles and Oxford, 1990), pp. 13–29.

Smith, Adam. *The Theory of Moral Sentiments* (Indianapolis, 1976).

Staël, Germaine Necker, madame de. *Lettres sur les écrits et la caractère de J.-J. Rousseau* (1788), Vol. I, in *Oeuvres complètes de Madame la baronne de Staël-Holstein* (Geneva, 1967).

Starobinski, Jean. *Jean-Jacques Rousseau: La Transparence et l'obstacle, suivi de sept essais sur Rousseau* (Paris, 1971).

Stern, J. P. *Lichtenberg: A Doctrine of Scattered Opinions* (Bloomington, 1959).

Taylor, Charles. *Philosophy and the Human Sciences: Philosophical Papers*, 2 vols. (Cambridge, 1985).

Sources of the Self (Cambridge, Mass., 1989).

The Malaise of Modernity (Concord, Ontario, 1991).

Thiers, Adolphe. *Histoire de la Révolution française*, 4 vols., 8th edn. (Paris, 1839).

Thucydides. *History of the Peloponnesian War*, trans. Rex Warner (Harmondsworth, 1986).

Trilling, Lionel. *Sincerity and Authenticity* (Cambridge, Mass., 1972).

Unger, Roberto M. *Social Theory: Its Situation and Its Task* (Cambridge, 1987).

Vernon, Richard. *Citizenship and Order: Studies in French Political Thought* (Toronto, 1986).

Viroli, Maurizio. *Jean-Jacques Rousseau and the Well-Ordered Society* (New York, 1988).

White, Hayden. *Metahistory: The Historical Imagination in Nineteenth-Century Europe* (Baltimore, 1973).

Tropics of Discourse: Essays in Cultural Criticism (Baltimore and London, 1978).

"The Politics of Historical Interpretation: Discipline and Desublimation," in *The Politics of Interpretation*, ed. W. J. T. Mitchell (Chicago and London, 1983), pp. 119–43.

Williams, Bernard. *Ethics and the Limits of Philosophy* (Cambridge, Mass., 1985).

Shame and Necessity (Berkeley, Los Angeles and London, 1993).

Zetterbaum, Marvin. *Tocqueville and the Problem of Democracy* (Stanford, 1967).

Index

socialism and, 92
the state and, 195–96
threats to, 15, 50, 92, 101–02, 104–05,
122, 123, 126, 127–28, 129, 132, 134,
137, 140, 144, 149, 153, 209, 210,
269
virtue and, 137
Lichtenberg, Andre, 228 n.1
Livy, Titus, 32
Loménie de Brienne, Etienne de, 240
London and Westminster Review, 109
Louis XIV, 118
Louis XVI, 124, 248
Louis-Napoleon, 75, 102, 109, 123,
128–29, 231
Louis-Philippe, 74, 77, 81, 193
Luther, Martin, 203
Lyons, 103

Mably, Gabriel-Bonnot de, 234
Machiavelli, Niccolò, 82, 82 n.19, 181–82
MacIntyre, Alasdair, 11, 271
Maine, Henry, 258
Maistre, Joseph de, 265
majority will, 141–42, 144
mal révolutionnaire, 13, 105, 198, 203,
238–39, 251, 252–53
Mallet du Pan, Jacques, 234, 252
Marquard, Odo, 68
Marrast, Armand, 99, 100
Martinists, 235
Marx, Karl, 258
materialism, 15, 20, 50, 60, 135–36, 151,
160, 166, 267
Mayer, J. P., 257
Mecklenburg, 211
Mélonio, Françoise, 7
men of letters, 100, 119, 126, 211, 231–33,
236, 239, 251, 267
Mesmerists, 235
Michelet, Jules, 30, 44
Michels, Robert, 269
middle class, 61, 181, 189, 190, 221, 223,
225
Mignet, François A., 22, 43, 44, 79
Mill, John Stuart, 43, 44 n.38, 44 n.40, 44
n.44, 45, 45 n.47, 109 n.3, 111, 111
n.5, 112, 115, 146, 146 n.50, 167
n.136
Mink, Louis, 11
Mirabeau, Honoré Gabriel Riqueti, comte
de, 62, 180
modern state formation, 6, 13, 24, 211–12,
219–20
modernity, 4, 14, 16, 19, 21, 44, 140, 154,
166, 214, 265, 266, 267

moeurs, 35–36, 39, 113, 121–22, 127, 209,
214, 235, 238, 247, 249, 263
Molé, Louis-Mathieu, comte, 83, 83 n.21
Mollien, François-Nicolas, comte, 219,
219 n.33
Monnard, Charles, 31, 31 n.7, 261 n.9
Montesquieu, Charles-Louis de Secondat,
baron de, 24, 30, 32, 36, 52, 135, 141,
142, 149, 151, 159, 171, 218, 233–34,
236, 242, 244, 245, 246, 267
morals and politics, 137, 147, 153–58, 165
Morellet, André, 236
Morocco, 92
Mounier, Jean-Joseph, 244–45, 250
Munster, 211

Napoleon I, 121, 123–25, 127, 128, 184
Napoleon III, *see* Louis-Napoleon
narrative in history, 10–13, 23, 40–41, 46,
49, 51, 54, 57, 65, 69, 76, 81–82, 94,
98, 103, 105–06
beginnings and ends, 82
concrete and particular in, 17–18, 41,
51, 55, 69, 85, 96, 106
fictional narrative contrasted with, 55, 81
historical structures and, 10–13, 23, 46,
76
ideological content of, 11
insights gained from, 11–12, 40–41
limitations of, 110–11
moral choice and, 65, 67, 90
natural law, 227, 232–33, 232 n.13
Necker, Jacques, 228–30, 248
Niethammer, Lutz, 265
Nietzsche, Friedrich, 7 n.12, 16, 258, 267
nobility, *see* aristocracy, differences between
English and French
noblesse, *see* aristocracy, differences between
English and French
Nussbaum, Martha, 51 n.61, 271

Oakeshott, Michael, 51
Olivier, Pierre d', 248 n.68
origins of community, 135, 141
Orléanist Monarchy, *see* July Monarchy
Orléans, Hélène-Louise-Elizabeth de
Mecklembourg-Schwerin, duchesse
d', 74, 77, 80, 80 n.13, 81–82, 89
Oudinot, Nicolas-Charles-Victor, 81–82
Ozouf, Mona, 260

pantheism, 271
Papacy, 102
Paraguay, 92
Pareto, Vilfredo, 269
parlement of Paris, 234, 240–41